The American Freshman

National Norms for Fall 2008

Prepared by the Staff of the
Cooperative Institutional Research Program

John H. Pryor
Sylvia Hurtado
Linda DeAngelo
Jessica Sharkness
Laura C. Romero
William S. Korn
Serge Tran

Higher Education Research Institute
Graduate School of Education & Information Studies
University of California, Los Angeles

December, 2008

Higher Education Research Institute
University of California, Los Angeles
Sylvia Hurtado, Professor and Director

HERI Affiliated Scholars

Walter R. Allen, Allan Murray Cartter Professor of Higher Education
Alexander W. Astin, Founding Director and Senior Scholar
Helen S. Astin, Senior Scholar
Mitchell J. Chang, Professor
Patricia M. McDonough, Professor
José Luis Santos, Assistant Professor
Linda J. Sax, Associate Professor
Rick Wagoner, Assistant Professor
Victor B. Sáenz, Assistant Professor, University of Texas at Austin

The Higher Education Research Institute (HERI) is based in the Graduate School of Education & Information Studies at the University of California, Los Angeles. The Institute serves as an interdisciplinary center for research, evaluation, information, policy studies, and research training in postsecondary education.

CIRP Advisory Committee

Betsy O. Barefoot
Co-Director and Senior Scholar
Policy Center on the First Year of College

Victor M. H. Borden
Associate Vice Chancellor and
Associate Professor
Indiana University

C. Anthony Broh
Consultant
Broh Consulting Services

Mark L. Gunty
Assistant Director of Institutional Research
University of Notre Dame

Kurt J. Keppler
Vice President for Student Affairs
Valdosta State University

David Shulenburger
Vice President for Academic Affairs
National Association of State Universities and
Land Grant Colleges

Sylvia Hurtado
Professor and Director, HERI
(ex-officio)

John H. Pryor
Director, CIRP
(ex-officio)

The authors wish to acknowledge Melissa Aragon and Kimberley R. Kelly for their assistance in the preparation of this report.
Cover design by Escott & Associates.
Page layout by The Oak Co.

Published by the Higher Education Research Institute. Suggested citation:

Pryor, J. H., Hurtado, S., DeAngelo, L., Sharkness, J., Romero, L. C., Korn, W. K., & Tran, S. (2008). *The American freshman: National norms for fall 2008.* Los Angeles: Higher Education Research Institute, UCLA.

Additional copies of this report may be purchased for $25.00 (CA residents add 7.5% sales tax, Los Angeles residents add 8.25% sales tax) plus $7.00 for shipping.

Please remit to: Higher Education Research Institute
UCLA Graduate School of Education & Information Studies
3005 Moore Hall/Mailbox 951521
Los Angeles, CA 90095-1521
Website: www.heri.ucla.edu
Telephone: 310-825-1925

The 2008 Freshman Norms monograph is dedicated to Bill Korn.

After 25 years of service,
Bill retired as HERI's Associate Director for Operations.
Bill has managed survey operations and interacted with
so many friends and colleagues of CIRP for so long that it is
hard to think about CIRP without thinking about Bill.
This monograph marks the "wizard's" final contribution
to computing the National Norms.
Thank You.

The American Freshman

National Norms for Fall 2008

CONTENTS

TABLES

FIGURES

The American Freshman:
National Norms for Fall 2008

This is the forty-third annual report of national normative data on the characteristics of students attending American colleges and universities as first-time, full-time freshmen. This series, initiated in the Fall of 1966, is a project of the Cooperative Institutional Research Program (CIRP), the longest-running and largest continuing longitudinal study of the American higher education system. CIRP is run by the Higher Education Research Institute (HERI), which is part of the Graduate School of Education & Information Studies at the University of California, Los Angeles. During the past 43 years, the CIRP has generated an array of normative, substantive, and methodological research on a wide range of issues in American higher education. The CIRP Freshman Survey instrument is revised annually to reflect the changing concerns of the academic community and others who use the information.

In the past few years, HERI faculty and staff published a variety of monographs examining long-term trends among all college freshmen (Pryor, Hurtado, Sáenz, Santos, & Korn, 2007) as well as trends among specific populations. In October of 2008 we released the most recent of these special-population reports in a report on Latino/a first-year students (Hurtado, Sáenz, Santos, & Cabrera, 2008). This report joins one on first-generation students (Sáenz,

Hurtado, Barrera, Wolf, & Yeung, 2007), Asian American students (Chang, Park, Lin, Poon, & Nakanishi, 2007), and Black undergraduates (Allen, Jayakumar, Griffin, Korn, & Hurtado, 2005). In addition to these HERI publications looking at CIRP data, this past year saw the release of HERI faculty affiliate Linda Sax's book on male and female first-year students: "The Gender Gap in College: Maximizing the Developmental Potential of Women and Men" (Sax, 2008).

A major purpose of CIRP is to provide initial information for longitudinal research. HERI conducts two follow-up surveys that enable institutions to examine changes amongst their students: the Your First College Year Survey (YFCY) which surveys students at the end of the first year of college, and the College Senior Survey (CSS), which surveys students during their last year of college. Longitudinal follow-up studies of CIRP students have been used in major studies of science students (Hurtado, Han, Sáenz, Espinosa, Cabrera, & Cerna, 2007; Chang, Cerna, Han, & Sáenz, 2008), retention (Astin & Oseguera, 2002), community service and citizenship (Sax, 2004; Vogelgesang & Astin, 2000), first-year adjustment (Hurtado et al., 2007, Keup & Stolzenberg, 2004); and diversity in higher education (Cole, 2007; Hurtado, 2006; Chang, Denson, Sáenz,

& Misa, 2006; Gurin, Dey, Hurtado, & Gurin, 2002).

The data reported in this monograph are weighted to provide a normative profile of the American freshman population for use by individuals engaged in policy analysis, educational research, college administration, human resource planning, and guidance and counseling. The data are also useful to the general community of current and future college students, their parents, and college faculty.

The normative data presented here are reported separately for men and women, and for 26 different institutional groupings. The major stratifying factors are institutional race (predominantly black, predominantly white), control (public, private non-sectarian, Roman Catholic, other religious), type (university, four-year college) and "selectivity level" of the institution. A complete discussion of the CIRP survey methodology, stratification scheme, and weighting procedures is presented in Appendix A.

An Overview of the 2008 Freshman Norms

The 2008 freshman norms are based on the weighted responses of 240,580 first-time, full-time students at 340 of the nation's baccalaureate colleges and universities. These data have been statistically adjusted to reflect the responses of the 1.4 million first-time, full-time students entering four-year colleges and universities as freshmen in 2008.

The Cooperative Institutional Research Program (CIRP) Freshman Survey was first administered nationally in 1966. It is the longest-running project of its kind, covering 43 years and containing data from over 13 million students. Over the years more than 1,700 colleges and universities have participated in the CIRP Freshman Survey, using their own institutional data both to more accurately understand the characteristics of their incoming students and to use as a baseline in future studies examining institutional effectiveness.

A Revival of Political Engagement

A record number of incoming college students are politically engaged, with 85.9 percent reporting that they frequently or occasionally discussed politics in the last year. The number of students who frequently discussed politics in the past year (35.6 percent) is the highest level of such involvement since CIRP has reported on political engagement. This level surpasses that recorded in 1968 (33.6 percent), a year characterized by students who were very politically active. The 2008 level is also higher than other recent Presidential election years, including 1992, when Bill Clinton was elected president (see Figure 1).

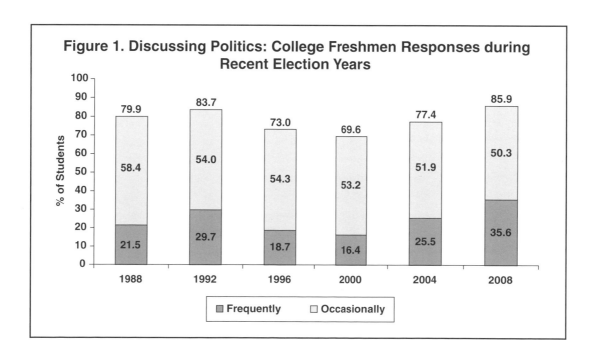

Figure 1. Discussing Politics: College Freshmen Responses during Recent Election Years

Steady increases have also occurred in the percentage of students who state that keeping up to date with political affairs is an "essential" or "very important" goal. After a record low of 28.1 percent was reported in 2000, post-9/11 freshmen have shown increased interest in keeping up to date in political affairs, rising to 39.5 percent in 2008. At the same time, however, these students have not yet surpassed their parents' generation (baby boomers): Over 60 percent of students in 1966 reported that keeping up to date with political affairs was an important personal goal. On average, baby boomers were more committed to keeping up with political affairs. Figure 2 compares the averages across the recent cohorts (2004–2008), the "echo boomers," with the earliest cohorts of "baby boomers" (1966–1970) in the CIRP Freshman Survey data on key political items. Data indicate that a higher proportion of echo boomers are committed to influencing the social and political structure. The echo boom generation is also somewhat more politically committed and engaged in terms of discussing politics. In addition, over one in ten (11.7 percent) worked on a local, state, or national political campaign in the last year.

Trends indicate that fewer students today characterize themselves as middle-of-the road in terms of their overall political view. This category has seen a steady decline and is at an all time low (43.3 percent), returning to roughly the same percentage as in 1970. Corresponding increases occurred in the proportion of students who characterized themselves as Liberal (31.0 percent), and Far Left (3.2 percent). This is the largest percentage of students categorizing themselves as liberal since 1973. Approximately one in five students in 2008 characterize themselves as conservative (20.7

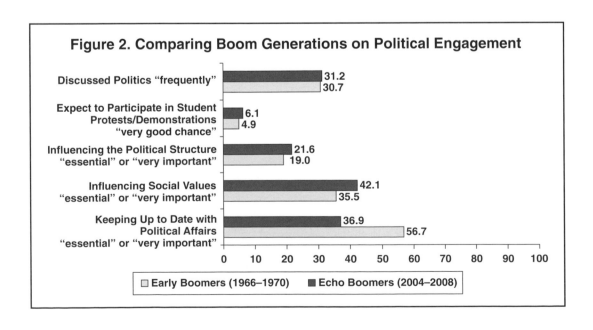

Figure 2. Comparing Boom Generations on Political Engagement

percent), a small decrease since the previous year (23.1 percent).

As more incoming students view themselves as liberal, the overall support for more liberal causes has also risen. Figure 3 features students' political views on a number of important issues in the last ten years. Steady increases have occurred in the percentage of students who support the right to legal marital status for same sex couples, indicating that now over two-thirds (66.2 percent) of entering freshmen support such rights. Support has also risen, since a low in 2002, for the statement that the wealthy should pay a larger share of taxes than they do now (60.4 percent).

Support for the legalization of marijuana has also steadily risen and is now at 41.3 percent, increasing 3.2 percentage points from the 38.1 percent recorded last year. One might expect that if support for legalization of mari-

juana is rising, it might indeed be tied to more marijuana users in the incoming student population. If this were self-serving we would expect that the national rates of marijuana use would be at least at the 41.3 percent rate for support of legalization of marijuana. Recent figures, however, on the 2008 high school seniors from the Monitoring the Future project indicate that only 32 percent had used marijuana at least once in the past year (Johnston, O'Malley, Bachman, & Schulenberg, 2008). Thus, this might be less of an indication of permissive marijuana usage and more about how one views government regulation of this area.

Freshman support for federal military spending has been on a steady decline since its highest point immediately after the 9/11 attacks (45.0 percent). Now only 28.0 percent of freshmen favor increases in military spending, a level more reflective of the mid-1980s. While

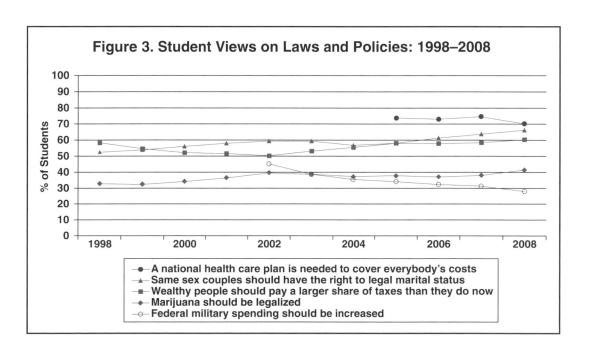

Figure 3. Student Views on Laws and Policies: 1998–2008

- A national health care plan is needed to cover everybody's costs
- Same sex couples should have the right to legal marital status
- Wealthy people should pay a larger share of taxes than they do now
- Marijuana should be legalized
- Federal military spending should be increased

5

freshmen overwhelmingly supported a national health care plan to cover everybody's costs, there was a slight decline this year to 70.3 percent. This may indicate support for a more moderate proposal, given the priorities of the two major party candidates at the time of the survey and the current economic context.

Skills for a Diverse Workplace

For more than a decade now, employers have articulated a need for workplace competencies associated with a diverse world—skills that are often in short supply among graduates of higher education (Bikson & Law, 1994; AAC&U, 2008). This year, a new set of items were placed on the survey to capture some of the key skills employers deem appropriate for participation in a diverse workplace. Together they constitute a factor called a *pluralistic orientation*, reflected now on the CIRP longitudinal surveys, and based on research about the relationship of these skills to diversity experiences in college (Engberg, 2006; Hurtado,

2005). Table 1 shows student responses on a number of items that capture skills for a diverse workplace by each racial/ethnic group. Students were asked to rate themselves compared with the average person their age, and included are responses from students who rated themselves "above average" or among the "top 10%" of their peers.

Overall, the majority of entering freshmen tend to rate themselves reasonably high on many of the items, with multi-racial students rating themselves higher than other racial/ethnic groups. In contrast, fewer American Indians rate themselves as highly as other groups on these items. All groups tend to rate themselves lower on a cognitive development item, "openness to having my own views challenged," while fewer Asian Americans tend to rate themselves highly on the "ability to discuss and negotiate controversial issues." By far, the biggest difference between men (69.4 percent) and women (58.5 percent) also occurs on this item. Students appear to have the most

Table 1. Skills for a Diverse Workplace, by Race/Ethnicity (percentages)

Reporting "Above Average" or "Top 10%"	White	African American	American Indian	Asian/PI American	Latina/o	Multi-Racial American
Ability to see the world from someone else's perspective	64.0	62.2	58.5	69.7	66.4	72.9
Tolerance of others with different beliefs	72.6	67.5	60.9	77.9	74.1	79.6
Openness to having my own views challenged	56.3	61.4	51.6	62.6	61.2	64.0
Ability to discuss and negotiate controversial issues	62.8	64.8	52.3	59.3	61.5	71.1
Ability to work cooperatively with diverse people	77.3	80.5	66.8	79.8	80.4	84.9

Note: PI = Pacific Islander

confidence in their tolerance of others with different beliefs and their ability to work cooperatively with diverse people. This may be a function of more diversity in the schools. Although 58.8 percent of all freshmen came from mostly White or all White high schools, slight increases were evident in those who came from mostly non-White (13.0 percent) and nearly a quarter (24.8 percent) came from roughly half non-White high schools. A continued decline in the percentage of White students among college freshmen was also evident this year: 71.9 percent of freshmen identified as White in 2008, compared with 81.8 percent of freshmen twenty years ago.

College Choice and Financial Issues

The number of students attending their first-choice college continues to decline, dropping 3.2 percentage points to 60.7 percent in 2008 from 63.9 percent in 2007. This is the lowest this figure has been since the question was first asked in 1974 (see Figure 4). Although this percentage was fairly stable from 1989 to 2005, hovering around 70 percent, it started a decline in 2006 that has only continued.

The percentage of incoming first-year students who had been accepted by their first-choice college also declined from 2007 (80.6 percent) to 2008 (77.8 percent). It remains the case that there is a gap between acceptances at first-choice colleges and actual attendance, and that gap is increasing—from 16.5 percent in 2007 to 17.1 percent in 2008. In terms of applications to college, students applying to four or more colleges reached a record high in 2008, moving up to 60.1 percent from 56.4 percent in 2007.

As we reported previously (Pryor, Hurtado, Sáenz, Korn, Santos, & Korn, 2006), students who were accepted by their first-choice college

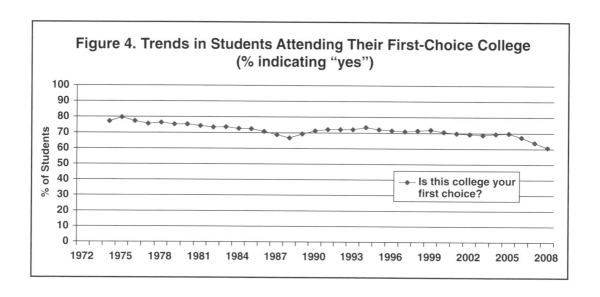

Figure 4. Trends in Students Attending Their First-Choice College (% indicating "yes")

7

but ultimately attend their second-choice institution are more likely to cite financial considerations as more important in deciding which college to attend. Specifically, when considering the many reasons why a student might choose a particular college to attend, the force that drives a student to decline a first-choice in favor of a second-choice institution is financial. More students report that being offered financial aid was a "very important" or "essential" consideration in choosing which school to attend than at any time in the past 36 years the question was asked (see Figure 5), and in the past year alone the percentage jumped from 39.7 percent in 2007 to 43.0 percent in 2008. The importance of the cost of attending the chosen college is also at a high, at 39.9 percent, up 3.1 percentage points from 2007. And, 8.5 percent specifically reported that not re-

ceiving aid from their first-choice college was very important in choosing where to attend, up 1.1 percent from 2007, and the highest percentage since the question was first asked in 1984.

Today's incoming students are more likely to look to multiple income sources to pay for college. Family resources (e.g., parents, relatives) are still the most likely source of funds, with 79.6 percent of students reporting that they will use family resources. Incoming first-year students in 2008, however, are more likely to report using their own savings and planning to work while in college than in previous years (64.7 percent in 2008). In fact, more students report that they will get a job in order to meet expenses while in college (49.4 percent in 2008) than in the 32 years CIRP surveys have asked the question. They are also more likely to be receiving funds from aid that

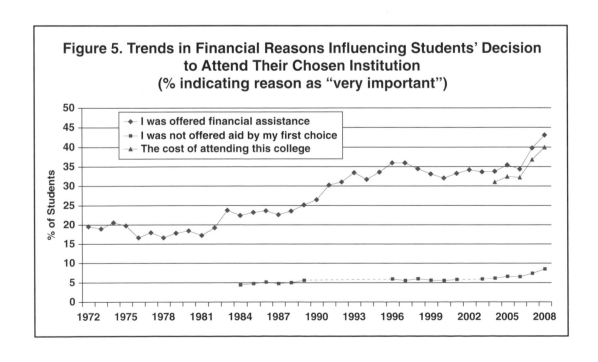

Figure 5. Trends in Financial Reasons Influencing Students' Decision to Attend Their Chosen Institution (% indicating reason as "very important")

need not be repaid, such as grants or scholarships (69.3 percent in 2008). With no subsequent decline in the use of other types of funding, such as loans, it seems that more students are using more than one source of funds to pay for college. Planning ahead to use multiple sources, as well as making the decision to attend a different college based upon financial circumstances, may explain why although financial issues drive college choice for some students, we are not seeing larger changes in the percentages of students concerned about their ability to pay for college.

College Readiness by Core High School Subject Areas

High-school students are considered ready for college if they meet a required number of years of study in certain subject areas. In the subjects of English (4 years), math (3 years), and history/American government (1 year), almost 100 percent of incoming freshmen indicate that they completed the necessary years of study. Fewer students, 92.9 percent, indicate that they completed two years of a foreign language, and 82.3 percent indicate that they completed at least a year of art and/or music in high school.

The story is different for the sciences. Since this set of questions was first asked on the 1984 CIRP Freshman Survey, the lowest level of achievement in terms of meeting college readiness has been completing two years of high school study in biological sciences. Although this is still the case, we see a new record of 49.5 percent in 2008, up from 46.8 percent in 2006. Physical science has also lagged behind compared to other subjects, although at a higher level of compliance than biological science, reaching a new record of 61.8 percent in 2008. Similarly, students show a lower level of achievement in completing half a year of computer science, at 60.8 percent in 2008. This shows a slight decrease from 2006 (61.6 percent) and even more of a drop from 2004, when a high of 62.5 percent of incoming freshmen reported computer readiness.

Perhaps more importantly, there are some distinct differences by race/ethnicity in the years of high school study devoted to core subject areas, particularly in the areas of physical and biological sciences. This can be seen in Table 2. Only 48.0 percent of African American, 49.4 percent of American Indian, and 59.8 percent of Latino/a freshmen report that they have completed two years of physical science in high school. In contrast, 63.2 percent of White freshmen and 67.3 percent of Asian American/Pacific Islander freshmen report that they completed two years of physical science in high school.

Disparities are less severe, but still widespread in the area of biological science preparation, especially when the comparison group is Asian American/Pacific Islander freshmen. Almost six out of ten (57.6 percent) Asian

Table 2. College Readiness* in Core High School Subject Areas, by Race/Ethnicity (percentages)

	English	Math	Foreign Language	Physical Sciences	Biological Sciences	History/ American Govt	Computer Science	Arts and/or Music
White	98.2	98.6	93.1	63.2	49.3	99.3	61.7	81.9
African American	96.9	97.8	89.0	48.0	43.7	97.1	61.4	76.5
American Indian	95.6	94.3	68.6	49.4	47.3	97.4	69.5	80.5
Asian/PI American	97.3	99.1	94.3	67.3	57.6	98.4	52.0	86.3
Latino/a	98.2	98.1	94.4	59.8	47.5	98.9	61.4	86.1
Multi-Racial American	98.2	98.3	93.5	61.3	49.7	99.0	59.3	85.7
Other	96.4	98.4	93.0	66.9	53.3	97.7	61.0	82.1
Total	97.9	98.5	92.9	61.8	49.5	98.9	60.8	82.3

Note: PI = Pacific Islander

* = College Readiness in each subject area is as follows: 4 or more years of English, 3 or more years of math, 2 or more years of foreign language, physical science and biological science, 1 or more years of history/American government, 1/2 or more years of computer science, and 1 or more years of Art/Music

American/Pacific Islander freshmen report two years of study in the biological sciences. This compares to 43.7 percent among African American freshmen, 47.3 percent of American Indian freshmen, and 47.5 percent of Latino/a freshmen. Interestingly, years of study devoted to computer science is the only core high school subject area where Asian American/Pacific Islander freshmen are less prepared at college entry. In this area only 52.0 percent have completed at least one half of a year of study in computer science, whereas among other racial/ethnic groups the figure is 60 percent or higher. These differences have considerable implications for entry into competitive colleges, success in introductory courses in the sciences, and retention in science related majors and careers.

Increasing Interest in Engineering

As shown in Figure 6, interest in the field of engineering as a major and career has rebounded from the decade lows of 7.5 percent (for the major) and 6.2 percent (for the probable career) that were reported among freshmen in 2007. This reverses a three-year decline, rising to 9.4 percent for the major and 7.4 percent for probable career in 2008. Although in line with interest in engineering among freshmen reported earlier this decade and through much of the 90s, these figures are still well under the highest levels of interest in the early 80s. At its peak in 1982, 11.9 percent (major) and 11.1 percent (probable career) of freshmen expressed an interest in engineering.

Men continue to far outpace women in terms of interest in both engineering as a major

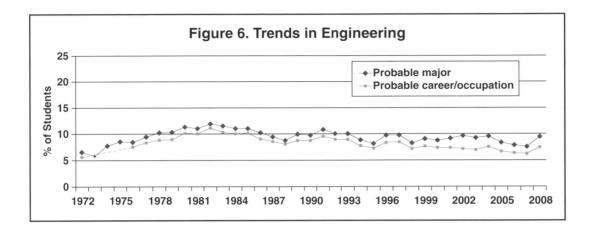

Figure 6. Trends in Engineering

(17.1 vs. 3.1 percent) and a career (13.4 vs. 2.5 percent). Despite this disparity, men and women's interest in engineering as a major grew at almost the same rate from 2007 to 2008, and women outpaced men in terms of growth in interest in engineering as a probable career during this period. From 2007 to 2008 interest in engineering as a major grew by 24.8 percent for men and 24.0 percent for women (from 13.7 percent of men and 2.5 percent of women interested in the major in 2007). Interest in engineering as a probable career grew by 18.6 percent for men and 25.0 percent for women (11.3 percent for men and 2.0 percent for women for a probable career in 2007).

More Students Reporting Learning Disabilities

Among the incoming 2008 freshmen, 3.3 percent report that they have a learning disability. This figure has steadily and slowly increased since the question was first asked in 1983, when only .05 percent reported that they had a learning disability (see Figure 7). During this time the percentage of freshmen reporting other disabilities has remained fairly stable, with the percentage of freshmen reporting partial or total blindness decreasing somewhat from 2.3 percent in 1983 to 1.4 percent in 2008.

Self-reported learning disabled students are more likely to anticipate that they will need extra time to complete their bachelor's degree and use campus counseling and tutoring services than freshmen overall (see Figure 8). Specifically, incoming first-year students reporting a learning disability are 5.2 percentage points more likely to expect that they will need extra time to complete their bachelor's degree (11.6 vs. 6.4 percent), 5.8 percentage points more likely to anticipate that they will seek personal counseling (15.0 vs. 9.2 percent), and 11.9 percentage points more likely to expect that they will need tutoring for specific courses (43.5 vs. 31.6 percent). These differences in expectations of needs are consistent with the

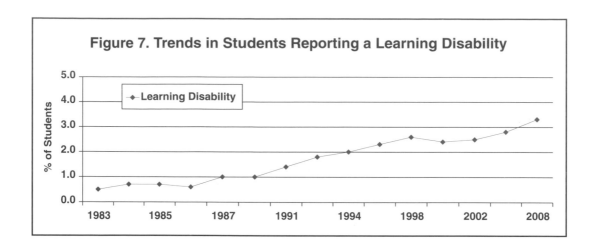

Figure 7. Trends in Students Reporting a Learning Disability

recent literature on students with learning disabilities. Both Heiman and Precel (2003) and Hall, Spruill, and Webster (2002) report that students with learning disabilities are more likely to experience psychological stress associated with their college experience than students without learning disabilities, especially as it relates to adjusting to the demands of college and dealing with the stress and anxiety associated with succeeding in the college environment. Findings from studies by these authors suggest one way students with learning disabilities cope positively with their learning difficulties is by putting intense and extra efforts toward their studies.

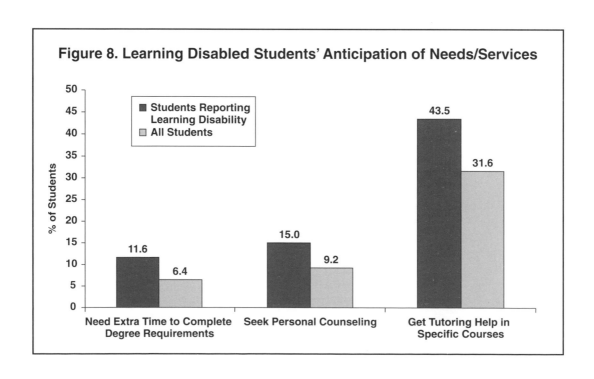

Figure 8. Learning Disabled Students' Anticipation of Needs/Services

Support for "Green" Initiatives

Concerns about the environment and global warming have been rising in recent years. Last year we reported an increase in the proportion of students who believe it is important to become involved in programs to clean up the environment, and this trend continues in 2008. Almost a third of the 2008 entering class (29.5 percent) report feeling that it is "essential" or "very important" to help clean up the environment; increasing from 26.7 percent in 2007 and 22.2 percent in 2006. Because the environment has become an important national concern, the 2008 CIRP Freshman Survey introduced two new questions on environmental issues to further explore entering students' beliefs. One of these questions asks students how important it is for them to adopt green practices to protect the environment, and almost half of students (45.3 percent) believe it "very important" or "essential." The second

new environment-related question assesses students' opinions regarding the federal government's role in combating global warming. Almost three-quarters of entering students (74.3 percent) agree with the statement that "addressing global warming should be a federal priority"; 34.5 percent agree strongly and 39.8 percent agree somewhat. Women are more likely than men to support both the personal adoption of "green" practices as well as an increased federal role in combating global warming. Almost half of women (49.6 percent) compared to 40.0 percent of men express the belief that it is "very important" or "essential" to protect the environment through the adoption of green practices. Over three-quarters of women (77.4 percent) compared to slightly fewer men (70.5 percent) believe the government should make it a priority to address global warming.

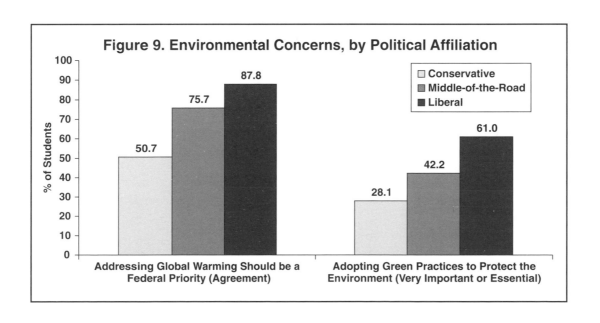

Figure 9. Environmental Concerns, by Political Affiliation

Students who identify themselves on opposite ends of the political spectrum express different attitudes on the new environmental items, as can be seen in Figure 9. Far more liberal students (87.8 percent) feel that the federal government should make it a priority to address global warming; compared to only half of conservative students (50.7 percent). Similarly, more than twice as many liberal students as conservative students believe that adopting "green" practices to protect the environment is a "very important" or "essential" life goal (61.0 percent vs. 28.1 percent).

How Incoming Students Use the Internet

Internet usage is becoming pervasive among America's high school seniors. As Table 3 shows, almost all entering students report using the internet in some capacity during their senior year of high school. The most common reported use of the internet was for research or homework—almost every first-year student (98.8 percent) reports turning to the internet for schoolwork at some point during their senior year of high school, and over three-

quarters (76.0 percent) report frequently doing so. Most students (86.5 percent) also indicate using the internet during senior year to read news sites. However, students generally read news less frequently than they did homework on the web—about the same proportion occasionally used the internet for news as frequently (43.6 and 42.9 percent, respectively). Despite these high numbers for internet usage overall, only 18.9 percent reported that information from a website was a very important factor in choosing which college to attend. Although this figure rose from 17.0 percent in 2007, one might expect larger numbers, given the heavy use of the internet for research in school.

These students do not only use the internet for information-gathering purposes in high school, many also report spending time during their senior year reading internet web logs, or "blogs," and, as a new survey question shows, some also spent time authoring blogs. Indeed, over half of these students as high school seniors (57.1 percent) report that they frequently or occasionally read blogs, and over a

Table 3. Incoming Freshmen's Internet Usage, by Race/Ethnicity (percentages)

"Frequent" Internet Usage	White	African American	American Indian	Asian/PI American	Latina/o	Multi-Racial American	Other
For Research or Homework	75.1	76.6	62.3	80.7	77.4	77.6	78.1
To Read News Sites	41.4	43.2	37.0	52.2	42.2	45.5	50.4
To Read Blogs	23.3	26.8	27.1	37.7	22.7	26.8	27.5
To Blog	13.1	16.3	18.5	22.0	14.1	15.7	15.9

Note: PI = Pacific Islander

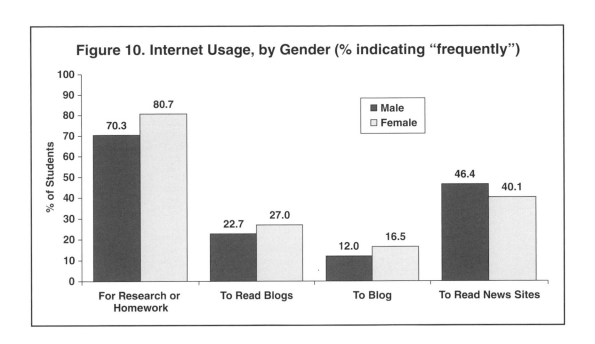

Figure 10. Internet Usage, by Gender (% indicating "frequently")

third (34.5 percent) frequently or occasionally wrote blogs. Most of the students who spent a significant amount of their time writing blogs also spent a lot of time reading others' blogs; 93.0 percent of those who wrote blogs frequently during high school also read blogs frequently. Virtually every student who blogged at any point also reports reading blogs— 96.8 percent who blogged occasionally or frequently during senior year also read blogs occasionally or frequently. By contrast, only 36.1 percent of students who never wrote a blog in the past year indicate reading blogs at all, and only 10.0 percent read blogs frequently.

Figure 10 illustrates differences in frequent internet usage between men and women entering college today. Women are more likely than men to frequently use the internet for research or homework (80.7 percent of women vs. 70.3 percent of men), to read blogs (27.0 vs.

22.7 percent), and to blog (16.5 vs. 12.0 percent). However, more men than women utilized the internet to frequently read news sites; 46.4 percent of men vs. 40.1 percent of women did this during their senior year.

Continued Decline in Student Drinking Behavior

This year's incoming college students are less likely to have experience drinking beer, wine, or liquor, and have spent less time partying as high school seniors than in previous years. Only 38.0 percent of incoming students drank beer occasionally or frequently as high school seniors. This figure is the lowest it has been in the 43 years of the CIRP Freshman Survey, and roughly half of the peak values seen in the late 1970s. Drinking wine or liquor occasionally or frequently is also at an all-time low, at 43.9 percent. In each case the drop

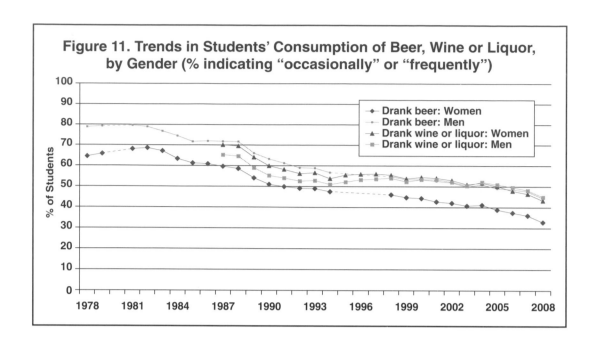

Figure 11. Trends in Students' Consumption of Beer, Wine or Liquor, by Gender (% indicating "occasionally" or "frequently")

from 2007 to 2008 was just over 3 percentage points. As indicated in Figure 11, the drop occurs for both men and women. Although, in both cases, men are more likely than women to use alcohol, the difference is even more prominent with beer.

A steady decline also is seen in the percentage of incoming students who, as high school seniors, partied an average of 6 or more hours a week. Since first measured in 1987, when 36.8 percent reported 6 or more hours a week of partying, this has dropped to half that amount, at 18.8 percent.

Rise in the Importance of Developing a Meaningful Philosophy of Life

A core set of questions in the CIRP Freshman Survey that have been asked since the origin of the project in 1966 are those that concern students' personal objectives or value commit-ments. In the 1960s and 1970s, "developing a meaningful philosophy of life" was one of the objectives that had the highest levels of agreement among incoming college students, with as many as 85 percent reporting this was an "essential" or "very important" personal goal. Over time, however, this percentage dropped drastically, to a low of 39.3 percent in 2003. Since 2003, we have seen an increase in importance of developing a meaningful philosophy of life to the point where now slightly over half of incoming students (51.4 percent) report such a goal. This marks a return to value levels not seen since the early 1980s.

Previous monographs have tracked mirror images of the search for a meaningful philosophy of life and one that asks about the importance of being well off financially. Thus we might expect that along with the 2008 increase in the importance of developing a meaningful philosophy of life we would see a corresponding decrease in the importance of being well off financially. This item, however, also rose in 2008. More than 3 out of 4 incoming first-year students (74.5 percent) report that being well off financially is an "essential" or "very important" objective in 2008, rising 2.3 percentage points from 76.8 percent in 2007. Fueling part of this overall increase is a convergence of male and female views. Whereas fewer women than men in the late 1980s reporting this as an important objective, lagging behind by about 8 percentage points, this gap diminished in the late 1990s to about 6 percentage points. In 2008 this gender gap closed even further, with men now at 77.8 percent and women at 76.1 percent.

References

Allen, W. R., Jayakumar, U. M., Griffin, K. A., Korn, W. S., & Hurtado, S. (2005). *Black under-graduates from* Bakke *to* Grutter: *Freshmen status, trends, and prospects, 1971–2004*. Los Angeles: Higher Education Research Institute, UCLA.

Astin, A. W., & Oseguera, L. (2002). *Degree attainment rates at American colleges and universities*. Los Angeles: Higher Education Research Institute, UCLA.

American Association of Colleges and Universities (2008). *How should colleges assess and improve student learning?* Retrieved December 16, 2008, from http://www.aacu.org/leap/documents/2008_Business_Leader_Poll.pdf

Bikson, T. K., & Law, S. A. (1994). *Global preparedness and human resources*. Santa Monica, CA: Rand Institute.

Chang, M. J., Cerna, O. S., Han, J. C., & Sáenz, V. B. (in press). The contradictory role of institutional status in retaining underrepresented minority students in biomedical and behavioral science majors. *Review of Higher Education*.

Chang, M. J., Denson, N., Sáenz, V., & Misa, K. (2006). The educational benefits of sustaining cross-racial interactions among undergraduates. *Journal of Higher Education 77*(3), 430–455.

Chang, M. J., Park, J. J., Lin, M. H., Poon, O. A., & Nakanishi, D. T. (2007). *Beyond myths: The growth and diversity of Asian American college freshmen, 1971–2005*. Los Angeles: Higher Education Research Institute, UCLA.

Cole, D. (2007). Do interracial interactions matter? An examination of student-faculty contact and intellectual self-concept. *The Journal of Higher Education, 78*(3), 249–281.

Engberg, M. (2007). Educating the workforce for the 21st century: A cross-disciplinary analysis of the impact of the undergraduate experience on students' pluralistic orientation. *Research in Higher Education, 48*(3), 283–317.

Gurin, P., Dey, E. L., Hurtado, S., & Gurin, G. (2002). Diversity and higher education: theory and impact on educational outcomes. *Harvard Educational Review, 72*(3), 330–366.

Heiman, T., & Precel, K. (2003). Students with learning disabilities in higher education: Academic strategies profile. *Journal of Learning Disabilities, 36*(3), 248–258.

Hurtado, S. (2006). Diversity and learning for a pluralistic democracy. In W. Allen, M. Bonous-Hammarth, & R. Teranishi (Eds.), *Higher Education in a Global Society: Achieving Diversity, Equity, and Excellence*. Oxford, England: Elsevier Publishers.

Hurtado, S., Han, J. C., Sáenz, V. B., Espinosa, L., Cabrera, N., & Cerna, O. S. (2007). Predicting transition and adjustment to college: biomedical and behavioral sciences aspirants' and minority students' first year of college. *Research in Higher Education, 48*(7), 841–887.

Hurtado, S. (2005). The next generation of diversity and intergroup relations research. *Journal of Social Issues, 61*(3), 595–610.

Hall, C. W., Spruill, K. L., & Webster, R. E. (2002). Motivational and attitudinal factors in college students with and without learning disabilities. *Learning Disabilities Quarterly, 28*, 79–86.

Johnston, L. D., O'Malley, P. M., Bachman, J. G., & Schulenberg, J. E. (2008). Various stimulant drugs show continuing gradual declines among teens in 2008, most illicit drugs hold steady, [Press Release]. University of Michigan News Service: Ann Arbor, MI. Retrieved 12/15/2008 from http://www.monitoringthefuture.org/pressreleases/08drugpr.pdf

Keup, J. R., & Stolzenberg, E. B. (2004). *The 2003 Your First College Year (YFCY) Survey: Exploring the academic and personal experiences of first-year students* (Monograph No. 40). Columbia, SC: University of South Carolina, National Resource Center for The First-Year Experience and Students in Transition.

Pryor, J. H., Hurtado, S., Sáenz, V. B., Korn, J. S., Santos, J. L., & Korn, W. S. (2006). *The American freshman: National norms for fall 2006.* Los Angeles: Higher Education Research Institute, UCLA.

Pryor, J. H., Hurtado, S., Sáenz, V. B., Santos, J. L., & Korn, W. S. (2007). *The American freshman: Forty year trends.* Los Angeles: Higher Education Research Institute, UCLA.

Sáenz, V. B., Hurtado, S., Barrera, D., Wolf, D., & Yeung, F. (2007). *First in my family: A profile of first-generation college students at four-year institutions since 1971.* Los Angeles: Higher Education Research Institute, UCLA.

Sax, L. J. (2008). *The gender gap in college: Maximizing the developmental potential of women and men.* San Francisco: Jossey-Bass.

Sax, L. J. (2004). Citizenship development and the American college student. *New Directions for Institutional Research, 122* (Summer), 65–80.

The 2008 Freshman Norms

2008 National Norms

Type of Institution and Control for All Freshmen

NOTES

These notes refer to report items that are followed by numbers in [brackets].

[1] Based on the recommendations of the National Commission on Excellence In Education.

[2] Percentage responding "frequently" only.

[3] Recategorization of this item from a longer list is shown in Appendix C.

[4] Percentages will add to more than 100.0 if any student marked more than one category.

WEIGHTED NATIONAL NORMS FOR ALL FRESHMEN, FALL 2008

	ALL BACC. INSTS.	ALL 4-YR. COLLEGES	ALL UNI-VERSITIES	ALL BLACK COLLEGES	FOUR-YEAR COLLEGES					UNIVERSITIES		BLACK COLLEGES	
					PUBLIC	ALL PRIV.	NONSECT.	CATHOLIC	OTH. REL.	PUBLIC	PRIVATE	PUBLIC	PRIVATE
How old will you be on December 31 of this year?													
16 or younger	0.0	0.0	0.0	0.0	0.0	0.1	0.0	0.0	0.1	0.0	0.1	0.0	0.0
17	1.6	1.5	1.7	1.8	1.4	1.6	1.8	1.8	1.3	1.6	2.0	1.1	3.0
18	69.5	69.2	69.9	69.6	70.5	67.4	69.9	69.5	63.2	69.6	71.3	68.8	71.0
19	27.3	27.2	27.5	25.6	26.0	28.8	25.8	27.4	33.5	27.9	25.8	26.6	24.0
20	1.0	1.2	0.6	1.8	1.1	1.4	1.6	0.8	1.4	0.5	0.7	2.2	1.2
21 to 24	0.5	0.7	0.3	1.0	0.7	0.5	0.7	0.3	0.5	0.3	0.2	1.2	0.6
25 to 29	0.1	0.1	0.0	0.1	0.1	0.1	0.1	0.1	0.0	0.0	0.0	0.1	0.1
30 to 39	0.0	0.0	0.0	0.0	0.1	0.0	0.0	0.0	0.0	0.0	0.0	0.0	0.0
40 to 54	0.0	0.0	0.0	0.0	0.1	0.0	0.0	0.0	0.0	0.0	0.0	0.0	0.0
55 or older	0.0	0.0	0.0	0.0	0.0	0.0	0.0	0.0	0.0	0.0	0.0	0.0	0.0
Is English your native language?													
Yes	91.2	93.0	88.3	97.8	92.6	93.5	91.7	93.1	96.0	88.3	88.3	97.9	97.7
No	8.8	7.0	11.7	2.2	7.4	6.5	8.3	6.9	4.0	11.7	11.7	2.1	2.3
In what year did you graduate from high school?													
2008	97.9	97.3	98.9	96.0	97.3	97.4	96.9	98.3	97.6	98.9	98.7	95.5	96.9
2007	1.2	1.6	0.7	2.7	1.5	1.6	2.0	1.0	1.5	0.6	1.0	3.0	2.0
2006	0.3	0.4	0.1	0.5	0.3	0.4	0.5	0.2	0.3	0.1	0.1	0.6	0.4
2005 or earlier	0.4	0.5	0.2	0.6	0.6	0.4	0.5	0.3	0.3	0.2	0.1	0.6	0.4
Did not graduate but passed G.E.D. test	0.1	0.2	0.0	0.2	0.2	0.1	0.1	0.1	0.2	0.1	0.0	0.2	0.2
Never completed high school	0.0	0.0	0.0	0.0	0.0	0.0	0.0	0.0	0.1	0.0	0.0	0.0	0.0
How many miles is this college from your permanent home?													
5 or less	5.4	7.0	2.9	6.8	8.2	5.3	5.5	7.0	4.2	2.7	3.4	8.4	4.0
6 to 10	5.8	7.6	3.1	5.7	8.6	6.2	6.8	8.4	4.3	2.7	4.3	6.2	4.9
11 to 50	24.3	28.2	18.1	14.1	31.3	24.0	23.7	32.7	20.1	18.3	17.0	13.8	14.5
51 to 100	17.3	17.1	17.7	15.5	17.7	16.3	14.5	15.5	18.9	19.9	9.2	18.8	9.9
101 to 500	33.0	26.9	43.0	36.0	24.9	29.6	27.0	24.9	35.3	45.6	33.1	40.0	29.2
Over 500	14.1	13.3	15.4	22.0	9.4	18.6	22.4	11.5	17.2	10.7	33.0	12.9	37.5
What was your average grade in high school?													
A or A+	22.3	17.4	30.3	10.5	15.2	20.3	18.6	19.1	23.1	27.5	40.7	7.6	15.3
A-	24.9	21.2	30.8	12.8	19.7	23.3	22.4	24.4	24.0	30.3	32.6	10.8	16.3
B+	21.0	21.8	19.8	21.4	22.4	21.0	21.6	22.9	19.4	20.9	15.9	21.7	21.0
B	20.1	23.6	14.4	23.6	26.0	20.5	21.4	21.4	19.0	16.0	8.3	23.8	23.2
B-	6.9	9.1	3.2	14.2	9.8	8.1	8.8	7.1	7.7	3.6	1.8	15.7	11.6
C+	3.4	4.9	1.1	12.3	5.1	4.6	5.0	3.5	4.7	1.2	0.4	14.7	8.2
C	1.3	1.9	0.4	4.8	1.8	1.9	2.1	1.5	2.0	0.5	0.2	5.1	4.4
D	0.1	0.1	0.0	0.4	0.1	0.1	0.2	0.0	0.1	0.0	0.0	0.6	0.0
From what kind of high school did you graduate?													
Public school (not charter or magnet)	77.8	77.6	78.1	78.4	82.8	70.7	69.4	65.8	74.9	82.1	62.8	84.6	67.7
Public charter school	1.9	2.1	1.5	3.1	2.4	1.7	1.7	1.9	1.6	1.6	1.1	2.0	4.9
Public magnet school	3.4	3.1	3.7	9.7	3.4	2.8	3.2	2.1	2.5	3.6	4.0	7.9	12.8
Private religious/parochial school	10.5	10.7	10.1	5.4	7.6	14.9	13.4	22.7	12.8	8.2	17.4	3.2	9.2
Private independent college-prep school	5.8	5.5	6.2	3.3	3.2	8.7	11.7	6.7	5.9	4.1	14.3	2.0	5.4
Home school	0.6	0.8	0.3	0.2	0.5	1.2	0.5	0.8	2.2	0.3	0.4	0.3	0.1
Prior to this term, have you ever taken courses for credit at this institution?													
No	95.4	95.1	95.8	91.0	94.8	95.6	95.6	95.4	95.7	95.8	96.1	93.2	87.2
Yes	4.6	4.9	4.2	9.0	5.2	4.4	4.4	4.6	4.3	4.2	3.9	6.8	12.8

WEIGHTED NATIONAL NORMS FOR ALL FRESHMEN, FALL 2008

	ALL BACC. INSTS.	ALL 4-YR. COLLEGES	ALL UNI-VERSITIES	ALL BLACK COLLEGES	FOUR-YEAR COLLEGES					UNIVERSITIES		BLACK COLLEGES	
					PUBLIC	ALL PRIV.	NONSECT.	CATHOLIC	OTH. REL.	PUBLIC	PRIVATE	PUBLIC	PRIVATE
Since leaving high school, have you ever taken courses, whether for credit or not for credit, at any other institution (university, 4- or 2-year college, technical, vocational, or business school)?													
No	88.5	89.0	87.8	86.7	89.0	88.9	89.5	89.2	88.0	87.5	88.6	86.9	86.5
Yes	11.5	11.0	12.2	13.3	11.0	11.1	10.5	10.8	12.0	12.5	11.4	13.1	13.5
Where do you plan to live during the fall term?													
With my family or other relatives	14.7	20.1	6.0	12.1	25.4	12.9	16.2	16.3	7.0	5.6	7.6	13.5	9.8
Other private home, apartment, or room	4.2	4.8	3.4	3.3	7.2	1.5	2.0	1.2	0.9	4.2	0.5	3.5	3.1
College residence hall	77.7	72.1	86.9	81.1	63.3	83.7	79.8	81.3	90.1	86.0	90.5	79.5	83.9
Fraternity or sorority house	0.5	0.2	0.9	0.0	0.1	0.2	0.4	0.0	0.1	1.1	0.1	0.0	0.0
Other campus student housing	2.5	2.5	2.6	2.9	3.3	1.4	1.4	0.9	1.7	2.9	1.3	2.9	2.8
Other	0.3	0.4	0.2	0.6	0.6	0.3	0.2	0.2	0.3	0.2	0.1	0.6	0.4
To how many colleges other than this one did you apply for admission this year?													
None	15.4	16.7	13.2	11.4	19.3	13.2	12.0	10.3	16.1	14.5	8.2	12.8	9.0
One	10.8	11.5	9.7	8.8	13.0	9.5	8.0	9.0	11.7	10.7	5.5	8.9	8.7
Two	13.7	14.9	11.7	16.3	16.3	12.9	10.7	13.5	15.4	12.9	7.2	17.8	13.9
Three	15.6	17.0	13.5	20.2	17.5	16.3	14.7	16.9	18.0	14.3	10.3	21.4	18.4
Four	13.0	13.7	11.9	16.7	13.0	14.5	14.4	15.4	14.1	12.2	11.1	16.5	17.1
Five	9.6	9.4	10.1	10.3	8.4	10.7	11.6	11.5	9.1	9.8	11.3	9.3	12.0
Six	7.2	6.4	8.6	5.9	5.6	7.5	8.9	8.1	5.5	7.9	11.0	5.1	7.3
Seven to ten	11.8	8.5	17.1	7.2	5.8	12.0	15.1	12.6	7.8	14.7	26.4	5.6	9.9
Eleven or more	2.9	2.1	4.3	3.0	1.2	3.4	4.6	2.7	2.2	3.0	9.0	2.6	3.8
Were you accepted by your first choice college?													
Yes	77.8	80.8	73.1	79.2	81.4	80.0	74.8	81.4	85.9	74.0	69.6	78.6	80.2
No	22.2	19.2	26.9	20.8	18.6	20.0	25.2	18.6	14.1	26.0	30.4	21.4	19.8
Is this college your:													
First choice?	60.7	60.8	60.4	46.0	60.5	61.2	57.9	60.7	65.6	60.8	59.0	41.2	54.1
Second choice?	26.1	27.0	24.7	30.5	27.8	25.9	27.2	28.2	23.1	24.6	25.2	31.9	28.0
Third choice?	8.6	8.3	9.1	14.6	8.1	8.6	9.8	7.9	7.5	8.9	9.9	16.2	11.7
Less than third choice?	4.6	3.9	5.8	9.0	3.6	4.3	5.1	3.2	3.8	5.7	5.8	10.6	6.3
Citizenship status													
U.S. citizen	96.3	96.8	95.3	98.5	97.5	95.9	94.3	97.3	97.2	95.9	93.1	98.5	98.5
Permanent resident (green card)	2.0	1.6	2.8	1.0	1.6	1.5	2.0	1.5	1.0	2.8	2.9	1.1	0.7
Neither	1.7	1.6	1.9	0.6	0.8	2.6	3.7	1.1	1.8	1.3	4.0	0.4	0.8
Are your parents:													
Both alive and living with each other?	70.3	67.2	75.5	36.9	65.7	69.1	66.7	71.2	71.1	74.5	79.3	35.6	39.2
Both alive, divorced or living apart?	25.9	28.7	21.4	54.6	30.0	26.8	29.1	24.8	25.0	22.3	17.8	55.6	52.9
One or both deceased?	3.8	4.2	3.1	8.4	4.2	4.1	4.2	4.0	3.9	3.2	2.9	8.7	7.9

WEIGHTED NATIONAL NORMS FOR ALL FRESHMEN, FALL 2008

	ALL BACC. INSTS.	ALL 4-YR. COLLEGES	ALL UNI- VERSITIES	ALL BLACK COLLEGES	FOUR-YEAR COLLEGES					UNIVERSITIES		BLACK COLLEGES	
					PUBLIC	ALL PRIV.	NONSECT.	CATHOLIC	OTH. REL.	PUBLIC	PRIVATE	PUBLIC	PRIVATE
During high school (grades 9-12) how many years did you study each of the following subjects? [1]													
English (4 years)	97.9	97.6	98.5	96.2	97.6	97.5	97.6	98.3	97.0	98.5	98.8	95.9	96.8
Mathematics (3 years)	98.5	98.1	99.1	97.1	97.9	98.4	98.7	99.1	97.8	99.0	99.5	96.4	98.1
Foreign Language (2 years)	92.9	91.1	95.7	85.2	90.2	92.4	92.7	94.6	91.0	95.2	97.6	82.7	89.6
Physical Science (2 years)	61.8	58.2	67.6	38.9	56.2	60.9	63.2	59.8	58.6	66.7	71.4	35.8	44.3
Biological Science (2 years)	49.5	47.4	52.7	39.6	45.6	49.8	49.6	50.4	49.8	52.5	53.6	37.0	44.0
History/Am. Govt. (1 year)	98.9	98.8	99.1	96.8	98.8	98.8	98.9	99.1	98.5	99.1	99.2	96.9	96.6
Computer Science (1/2 year)	60.8	63.7	56.0	63.2	66.6	59.9	57.5	62.1	61.8	56.8	53.1	63.9	62.0
Arts and/or Music (1 year)	82.3	81.3	84.1	74.7	80.3	82.6	84.0	80.4	81.8	83.7	85.6	72.6	78.3
WHAT IS THE HIGHEST ACADEMIC DEGREE THAT YOU INTEND TO OBTAIN?													
Highest planned													
None	0.9	1.1	0.6	1.6	1.0	1.1	1.3	1.0	1.1	0.6	0.5	1.5	1.6
Vocational certificate	0.1	0.2	0.1	0.2	0.2	0.3	0.3	0.1	0.2	0.1	0.0	0.3	0.2
Associate (A.A. or equivalent)	0.6	0.8	0.3	0.5	0.8	0.7	0.6	0.7	0.9	0.3	0.1	0.7	0.3
Bachelor's degree (B.A., B.S., etc.)	22.6	25.6	18.1	14.7	27.6	22.9	21.8	20.3	25.7	19.6	12.1	18.5	8.3
Master's degree (M.A., M.S., etc.)	42.4	43.1	41.2	36.8	43.5	42.5	43.4	44.6	40.2	41.6	39.7	40.6	30.4
Ph.D. or Ed.D.	18.0	16.6	20.2	26.7	16.0	17.4	17.3	17.2	17.5	19.8	21.7	24.8	29.8
M.D., D.O., D.D.S., D.V.M.	9.4	7.0	13.0	10.8	6.1	8.2	7.6	9.7	8.1	12.3	15.9	6.6	17.7
J.D. (Law)	4.1	3.5	5.1	5.6	2.9	4.3	4.8	4.3	3.6	4.4	8.0	3.5	9.0
B.D. or M.DIV. (Divinity)	0.3	0.4	0.2	0.8	0.3	0.5	0.5	0.3	0.6	0.2	0.3	0.9	0.7
Other	1.6	1.8	1.3	2.4	1.6	2.1	2.3	1.7	2.0	1.2	1.6	2.6	2.1
Highest planned at this college													
None	1.4	1.8	0.8	3.1	2.2	1.3	1.3	1.1	1.6	0.8	0.5	3.9	1.7
Vocational certificate	0.2	0.2	0.1	0.3	0.2	0.2	0.2	0.1	0.3	0.1	0.1	0.4	0.2
Associate (A.A. or equivalent)	2.2	3.0	1.0	3.3	3.6	2.3	1.9	2.3	2.8	1.1	0.7	4.0	2.2
Bachelor's degree (B.A., B.S., etc.)	69.7	71.6	66.9	65.4	69.2	74.6	75.8	66.9	77.1	66.8	67.2	63.7	68.4
Master's degree (M.A., M.S., etc.)	19.4	18.1	21.4	18.0	19.5	16.2	15.9	22.2	13.5	21.6	20.6	19.5	15.6
Ph.D. or Ed.D.	3.3	2.5	4.6	5.6	2.1	2.4	2.1	3.9	2.0	4.7	4.6	5.1	6.3
M.D., D.O., D.D.S., D.V.M.	1.7	0.7	3.4	1.3	0.6	0.7	0.7	1.2	0.6	3.3	3.5	0.5	2.6
J.D. (Law)	0.6	0.4	0.9	0.7	0.3	0.5	0.4	0.7	0.5	0.7	1.5	0.6	0.8
B.D. or M.DIV. (Divinity)	0.2	0.2	0.1	0.6	0.2	0.2	0.2	0.2	0.3	0.1	0.2	0.5	0.6
Other	1.2	1.4	0.9	1.7	1.4	1.5	1.4	1.5	1.5	0.8	1.2	1.8	1.6
HOW WOULD YOU DESCRIBE THE RACIAL COMPOSITION OF THE:													
High school I last attended													
Completely non-White	3.4	3.8	2.9	15.6	4.2	3.3	3.8	4.1	2.3	3.0	2.4	15.5	15.7
Mostly non-White	13.0	12.5	13.8	34.5	13.8	10.9	11.8	11.2	9.6	14.6	10.6	35.8	32.1
Roughly half non-White	24.8	24.9	24.5	26.8	26.1	23.2	23.8	19.1	24.7	25.1	22.4	28.3	24.2
Mostly White	51.2	50.9	51.6	21.3	48.6	54.0	52.8	56.5	54.2	50.2	56.7	19.3	24.5
Completely White	7.6	7.9	7.3	2.0	7.3	8.6	7.9	9.2	9.2	7.1	7.9	1.1	3.4
Neighborhood where I grew up													
Completely non-White	6.1	6.9	4.8	29.1	7.4	6.4	7.3	6.8	5.0	4.9	4.5	29.7	28.2
Mostly non-White	11.5	11.6	11.4	33.0	12.4	10.6	11.8	10.6	9.0	11.8	9.7	33.4	32.3
Roughly half non-White	13.6	13.5	13.9	18.9	14.2	12.6	12.8	12.3	12.4	14.0	13.6	19.0	18.8
Mostly White	48.9	47.4	51.3	15.9	46.5	48.7	48.1	47.4	50.1	50.7	53.6	15.2	17.1
Completely White	19.8	20.5	18.6	3.1	19.6	21.8	20.0	22.9	23.5	18.7	18.5	2.8	3.6

	ALL BACC. INSTS.	ALL 4-YR. COLLEGES	ALL UNI-VERSITIES	ALL BLACK COLLEGES	FOUR-YEAR COLLEGES					UNIVERSITIES		BLACK COLLEGES	
					PUBLIC	ALL PRIV.	NONSECT.	CATHOLIC	OTH. REL.	PUBLIC	PRIVATE	PUBLIC	PRIVATE
Do you have a disability?													
Hearing	0.6	0.6	0.5	0.2	0.6	0.6	0.7	0.6	0.7	0.5	0.4	0.2	0.3
Speech	0.3	0.3	0.2	0.3	0.3	0.3	0.3	0.3	0.3	0.2	0.2	0.3	0.2
Orthopedic	0.5	0.5	0.4	0.4	0.5	0.5	0.6	0.5	0.6	0.4	0.4	0.4	0.4
Learning disability	3.3	4.0	2.1	2.0	3.3	5.0	5.7	3.9	4.6	1.9	2.7	1.7	2.5
Partially sighted or blind	1.4	1.4	1.2	1.3	1.5	1.2	1.2	1.1	1.3	1.4	1.3	1.2	1.4
Health-related	1.4	1.5	1.2	1.8	1.4	1.6	1.6	1.6	1.7	1.2	1.3	1.6	2.0
Other	1.3	1.4	1.0	1.1	1.3	1.5	1.5	1.3	1.6	1.0	1.0	0.9	1.4
HOW MUCH OF YOUR FIRST YEAR'S EDUCATIONAL EXPENSES (ROOM, BOARD TUITION, AND FEES) DO YOU EXPECT TO COVER FROM:													
Family resources (parents, relatives, spouse, etc.)													
None	20.4	23.5	15.4	40.2	26.7	19.2	19.5	18.5	19.2	16.5	11.4	44.7	32.5
Less than $1,000	11.7	13.5	8.7	19.8	15.6	10.8	9.7	10.6	12.3	9.6	5.2	22.4	15.4
$1,000 to 2,999	13.8	15.3	11.4	16.7	17.2	12.7	11.4	13.6	14.1	12.5	7.2	16.2	17.6
$3,000 to 5,999	12.6	13.0	11.8	10.1	13.5	12.4	11.2	13.2	13.5	12.8	7.9	9.0	12.1
$6,000 to 9,999	10.5	10.1	11.1	4.9	9.5	10.8	10.2	11.4	11.2	11.7	8.7	3.7	7.0
$10,000 +	31.1	24.6	41.5	8.2	17.4	34.1	38.1	32.7	29.7	36.9	59.5	4.1	15.4
My own resources (savings from work, work-study, other income)													
None	35.3	36.4	33.5	55.8	37.8	34.5	36.2	30.3	34.4	32.4	37.7	58.7	50.9
Less than $1,000	27.1	28.0	25.8	25.6	29.9	25.5	24.7	26.0	26.2	26.5	22.7	25.1	26.3
$1,000 to 2,999	23.8	22.7	25.7	13.3	21.4	24.3	23.9	25.9	24.1	26.1	24.0	11.9	15.6
$3,000 to 5,999	8.8	8.3	9.7	3.2	7.4	9.4	9.0	10.8	9.3	9.9	8.9	2.6	4.3
$6,000 to 9,999	2.6	2.5	2.8	1.2	2.0	3.1	2.8	3.6	3.1	2.8	3.1	1.0	1.5
$10,000 +	2.4	2.3	2.5	0.9	1.6	3.2	3.4	3.4	2.9	2.2	3.6	0.7	1.4
Aid which _not_ be repaid (grants, scholarships, military funding, etc.)													
None	30.7	29.5	32.8	26.9	36.0	20.8	25.9	16.7	16.2	34.2	27.3	27.9	25.4
Less than $1,000	7.2	7.0	7.4	6.3	9.4	3.8	4.4	3.5	3.3	8.4	3.5	6.7	5.5
$1,000 to 2,999	13.7	14.0	13.1	15.3	17.9	8.8	9.1	8.6	8.5	14.7	7.2	16.3	13.4
$3,000 to 5,999	13.5	14.3	12.2	19.6	16.0	12.0	11.9	12.1	12.1	13.5	7.0	21.3	16.7
$6,000 to 9,999	10.8	11.1	10.3	12.8	8.6	14.4	13.4	15.7	15.1	10.8	8.6	12.6	13.2
$10,000 +	24.1	24.0	24.2	19.0	11.9	40.2	35.4	43.3	44.7	18.4	46.4	15.1	25.8
Aid which _must_ be repaid (loans, etc.)													
None	50.6	48.6	53.9	41.3	55.4	39.5	42.7	34.8	37.8	54.4	51.8	45.7	33.7
Less than $1,000	3.9	4.3	3.2	5.7	5.0	3.3	3.0	3.7	3.6	3.5	2.1	6.5	4.3
$1,000 to 2,999	9.5	10.4	8.1	12.8	10.9	9.8	8.8	10.9	10.5	8.2	7.7	14.8	9.3
$3,000 to 5,999	15.3	15.9	14.3	16.3	14.3	18.0	15.9	20.2	19.7	14.3	14.0	17.3	14.6
$6,000 to 9,999	8.9	9.4	8.2	10.5	7.2	12.2	11.1	13.0	13.3	8.3	7.9	9.4	12.3
$10,000 +	11.8	11.5	12.4	13.5	7.2	17.1	18.6	17.5	15.1	11.3	16.4	6.3	25.9
Other than above													
None	93.6	93.4	94.0	92.0	93.9	92.6	93.2	91.6	92.3	94.1	93.7	92.2	91.6
Less than $1,000	2.5	2.6	2.3	2.9	2.6	2.5	2.2	3.0	2.7	2.4	1.9	2.8	3.0
$1,000 to 2,999	1.5	1.6	1.4	2.0	1.6	1.6	1.4	1.8	1.7	1.5	1.3	2.2	1.6
$3,000 to 5,999	0.9	0.9	0.8	1.2	0.8	1.2	1.1	1.2	1.2	0.8	0.8	1.2	1.3
$6,000 to 9,999	0.5	0.5	0.5	0.6	0.3	0.7	0.7	0.7	0.7	0.5	0.6	0.6	0.7
$10,000 +	1.0	1.1	1.0	1.4	0.8	1.5	1.5	1.7	1.4	0.8	1.8	1.1	1.9

WEIGHTED NATIONAL NORMS FOR ALL FRESHMEN, FALL 2008

	ALL BACC. INSTS.	ALL 4-YR. COLLEGES	ALL UNI-VERSITIES	ALL BLACK COLLEGES	FOUR-YEAR COLLEGES PUBLIC	ALL PRIV.	NONSECT.	CATHOLIC	OTH. REL.	UNIVERSITIES PUBLIC	PRIVATE	BLACK COLLEGES PUBLIC	PRIVATE
What is your best estimate of your parents' total income last year? Consider income from all sources before taxes													
Less than $10,000	3.7	4.4	2.6	13.1	4.6	4.0	4.1	4.1	3.9	2.7	1.9	14.5	10.8
$10,000 to 14,999	2.8	3.3	2.1	6.5	3.6	2.9	2.9	2.9	2.8	2.2	1.4	6.6	6.4
$15,000 to 19,999	2.5	2.8	2.0	6.1	3.0	2.5	2.6	2.6	2.4	2.1	1.5	6.5	5.3
$20,000 to 24,999	3.4	3.8	2.8	7.6	4.1	3.4	3.2	3.6	3.6	3.0	1.8	7.8	7.3
$25,000 to 29,999	3.3	3.7	2.6	6.5	3.9	3.4	3.3	3.0	3.7	2.8	1.7	6.9	6.0
$30,000 to 39,999	6.3	6.9	5.3	10.7	7.2	6.6	6.3	6.7	6.9	5.6	4.0	11.5	9.5
$40,000 to 49,999	7.3	8.2	5.9	10.4	8.4	7.8	7.3	7.7	8.6	6.3	4.4	11.0	9.3
$50,000 to 59,999	8.3	9.1	7.1	8.3	9.3	8.9	8.5	8.7	9.5	7.5	5.4	8.1	8.6
$60,000 to 74,999	11.0	11.8	9.7	9.6	12.1	11.5	10.7	11.7	12.4	10.2	8.1	9.2	10.2
$75,000 to 99,999	14.2	14.1	14.5	8.3	14.1	14.1	13.5	14.8	14.4	14.9	13.0	7.6	9.4
$100,000 to 149,999	17.6	15.8	20.4	6.8	15.8	15.7	15.7	16.6	15.4	20.4	20.5	6.2	7.8
$150,000 to 199,999	8.0	7.0	9.7	3.0	6.7	7.4	8.1	7.8	6.4	9.3	11.0	2.4	4.2
$200,000 to 249,999	4.1	3.3	5.5	1.3	2.8	4.0	4.4	3.7	3.5	5.0	7.6	0.9	1.8
$250,000 or more	7.4	5.8	9.9	1.7	4.5	7.7	9.4	6.0	6.5	8.0	17.5	0.8	3.3
Do you have any concern about your ability to finance your college education?													
None (I am confident that I will have sufficient funds)	35.9	35.8	36.1	29.9	36.8	34.4	35.1	32.1	34.6	35.4	38.9	31.4	27.2
Some (but I probably will have enough funds)	53.2	53.0	53.5	50.1	52.3	53.9	52.6	56.0	54.4	54.0	51.5	50.6	49.4
Major (not sure I will have enough funds to complete college)	10.9	11.2	10.4	20.0	10.9	11.7	12.3	11.9	11.0	10.6	9.6	18.0	23.5
Your current religious preference													
Baptist	10.6	13.5	5.9	50.4	14.6	12.2	9.0	7.0	18.9	6.1	5.4	52.3	47.3
Buddhist	1.3	0.8	2.0	0.3	0.8	0.9	1.2	0.8	0.5	2.1	1.5	0.1	0.6
Church of Christ	4.4	5.0	3.3	9.6	5.3	4.6	4.7	3.5	5.1	3.6	1.9	10.5	8.1
Eastern Orthodox	0.7	0.5	0.8	0.0	0.5	0.6	0.7	0.7	0.4	0.7	1.2	0.0	0.1
Episcopalian	1.3	1.3	1.4	0.6	1.2	1.6	1.9	0.9	1.6	1.2	1.8	0.4	0.9
Hindu	0.8	0.4	1.5	0.1	0.3	0.5	0.8	0.3	0.3	1.4	1.9	0.1	0.1
Jewish	2.6	1.7	4.1	0.0	1.5	2.0	3.4	0.4	1.0	3.5	6.6	0.0	0.1
LDS (Mormon)	2.3	2.2	2.5	0.1	3.7	0.1	0.1	0.1	0.2	3.1	0.2	0.1	0.0
Lutheran	3.6	3.2	4.1	0.3	2.6	4.0	2.3	3.5	6.4	4.5	2.3	0.3	0.3
Methodist	4.5	4.7	4.1	5.5	4.7	4.8	3.4	2.7	7.5	4.4	3.1	5.5	5.5
Muslim	0.9	0.8	1.1	0.6	0.8	0.8	1.1	0.7	0.4	1.0	1.6	0.4	1.0
Presbyterian	3.1	2.8	3.6	0.8	2.6	3.1	2.6	1.7	4.4	3.7	3.3	0.8	0.7
Quaker	0.2	0.2	0.2	0.1	0.2	0.3	0.3	0.1	0.4	0.2	0.2	0.1	0.1
Roman Catholic	25.4	24.9	26.2	5.6	23.7	26.6	26.2	52.7	13.6	24.5	32.6	3.8	8.7
Seventh Day Adventist	0.5	0.5	0.3	1.3	0.4	0.8	0.5	0.3	1.3	0.3	0.2	1.5	1.0
United Church of Christ/Congregational	0.7	0.8	0.6	0.8	0.7	0.9	1.0	0.7	0.9	0.6	0.6	0.9	0.5
Other Christian	12.9	14.1	11.0	14.9	13.8	14.6	11.0	9.3	21.9	11.7	8.5	13.9	16.6
Other Religion	3.0	3.1	2.9	2.9	3.2	2.9	3.4	2.1	2.6	2.9	2.7	3.1	2.7
None	21.2	19.2	24.6	6.0	19.4	18.8	26.3	12.3	12.6	24.6	24.6	6.1	5.8

WEIGHTED NATIONAL NORMS FOR ALL FRESHMEN, FALL 2008

	ALL BACC. INSTS.	ALL 4-YR. COLLEGES	ALL UNI-VERSITIES	ALL BLACK COLLEGES	FOUR-YEAR COLLEGES					UNIVERSITIES		BLACK COLLEGES	
					PUBLIC	ALL PRIV.	NONSECT.	CATHOLIC	OTH. REL.	PUBLIC	PRIVATE	PUBLIC	PRIVATE
Father's current religious preference													
Baptist	10.6	13.4	6.2	48.3	14.7	11.8	8.9	6.6	18.1	6.3	5.6	50.6	44.6
Buddhist	1.7	0.9	2.9	0.5	0.9	0.9	1.3	0.8	0.5	3.1	2.2	0.2	0.8
Church of Christ	4.4	5.0	3.5	8.1	5.2	4.6	5.0	3.6	4.7	3.8	2.2	8.6	7.2
Eastern Orthodox	0.8	0.7	0.9	0.0	0.6	0.8	1.0	0.9	0.4	0.8	1.3	0.0	0.1
Episcopalian	1.7	1.6	1.7	0.6	1.4	1.9	2.3	1.1	1.8	1.5	2.5	0.5	0.7
Hindu	1.0	0.5	1.8	0.1	0.4	0.6	1.0	0.3	0.3	1.7	2.3	0.1	0.0
Jewish	3.4	2.4	5.0	0.2	2.0	3.0	5.0	0.8	1.5	4.2	7.8	0.2	0.1
LDS (Mormon)	2.4	2.3	2.6	0.1	3.9	0.2	0.2	0.1	0.3	3.2	0.2	0.1	0.0
Lutheran	4.3	3.9	4.9	0.4	3.2	4.7	2.8	4.3	7.3	5.4	3.0	0.4	0.3
Methodist	4.9	5.0	4.7	4.6	5.0	5.0	4.0	3.0	7.4	4.9	3.7	4.5	4.6
Muslim	1.3	1.2	1.5	1.8	1.2	1.2	1.7	1.0	0.6	1.4	2.0	1.5	2.3
Presbyterian	3.7	3.4	4.1	0.8	3.1	3.6	3.3	2.1	4.9	4.1	4.0	1.0	0.6
Quaker	0.2	0.2	0.2	0.0	0.2	0.3	0.3	0.1	0.3	0.2	0.2	0.0	0.1
Roman Catholic	28.6	28.2	29.2	6.4	27.1	29.5	30.3	53.5	16.1	27.5	35.5	4.3	10.0
Seventh Day Adventist	0.5	0.6	0.4	1.2	0.4	0.8	0.5	0.4	1.3	0.4	0.3	1.3	0.9
United Church of Christ/Congregational	0.8	0.8	0.7	0.8	0.8	1.0	1.1	0.7	0.9	0.7	0.7	0.8	0.6
Other Christian	11.9	12.9	10.3	13.1	12.6	13.3	10.5	8.3	19.4	10.9	8.0	12.3	14.4
Other Religion	2.1	2.2	2.1	2.8	2.3	2.0	2.3	1.7	1.9	2.1	1.8	2.8	2.7
None	15.8	14.9	17.4	10.3	14.9	14.8	18.6	10.5	12.1	17.6	16.6	10.7	9.7
Mother's current religious preference													
Baptist	11.4	14.4	6.6	51.4	15.5	12.9	10.0	7.5	19.3	6.7	6.0	52.8	49.1
Buddhist	1.8	1.0	3.1	0.5	0.9	1.0	1.4	0.8	0.5	3.3	2.5	0.3	0.8
Church of Christ	4.9	5.6	3.8	9.6	5.9	5.1	5.6	3.9	5.1	4.2	2.5	10.7	7.6
Eastern Orthodox	0.8	0.6	1.0	0.1	0.6	0.7	0.9	0.8	0.5	0.9	1.4	0.1	0.1
Episcopalian	1.9	1.8	2.0	0.8	1.5	2.1	2.7	1.1	2.0	1.8	2.6	0.6	1.0
Hindu	1.0	0.5	1.8	0.1	0.4	0.6	0.9	0.3	0.3	1.6	2.3	0.1	0.0
Jewish	3.2	2.2	4.8	0.0	1.9	2.5	4.3	0.5	1.3	4.1	7.4	0.0	0.0
LDS (Mormon)	2.5	2.4	2.6	0.1	4.1	0.2	0.2	0.2	0.2	3.3	0.2	0.1	0.0
Lutheran	4.4	4.0	5.0	0.3	3.3	5.0	3.3	4.2	7.6	5.5	3.1	0.3	0.4
Methodist	5.5	5.7	5.2	5.7	5.7	5.6	4.4	3.3	8.4	5.5	4.0	5.8	5.4
Muslim	1.0	0.9	1.3	0.6	0.9	0.9	1.3	0.7	0.5	1.2	1.7	0.4	0.9
Presbyterian	3.9	3.6	4.5	0.7	3.3	3.9	3.7	2.2	5.2	4.5	4.3	0.7	0.7
Quaker	0.2	0.3	0.2	0.1	0.2	0.3	0.3	0.2	0.4	0.2	0.2	0.1	0.2
Roman Catholic	30.3	29.6	31.3	6.2	28.7	30.9	31.9	56.1	16.6	29.6	38.1	4.6	8.8
Seventh Day Adventist	0.5	0.6	0.4	1.5	0.5	0.8	0.6	0.4	1.4	0.4	0.3	1.8	1.0
United Church of Christ/Congregational	0.9	1.0	0.8	0.8	0.9	1.2	1.3	0.8	1.1	0.8	0.8	0.9	0.6
Other Christian	13.1	14.2	11.4	14.5	13.9	14.6	12.1	9.3	20.5	12.1	8.9	13.2	16.6
Other Religion	2.3	2.3	2.2	3.0	2.4	2.2	2.5	1.7	2.0	2.2	1.9	3.2	2.6
None	10.5	9.5	12.0	4.2	9.4	9.5	12.8	6.0	7.1	12.1	11.8	4.3	4.0

WEIGHTED NATIONAL NORMS FOR ALL FRESHMEN, FALL 2008

	ALL BACC. INSTS.	ALL 4-YR. COLLEGES	ALL UNI-VERSITIES	ALL BLACK COLLEGES	FOUR-YEAR COLLEGES PUBLIC	ALL PRIV.	NONSECT.	CATHOLIC	OTH. REL.	UNIVERSITIES PUBLIC	PRIVATE	BLACK COLLEGES PUBLIC	PRIVATE
During the past year, student "frequently" or "occasionally":													
Attended a religious service	75.8	76.9	74.1	91.4	76.0	78.0	70.0	83.2	85.7	73.9	74.9	90.8	92.5
Was bored in class [2]	39.5	39.1	40.1	34.9	41.0	36.5	36.6	34.6	37.2	40.6	38.1	37.5	30.5
Participated in political demonstrations	25.7	25.5	26.1	37.4	24.8	26.5	27.0	26.6	25.8	26.0	26.4	37.0	38.2
Tutored another student	56.4	51.6	64.2	58.0	51.4	51.8	50.8	53.6	52.1	62.7	69.8	53.6	65.3
Studied with other students	87.7	86.1	90.2	87.2	85.5	87.0	86.1	88.9	87.0	90.0	90.7	86.5	88.6
Was a guest in a teacher's home	21.5	21.8	21.0	20.3	20.3	23.8	22.4	18.9	27.9	20.3	23.4	18.9	22.6
Smoked cigarettes [2]	4.4	5.1	3.3	1.9	5.4	4.7	5.9	3.9	3.5	3.4	3.0	1.9	1.9
Drank beer	38.0	37.5	38.9	12.7	36.4	38.9	45.5	38.7	30.6	38.1	42.0	14.1	10.2
Drank wine or liquor	43.9	43.9	44.1	34.9	42.9	45.2	52.3	44.9	36.2	43.2	47.5	36.6	31.9
Felt overwhelmed by all I had to do [2]	28.2	28.8	27.1	27.4	28.4	29.4	29.3	29.2	29.5	26.9	28.0	27.9	26.5
Felt depressed [2]	6.9	7.6	5.7	10.6	7.6	7.5	8.1	6.7	7.1	5.7	5.9	11.6	8.8
Performed volunteer work	84.4	82.2	88.1	81.7	79.9	85.2	83.3	87.0	86.7	87.3	91.2	79.3	85.8
Played a musical instrument	44.5	42.3	48.1	39.4	41.6	43.4	42.2	38.7	47.2	47.4	50.9	38.5	40.9
Asked a teacher for advice after class [2]	28.0	27.5	28.8	29.3	26.0	29.6	29.9	29.5	29.3	28.3	30.9	26.0	36.6
Voted in a student election [2]	22.6	22.2	23.4	31.6	21.5	23.0	22.6	24.3	22.9	22.8	25.9	28.7	36.4
Socialized with someone of another racial/ethnic group [2]	69.8	68.6	71.8	69.8	68.9	68.3	70.0	66.1	67.2	71.2	73.9	67.6	73.6
Came late to class	60.5	60.3	60.8	68.3	61.4	58.7	60.6	55.8	57.8	61.1	59.4	68.8	67.4
Used the Internet: [2]													
For research or homework	76.0	73.3	80.5	76.5	71.1	76.2	77.0	79.3	73.6	79.4	84.5	74.5	80.0
To read news sites	42.9	40.6	46.8	43.6	38.8	42.9	45.2	44.3	39.2	44.9	54.1	41.7	46.9
To read blogs	25.1	24.5	26.1	27.3	23.8	25.4	26.1	24.8	24.7	25.7	27.5	26.5	28.6
To blog	14.5	14.7	14.2	17.1	14.4	15.1	14.4	15.1	15.8	14.4	13.4	16.9	17.4
Performed community service as part of a class	58.4	57.6	59.6	57.9	55.3	60.8	59.1	66.1	60.2	58.7	62.7	54.2	64.2
Discussed religion [2]	31.8	31.4	32.4	31.7	29.8	33.6	29.6	32.8	39.1	31.2	36.9	27.7	38.6
Discussed politics [2]	35.6	33.0	39.8	31.4	31.8	34.6	35.7	33.8	33.4	38.5	44.7	27.9	37.4
Worked on a local, state or national political campaign	11.7	11.0	12.9	16.5	10.5	11.7	11.6	12.0	11.6	12.5	14.5	14.8	19.5
Student rated self "above average" or "highest 10%" as compared with the average person of his/her age in:													
Academic ability	69.5	62.5	80.9	60.4	61.0	64.5	63.4	65.4	65.4	79.2	87.5	54.9	69.8
Artistic ability	30.6	30.1	31.4	29.1	28.8	31.7	35.9	24.9	29.9	30.4	35.1	27.0	32.6
Computer skills	38.4	36.9	40.9	45.5	38.0	35.4	36.4	36.6	33.4	40.6	41.8	44.7	46.9
Cooperativeness	73.7	72.2	76.0	73.0	71.6	73.1	72.3	75.1	73.1	75.8	76.7	70.8	76.7
Creativity	56.8	56.3	57.5	61.9	55.1	57.9	61.2	53.8	55.8	56.6	61.1	60.4	64.5
Drive to achieve	75.2	72.6	79.4	80.8	70.9	74.8	75.1	76.2	73.7	78.3	83.8	78.0	85.7
Emotional health	54.5	51.8	58.9	56.4	51.2	52.5	51.3	53.4	53.5	58.6	60.0	53.8	60.9
Leadership ability	61.8	60.0	64.8	69.1	59.4	60.8	59.9	61.5	61.6	64.0	68.2	66.5	73.5
Mathematical ability	44.9	38.5	55.2	37.7	38.6	38.4	37.7	39.4	38.8	53.5	61.8	35.4	41.5
Physical health	55.8	54.0	58.8	53.3	53.0	55.3	54.0	56.8	56.2	58.6	59.4	50.7	57.7
Popularity	39.4	38.6	40.6	49.2	38.4	38.9	39.4	39.1	38.1	39.8	43.3	48.0	51.3
Public speaking ability	37.7	35.7	41.0	40.5	35.3	36.3	36.7	35.3	36.4	39.4	46.9	37.9	44.9
Self-confidence (intellectual)	60.7	57.6	65.6	74.9	57.0	58.5	58.4	57.6	59.0	64.4	70.2	73.1	77.8
Self-confidence (social)	52.5	51.9	53.6	70.4	52.2	51.4	51.3	52.0	51.3	53.6	53.7	69.9	71.3
Self-understanding	58.5	56.5	61.6	71.6	55.6	57.7	58.6	56.6	57.2	60.9	64.0	69.7	74.9
Spirituality	39.9	40.3	39.2	59.3	40.0	40.7	35.9	40.0	47.3	39.1	39.6	58.0	61.6
Understanding of others	67.2	66.0	69.2	67.4	65.3	66.8	67.2	67.2	66.1	68.7	71.2	65.9	70.0
Writing ability	47.5	44.9	51.8	48.0	43.4	46.9	48.3	46.6	45.3	50.0	58.9	44.6	53.9

WEIGHTED NATIONAL NORMS FOR ALL FRESHMEN, FALL 2008

	ALL BACC. INSTS.	ALL 4-YR. COLLEGES	ALL UNI-VERSITIES	ALL BLACK COLLEGES	FOUR-YEAR COLLEGES PUBLIC	FOUR-YEAR COLLEGES ALL PRIV.	FOUR-YEAR COLLEGES NONSECT.	FOUR-YEAR COLLEGES CATHOLIC	FOUR-YEAR COLLEGES OTH. REL.	UNIVERSITIES PUBLIC	UNIVERSITIES PRIVATE	BLACK COLLEGES PUBLIC	BLACK COLLEGES PRIVATE
Student rated self "above average" or "highest 10%" as compared with the average person of his/her age in:													
Ability to see the world from someone else's perspective	65.3	62.4	70.2	59.3	61.7	63.2	65.0	62.4	61.4	69.1	74.1	55.9	65.1
Tolerance of others with different beliefs	73.2	70.0	78.5	63.0	69.4	70.7	73.2	71.1	67.4	77.7	81.5	59.2	69.4
Openness to having my own views challenged	58.4	56.7	61.4	60.2	56.3	57.1	59.9	56.1	53.9	60.6	64.5	57.0	65.5
Ability to discuss and negotiate controversial issues	63.4	60.8	67.7	63.2	60.7	60.9	63.2	60.1	58.4	66.7	71.8	60.1	68.4
Ability to work cooperatively with diverse people	78.7	76.6	82.1	76.5	76.4	76.9	78.1	77.5	75.0	81.5	84.2	73.8	81.1
WHAT IS THE HIGHEST LEVEL OF FORMAL EDUCATION OBTAINED BY YOUR PARENTS?													
Father													
Grammar school or less	4.1	4.5	3.5	5.9	5.1	3.6	3.8	4.1	3.0	3.8	2.1	5.5	6.4
Some high school	5.1	5.9	3.7	10.5	6.5	5.1	5.3	5.1	4.9	3.9	2.7	11.6	8.6
High school graduate	19.7	23.2	14.1	34.8	24.6	21.4	20.6	22.5	22.0	15.1	10.1	37.7	30.0
Postsecondary school other than college	3.4	3.7	2.9	4.2	3.7	3.7	3.3	4.6	3.9	3.0	2.2	4.3	4.0
Some college	15.0	16.0	13.3	18.6	17.0	14.8	14.1	15.4	15.2	14.0	10.3	18.0	19.5
College degree	27.4	25.9	29.9	15.7	25.2	26.8	26.0	26.9	27.7	30.2	29.1	15.0	16.8
Some graduate school	2.2	1.9	2.6	1.1	1.6	2.2	2.2	2.1	2.3	2.5	3.2	0.8	1.5
Graduate degree	23.2	18.9	30.1	9.4	16.3	22.4	24.7	19.2	21.0	27.4	40.3	7.0	13.3
Mother													
Grammar school or less	3.8	4.1	3.2	5.7	4.7	3.2	3.3	3.6	2.8	3.6	1.9	5.3	6.3
Some high school	3.8	4.2	3.1	6.2	4.7	3.4	3.8	3.5	2.9	3.3	2.0	6.6	5.5
High school graduate	17.9	20.2	14.0	22.9	21.3	18.8	18.0	20.5	19.0	15.0	10.2	24.9	19.5
Postsecondary school other than college	3.6	3.9	3.0	3.9	4.0	3.9	3.6	4.6	3.9	3.1	2.6	3.8	4.1
Some college	17.5	18.7	15.6	22.6	20.0	16.9	15.6	17.1	18.5	16.6	11.9	23.5	21.2
College degree	32.5	30.4	35.7	24.1	29.2	32.1	31.5	31.9	33.0	35.3	37.3	24.1	24.0
Some graduate school	2.7	2.4	3.3	1.5	2.0	2.9	3.1	2.5	2.8	3.1	4.1	1.2	2.1
Graduate degree	18.3	16.1	22.0	13.1	14.0	18.8	21.1	16.4	17.1	19.9	29.9	10.6	17.4
During the past year, did you "frequently":													
Ask questions in class	53.9	52.7	55.7	56.3	51.2	54.8	55.5	55.1	53.7	54.3	61.5	52.3	63.1
Support your opinions with a logical argument	57.9	54.4	63.6	51.5	53.3	55.9	58.5	54.7	53.2	61.4	71.7	47.6	58.3
Seek solutions to problems and explain them to others	51.7	48.3	57.1	48.8	47.3	49.7	51.5	49.5	47.5	54.9	65.4	45.4	54.5
Revise your papers to improve your writing	46.6	45.4	48.7	49.9	42.9	48.7	48.3	50.3	48.5	47.2	54.3	48.4	52.3
Evaluate the quality or reliability of information you received	37.0	34.6	41.1	38.1	33.5	36.0	37.3	36.1	34.3	39.3	47.8	35.8	41.9
Take a risk because you feel you have more to gain	40.0	40.0	40.0	41.1	39.9	40.1	41.7	39.6	38.3	39.4	42.1	41.2	41.0
Seek alternative solutions to a problem	44.3	42.9	46.5	45.1	42.3	43.7	45.3	43.6	41.7	45.3	51.0	42.5	49.6
Look up scientific research articles and resources	22.1	20.3	25.1	21.2	19.8	21.0	21.8	22.0	19.5	23.9	29.5	18.3	26.2
Explore topics on your own, even though it was not required for a class	31.4	29.8	34.0	27.7	29.2	30.6	33.5	28.4	27.9	32.6	39.7	25.2	31.8
Accept mistakes as part of the learning process	51.6	50.8	52.9	57.5	50.9	50.8	52.3	50.7	48.8	52.6	53.9	55.7	60.5
Seek feedback on your academic work	47.7	46.7	49.5	55.8	45.0	48.8	50.3	49.6	46.5	48.3	54.1	53.4	60.1
Take notes during class	65.8	65.4	66.5	76.2	62.7	69.1	69.4	72.5	67.0	65.2	71.1	76.6	75.6

WEIGHTED NATIONAL NORMS FOR ALL FRESHMEN, FALL 2008

	ALL BACC. INSTS.	ALL 4-YR. COLLEGES	ALL UNI-VERSITIES	ALL BLACK COLLEGES	FOUR-YEAR COLLEGES					UNIVERSITIES		BLACK COLLEGES	
					PUBLIC	ALL PRIV.	NONSECT.	CATHOLIC	OTH. REL.	PUBLIC	PRIVATE	PUBLIC	PRIVATE
Your probable career occupation													
Accountant or actuary	2.4	2.5	2.2	2.8	2.4	2.7	2.7	3.3	2.4	2.3	1.9	3.2	2.2
Actor or entertainer	1.4	1.6	0.9	1.4	1.6	1.7	2.3	0.8	1.4	0.8	1.4	1.5	1.4
Architect or urban planner	0.8	0.5	1.3	0.7	0.5	0.5	0.6	0.2	0.4	1.3	1.5	0.8	0.5
Artist	2.7	3.4	1.5	1.2	2.5	4.6	8.1	1.1	2.0	1.5	1.4	1.6	0.6
Business (clerical)	0.7	0.7	0.7	0.7	0.7	0.8	0.8	0.8	0.7	0.7	0.5	0.7	0.6
Business executive (management, administrator)	7.5	6.9	8.5	6.6	6.2	7.8	8.5	8.3	6.7	8.0	10.4	6.5	6.8
Business owner or proprietor	3.3	3.5	2.9	4.2	3.4	3.6	4.0	3.2	3.3	2.9	3.2	3.9	4.8
Business salesperson or buyer	0.9	1.0	0.8	0.6	1.0	1.0	1.1	1.0	0.7	0.9	0.7	0.6	0.6
Clergy (minister, priest)	0.2	0.2	0.1	0.0	0.1	0.4	0.1	0.2	1.0	0.1	0.1	0.0	0.1
Clergy (other religious)	0.1	0.1	0.0	0.0	0.0	0.2	0.0	0.1	0.4	0.0	0.1	0.0	0.0
Clinical psychologist	1.4	1.5	1.2	2.4	1.5	1.5	1.4	1.7	1.5	1.2	1.1	2.4	2.3
College administrator/staff	0.0	0.0	0.0	0.1	0.0	0.1	0.0	0.1	0.1	0.0	0.0	0.0	0.2
College teacher	0.5	0.5	0.5	0.3	0.4	0.6	0.7	0.3	0.7	0.4	0.8	0.3	0.3
Computer programmer or analyst	1.7	1.6	1.9	3.6	1.9	1.2	1.1	1.1	1.3	2.0	1.8	4.5	2.1
Conservationist or forester	0.3	0.2	0.4	0.1	0.2	0.3	0.3	0.1	0.3	0.4	0.2	0.1	0.1
Dentist (including orthodontist)	1.2	1.1	1.4	1.6	1.2	0.9	0.7	1.3	1.0	1.4	1.2	1.1	2.5
Dietitian or nutritionist	0.5	0.4	0.6	0.1	0.5	0.3	0.2	0.5	0.4	0.7	0.2	0.1	0.0
Engineer	7.4	4.4	12.3	5.1	5.5	2.9	3.0	3.4	2.5	12.7	10.7	5.8	3.8
Farmer or rancher	0.2	0.2	0.3	0.1	0.2	0.2	0.2	0.1	0.3	0.4	0.1	0.1	0.1
Foreign service worker (including diplomat)	0.8	0.7	1.1	0.1	0.4	0.9	1.1	0.7	0.9	0.8	2.0	0.0	0.4
Homemaker (full-time)	0.1	0.1	0.1	0.0	0.1	0.1	0.1	0.1	0.2	0.1	0.0	0.0	0.0
Interior decorator (including designer)	0.4	0.4	0.4	0.0	0.4	0.4	0.7	0.2	0.3	0.4	0.2	0.0	0.0
Lab technician or hygienist	0.2	0.2	0.2	0.2	0.2	0.2	0.2	0.3	0.1	0.2	0.1	0.2	0.1
Law enforcement officer	1.2	1.6	0.5	1.4	1.8	1.3	1.2	1.5	1.4	0.5	0.4	1.7	0.9
Lawyer (attorney) or judge	3.4	3.0	4.1	5.3	2.6	3.5	3.8	3.8	3.1	3.7	5.7	3.8	7.9
Military service (career)	1.7	2.4	0.5	0.7	3.9	0.4	0.4	0.6	0.4	0.6	0.4	0.7	0.7
Musician (performer, composer)	1.7	1.9	1.4	1.7	1.9	1.8	1.3	0.8	3.0	1.3	1.8	1.5	2.0
Nurse	4.5	5.9	2.3	8.7	6.8	4.6	2.5	9.2	4.8	2.4	1.7	11.3	4.3
Optometrist	0.4	0.3	0.4	0.4	0.4	0.3	0.2	0.4	0.3	0.4	0.3	0.4	0.5
Pharmacist	2.0	1.7	2.5	3.7	1.8	1.7	1.3	2.9	1.6	2.6	2.0	1.7	7.0
Physician	6.3	4.4	9.3	7.8	3.6	5.6	4.9	7.2	5.7	8.4	12.4	3.9	14.2
Policymaker/Government	0.9	0.8	1.1	0.5	0.7	1.0	1.1	0.9	0.9	1.0	1.8	0.4	0.9
School counselor	0.3	0.4	0.2	0.5	0.4	0.4	0.2	0.5	0.5	0.2	0.1	0.5	0.6
School principal or superintendent	0.0	0.0	0.0	0.1	0.0	0.0	0.0	0.0	0.0	0.0	0.0	0.1	0.1
Scientific researcher	2.0	1.5	2.7	0.7	1.3	1.7	2.0	1.2	1.7	2.6	3.3	0.7	0.7
Social, welfare, or recreation worker	1.1	1.3	0.7	2.8	1.4	1.1	0.8	1.1	1.5	0.8	0.5	3.3	2.0
Therapist (physical, occupational, speech)	2.9	3.4	2.3	2.7	3.6	3.1	2.0	3.9	4.0	2.4	1.7	3.3	1.7
Teacher or administrator (elementary)	4.1	5.3	2.0	4.7	5.9	4.6	3.3	5.1	5.9	2.2	1.1	6.1	2.3
Teacher or administrator (secondary)	4.2	5.2	2.5	3.1	5.7	4.6	3.2	4.6	6.3	2.7	1.5	4.1	1.5
Veterinarian	1.2	1.1	1.4	0.6	0.8	1.4	1.8	0.7	1.3	1.6	0.5	0.3	1.0
Writer or journalist	2.8	2.7	2.8	2.3	2.3	3.3	3.6	2.9	3.1	2.6	3.7	2.0	2.7
Skilled trades	0.3	0.3	0.2	0.2	0.4	0.3	0.3	0.2	0.3	0.2	0.1	0.2	0.1
Laborer (unskilled)	0.3	0.3	0.3	0.2	0.4	0.3	0.3	0.3	0.3	0.3	0.1	0.2	0.1
Semi-skilled worker	0.2	0.2	0.2	0.2	0.3	0.2	0.2	0.2	0.2	0.2	0.1	0.2	0.1
Unemployed	1.3	1.3	1.2	2.8	1.4	1.3	1.2	1.3	1.4	1.2	0.9	3.1	2.2
Other	8.7	9.5	7.5	9.8	9.1	10.0	10.5	9.1	9.8	7.9	5.9	9.4	10.6
Undecided	14.1	13.6	14.8	6.9	12.9	14.6	16.0	12.7	14.0	14.9	14.3	7.2	6.4

WEIGHTED NATIONAL NORMS FOR ALL FRESHMEN, FALL 2008

	ALL BACC. INSTS.	ALL 4-YR. COLLEGES	ALL UNI-VERSITIES	ALL BLACK COLLEGES	FOUR-YEAR COLLEGES					UNIVERSITIES		BLACK COLLEGES	
					PUBLIC	ALL PRIV.	NONSECT.	CATHOLIC	OTH. REL.	PUBLIC	PRIVATE	PUBLIC	PRIVATE
Your father's occupation [3]													
Artist	1.2	1.2	1.2	1.2	1.0	1.5	2.0	0.9	1.3	1.1	1.3	1.1	1.3
Business	27.1	25.5	29.6	14.3	24.3	27.1	28.0	27.9	25.7	28.5	33.8	13.5	15.6
Business (clerical)	1.3	1.3	1.3	1.2	1.3	1.3	1.3	1.3	1.3	1.3	1.3	1.1	1.4
Clergy	0.8	1.0	0.6	1.7	0.7	1.4	0.6	0.5	2.8	0.6	0.7	1.6	1.8
College teacher	0.7	0.6	0.9	0.4	0.4	1.0	1.1	0.5	1.0	0.7	1.5	0.2	0.7
Doctor (MD or DDS)	2.8	2.0	4.1	0.7	1.4	2.8	3.2	2.3	2.7	3.4	6.8	0.1	1.7
Education (secondary)	2.2	2.3	2.0	1.7	2.2	2.4	2.1	2.0	2.9	2.0	1.8	1.5	2.0
Education (elementary)	0.7	0.7	0.7	0.6	0.6	0.8	0.7	0.7	0.9	0.7	0.5	0.5	0.7
Engineer	8.7	7.3	10.8	4.8	7.7	6.8	6.7	7.2	6.8	11.1	9.5	4.6	5.1
Farmer or forester	1.4	1.3	1.5	0.6	1.2	1.3	0.7	1.0	2.2	1.7	0.7	0.7	0.4
Health professional	1.4	1.3	1.6	1.2	1.2	1.4	1.4	1.3	1.4	1.6	1.6	1.3	1.1
Homemaker (full-time)	0.3	0.3	0.3	0.1	0.3	0.3	0.3	0.2	0.3	0.3	0.2	0.1	0.2
Lawyer	2.4	1.9	3.2	0.9	1.4	2.6	3.2	2.2	2.0	2.7	5.3	0.5	1.6
Military (career)	1.7	2.0	1.2	4.4	2.6	1.3	1.1	1.2	1.5	1.3	0.8	4.7	3.8
Nurse	0.5	0.6	0.5	0.7	0.6	0.5	0.5	0.6	0.5	0.5	0.4	0.7	0.5
Research scientist	0.8	0.5	1.2	0.2	0.5	0.6	0.8	0.4	0.5	1.1	1.6	0.2	0.1
Social/welfare/rec worker	0.6	0.6	0.5	1.1	0.7	0.6	0.5	0.6	0.6	0.5	0.4	1.0	1.3
Skilled worker	7.0	7.8	5.7	7.1	8.3	7.1	6.7	7.9	7.1	6.0	4.5	7.2	6.8
Semi-skilled worker	2.8	3.0	2.5	3.5	3.3	2.6	2.3	2.9	2.7	2.8	1.6	3.7	3.0
Unskilled worker	3.1	3.5	2.6	4.3	3.9	2.9	2.6	3.6	2.9	2.9	1.4	4.7	3.7
Unemployed	3.2	3.5	2.8	9.1	3.6	3.4	3.7	3.6	3.0	2.9	2.2	9.9	7.6
Other	29.4	31.9	25.4	40.4	32.9	30.4	30.4	31.2	30.0	26.2	22.3	40.9	39.7
Your mother's occupation [3]													
Artist	2.0	1.9	2.1	0.7	1.5	2.3	3.0	1.4	2.0	2.0	2.7	0.5	1.0
Business	16.4	16.1	16.9	16.1	16.3	15.8	16.0	16.2	15.4	16.8	17.2	15.5	17.2
Business (clerical)	4.1	4.2	4.0	3.6	4.2	4.2	4.2	4.3	4.2	4.1	3.5	3.3	4.3
Clergy	0.2	0.3	0.2	0.3	0.2	0.4	0.2	0.2	0.7	0.2	0.3	0.3	0.3
College teacher	0.5	0.5	0.6	0.4	0.3	0.7	0.7	0.4	0.7	0.5	0.9	0.5	0.3
Doctor (MD or DDS)	1.4	1.2	1.8	1.0	0.9	1.5	1.8	1.2	1.3	1.5	3.0	0.5	1.8
Education (secondary)	4.5	4.5	4.5	4.7	4.4	4.7	4.5	4.1	5.2	4.5	4.5	4.4	5.1
Education (elementary)	7.9	7.8	7.9	6.1	7.7	8.0	7.2	8.0	9.1	8.1	7.0	6.0	6.3
Engineer	0.9	0.6	1.3	0.6	0.7	0.6	0.7	0.5	0.5	1.3	1.5	0.6	0.7
Farmer or forester	0.2	0.2	0.2	0.1	0.2	0.2	0.2	0.2	0.3	0.3	0.2	0.0	0.1
Health professional	3.4	3.2	3.8	2.7	3.0	3.3	3.4	3.4	3.2	3.9	3.8	3.0	2.3
Homemaker (full-time)	8.7	7.5	10.7	1.6	6.7	8.6	8.3	8.3	9.1	9.9	13.4	1.4	2.1
Lawyer	1.0	0.8	1.4	0.7	0.6	1.1	1.5	0.6	0.8	1.1	2.4	0.5	1.0
Military (career)	0.2	0.3	0.2	0.8	0.3	0.2	0.2	0.2	0.2	0.2	0.1	0.8	0.8
Nurse	8.2	8.7	7.4	9.4	8.9	8.4	7.7	9.5	8.7	7.6	7.0	9.8	8.8
Research scientist	0.4	0.3	0.7	0.2	0.3	0.3	0.4	0.2	0.3	0.6	0.9	0.1	0.3
Social/welfare/rec worker	1.8	1.9	1.6	3.8	1.8	1.9	1.9	2.0	1.9	1.6	1.6	4.2	3.2
Skilled worker	1.5	1.6	1.4	2.0	1.8	1.4	1.4	1.5	1.4	1.5	1.0	2.2	1.5
Semi-skilled worker	1.8	1.9	1.8	1.7	2.0	1.6	1.5	1.8	1.6	1.9	1.3	1.7	1.7
Unskilled worker	1.7	1.8	1.6	2.1	2.1	1.4	1.2	1.6	1.4	1.8	0.9	2.6	1.3
Unemployed	6.8	7.0	6.6	8.0	7.4	6.4	6.6	6.6	6.1	6.7	6.3	8.4	7.4
Other	26.1	27.9	23.2	33.3	28.6	27.0	27.4	28.0	26.0	24.0	20.5	33.7	32.7
How would you characterize your political views?													
Far left	3.2	3.2	3.3	4.1	2.8	3.7	4.8	2.5	2.8	3.1	4.1	4.5	3.4
Liberal	31.0	28.4	35.0	35.6	27.0	30.3	37.0	29.3	22.5	34.1	38.3	33.2	39.5
Middle-of-the-road	43.3	45.1	40.4	40.4	46.9	42.7	41.9	45.7	42.2	41.2	37.6	40.1	40.9
Conservative	20.7	21.3	19.8	17.3	21.2	21.4	14.9	20.8	29.8	20.1	18.6	19.3	14.2
Far right	1.8	2.0	1.5	2.6	2.1	1.9	1.4	1.7	2.7	1.5	1.4	2.9	2.1

WEIGHTED NATIONAL NORMS FOR ALL FRESHMEN, FALL 2008

Student agrees "strongly" or "somewhat":	ALL BACC. INSTS.	ALL 4-YR. COLLEGES	ALL UNI-VERSITIES	ALL BLACK COLLEGES	FOUR-YEAR COLLEGES					UNIVERSITIES		BLACK COLLEGES	
					PUBLIC	ALL PRIV.	NONSECT.	CATHOLIC	OTH. REL.	PUBLIC	PRIVATE	PUBLIC	PRIVATE
There is too much concern in the courts for the rights of criminals	57.4	58.8	55.1	49.6	61.0	55.9	52.4	58.0	59.2	56.0	51.8	52.3	45.2
Abortion should be legal	58.2	55.2	63.2	50.1	55.1	55.3	66.3	51.6	43.7	62.4	66.6	48.8	52.1
The death penalty should be abolished	34.9	33.6	37.2	44.7	30.3	38.0	41.2	38.9	33.6	35.1	45.0	44.5	45.0
Marijuana should be legalized	41.3	40.7	42.3	41.7	40.3	41.1	48.2	38.2	33.8	41.9	43.9	43.1	39.3
It is important to have laws prohibiting homosexual relationships	23.4	25.5	20.0	35.6	25.3	25.7	18.5	22.9	36.0	20.7	17.2	37.2	33.0
Racial discrimination is no longer a major problem in America	20.1	20.7	19.1	14.7	21.5	19.7	18.1	19.2	22.1	19.3	18.5	14.9	14.2
Realistically, an individual can do little to bring about changes in our society	27.3	28.8	24.9	35.5	29.9	27.3	27.4	27.2	27.1	25.3	23.4	38.3	30.9
Wealthy people should pay a larger share of taxes than they do now	60.4	61.0	59.4	64.3	60.3	62.0	64.9	61.8	58.5	59.6	58.3	64.0	64.8
Same-sex couples should have the right to legal marital status	66.2	63.9	70.1	51.5	64.0	63.7	73.5	66.5	50.2	69.2	73.7	50.1	53.7
Affirmative action in college admissions should be abolished	47.6	44.2	53.0	33.6	44.0	44.6	45.0	45.1	43.8	52.1	56.2	36.0	29.7
Federal military spending should be increased	28.0	30.6	23.7	33.4	32.6	27.8	24.2	28.6	31.8	23.9	22.9	36.5	28.5
The federal government should do more to control the sale of handguns	72.2	71.6	73.3	79.9	69.8	74.0	77.7	75.8	68.5	72.2	77.3	79.5	80.5
Only volunteers should serve in the armed forces	66.6	65.4	68.8	63.6	64.3	66.8	70.3	66.1	62.8	67.9	72.1	61.1	67.7
The federal government is not doing enough to control environmental pollution	79.0	77.9	80.9	79.3	77.1	79.0	83.3	79.1	73.8	80.4	82.8	79.0	79.7
A national health care plan is needed to cover everybody's medical costs	70.3	71.7	67.8	85.1	70.9	72.9	77.4	74.5	66.4	67.7	68.3	86.1	83.5
Undocumented immigrants should be denied access to public education	47.2	48.5	45.1	41.8	50.5	45.7	42.3	47.2	49.2	46.1	41.2	43.8	38.6
Through hard work, everybody can succeed in American society	78.6	79.1	77.9	77.1	81.1	76.5	73.8	79.4	78.3	79.0	73.7	78.6	74.7
Dissent is a critical component of the political process	62.2	59.2	67.0	56.2	58.4	60.4	61.9	58.8	59.5	65.1	73.8	57.1	54.7
Colleges have the right to ban extreme speakers from campus	40.5	41.5	38.7	42.2	41.2	41.9	37.5	42.9	46.8	38.2	40.7	42.7	41.5
Students from disadvantaged social backgrounds should be given preferential treatment in college admissions	39.5	40.9	37.2	56.8	40.5	41.4	42.0	39.4	41.7	37.3	36.6	57.7	55.3
The federal government should raise taxes to reduce the deficit	28.3	25.9	32.3	22.9	25.0	27.1	29.1	25.3	25.6	31.7	34.4	21.3	25.6
Addressing global warming should be a federal priority	74.3	73.1	76.3	73.3	72.0	74.5	80.3	75.8	66.6	75.5	79.2	77.3	80.0

WEIGHTED NATIONAL NORMS FOR ALL FRESHMEN, FALL 2008

	ALL BACC. INSTS.	ALL 4-YR. COLLEGES	ALL UNI-VERSITIES	ALL BLACK COLLEGES	FOUR-YEAR COLLEGES					UNIVERSITIES		BLACK COLLEGES	
					PUBLIC	ALL PRIV.	NONSECT.	CATHOLIC	OTH. REL.	PUBLIC	PRIVATE	PUBLIC	PRIVATE
DURING YOUR LAST YEAR IN HIGH SCHOOL, HOW MUCH TIME DID YOU SPEND DURING A TYPICAL WEEK DOING THE FOLLOWING?													
Studying/homework													
None	2.0	2.3	1.4	2.7	2.6	1.8	1.9	1.5	2.0	1.5	1.3	3.1	2.0
Less than one hour	10.8	12.5	8.0	11.8	14.2	10.2	10.4	9.1	10.6	8.6	5.7	13.5	9.1
1 to 2 hours	22.0	24.6	17.8	30.2	26.9	21.5	21.1	21.2	22.2	19.0	13.3	31.9	27.3
3 to 5 hours	28.7	29.1	28.1	28.3	29.4	28.7	27.7	29.2	29.5	29.4	23.1	29.9	25.6
6 to 10 hours	19.5	17.7	22.5	15.3	16.1	19.9	19.5	21.5	19.5	22.2	23.8	13.1	18.9
11 to 15 hours	9.1	7.6	11.6	6.2	6.1	9.5	9.8	9.7	8.9	10.6	15.4	4.7	8.8
16 to 20 hours	4.5	3.6	6.0	2.9	2.7	4.9	5.4	4.6	4.3	5.1	9.5	2.0	4.2
Over 20 hours	3.3	2.6	4.6	2.7	1.9	3.6	4.1	3.2	3.0	3.7	8.0	1.8	4.1
Socializing with friends													
None	0.3	0.3	0.3	0.7	0.3	0.3	0.3	0.3	0.3	0.3	0.3	0.6	0.8
Less than one hour	1.5	1.7	1.2	2.5	1.8	1.5	1.5	1.3	1.6	1.2	1.0	2.6	2.4
1 to 2 hours	6.5	6.7	6.2	9.2	7.1	6.1	5.9	6.1	6.5	6.4	5.5	9.5	8.8
3 to 5 hours	19.5	19.3	19.7	22.9	19.6	18.9	18.4	18.2	19.9	19.9	18.9	23.6	21.8
6 to 10 hours	26.7	25.6	28.3	22.8	25.3	26.1	25.4	26.6	26.7	28.1	29.1	22.6	23.1
11 to 15 hours	18.6	18.1	19.4	14.2	17.6	18.8	18.7	19.2	18.7	19.2	20.1	13.4	15.6
16 to 20 hours	11.3	11.5	11.1	9.1	11.1	12.0	12.5	12.4	11.2	11.0	11.5	9.1	9.0
Over 20 hours	15.6	16.7	13.8	18.5	17.1	16.2	17.2	16.0	15.1	13.8	13.5	18.5	18.5
Talking with teachers outside of class													
None	9.3	9.8	8.5	10.4	10.8	8.5	8.5	8.3	8.6	9.0	6.6	12.1	7.6
Less than one hour	41.7	41.2	42.6	34.9	42.7	39.3	37.9	40.9	40.2	43.8	37.8	36.7	31.9
1 to 2 hours	32.0	31.5	32.9	30.5	30.4	32.9	33.0	32.5	33.0	32.0	36.2	29.7	31.7
3 to 5 hours	11.8	11.9	11.6	15.0	10.9	13.2	13.9	12.8	12.4	11.0	14.1	13.4	17.6
6 to 10 hours	3.2	3.4	2.9	5.4	3.1	3.8	4.0	3.5	3.6	2.7	3.5	5.0	6.1
11 to 15 hours	1.1	1.2	0.9	2.0	1.1	1.3	1.5	1.0	1.2	0.8	1.0	1.6	2.7
16 to 20 hours	0.4	0.4	0.3	0.7	0.4	0.5	0.5	0.5	0.4	0.3	0.4	0.6	1.0
Over 20 hours	0.5	0.6	0.4	1.2	0.5	0.6	0.7	0.6	0.6	0.3	0.4	1.0	1.4
Exercise or sports													
None	4.7	5.2	3.7	9.7	5.4	4.9	5.6	4.2	4.5	3.9	3.3	10.1	9.1
Less than one hour	8.9	9.2	8.5	12.3	9.8	8.4	8.9	7.6	8.1	8.7	7.7	13.2	10.8
1 to 2 hours	15.2	15.3	15.2	17.9	15.9	14.4	14.9	14.4	13.8	15.4	14.4	18.4	17.2
3 to 5 hours	19.3	18.4	20.7	18.9	18.9	17.8	18.1	18.5	17.0	20.4	21.5	18.7	19.2
6 to 10 hours	18.8	17.7	20.6	14.7	17.7	17.7	17.7	18.1	17.5	20.5	20.8	14.5	15.0
11 to 15 hours	14.0	13.8	14.4	8.6	13.3	14.4	13.9	15.4	14.6	14.3	14.8	7.9	9.7
16 to 20 hours	8.5	8.7	8.1	5.8	8.1	9.6	9.2	9.3	10.2	8.0	8.3	5.6	6.0
Over 20 hours	10.6	11.7	8.8	12.0	10.9	12.8	11.8	12.5	14.1	8.7	9.1	11.5	12.9
Partying													
None	28.9	28.9	29.0	20.6	28.2	29.8	25.6	25.6	37.3	29.5	27.0	21.5	19.2
Less than one hour	15.1	14.5	16.0	11.8	14.5	14.5	14.1	14.3	15.2	16.1	15.9	11.0	13.0
1 to 2 hours	18.2	17.7	19.1	19.9	17.9	17.3	17.6	18.7	16.3	19.2	18.8	19.7	20.3
3 to 5 hours	18.9	18.8	19.3	25.4	18.9	18.6	20.2	20.7	15.6	18.9	20.5	25.5	25.1
6 to 10 hours	10.6	10.9	10.2	11.8	10.9	10.8	12.3	12.0	8.3	9.9	11.1	11.9	11.7
11 to 15 hours	4.3	4.7	3.6	4.6	4.8	4.6	5.3	4.8	3.7	3.6	3.6	4.1	5.5
16 to 20 hours	1.8	2.1	1.4	2.0	2.1	2.0	2.4	1.8	1.6	1.4	1.5	2.1	1.8
Over 20 hours	2.1	2.4	1.4	3.9	2.6	2.2	2.5	2.1	1.9	1.4	1.5	4.2	3.5

WEIGHTED NATIONAL NORMS FOR ALL FRESHMEN, FALL 2008

	ALL BACC. INSTS.	ALL 4-YR. COLLEGES	A.L UNI-VERSITIES	ALL BLACK COLLEGES	FOUR-YEAR COLLEGES					UNIVERSITIES		BLACK COLLEGES	
					P.JBLIC	ALL PRIV.	NONSECT.	CATHOLIC	OTH. REL.	PUBLIC	PRIVATE	PUBLIC	PRIVATE
DURING YOUR LAST YEAR IN HIGH SCHOOL, HOW MUCH TIME DID YOU SPEND DURING A TYPICAL WEEK DOING THE FOLLOWING?													
Working (for pay)													
None	33.6	31.0	37.8	33.0	29.7	32.8	34.3	29.1	32.9	36.1	43.9	31.1	36.0
Less than one hour	2.9	2.7	3.2	2.3	2.5	3.0	3.1	2.7	3.2	3.1	3.8	2.4	2.1
1 to 2 hours	4.2	3.9	4.7	3.3	3.6	4.3	4.2	3.8	4.7	4.4	5.7	3.2	3.4
3 to 5 hours	7.8	7.6	8.1	6.9	7.3	8.1	7.7	8.3	8.5	7.8	9.1	7.1	6.6
6 to 10 hours	12.3	12.4	12.3	12.6	11.8	13.0	12.5	14.3	13.1	12.5	11.4	13.4	11.2
11 to 15 hours	12.5	12.7	12.3	9.1	13.0	12.4	11.9	14.0	12.2	12.8	10.1	8.7	9.6
16 to 20 hours	12.8	13.8	11.2	12.3	14.9	12.3	12.4	13.3	11.7	12.0	8.4	12.6	11.8
Over 20 hours	13.8	15.9	10.4	20.7	17.2	14.0	13.9	14.6	13.9	11.2	7.6	21.5	19.3
Volunteer work													
None	27.6	30.1	23.5	27.8	32.8	26.5	28.6	23.9	25.2	24.6	19.4	32.0	20.8
Less than one hour	22.0	21.6	22.6	14.2	21.9	21.1	20.0	20.9	22.7	23.1	20.6	14.8	13.1
1 to 2 hours	25.2	23.8	27.5	23.0	22.6	25.2	24.4	26.5	25.6	27.0	29.4	21.9	24.9
3 to 5 hours	14.3	13.5	15.7	17.6	12.4	14.9	14.6	16.1	14.7	15.0	18.4	16.2	19.8
6 to 10 hours	5.8	5.6	6.1	7.9	5.2	6.2	6.0	6.6	6.2	5.9	7.1	6.4	10.2
11 to 15 hours	2.2	2.2	2.1	3.8	2.0	2.5	2.6	2.4	2.5	2.0	2.4	3.7	4.0
16 to 20 hours	1.1	1.2	1.0	2.0	1.1	1.3	1.4	1.3	1.2	1.0	1.0	1.9	2.1
Over 20 hours	1.9	2.1	1.5	3.9	2.0	2.2	2.3	2.3	2.0	1.5	1.7	3.2	5.2
Student clubs/groups													
None	28.4	32.2	22.0	28.5	34.8	28.7	29.4	26.3	28.9	24.1	14.4	33.3	20.7
Less than one hour	14.1	14.1	14.2	10.6	14.4	13.6	12.7	14.2	14.5	14.8	11.8	10.4	10.8
1 to 2 hours	25.0	23.4	27.6	23.7	22.6	24.5	24.2	25.6	24.3	27.3	28.7	24.0	23.2
3 to 5 hours	17.2	15.8	19.6	18.4	14.4	17.6	17.6	18.3	17.2	18.5	23.8	16.9	20.8
6 to 10 hours	7.9	7.4	8.9	8.8	6.8	8.1	8.2	8.2	7.9	8.3	11.4	7.5	10.9
11 to 15 hours	3.4	3.3	3.7	4.1	3.1	3.6	3.6	3.5	3.5	3.4	4.7	3.0	5.8
16 to 20 hours	1.7	1.6	1.8	2.0	1.5	1.7	1.9	1.6	1.5	1.6	2.3	1.7	2.6
Over 20 hours	2.3	2.3	2.2	3.9	2.4	2.2	2.3	2.2	2.1	2.1	2.8	3.1	5.3
Watching TV													
None	6.6	6.3	7.1	4.7	6.0	6.7	7.4	5.1	6.6	7.0	7.6	4.6	4.9
Less than one hour	14.8	14.8	14.7	11.6	15.4	14.1	13.9	14.5	14.0	15.0	13.7	11.6	11.5
1 to 2 hours	24.8	24.6	25.2	21.1	25.0	24.1	24.1	24.3	24.0	25.4	24.2	21.5	20.5
3 to 5 hours	27.5	27.2	28.1	25.7	27.0	27.5	27.2	28.3	27.5	28.0	28.6	26.1	25.2
6 to 10 hours	15.3	15.4	15.3	16.3	15.1	15.8	15.3	16.4	16.1	15.0	16.1	15.8	17.1
11 to 15 hours	5.7	5.9	5.3	9.1	5.8	6.1	6.2	6.0	6.0	5.2	5.4	9.2	9.0
16 to 20 hours	2.3	2.5	2.0	4.2	2.5	2.3	2.3	2.3	2.5	2.0	2.2	4.2	4.2
Over 20 hours	2.9	3.3	2.3	7.2	3.2	3.3	3.5	3.2	3.3	2.4	2.2	6.9	7.7
Household/childcare duties													
None	18.2	18.6	17.5	17.4	18.3	19.1	20.9	15.5	18.8	17.2	18.8	17.9	16.6
Less than one hour	19.6	18.7	21.2	14.2	18.6	18.8	18.9	18.2	19.1	21.2	21.2	15.0	12.9
1 to 2 hours	31.0	30.1	32.6	26.6	30.0	30.2	29.3	31.5	30.6	32.6	32.5	27.2	25.6
3 to 5 hours	19.4	19.6	19.1	20.5	19.9	19.3	18.5	21.2	19.4	19.2	18.6	20.1	21.3
6 to 10 hours	6.8	7.3	6.0	10.2	7.4	7.0	7.0	7.7	6.7	6.0	5.7	9.7	11.1
11 to 15 hours	2.3	2.6	1.8	4.0	2.7	2.6	2.5	2.9	2.5	1.8	1.7	3.3	5.2
16 to 20 hours	1.0	1.2	0.8	2.5	1.2	1.1	1.1	1.1	1.1	0.8	0.6	2.6	2.4
Over 20 hours	1.6	1.9	1.1	4.6	2.0	1.8	1.8	1.9	1.8	1.2	0.9	4.3	5.0

DURING YOUR LAST YEAR IN HIGH SCHOOL, HOW MUCH TIME DID YOU SPEND DURING A TYPICAL WEEK DOING THE FOLLOWING?

	ALL BACC. INSTS.	ALL 4-YR. COLLEGES	ALL UNI-VERSITIES	ALL BLACK COLLEGES	FOUR-YEAR COLLEGES					UNIVERSITIES		BLACK COLLEGES	
					PUBLIC	ALL PRIV.	NONSECT.	CATHOLIC	OTH. REL.	PUBLIC	PRIVATE	PUBLIC	PRIVATE
Reading for pleasure													
None	24.6	26.6	21.3	26.0	28.0	24.8	23.6	25.4	26.0	22.3	17.8	28.9	21.2
Less than one hour	23.9	23.3	24.9	23.2	23.6	22.8	22.3	24.4	22.5	25.2	24.0	23.8	22.2
1 to 2 hours	23.8	22.6	25.9	24.1	22.1	23.3	23.6	24.2	22.4	25.5	27.4	23.4	25.2
3 to 5 hours	15.6	14.9	16.6	13.6	14.1	16.0	16.7	14.5	15.7	16.2	18.3	12.8	14.8
6 to 10 hours	7.0	7.1	6.9	6.6	6.7	7.5	7.7	6.4	7.8	6.7	7.8	5.7	8.1
11 to 15 hours	2.7	2.8	2.5	2.8	2.7	3.0	3.2	2.7	3.0	2.4	2.7	2.3	3.7
16 to 20 hours	1.1	1.2	0.8	1.5	1.2	1.2	1.3	1.1	1.2	0.8	1.0	1.3	1.9
Over 20 hours	1.3	1.4	1.0	2.2	1.4	1.5	1.6	1.2	1.4	0.9	1.1	1.7	2.9
Playing video/computer games													
None	39.8	39.8	39.9	41.5	39.1	40.8	40.8	42.5	40.0	39.4	41.8	39.8	44.3
Less than one hour	19.9	20.1	19.5	18.7	20.3	19.9	19.5	20.3	20.3	19.7	18.8	19.1	18.1
1 to 2 hours	15.8	15.9	15.7	16.1	16.1	15.6	15.6	15.3	15.9	15.7	15.5	16.7	15.2
3 to 5 hours	12.0	11.7	12.4	11.3	11.6	11.8	12.3	11.2	11.5	12.5	12.2	11.9	10.2
6 to 10 hours	6.4	6.3	6.6	5.9	6.5	6.1	6.0	5.8	6.4	6.6	6.5	6.2	5.5
11 to 15 hours	2.9	2.9	2.9	2.6	2.9	2.8	2.8	2.5	2.9	3.0	2.7	2.6	2.7
16 to 20 hours	1.3	1.3	1.2	1.4	1.4	1.2	1.2	1.1	1.2	1.3	1.1	1.4	1.5
Over 20 hours	1.9	1.9	1.8	2.4	2.1	1.8	1.9	1.3	1.9	1.9	1.5	2.3	2.5
Online social networks (MySpace, Facebook, etc.)													
None	11.1	11.4	10.5	9.3	12.7	9.7	9.2	10.1	10.2	11.2	7.9	9.4	9.0
Less than one hour	18.5	18.3	18.7	15.9	19.6	16.6	16.8	17.5	15.9	19.4	16.1	15.9	15.8
1 to 2 hours	27.3	26.7	28.4	24.7	26.7	26.7	26.6	27.2	26.6	28.3	28.6	25.9	22.6
3 to 5 hours	23.6	23.0	24.6	21.3	21.6	24.9	25.0	24.5	24.9	23.9	27.1	21.7	20.5
6 to 10 hours	10.7	10.9	10.4	12.8	10.3	11.7	11.6	11.0	12.1	9.9	11.9	12.4	13.4
11 to 15 hours	4.2	4.5	3.8	6.3	4.2	4.9	5.0	4.7	4.9	3.6	4.2	5.5	7.7
16 to 20 hours	1.9	2.1	1.6	3.8	1.9	2.3	2.5	2.2	2.2	1.5	1.8	3.5	4.3
Over 20 hours	2.7	3.0	2.1	6.1	3.0	3.1	3.3	2.7	3.1	2.1	2.3	5.7	6.7
Are you: [4]													
White/Caucasian	71.9	72.6	70.7	4.2	71.0	74.7	71.0	74.0	79.8	70.8	70.6	4.5	3.7
African American/Black	11.3	14.4	6.2	93.7	14.1	14.8	16.0	13.8	13.9	6.1	6.6	93.2	94.7
American Indian/Alaska Native	2.6	3.0	1.9	3.5	3.5	2.3	2.4	1.7	2.6	2.0	1.7	3.5	3.5
Asian American/Asian	8.8	4.9	15.4	1.6	4.4	5.4	7.2	5.0	3.3	14.9	17.2	0.7	3.1
Native Hawaiian/Pacific Islander	1.3	1.3	1.4	0.5	1.5	0.9	0.9	1.6	0.7	1.5	1.0	0.4	0.6
Mexican American/Chicano	5.7	5.3	6.3	0.6	7.4	2.7	1.8	4.5	2.8	7.0	3.4	0.6	0.5
Puerto Rican	1.4	1.6	1.1	2.1	1.2	2.2	3.2	2.0	1.1	0.9	1.7	2.4	1.4
Other Latino	4.2	4.2	4.2	1.7	4.5	3.8	4.8	4.0	2.5	3.9	5.5	1.5	2.2
Other	4.0	4.1	3.9	4.2	4.1	4.1	4.9	3.5	3.4	3.7	4.3	4.0	4.5

WEIGHTED NATIONAL NORMS FOR ALL FRESHMEN, FALL 2008

	ALL BACC. INSTS.	ALL 4-YR. COLLEGES	ALL UNI-VERSITIES	ALL BLACK COLLEGES	FOUR-YEAR COLLEGES					UNIVERSITIES		BLACK COLLEGES	
					PUBLIC	ALL PFIV.	NONSECT.	CATHOLIC	OTH. REL.	PUBLIC	PRIVATE	PUBLIC	PRIVATE
Reasons noted as "very important" in influencing student's decision to attend this particular college													
My parents wanted me to come here	14.7	15.5	13.3	22.4	15.7	15.3	13.8	16.9	16.3	13.0	14.2	21.9	23.3
My relatives wanted me to come here	5.8	6.3	4.9	14.3	6.6	6.0	5.4	6.7	6.4	4.9	5.0	14.3	14.3
My teacher advised me	6.9	7.5	5.9	10.0	7.4	7.6	8.7	7.5	6.2	5.7	6.6	10.1	10.0
This college has a very good academic reputation	64.7	61.5	69.9	58.5	57.9	66.3	66.7	71.1	63.5	67.0	80.5	48.9	73.8
This college has a good reputation for its social activities	38.4	36.6	41.4	38.5	35.4	38.2	37.3	39.6	38.5	41.9	39.7	34.0	45.8
I was offered financial assistance	43.0	46.8	36.8	52.0	37.3	59.2	54.2	64.5	62.9	33.7	47.8	55.5	46.3
The cost of attending this college	39.9	42.8	34.9	50.6	49.5	33.9	34.2	37.1	32.0	37.1	27.1	59.0	37.1
High school counselor advised me	10.2	11.1	8.5	15.1	11.3	11.0	12.8	12.2	8.2	8.0	10.3	15.4	14.7
Private college counselor advised me	3.6	4.1	2.8	6.4	3.0	5.7	5.9	5.2	5.6	2.3	4.5	5.4	7.9
I wanted to live near home	20.1	23.4	14.4	20.7	25.4	20.8	19.7	26.5	19.3	15.0	12.1	22.9	17.1
Not offered aid by first choice	8.5	8.7	8.1	14.8	8.1	9.5	9.4	10.8	9.1	8.0	8.4	15.7	13.4
Could not afford first choice	11.2	11.7	10.3	17.7	12.9	10.1	10.2	11.8	9.1	11.0	7.9	20.0	14.1
This college's graduates gain admission to top graduate/professional schools	35.1	32.0	40.3	40.9	28.3	36.9	39.2	39.4	32.7	37.2	51.6	30.4	57.9
This college's graduates get good jobs	54.2	52.2	57.6	56.5	48.3	57.3	59.3	62.0	52.3	54.5	69.2	48.9	68.7
I was attracted by the religious affiliation/orientation of the college	7.5	9.1	4.7	13.0	4.2	15.6	5.3	16.6	28.2	3.2	10.3	8.6	19.9
I wanted to go to a school about the size of this college	38.5	41.7	33.2	35.8	34.5	51.2	48.5	52.2	54.0	30.9	41.7	33.9	38.9
Rankings in national magazines	17.6	13.3	24.8	22.1	11.2	16.0	18.1	16.3	13.0	22.9	31.9	14.3	34.5
Information from a website	18.9	18.5	19.5	27.2	17.1	20.4	23.4	19.1	17.3	18.2	24.2	23.0	34.0
I was admitted through an Early Action or Early Decision program	11.8	11.2	12.7	11.5	8.9	14.4	16.2	13.7	12.3	10.1	22.1	9.4	15.1
The athletic department recruited me	8.4	11.2	3.8	9.0	7.2	16.4	13.8	13.5	21.1	3.2	6.0	9.4	8.5
A visit to campus	41.4	42.4	39.8	37.5	36.1	50.6	51.5	47.9	50.8	37.4	48.6	36.1	39.8

WEIGHTED NATIONAL NORMS FOR ALL FRESHMEN, FALL 2008

YOUR PROBABLE MAJOR	ALL BACC. INSTS.	ALL 4-YR. COLLEGES	ALL UNI-VERSITIES	ALL BLACK COLLEGES	FOUR-YEAR COLLEGES					UNIVERSITIES		BLACK COLLEGES	
					PUBLIC	ALL PRIV.	NONSECT.	CATHOLIC	OTH. REL.	PUBLIC	PRIVATE	PUBLIC	PRIVATE
Arts and Humanities													
Art, fine and applied	3.2	4.0	1.9	1.0	3.0	5.4	9.4	1.5	2.4	2.0	1.6	1.4	0.5
English (language & literature)	1.9	1.9	1.9	1.2	1.6	2.4	2.7	2.0	2.3	1.8	2.2	0.7	2.0
History	1.5	1.6	1.2	0.3	1.6	1.6	1.5	1.4	1.7	1.2	1.5	0.2	0.5
Journalism	1.6	1.6	1.8	1.2	1.5	1.7	1.8	2.0	1.4	1.7	2.2	0.9	1.6
Language and Literature (except English)	0.6	0.6	0.7	0.1	0.5	0.7	0.7	0.4	0.7	0.7	0.8	0.0	0.2
Music	1.6	1.8	1.3	1.8	1.8	1.8	1.1	0.7	3.1	1.2	1.9	1.6	2.1
Philosophy	0.3	0.3	0.4	0.2	0.2	0.4	0.4	0.4	0.3	0.3	0.4	0.0	0.4
Speech	0.1	0.1	0.1	0.1	0.1	0.1	0.1	0.1	0.1	0.1	0.1	0.1	0.1
Theater or Drama	1.2	1.5	0.9	0.6	1.5	1.5	2.0	0.6	1.3	0.8	1.2	0.5	0.8
Theology or Religion	0.2	0.3	0.1	0.0	0.0	0.6	0.1	0.3	1.5	0.0	0.1	0.0	0.0
Other Arts and Humanities	1.3	1.3	1.2	0.5	1.2	1.5	2.2	0.6	1.1	1.1	1.4	0.6	0.4
Biological Science													
Biology (general)	5.2	4.4	6.4	9.3	3.8	5.2	4.6	6.9	5.1	6.2	7.1	6.8	13.5
Biochemistry or Biophysics	1.4	1.0	2.2	0.4	0.9	1.0	0.9	1.1	1.2	2.3	1.8	0.2	0.7
Botany	0.0	0.0	0.1	0.1	0.0	0.0	0.1	0.0	0.0	0.1	0.1	0.1	0.0
Environmental Science	0.8	0.7	0.9	0.2	0.5	0.9	1.0	0.5	1.0	1.0	0.6	0.2	0.1
Marine (Life) Science	0.4	0.4	0.4	0.3	0.5	0.4	0.4	0.2	0.4	0.4	0.2	0.4	0.0
Microbiology or Bacteriology	0.3	0.1	0.6	0.1	0.2	0.1	0.2	0.1	0.1	0.7	0.3	0.1	0.2
Zoology	0.4	0.4	0.4	0.1	0.4	0.3	0.4	0.1	0.4	0.5	0.1	0.0	0.1
Other Biological Science	0.8	0.5	1.2	0.3	0.5	0.5	0.7	0.4	0.4	1.3	1.0	0.3	0.4
Business													
Accounting	2.5	2.7	2.1	3.3	2.6	2.7	2.8	3.2	2.4	2.3	1.6	3.7	2.7
Business Admin. (general)	3.8	4.0	3.4	4.3	4.0	4.1	4.1	3.6	4.3	3.5	3.0	4.7	3.6
Finance	1.8	1.3	2.4	1.0	1.1	1.6	1.9	2.1	0.9	2.0	3.9	0.7	1.5
International Business	1.5	1.4	1.8	1.0	1.1	1.7	2.0	1.9	1.3	1.6	2.4	0.6	1.5
Marketing	2.6	2.7	2.5	2.9	2.7	2.7	2.8	3.4	2.2	2.5	2.4	2.9	2.9
Management	3.6	4.0	3.0	4.7	3.8	4.3	4.7	4.0	3.9	3.2	2.4	5.3	3.7
Secretarial Studies	0.0	0.0	0.0	0.0	0.0	0.0	0.0	0.0	0.0	0.0	0.0	0.0	0.0
Other Business	0.9	0.9	1.0	0.5	0.8	1.1	1.4	0.9	0.9	0.9	1.1	0.6	0.3
Education													
Business Education	0.1	0.1	0.1	0.2	0.1	0.1	0.1	0.1	0.1	0.1	0.1	0.2	0.2
Elementary Education	3.6	4.7	1.7	4.8	5.2	4.1	3.0	4.5	5.2	1.9	1.0	6.2	2.4
Music or Art Education	0.8	1.0	0.4	0.7	1.2	0.8	0.6	0.4	1.2	0.4	0.2	0.8	0.5
Physical Education or Recreation	0.8	1.2	0.3	1.6	1.2	1.1	0.9	0.5	1.7	0.3	0.1	2.2	0.6
Secondary Education	2.1	2.7	1.1	2.1	2.7	2.6	1.8	2.9	3.4	1.2	0.7	2.6	1.2
Special Education	0.5	0.7	0.3	0.4	0.7	0.6	0.4	0.9	0.7	0.2	0.1	0.5	0.2
Other Education	0.4	0.5	0.2	0.7	0.6	0.3	0.2	0.2	0.4	0.2	0.1	1.0	0.2
Engineering													
Aeronautical or Astronautical Engineering	1.0	0.7	1.4	0.2	1.1	0.2	0.2	0.2	0.1	1.6	0.8	0.2	0.1
Civil Engineering	1.2	0.9	1.7	0.7	1.3	0.5	0.2	0.9	0.5	1.8	1.6	0.8	0.6
Chemical Engineering	0.8	0.3	1.7	0.2	0.3	0.2	0.2	0.3	0.2	1.7	2.0	0.0	0.4
Computer Engineering	1.1	0.8	1.7	2.1	1.0	0.5	0.5	0.5	0.4	1.8	1.2	2.3	1.9
Electrical or Electronic Engineering	1.0	0.7	1.5	1.1	0.9	0.4	0.4	0.5	0.3	1.6	1.3	1.4	0.5
Industrial Engineering	0.2	0.1	0.3	0.3	0.1	0.1	0.1	0.0	0.0	0.4	0.3	0.3	0.1
Mechanical Engineering	2.4	1.6	3.7	1.1	2.1	1.0	1.1	1.3	0.8	3.8	3.1	1.2	0.9
Other Engineering	1.6	0.8	2.9	0.5	1.1	0.5	0.6	0.4	0.5	2.8	3.5	0.4	0.6

WEIGHTED NATIONAL NORMS FOR ALL FRESHMEN, FALL 2008

	ALL BACC. INSTS.	ALL 4-YR. COLLEGES	ALL UNI-VERSITIES	ALL BLACK COLLEGES	FOUR-YEAR COLLEGES					UNIVERSITIES		BLACK COLLEGES	
					PUBLIC	ALL PRIV.	NONSECT.	CATHOLIC	OTH. REL.	PUBLIC	PRIVATE	PUBLIC	PRIVATE
YOUR PROBABLE MAJOR													
Physical Science													
Astronomy	0.1	0.1	0.2	0.0	0.1	0.1	0.1	0.0	0.1	0.2	0.1	0.0	0.0
Atmospheric Science (incl. Meteorology)	0.1	0.1	0.1	0.1	0.1	0.1	0.0	0.0	0.1	0.1	0.1	0.1	0.0
Chemistry	1.2	1.1	1.4	1.7	1.1	1.1	1.0	1.4	1.2	1.4	1.6	0.9	3.0
Earth Science	0.1	0.1	0.2	0.0	0.1	0.1	0.2	0.1	0.1	0.2	0.1	0.0	0.0
Marine Science (incl. Oceanography)	0.1	0.2	0.1	0.1	0.2	0.1	0.1	0.1	0.2	0.1	0.1	0.1	0.0
Mathematics	0.8	0.7	1.0	0.4	0.6	0.8	0.7	0.7	0.9	1.0	1.2	0.4	0.3
Physics	0.6	0.4	0.8	0.2	0.4	0.4	0.5	0.2	0.5	0.7	1.2	0.1	0.3
Other Physical Science	0.2	0.2	0.2	0.1	0.2	0.2	0.2	0.2	0.2	0.2	0.2	0.2	0.1
Professional													
Architecture or Urban Planning	0.6	0.3	1.1	0.3	0.3	0.3	0.4	0.1	0.3	1.0	1.4	0.3	0.2
Family & Consumer Sciences	0.2	0.2	0.3	0.1	0.2	0.1	0.1	0.1	0.1	0.4	0.2	0.2	0.0
Health Technology (medical, dental, laboratory)	0.6	0.6	0.5	0.5	0.7	0.5	0.4	0.8	0.4	0.5	0.3	0.4	0.6
Library or Archival Science	0.1	0.1	0.1	0.2	0.0	0.1	0.1	0.1	0.1	0.1	0.0	0.0	0.4
Medicine, Dentistry, Veterinary Medicine	3.8	3.2	4.7	3.9	2.7	3.9	3.7	4.3	4.1	4.5	5.6	1.8	7.5
Nursing	4.5	5.9	2.2	8.0	6.9	4.7	2.8	9.1	4.8	2.3	1.8	10.4	3.9
Pharmacy	1.4	1.2	1.8	2.7	1.2	1.3	1.0	2.1	1.1	1.8	1.8	1.2	5.2
Therapy (occupational, physical, speech)	1.9	2.2	1.5	1.4	2.2	2.2	1.4	2.9	2.9	1.6	1.1	1.9	0.7
Other Professional	0.7	0.8	0.6	0.5	0.7	0.9	0.8	1.4	0.7	0.6	0.7	0.5	0.5
Social Science													
Anthropology	0.5	0.4	0.6	0.1	0.4	0.4	0.5	0.2	0.4	0.6	0.6	0.1	0.2
Economics	0.8	0.5	1.1	0.5	0.3	0.9	1.5	0.4	0.4	0.9	2.1	0.0	1.2
Ethnic Studies	0.1	0.1	0.1	0.0	0.0	0.1	0.1	0.0	0.1	0.1	0.1	0.0	0.1
Geography	0.1	0.1	0.1	0.1	0.1	0.1	0.1	0.0	0.0	0.1	0.0	0.0	0.1
Political Science (gov't., international relations)	3.1	2.7	3.7	2.6	2.4	3.1	3.4	2.8	2.8	3.2	5.6	1.6	4.2
Psychology	5.1	5.3	4.6	7.5	5.5	5.1	5.0	5.6	4.9	4.9	3.7	7.1	8.0
Public Policy	0.1	0.1	0.2	0.0	0.0	0.1	0.1	0.1	0.1	0.1	0.3	0.0	0.0
Social Work	0.6	0.9	0.3	2.3	1.0	0.7	0.6	0.7	0.9	0.3	0.2	3.0	1.0
Sociology	0.7	0.7	0.8	0.8	0.8	0.6	0.5	0.7	0.7	0.8	0.4	0.4	1.3
Women's Studies	0.0	0.0	0.0	0.0	0.0	0.0	0.0	0.0	0.0	0.0	0.0	0.0	0.0
Other Social Science	0.4	0.4	0.4	0.6	0.4	0.4	0.3	0.3	0.4	0.4	0.3	0.6	0.7
Technical													
Building Trades	0.0	0.0	0.1	0.0	0.0	0.0	0.0	0.0	0.1	0.1	0.0	0.0	0.0
Data Processing or Computer Programming	0.5	0.5	0.5	0.9	0.6	0.4	0.5	0.3	0.4	0.5	0.5	1.3	0.2
Drafting or Design	0.3	0.3	0.2	0.5	0.3	0.4	0.6	0.1	0.3	0.2	0.1	0.7	0.2
Electronics	0.1	0.1	0.1	0.2	0.1	0.0	0.0	0.0	0.1	0.1	0.0	0.3	0.0
Mechanics	0.0	0.0	0.0	0.0	0.0	0.0	0.0	0.1	0.0	0.1	0.0	0.0	0.0
Other Technical	0.1	0.1	0.1	0.0	0.1	0.1	0.0	0.1	0.1	0.1	0.0	0.0	0.0
Other Fields													
Agriculture	0.4	0.2	0.7	0.3	0.3	0.2	0.2	0.0	0.2	0.8	0.1	0.5	0.0
Communications	1.8	1.9	1.6	2.1	1.8	2.0	2.0	2.0	2.1	1.4	2.2	2.4	1.7
Computer Science	1.0	1.0	1.1	2.5	1.2	0.7	0.6	0.7	0.9	1.1	1.3	3.0	1.7
Forestry	0.1	0.1	0.2	0.1	0.1	0.0	0.0	0.0	0.1	0.2	0.0	0.2	0.0
Kinesiology	0.7	0.8	0.6	0.1	1.1	0.4	0.1	0.2	0.9	0.7	0.2	0.0	0.3
Law Enforcement	1.4	1.9	0.4	2.4	2.1	1.7	1.7	1.8	1.6	0.4	0.5	2.6	2.1
Military Science	0.1	0.2	0.0	0.1	0.2	0.1	0.0	0.1	0.1	0.0	0.0	0.2	0.1
Other Field	1.5	1.7	1.1	1.5	1.5	2.0	2.1	1.7	1.9	1.2	0.9	1.6	1.4
Undecided	6.2	6.4	5.9	2.6	6.6	6.2	6.2	6.2	6.3	6.0	5.3	2.7	2.3

WEIGHTED NATIONAL NORMS FOR ALL FRESHMEN, FALL 2008

	ALL BACC. INSTS.	ALL 4-YR. COLLEGES	ALL UNI-VERSITIES	ALL BLACK COLLEGES	FOUR-YEAR COLLEGES					UNIVERSITIES		BLACK COLLEGES	
					PUBLIC	ALL PRIV.	NONSECT.	CATHOLIC	OTH. REL.	PUBLIC	PRIVATE	PUBLIC	PRIVATE
Objectives considered to be "essential" or "very important":													
Becoming accomplished in one of the performing arts (acting, dancing, etc.)	16.6	17.6	15.1	24.0	17.0	18.4	19.7	13.9	19.1	14.3	17.7	23.2	25.2
Becoming an authority in my field	60.2	59.6	61.2	75.5	59.5	59.9	61.4	60.5	57.6	59.9	65.8	75.3	76.0
Obtaining recognition from my colleagues for contributions to my special field	57.6	56.7	59.1	68.9	56.4	57.1	60.1	58.7	52.5	58.3	62.0	68.8	69.1
Influencing the political structure	22.3	22.3	22.2	38.8	21.9	22.9	24.2	23.4	21.2	21.5	24.8	37.6	40.7
Influencing social values	44.7	45.8	42.8	60.0	44.6	47.3	46.4	48.5	47.8	42.1	45.5	59.6	60.7
Raising a family	75.5	75.8	75.1	77.7	76.2	75.3	71.6	79.7	77.7	75.3	74.4	78.3	76.7
Being very well off financially	76.8	76.9	76.8	89.3	79.2	73.7	75.2	79.5	69.0	77.6	74.1	90.1	88.0
Helping others who are in difficulty	69.7	69.8	69.6	79.3	68.7	71.1	68.8	73.9	72.6	69.0	72.0	78.2	81.0
Making a theoretical contribution to science	21.3	19.0	25.3	29.7	19.1	18.9	18.9	21.1	17.8	25.1	26.1	26.8	34.4
Writing original works (poems, novels, short stories, etc.)	16.6	17.4	15.3	26.3	16.2	18.9	21.2	15.6	17.6	14.6	18.0	26.0	26.9
Creating artistic works (painting, sculpture, decorating, etc.)	16.9	17.9	15.1	19.7	16.6	19.7	24.3	14.3	16.8	14.8	16.1	20.0	19.2
Becoming successful in a business of my own	43.4	43.5	43.1	66.8	42.9	44.4	47.9	44.0	40.3	43.3	42.5	66.0	68.1
Becoming involved in programs to clean up the environment	29.5	28.1	31.8	40.3	26.8	29.8	32.4	29.4	26.7	31.5	33.1	40.2	40.5
Developing a meaningful philosophy of life	51.4	49.9	53.8	57.2	48.3	52.1	53.3	50.4	51.5	52.5	58.3	55.6	59.9
Participating in a community action program	30.3	29.5	31.6	49.4	27.4	32.2	31.5	34.0	32.3	30.1	37.0	46.7	53.6
Helping to promote racial understanding	37.3	37.2	37.5	62.1	36.1	38.6	40.4	39.0	36.2	36.8	40.1	60.0	65.4
Keeping up to date with political affairs	39.5	37.0	43.8	51.8	35.5	39.0	41.5	38.3	36.0	42.1	49.7	49.6	55.4
Becoming a community leader	36.2	35.8	36.9	54.6	34.7	37.2	36.8	38.5	37.1	35.5	42.0	52.6	57.9
Improving my understanding of other countries and cultures	52.8	50.4	56.8	58.4	47.7	54.1	57.1	52.1	51.4	55.0	63.5	55.2	63.5
Adopting "green" practices to protect the environment	45.3	42.5	49.9	43.7	40.4	45.3	50.0	45.3	39.5	49.1	52.7	42.9	44.9

42

WEIGHTED NATIONAL NORMS FOR ALL FRESHMEN, FALL 2008

	ALL BACC. INSTS.	ALL 4-YR. COLLEGES	ALL UNI-VERSITIES	ALL BLACK COLLEGES	FOUR-YEAR COLLEGES					UNIVERSITIES		BLACK COLLEGES	
					PUBLIC	ALL PRIV.	NONSECT.	CATHOLIC	OTH. REL.	PUBLIC	PRIVATE	PUBLIC	PRIVATE
Student estimates chances are "very good" that he/she will:													
Change major field	13.4	12.5	14.9	10.4	12.8	12.2	13.0	11.4	11.7	15.1	14.2	11.0	9.4
Change career choice	13.1	12.0	14.9	8.4	11.4	12.7	13.5	11.4	12.3	14.7	15.4	8.9	7.5
Participate in student government	7.1	7.0	7.3	15.0	6.7	7.4	7.6	7.7	7.1	6.8	9.1	13.0	18.2
Get a job to help pay for college expenses	49.4	49.7	48.9	43.6	49.5	49.9	49.5	52.2	49.1	50.0	44.8	44.1	42.9
Work full-time while attending college	7.6	9.0	5.3	11.5	10.9	6.6	7.2	6.9	5.6	5.6	4.0	12.3	10.4
Join a social fraternity or sorority	10.4	9.9	11.2	36.8	11.0	8.6	8.4	7.0	9.5	11.2	11.5	35.1	39.6
Play varsity/intercollegiate athletics	16.9	20.3	11.0	21.3	16.1	25.8	23.8	22.4	30.1	10.3	13.7	23.1	18.5
Make at least a "B" average	62.3	60.0	66.2	65.2	56.8	64.2	65.0	65.7	62.5	64.5	72.3	62.0	70.2
Need extra time to complete your degree requirements	6.4	7.0	5.6	11.9	7.5	6.2	5.9	6.2	6.7	6.0	4.0	12.9	10.4
Participate in student protests or demonstrations	6.3	6.1	6.6	10.5	5.5	7.0	8.0	6.2	6.0	6.2	7.9	9.4	12.3
Transfer to another college before graduating	7.6	9.4	4.7	13.8	11.3	6.8	6.5	6.0	7.5	5.2	2.9	16.9	8.9
Be satisfied with your college	55.3	52.2	60.4	44.5	48.8	56.7	56.6	57.6	56.4	58.7	66.7	37.4	55.9
Participate in volunteer or community service work	28.3	26.2	31.9	42.5	22.0	31.6	29.3	33.8	33.4	28.9	42.8	41.8	43.7
Seek personal counseling	9.2	9.0	9.5	13.8	9.0	9.0	9.3	9.4	8.6	9.7	8.7	12.5	15.8
Communicate regularly with your professors	36.4	35.7	37.4	40.4	32.1	40.6	42.0	39.6	39.2	34.8	46.8	34.3	50.1
Socialize with someone of another racial/ethnic group	65.4	62.7	70.1	56.8	60.7	65.3	67.2	63.4	64.0	68.5	75.6	54.9	60.0
Participate in student clubs/groups	45.6	41.5	52.5	45.3	38.9	44.9	46.2	46.5	42.4	49.7	62.4	41.1	51.9
Participate in a study abroad program	29.6	26.8	34.3	25.8	21.3	34.0	37.0	32.2	31.0	31.6	44.1	23.3	29.9
Have a roommate of different race/ethnicity	29.3	26.6	33.8	19.8	25.5	28.2	31.2	24.0	26.4	32.0	40.4	21.1	17.7
Discuss course content with students outside of class	46.9	42.2	54.7	40.0	39.1	46.4	47.8	45.1	45.4	52.5	62.7	36.8	45.3
Work on a professor's research project	29.8	30.8	28.2	45.5	30.7	30.8	32.8	29.4	29.0	27.1	32.0	44.4	47.5
Get tutoring help in specific courses	31.6	31.8	31.3	50.4	32.9	30.4	30.0	32.2	29.9	32.3	27.8	47.9	54.4
Do you give the Higher Education Research Institute (HERI) permission to include your ID number should your college request the data for additional research analyses?													
Yes	67.8	70.4	63.3	65.1	73.7	66.0	63.8	66.1	68.8	64.4	59.2	66.2	63.3
No	32.2	29.6	36.7	34.9	26.3	34.0	36.2	33.9	31.2	35.6	40.8	33.8	36.7

2008 National Norms

Type of Institution and Control for Men

NOTES

These notes refer to report items that are followed by numbers in [brackets].

[1] Based on the recommendations of the National Commission on Excellence In Education.

[2] Percentage responding "frequently" only.

[3] Recategorization of this item from a longer list is shown in Appendix C.

[4] Percentages will add to more than 100.0 if any student marked more than one category.

WEIGHTED NATIONAL NORMS FOR FRESHMAN MEN, FALL 2008

	ALL BACC. INSTS.	ALL 4-YR. COLLEGES	ALL UNI-VERSITIES	ALL BLACK COLLEGES	FOUR-YEAR COLLEGES					UNIVERSITIES		BLACK COLLEGES	
					PUBLIC	ALL PRIV.	NONSECT.	CATHOLIC	OTH. REL.	PUBLIC	PRIVATE	PUBLIC	PRIVATE
How old will you be on December 31 of this year?													
16 or younger	0.0	0.0	0.0	0.0	0.0	0.0	0.0	0.0	0.0	0.0	0.1	0.0	0.0
17	1.2	1.1	1.4	1.4	1.1	1.2	1.4	1.3	0.9	1.3	1.7	0.9	2.3
18	65.2	64.6	66.2	66.9	66.3	62.3	65.2	64.5	57.4	65.9	67.2	66.7	67.3
19	31.3	31.4	31.1	28.0	29.7	33.7	30.1	32.5	39.0	31.4	29.9	28.2	27.8
20	1.3	1.7	0.7	2.4	1.5	1.9	2.1	1.2	2.0	0.7	0.9	2.7	1.9
21 to 24	0.8	1.0	0.5	1.2	1.1	0.8	1.0	0.4	0.6	0.5	0.3	1.6	0.6
25 to 29	0.1	0.1	0.1	0.0	0.1	0.1	0.1	0.1	0.0	0.1	0.0	0.0	0.1
30 to 39	0.0	0.0	0.0	0.0	0.1	0.0	0.0	0.0	0.0	0.0	0.0	0.0	0.0
40 to 54	0.0	0.0	0.0	0.0	0.1	0.0	0.0	0.0	0.0	0.0	0.0	0.0	0.0
55 or older	0.0	0.0	0.0	0.0	0.0	0.0	0.0	0.0	0.0	0.0	0.0	0.0	0.0
Is English your native language?													
Yes	91.6	93.5	88.9	97.0	93.0	94.1	92.5	93.9	96.1	88.9	88.8	97.4	96.3
No	8.4	6.5	11.1	3.0	7.0	5.9	7.5	6.1	3.9	11.1	11.2	2.6	3.7
In what year did you graduate from high school?													
2008	97.4	96.6	98.6	95.5	96.4	96.8	96.3	97.9	97.1	98.6	98.6	95.4	95.7
2007	1.5	2.0	0.8	3.1	2.1	2.0	2.2	1.3	2.0	0.7	1.1	3.0	3.1
2006	0.4	0.5	0.2	0.6	0.5	0.6	0.8	0.3	0.5	0.2	0.1	0.7	0.6
2005 or earlier	0.6	0.7	0.4	0.6	0.9	0.5	0.6	0.3	0.4	0.4	0.2	0.6	0.5
Did not graduate but passed G.E.D. test	0.1	0.2	0.1	0.2	0.2	0.1	0.1	0.1	0.1	0.1	0.0	0.3	0.1
Never completed high school	0.0	0.0	0.0	0.0	0.0	0.0	0.0	0.0	0.0	0.0	0.1	0.0	0.0
How many miles is this college from your permanent home?													
5 or less	5.5	7.1	2.9	6.2	8.4	5.3	5.6	7.0	4.3	2.8	3.3	6.7	5.3
6 to 10	5.3	6.9	2.9	6.2	7.8	5.6	6.6	7.4	3.5	2.6	4.1	6.3	6.0
11 to 50	24.3	27.9	18.7	14.9	31.1	23.5	23.9	32.2	19.1	19.1	17.3	14.1	16.3
51 to 100	16.6	16.1	17.3	14.0	16.1	16.1	14.4	15.2	18.9	19.5	8.7	17.3	8.0
101 to 500	33.9	27.6	43.3	38.2	25.0	31.4	28.4	26.4	37.4	45.7	34.3	44.0	27.7
Over 500	14.5	14.3	14.8	20.5	11.6	18.0	21.2	11.8	16.8	10.3	32.4	11.6	36.7
What was your average grade in high school?													
A or A+	19.5	14.3	27.5	7.5	13.5	15.4	14.5	14.7	16.9	24.7	38.0	5.1	11.9
A-	23.0	18.7	29.5	9.9	17.4	20.6	19.8	21.9	21.0	29.0	31.5	7.5	14.3
B+	20.7	20.7	20.8	17.5	20.5	20.9	20.7	23.4	19.9	21.7	17.3	15.7	20.7
B	21.9	25.6	16.2	24.9	27.2	23.4	24.3	24.3	21.6	17.8	9.9	25.0	24.7
B-	8.3	11.1	4.0	17.3	11.9	10.1	10.7	8.6	10.1	4.4	2.3	19.8	12.7
C+	4.5	6.6	1.4	15.0	6.7	6.4	6.6	4.8	6.9	1.6	0.7	18.0	9.7
C	1.9	2.8	0.6	7.1	2.6	3.0	3.0	2.3	3.4	0.7	0.3	7.6	6.1
D	0.1	0.2	0.0	0.8	0.2	0.2	0.3	0.1	0.1	0.0	0.0	1.2	0.0
From what kind of high school did you graduate?													
Public school (not charter or magnet)	76.6	76.2	77.2	76.5	81.5	68.8	67.1	61.6	74.3	81.4	61.1	83.8	63.5
Public charter school	1.8	2.0	1.5	3.0	2.4	1.4	1.4	1.5	1.5	1.6	1.0	2.3	4.3
Public magnet school	3.1	2.9	3.4	9.1	3.3	2.4	2.9	1.7	2.1	3.3	3.9	7.1	12.7
Private religious/parochial school	11.4	11.9	10.7	7.1	8.6	16.4	15.4	26.3	13.2	8.8	18.1	4.1	12.6
Private independent college-prep school	6.5	6.2	6.9	4.2	3.7	9.8	12.7	8.0	6.9	4.7	15.6	2.7	6.9
Home school	0.6	0.8	0.3	0.0	0.6	1.1	0.5	0.9	2.1	0.3	0.4	0.0	0.1
Prior to this term, have you ever taken courses for credit at this institution?													
No	95.3	95.2	95.5	89.4	95.1	95.3	95.3	95.0	95.5	95.4	95.7	92.5	84.0
Yes	4.7	4.8	4.5	10.6	4.9	4.7	4.7	5.0	4.5	4.6	4.3	7.5	16.0

WEIGHTED NATIONAL NORMS FOR FRESHMAN MEN, FALL 2008

	ALL BACC. INSTS.	ALL 4-YR. COLLEGES	ALL UNI-VERSITIES	ALL BLACK COLLEGES	FOUR-YEAR COLLEGES					UNIVERSITIES		BLACK COLLEGES	
					PUBLIC	ALL PRIV.	NONSECT.	CATHOLIC	OTH. REL.	PUBLIC	PRIVATE	PUBLIC	PRIVATE
Since leaving high school, have you ever taken courses, whether for credit or not for credit, at any other institution (university, 4- or 2-year college, technical, vocational, or business school)?													
No	89.9	90.7	88.8	88.6	90.8	90.5	90.8	90.6	90.0	88.7	89.1	89.5	86.8
Yes	10.1	9.3	11.2	11.4	9.2	9.5	9.2	9.4	10.0	11.3	10.9	10.5	13.2
Where do you plan to live during the fall term?													
With my family or other relatives	14.8	20.6	6.0	14.0	25.9	13.3	17.1	16.2	6.9	5.7	7.1	14.3	13.5
Other private home, apartment, or room	4.3	4.9	3.4	3.7	7.3	1.7	2.2	1.4	1.1	4.1	0.6	3.4	4.3
College residence hall	77.4	71.2	86.8	78.7	62.9	82.6	77.9	80.8	89.5	85.8	90.8	79.0	78.2
Fraternity or sorority house	0.6	0.3	1.2	0.1	0.2	0.4	0.8	0.0	0.1	1.4	0.1	0.1	0.0
Other campus student housing	2.4	2.5	2.4	2.8	3.0	1.7	1.6	1.2	2.0	2.7	1.3	2.6	3.2
Other	0.4	0.6	0.2	0.7	0.7	0.4	0.4	0.3	0.4	0.3	0.1	0.6	0.9
To how many colleges other than this one did you apply for admission this year?													
None	16.3	17.7	14.3	12.0	20.7	13.4	12.6	10.5	15.7	15.7	8.7	13.3	9.7
One	10.7	11.3	9.8	7.6	12.8	9.3	8.3	9.0	10.7	10.9	5.6	7.2	8.3
Two	13.6	14.6	12.0	16.3	16.1	12.6	10.5	13.7	14.7	13.1	7.5	17.7	13.7
Three	16.1	17.5	13.9	21.3	17.8	17.1	15.4	18.1	18.9	14.7	10.4	23.0	18.4
Four	13.0	13.7	11.9	16.5	13.0	14.7	14.2	15.2	15.1	12.0	11.6	16.4	16.9
Five	9.6	9.3	10.0	10.3	8.1	11.0	11.9	11.7	9.4	9.7	11.1	9.1	12.5
Six	6.9	5.9	8.3	5.3	4.9	7.4	8.8	7.6	5.4	7.6	11.1	4.5	6.9
Seven to ten	11.1	7.9	15.9	7.1	5.5	11.3	13.9	11.6	7.8	13.4	25.5	5.6	10.0
Eleven or more	2.8	2.1	3.9	3.4	1.2	3.3	4.3	2.5	2.3	2.7	8.6	3.2	3.7
Were you accepted by your first choice college?													
Yes	75.8	79.0	71.0	77.4	79.8	77.9	72.6	79.9	83.8	72.1	66.7	76.6	78.8
No	24.2	21.0	29.0	22.6	20.2	22.1	27.4	20.1	16.2	27.9	33.3	23.4	21.2
Is this college your:													
First choice?	61.0	61.2	60.6	44.7	62.1	59.9	57.0	60.9	63.1	61.2	58.4	40.1	53.0
Second choice?	25.6	26.5	24.3	29.4	26.6	26.2	27.4	28.0	23.9	24.0	25.2	29.5	29.3
Third choice?	8.7	8.4	9.2	15.4	7.8	10.1	10.1	8.1	8.5	9.0	10.1	17.7	11.2
Less than third choice?	4.7	4.0	5.9	10.5	3.4	4.7	5.4	3.0	4.5	5.7	6.3	12.8	6.5
Citizenship status													
U.S. citizen	96.0	96.6	94.9	98.2	97.3	95.6	94.4	97.0	96.7	95.5	92.8	98.3	98.0
Permanent resident (green card)	2.1	1.6	2.9	0.8	1.7	1.4	1.6	1.5	1.0	2.9	2.9	0.9	0.7
Neither	1.9	1.8	2.1	1.0	0.9	3.0	4.1	1.5	2.3	1.6	4.3	0.8	1.4
Are your parents:													
Both alive and living with each other?	73.1	70.1	77.8	40.7	69.1	71.4	69.4	74.3	72.7	76.9	81.5	38.2	45.1
Both alive, divorced or living apart?	23.3	26.0	19.2	50.9	27.0	24.6	26.3	22.1	23.6	20.1	15.8	53.4	46.5
One or both deceased?	3.6	3.9	3.0	8.4	3.9	4.0	4.3	3.6	3.7	3.1	2.7	8.4	8.4

WEIGHTED NATIONAL NORMS FOR FRESHMAN MEN, FALL 2008

	ALL BACC. INSTS.	ALL 4-YR. COLLEGES	ALL UNI-VERSITIES	ALL BLACK COLLEGES	FOUR-YEAR COLLEGES					UNIVERSITIES		BLACK COLLEGES	
					PUBLIC	ALL PRIV.	NONSECT.	CATHOLIC	OTH. REL.	PUBLIC	PRIVATE	PUBLIC	PRIVATE
During high school (grades 9-12) how many years did you study each of the following subjects? [1]													
English (4 years)	97.6	97.2	98.4	95.5	97.2	97.1	97.1	98.1	96.7	98.3	98.6	95.2	96.0
Mathematics (3 years)	98.5	98.1	99.1	96.8	97.8	98.4	98.5	99.0	97.8	99.1	99.4	96.1	98.1
Foreign Language (2 years)	91.8	89.6	95.1	82.7	88.7	90.9	91.3	93.3	89.1	94.5	97.3	79.5	88.2
Physical Science (2 years)	65.9	61.9	72.0	42.2	60.5	63.9	65.5	61.7	62.9	71.2	74.9	40.8	44.8
Biological Science (2 years)	47.7	46.4	49.7	41.9	44.8	48.5	48.2	47.7	49.3	49.7	50.1	41.0	43.7
History/Am. Govt. (1 year)	99.0	98.8	99.2	97.3	98.9	98.7	98.7	99.2	98.6	99.2	99.2	97.5	96.8
Computer Science (1/2 year)	65.8	68.7	61.3	67.6	71.6	64.8	62.9	67.2	66.0	62.1	58.2	67.2	68.4
Arts and/or Music (1 year)	78.2	77.1	79.9	74.9	76.5	77.8	79.2	76.5	76.7	79.4	82.0	72.7	79.1
WHAT IS THE HIGHEST ACADEMIC DEGREE THAT YOU INTEND TO OBTAIN?													
Highest planned													
None	1.0	1.2	0.6	1.8	1.1	1.3	1.5	0.9	1.4	0.6	0.5	1.6	2.1
Vocational certificate	0.2	0.2	0.0	0.4	0.2	0.3	0.4	0.1	0.2	0.1	0.0	0.6	0.2
Associate (A.A. or equivalent)	0.6	0.8	0.3	0.4	0.7	0.8	0.6	0.7	1.2	0.3	0.2	0.5	0.3
Bachelor's degree (B.A., B.S., etc.)	24.3	27.7	19.3	18.8	29.7	24.9	23.9	21.8	27.7	20.9	12.9	23.9	10.1
Master's degree (M.A., M.S., etc.)	42.2	42.3	42.0	39.6	42.5	42.0	43.4	44.3	39.0	42.4	40.1	42.0	35.4
Ph.D. or Ed.D.	17.6	15.8	20.2	22.8	15.5	16.2	16.3	15.3	16.6	19.6	22.5	21.2	25.7
M.D., D.O., D.D.S., D.V.M.	8.0	6.0	11.0	7.8	5.3	6.9	6.0	9.3	6.8	10.4	13.6	3.8	14.9
J.D. (Law)	4.4	3.8	5.2	5.3	3.1	4.7	5.0	5.3	3.9	4.5	8.2	3.3	8.9
B.D. or M.DIV. (Divinity)	0.4	0.5	0.2	0.8	0.3	0.7	0.6	0.4	0.9	0.2	0.4	0.9	0.6
Other	1.5	1.8	1.1	2.2	1.5	2.2	2.3	1.8	2.3	1.0	1.6	2.4	1.8
Highest planned at this college													
None	1.7	2.2	0.9	3.2	2.7	1.6	1.6	1.1	1.9	0.9	0.7	3.8	1.9
Vocational certificate	0.2	0.3	0.1	0.3	0.3	0.2	0.3	0.1	0.3	0.1	0.1	0.5	0.0
Associate (A.A. or equivalent)	2.1	3.0	0.9	2.9	3.5	2.2	1.8	2.1	2.8	0.9	0.6	3.7	1.6
Bachelor's degree (B.A., B.S., etc.)	69.3	72.3	65.1	65.6	71.1	73.9	74.5	66.7	76.5	65.2	64.8	64.8	67.2
Master's degree (M.A., M.S., etc.)	19.6	17.0	23.3	17.7	17.5	16.4	16.5	22.5	13.4	23.4	22.7	19.0	15.3
Ph.D. or Ed.D.	3.4	2.4	4.9	5.3	2.4	2.4	2.4	3.3	2.1	4.9	4.8	4.7	6.5
M.D., D.O., D.D.S., D.V.M.	1.6	0.6	3.0	1.7	0.5	0.7	0.6	1.4	0.5	2.9	3.3	0.5	3.8
J.D. (Law)	0.6	0.4	0.9	1.0	0.3	0.6	0.6	1.0	0.5	0.7	1.6	1.0	1.0
B.D. or M.DIV. (Divinity)	0.2	0.3	0.1	0.8	0.2	0.3	0.3	0.2	0.4	0.1	0.2	0.8	0.7
Other	1.2	1.5	0.9	1.5	1.4	1.6	1.5	1.7	1.8	0.8	1.2	1.2	2.0
HOW WOULD YOU DESCRIBE THE RACIAL COMPOSITION OF THE:													
High school I last attended													
Completely non-White	3.2	3.7	2.6	16.5	4.1	3.1	3.5	3.6	2.4	2.6	2.3	16.3	16.8
Mostly non-White	12.4	11.9	13.0	35.2	13.2	10.1	10.8	10.2	9.1	13.9	9.7	35.7	34.2
Roughly half non-White	23.4	23.5	23.2	26.8	24.6	22.1	22.5	17.5	23.5	23.8	21.1	28.3	24.1
Mostly White	52.8	52.4	53.5	19.5	50.3	55.4	54.3	59.4	55.0	52.1	58.9	18.6	21.0
Completely White	8.1	8.4	7.7	2.0	7.8	9.3	8.8	9.2	9.9	7.6	7.9	1.0	3.8
Neighborhood where I grew up													
Completely non-White	5.9	6.9	4.3	33.0	7.1	6.5	7.4	6.6	5.3	4.3	4.3	33.0	33.0
Mostly non-White	11.2	11.3	11.0	31.7	11.9	10.5	11.5	10.5	9.0	11.4	9.3	32.5	30.2
Roughly half non-White	13.3	13.1	13.7	17.8	13.9	11.9	11.8	11.7	12.1	13.8	13.2	17.3	18.5
Mostly White	49.1	47.5	51.7	14.3	46.7	48.4	47.9	48.5	49.1	51.1	54.2	14.0	15.1
Completely White	20.5	21.3	19.3	3.2	20.3	22.7	21.3	22.7	24.4	19.3	19.0	3.1	3.3

WEIGHTED NATIONAL NORMS FOR FRESHMAN MEN, FALL 2008

	ALL BACC. INSTS.	ALL 4-YR. COLLEGES	ALL UNI-VERSITIES	ALL BLACK COLLEGES	FOUR-YEAR COLLEGES					UNIVERSITIES		BLACK COLLEGES	
					PUBLIC	ALL PRIV.	NONSECT.	CATHOLIC	OTH. REL.	PUBLIC	PRIVATE	PUBLIC	PRIVATE
Do you have a disability?													
Hearing	0.6	0.7	0.5	0.3	0.7	0.7	0.7	0.5	0.7	0.5	0.4	0.3	0.3
Speech	0.4	0.4	0.3	0.5	0.4	0.5	0.5	0.5	0.5	0.3	0.3	0.4	0.5
Orthopedic	0.4	0.4	0.4	0.3	0.4	0.5	0.5	0.4	0.5	0.3	0.4	0.2	0.4
Learning disability	3.8	4.8	2.3	2.7	4.0	5.9	6.7	4.5	5.4	2.1	3.1	2.4	3.4
Partially sighted or blind	1.6	1.6	1.5	1.2	1.8	1.3	1.2	1.3	1.3	1.6	1.5	1.4	1.0
Health-related	1.2	1.2	1.1	1.4	1.1	1.4	1.5	1.1	1.3	1.1	1.3	1.4	1.6
Other	1.4	1.5	1.2	0.9	1.4	1.6	1.7	1.4	1.7	1.2	1.3	0.6	1.5
HOW MUCH OF YOUR FIRST YEAR'S EDUCATIONAL EXPENSES (ROOM, BOARD TUITION, AND FEES) DO YOU EXPECT TO COVER FROM:													
Family resources (parents, relatives, spouse, etc.)													
None	21.2	25.2	15.1	41.2	29.3	19.6	20.4	18.4	19.2	16.0	11.5	45.1	34.4
Less than $1,000	10.6	12.3	7.9	17.7	14.1	9.8	8.6	9.0	11.7	8.8	4.6	19.3	14.7
$1,000 to 2,999	13.3	15.0	10.7	17.0	16.8	12.4	10.9	13.4	14.0	11.8	6.7	17.4	16.4
$3,000 to 5,999	12.4	13.0	11.4	10.5	13.4	12.3	11.3	12.9	13.4	12.4	7.5	10.0	11.5
$6,000 to 9,999	10.3	9.7	11.2	5.1	9.1	10.7	10.2	11.3	11.0	11.9	8.3	3.9	7.3
$10,000 +	32.2	24.8	43.6	8.4	17.3	35.2	38.7	35.1	30.7	39.1	61.4	4.3	15.8
My own resources (savings from work, work-study, other income)													
None	37.0	38.8	34.2	56.5	40.4	36.6	37.9	33.2	36.4	33.1	38.5	59.6	51.0
Less than $1,000	24.5	24.9	23.7	23.6	26.4	23.0	22.0	23.9	23.8	24.4	21.0	22.9	24.9
$1,000 to 2,999	23.9	22.6	25.9	13.5	21.6	23.9	23.5	24.5	24.0	26.4	23.7	12.2	15.8
$3,000 to 5,999	9.3	8.6	10.3	3.8	7.9	9.7	9.6	10.9	9.4	10.5	9.6	3.0	5.1
$6,000 to 9,999	2.8	2.6	3.2	1.5	2.1	3.3	3.2	3.8	3.2	3.2	3.4	1.4	1.6
$10,000 +	2.6	2.5	2.7	1.1	1.6	3.6	3.8	3.8	3.2	2.4	3.9	0.8	1.6
Aid which need not be repaid (grants, scholarships, military funding, etc.)													
None	33.7	32.6	35.4	32.8	39.0	23.7	28.5	19.8	19.1	37.0	29.1	35.4	28.2
Less than $1,000	7.0	6.8	7.2	6.0	9.0	3.7	4.2	3.2	3.2	8.2	3.4	6.7	4.8
$1,000 to 2,999	12.9	13.0	12.7	13.5	16.6	8.0	8.2	7.8	7.9	14.3	6.5	14.5	11.8
$3,000 to 5,999	12.6	13.3	11.5	17.4	14.4	11.7	11.7	11.4	11.9	12.7	6.7	18.0	16.4
$6,000 to 9,999	9.9	9.9	9.8	11.2	7.5	13.4	12.3	14.8	14.1	10.3	7.8	11.3	11.0
$10,000 +	24.0	24.4	23.4	19.0	13.6	39.5	35.1	42.9	43.8	17.6	46.5	14.0	27.8
Aid which must be repaid (loans, etc.)													
None	53.1	51.8	55.2	44.3	58.7	42.1	45.1	38.9	39.7	55.8	53.2	48.1	37.5
Less than $1,000	3.8	4.3	3.0	5.6	4.8	3.5	3.1	3.5	4.1	3.2	2.1	6.4	4.2
$1,000 to 2,999	9.1	10.0	7.9	13.3	10.1	9.8	8.8	10.8	10.6	7.9	7.7	15.2	9.9
$3,000 to 5,999	14.3	14.8	13.6	14.9	13.1	17.0	15.3	18.4	18.6	13.8	13.0	16.2	12.5
$6,000 to 9,999	8.3	8.4	8.2	9.4	6.3	11.3	10.1	12.3	12.6	8.2	7.9	7.8	12.4
$10,000 +	11.4	10.9	12.1	12.4	7.0	16.2	17.6	16.1	14.5	11.1	16.2	6.2	23.6
Other than above													
None	93.1	92.7	93.7	90.6	93.3	91.9	92.4	91.2	91.6	93.9	93.2	90.6	90.5
Less than $1,000	2.7	2.8	2.5	3.1	2.9	2.7	2.4	3.1	2.9	2.6	2.2	3.1	3.2
$1,000 to 2,999	1.6	1.8	1.5	2.2	1.8	1.8	1.6	2.0	1.9	1.5	1.4	2.8	1.1
$3,000 to 5,999	0.9	1.0	0.9	1.7	0.8	1.2	1.1	1.4	1.3	0.8	0.9	1.6	1.8
$6,000 to 9,999	0.5	0.5	0.5	0.6	0.3	0.7	0.7	0.7	0.8	0.5	0.6	0.5	0.8
$10,000 +	1.2	1.3	1.0	1.8	1.0	1.7	1.8	1.7	1.5	0.8	1.7	1.4	2.6

WEIGHTED NATIONAL NORMS FOR FRESHMAN MEN, FALL 2008

	ALL BACC. INSTS.	ALL 4-YR. COLLEGES	ALL UNI-VERSITIES	ALL BLACK COLLEGES	FOUR-YEAR COLLEGES					UNIVERSITIES		BLACK COLLEGES	
					PUBLIC	ALL PRIV.	NONSECT.	CATHOLIC	OTH. REL.	PUBLIC	PRIVATE	PUBLIC	PRIVATE
What is your best estimate of your parents' total income last year? Consider income from all sources before taxes													
Less than $10,000	2.9	3.5	2.1	11.6	3.6	3.4	3.3	3.2	3.6	2.2	1.7	12.9	9.2
$10,000 to 14,999	2.2	2.5	1.6	4.7	2.7	2.3	2.5	2.3	2.2	1.7	1.2	4.5	4.9
$15,000 to 19,999	2.1	2.3	1.7	5.9	2.6	2.0	2.0	1.8	2.1	1.9	1.3	6.3	5.2
$20,000 to 24,999	2.8	3.1	2.4	6.9	3.2	2.9	2.6	3.2	3.1	2.6	1.6	6.7	7.2
$25,000 to 29,999	2.8	3.1	2.2	5.9	3.3	3.0	2.9	2.3	3.3	2.4	1.5	5.8	5.9
$30,000 to 39,999	5.4	6.0	4.6	10.4	6.3	5.7	5.5	5.5	6.0	4.8	3.4	12.1	7.4
$40,000 to 49,999	6.3	7.0	5.2	10.4	7.2	6.6	6.0	6.2	7.6	5.5	3.8	11.8	8.1
$50,000 to 59,999	8.0	8.9	6.6	8.3	9.2	8.4	7.9	8.1	9.0	7.0	5.2	7.6	9.5
$60,000 to 74,999	10.7	11.7	9.1	10.7	11.9	11.5	11.0	11.1	12.3	9.5	7.5	10.6	10.9
$75,000 to 99,999	15.2	15.3	15.1	10.0	15.4	15.3	14.5	16.3	15.7	15.5	13.5	9.1	11.5
$100,000 to 149,999	20.0	18.2	22.6	7.7	18.6	17.7	17.6	19.1	17.1	22.9	21.8	6.5	9.7
$150,000 to 199,999	8.8	7.8	10.3	4.0	7.6	8.2	9.0	9.1	6.8	10.0	11.3	3.5	4.9
$200,000 to 249,999	4.6	3.8	5.9	1.7	3.4	4.3	4.8	4.6	3.6	5.5	7.9	1.6	1.8
$250,000 or more	8.3	6.7	10.6	2.0	5.2	8.9	10.4	7.3	7.7	8.6	18.5	0.9	3.8
Do you have any concern about your ability to finance your college education?													
None (I am confident that I will have sufficient funds)	42.8	43.4	41.9	35.1	45.0	41.2	41.9	40.1	40.9	41.3	44.3	36.7	32.1
Some (but I probably will have enough funds)	48.7	47.9	50.0	48.1	46.8	49.4	48.4	51.1	50.0	50.6	47.8	49.2	46.1
Major (not sure I will have enough funds to complete college)	8.4	8.7	8.1	16.8	8.2	9.3	9.7	8.9	9.1	8.2	7.9	14.1	21.8
Your current religious preference													
Baptist	10.0	12.9	5.5	49.6	13.3	12.3	8.8	6.9	19.4	5.7	5.0	52.5	44.6
Buddhist	1.4	0.9	2.0	0.6	0.9	1.0	1.3	1.1	0.6	2.2	1.5	0.2	1.4
Church of Christ	4.8	5.6	3.7	10.8	5.8	5.2	5.3	4.2	5.7	4.1	2.1	12.7	7.4
Eastern Orthodox	0.7	0.6	0.8	0.1	0.6	0.6	0.6	0.8	0.4	0.7	1.2	0.0	0.2
Episcopalian	1.2	1.2	1.2	0.4	1.2	1.4	1.4	0.8	1.6	1.1	1.7	0.1	0.8
Hindu	0.9	0.5	1.6	0.2	0.4	0.6	0.9	0.4	0.3	1.6	2.0	0.2	0.2
Jewish	2.8	1.9	4.3	0.1	1.7	2.1	3.5	0.4	1.1	3.6	7.2	0.0	0.2
LDS (Mormon)	2.2	2.3	2.1	0.0	3.9	0.1	0.1	0.1	0.1	2.5	0.2	0.0	0.0
Lutheran	3.5	3.2	3.9	0.3	2.6	3.9	2.1	3.4	6.4	4.4	2.0	0.3	0.3
Methodist	4.2	4.4	3.9	5.0	4.3	4.6	3.1	2.4	7.6	4.2	2.7	4.7	5.4
Muslim	1.0	0.7	1.3	0.7	0.7	0.8	1.0	0.8	0.4	1.2	1.6	0.5	1.1
Presbyterian	3.0	2.7	3.5	1.0	2.5	3.0	2.5	1.7	4.3	3.6	3.2	1.2	0.8
Quaker	0.2	0.2	0.2	0.2	0.2	0.3	0.4	0.1	0.3	0.2	0.2	0.1	0.3
Roman Catholic	25.3	25.3	25.4	6.7	24.0	27.1	28.0	52.5	14.4	23.7	32.1	3.8	11.9
Seventh Day Adventist	0.4	0.5	0.3	1.7	0.4	0.7	0.5	0.3	1.3	0.2	0.3	1.9	1.2
United Church of Christ/Congregational	0.6	0.7	0.5	0.5	0.7	0.7	0.7	0.6	0.7	0.5	0.6	0.8	0.1
Other Christian	11.8	12.9	10.1	13.5	12.8	13.0	10.1	8.1	18.9	10.8	7.5	12.1	15.9
Other Religion	2.8	2.8	2.8	2.3	3.0	2.4	2.8	1.9	2.2	2.9	2.6	2.2	2.4
None	23.2	20.8	26.8	6.3	21.4	20.0	26.9	13.6	14.1	26.8	26.6	6.6	5.8

WEIGHTED NATIONAL NORMS FOR FRESHMAN MEN, FALL 2008

	ALL BACC. INSTS.	ALL 4-YR. COLLEGES	ALL UNI-VERSITIES	ALL BLACK COLLEGES	FOUR-YEAR COLLEGES					UNIVERSITIES		BLACK COLLEGES	
					PUBLIC	ALL PRIV.	NONSECT.	CATHOLIC	OTH. REL.	PUBLIC	PRIVATE	PUBLIC	PRIVATE
Father's current religious preference													
Baptist	10.4	13.4	5.9	50.4	14.2	12.3	9.1	6.8	19.2	6.0	5.4	53.9	44.1
Buddhist	1.8	1.0	2.9	0.8	1.1	0.9	1.2	1.0	0.5	3.1	2.2	0.3	1.8
Church of Christ	5.0	5.7	4.1	9.3	5.8	5.4	5.8	4.5	5.3	4.5	2.6	10.4	7.3
Eastern Orthodox	0.8	0.7	0.9	0.1	0.7	0.8	0.9	0.9	0.5	0.8	1.3	0.0	0.2
Episcopalian	1.6	1.6	1.7	0.3	1.4	1.8	2.0	1.1	1.9	1.5	2.5	0.1	0.7
Hindu	1.2	0.6	2.1	0.2	0.5	0.7	1.1	0.4	0.4	2.0	2.5	0.3	0.0
Jewish	3.7	2.6	5.4	0.2	2.2	3.2	5.2	0.9	1.7	4.5	8.8	0.3	0.1
LDS (Mormon)	2.4	2.5	2.2	0.0	4.2	0.2	0.2	0.1	0.3	2.7	0.2	0.0	0.0
Lutheran	4.3	3.8	4.9	0.2	3.3	4.6	2.6	4.2	7.5	5.5	2.9	0.3	0.1
Methodist	4.8	4.9	4.7	3.6	4.8	5.1	3.8	2.8	7.9	5.1	3.5	3.0	4.9
Muslim	1.3	1.1	1.6	1.7	1.1	1.1	1.5	1.0	0.6	1.5	2.0	1.5	2.1
Presbyterian	3.6	3.4	4.1	1.0	3.2	3.6	3.2	2.1	5.0	4.1	4.0	1.0	1.0
Quaker	0.2	0.2	0.2	0.1	0.2	0.3	0.3	0.1	0.3	0.2	0.2	0.0	0.2
Roman Catholic	28.8	28.8	28.7	7.5	27.8	30.2	31.9	54.5	16.7	27.0	35.1	4.1	13.6
Seventh Day Adventist	0.4	0.5	0.3	0.9	0.4	0.8	0.5	0.6	1.3	0.3	0.3	1.0	0.7
United Church of Christ/Congregational	0.7	0.8	0.7	0.7	0.8	0.8	0.9	0.6	0.8	0.7	0.7	0.8	0.5
Other Christian	11.5	12.4	10.1	12.3	12.3	12.5	10.4	7.9	17.4	10.8	7.6	11.6	13.5
Other Religion	1.9	1.8	2.0	2.3	1.8	1.8	2.0	1.4	1.6	2.0	1.8	2.1	2.6
None	15.5	14.1	17.5	8.4	14.4	13.8	17.4	9.3	11.3	17.8	16.4	9.3	6.8
Mother's current religious preference													
Baptist	10.9	14.0	6.3	51.2	14.6	13.2	9.9	7.4	20.1	6.5	5.7	53.5	47.0
Buddhist	1.9	1.0	3.2	0.9	1.0	1.0	1.3	1.0	0.6	3.4	2.3	0.5	1.8
Church of Christ	5.6	6.3	4.5	10.9	6.6	6.0	6.4	4.8	5.9	4.9	2.8	12.6	8.0
Eastern Orthodox	0.8	0.7	1.0	0.2	0.7	0.7	0.8	0.9	0.5	0.9	1.4	0.1	0.2
Episcopalian	1.8	1.7	1.9	0.3	1.5	1.9	2.1	1.1	2.0	1.7	2.7	0.1	0.6
Hindu	1.1	0.6	2.0	0.2	0.5	0.7	1.0	0.5	0.4	1.9	2.4	0.4	0.0
Jewish	3.4	2.3	5.1	0.0	2.1	2.7	4.6	0.6	1.3	4.3	8.3	0.0	0.0
LDS (Mormon)	2.5	2.6	2.3	0.0	4.3	0.2	0.2	0.1	0.2	2.8	0.3	0.0	0.0
Lutheran	4.4	4.0	5.1	0.2	3.4	4.8	2.9	4.0	7.7	5.6	2.8	0.2	0.1
Methodist	5.3	5.5	5.1	4.8	5.5	5.4	4.0	3.2	8.3	5.4	3.8	4.6	5.0
Muslim	1.0	0.8	1.4	0.4	0.8	0.8	1.1	0.7	0.5	1.3	1.7	0.1	1.0
Presbyterian	3.9	3.6	4.5	0.9	3.3	3.9	3.6	2.2	5.2	4.5	4.4	0.9	0.7
Quaker	0.3	0.3	0.2	0.1	0.3	0.3	0.3	0.2	0.3	0.2	0.2	0.0	0.3
Roman Catholic	30.4	30.2	30.8	7.6	29.3	31.5	33.5	56.5	17.3	29.0	37.9	5.1	12.1
Seventh Day Adventist	0.5	0.6	0.3	1.8	0.4	0.8	0.6	0.2	1.4	0.3	0.3	2.1	1.1
United Church of Christ/Congregational	0.8	0.9	0.7	0.7	0.8	0.9	1.0	0.7	0.9	0.7	0.8	1.0	0.3
Other Christian	12.5	13.5	11.1	13.4	13.6	13.4	11.5	8.7	18.2	11.8	8.4	11.8	16.3
Other Religion	1.9	1.9	2.0	2.3	1.9	1.8	2.1	1.4	1.7	2.1	1.7	2.5	2.1
None	10.7	9.6	12.5	4.0	9.4	9.7	12.8	5.7	7.6	12.6	12.1	4.4	3.4

WEIGHTED NATIONAL NORMS FOR FRESHMAN MEN, FALL 2008

	ALL BACC. INSTS.	ALL 4-YR. COLLEGES	ALL UNI-VERSITIES	ALL BLACK COLLEGES	FOUR-YEAR COLLEGES					UNIVERSITIES		BLACK COLLEGES	
					PUBLIC	ALL PFIV.	NONSECT.	CATHOLIC	OTH. REL.	PUBLIC	PRIVATE	PUBLIC	PRIVATE
During the past year, student "frequently" or "occasionally":													
Attended a religious service	73.5	74.6	71.9	89.9	73.6	76.0	68.5	81.4	83.1	71.7	72.7	89.2	91.3
Was bored in class [2]	41.4	41.1	41.9	35.6	42.7	38.8	37.9	37.4	40.5	42.6	39.4	38.1	31.0
Participated in political demonstrations	25.7	25.9	25.2	39.7	25.4	26.7	26.9	26.8	26.4	25.1	26.0	39.4	40.2
Tutored another student	54.3	49.1	62.4	56.0	49.8	48.1	47.4	49.9	48.2	61.0	67.9	50.8	65.4
Studied with other students	84.7	82.9	87.5	86.4	82.2	83.9	83.1	85.6	84.1	87.4	88.1	85.5	88.0
Was a guest in a teacher's home	22.1	22.8	21.0	23.5	21.3	24.8	23.4	20.3	28.8	20.3	23.7	21.6	26.8
Smoked cigarettes [2]	4.7	5.2	3.8	2.8	5.6	4.8	5.7	4.4	3.7	3.9	3.3	2.4	3.6
Drank beer	44.3	44.3	44.2	20.4	42.1	47.4	53.8	47.3	39.2	43.4	47.7	20.7	19.9
Drank wine or liquor	44.9	45.1	44.5	39.8	43.2	47.7	54.2	47.7	39.3	43.5	48.5	39.6	40.0
Felt overwhelmed by all I had to do [2]	17.0	17.6	16.2	17.7	17.3	18.0	18.3	16.9	18.1	16.0	16.9	17.7	17.8
Felt depressed [2]	5.3	5.7	4.6	7.0	5.7	5.6	6.1	5.0	5.2	4.6	4.9	7.2	6.8
Performed volunteer work	80.9	78.5	84.5	77.5	76.4	81.4	79.5	83.7	82.8	83.5	88.3	74.1	83.7
Played a musical instrument	48.2	45.9	51.8	44.5	46.7	44.8	43.6	41.7	47.8	51.0	54.6	42.0	49.1
Asked a teacher for advice after class [2]	25.0	24.6	25.6	28.5	23.1	26.8	27.7	25.8	26.1	25.0	27.8	25.5	33.9
Voted in a student election [2]	20.9	20.6	21.3	29.1	20.1	21.5	21.5	22.4	21.0	20.6	23.7	26.9	33.2
Socialized with someone of another racial/ethnic group [2]	69.0	67.9	70.7	66.8	68.3	67.4	68.2	66.5	66.9	70.1	72.9	65.9	68.6
Came late to class	62.4	62.5	62.2	69.8	63.0	61.7	62.9	60.6	60.5	62.4	61.3	71.6	66.6
Used the Internet: [2]													
For research or homework	70.3	66.9	75.5	69.9	65.0	69.5	70.9	73.2	66.1	74.2	80.3	67.8	73.8
To read news sites	46.4	43.6	50.7	43.9	41.8	46.1	48.7	47.3	42.2	48.8	58.1	42.4	46.7
To read blogs	22.7	21.7	24.3	26.1	20.8	23.0	24.1	21.7	22.0	23.7	26.5	25.7	26.8
To blog	12.0	12.2	11.6	16.7	11.8	12.9	12.8	12.1	13.3	11.7	11.6	16.2	17.7
Performed community service as part of a class	54.7	54.0	55.8	55.6	51.0	58.1	56.7	63.7	57.3	54.6	60.3	51.0	63.9
Discussed religion [2]	30.6	30.3	31.0	28.0	29.7	31.2	28.4	31.4	34.7	29.6	36.0	23.7	35.6
Discussed politics [2]	37.9	35.7	41.3	30.6	35.8	35.5	36.2	35.8	34.3	40.0	46.2	28.0	35.4
Worked on a local, state or national political campaign	12.2	11.8	12.8	18.9	11.3	12.6	12.4	13.3	12.5	12.4	14.7	16.6	23.1
Student rated self "above average" or "highest 10%" as compared with the average person of his/her age in:													
Academic ability	73.4	66.3	84.3	66.0	66.4	66.2	65.4	69.7	65.5	83.0	89.6	61.8	73.7
Artistic ability	29.4	29.6	29.2	36.6	29.1	30.2	33.2	24.6	28.8	28.3	32.8	35.1	39.3
Computer skills	48.4	45.5	53.0	52.1	46.9	45.4	44.4	45.2	41.3	52.6	54.7	51.2	53.7
Cooperativeness	72.8	71.4	74.8	72.5	70.8	72.3	71.6	75.1	71.9	74.6	75.7	70.7	75.7
Creativity	57.3	57.2	57.6	65.0	56.4	58.2	60.9	55.8	56.0	56.5	61.7	64.1	66.7
Drive to achieve	72.6	70.5	75.9	78.8	69.1	72.4	72.7	74.1	71.1	74.7	80.8	76.2	83.5
Emotional health	61.9	59.9	65.1	62.9	59.2	60.8	59.8	62.4	61.5	64.8	66.1	61.0	66.2
Leadership ability	65.7	65.1	66.6	71.1	64.5	65.9	65.2	66.8	66.5	65.5	70.7	69.1	74.8
Mathematical ability	55.0	47.4	66.7	45.9	48.7	45.6	44.7	48.1	45.5	65.4	71.7	43.6	50.1
Physical health	67.8	67.5	68.3	68.4	66.5	69.0	67.0	71.8	70.2	68.5	67.5	66.3	72.3
Popularity	47.5	47.9	47.0	55.1	46.6	49.8	50.3	50.1	48.9	46.1	50.3	52.9	59.0
Public speaking ability	41.8	40.5	43.9	42.7	40.3	40.8	41.1	40.0	40.8	42.1	50.5	40.2	47.1
Self-confidence (intellectual)	69.5	66.8	73.6	78.3	66.5	67.2	66.8	67.6	67.4	72.6	77.7	76.4	81.8
Self-confidence (social)	57.9	58.4	57.1	70.9	58.2	58.7	58.5	59.3	58.6	57.0	57.4	70.2	72.3
Self-understanding	63.5	62.1	65.5	74.8	61.4	63.2	64.1	63.4	61.9	64.9	67.9	72.7	78.5
Spirituality	39.3	40.1	38.0	57.3	40.2	39.9	35.9	39.6	45.3	37.7	39.4	55.6	60.3
Understanding of others	65.3	64.4	66.7	67.8	63.7	65.3	66.0	65.6	64.1	66.0	69.3	66.7	69.8
Writing ability	45.5	43.0	49.2	45.5	42.3	44.1	45.6	45.9	41.4	47.1	57.1	41.3	53.3

WEIGHTED NATIONAL NORMS FOR FRESHMAN MEN, FALL 2008

	ALL BACC. INSTS.	ALL 4-YR. COLLEGES	ALL UNI-VERSITIES	ALL BLACK COLLEGES	FOUR-YEAR COLLEGES PUBLIC	ALL PRIV.	NONSECT.	CATHOLIC	OTH. REL.	UNIVERSITIES PUBLIC	PRIVATE	BLACK COLLEGES PUBLIC	PRIVATE
Student rated self "above average" or "highest 10%" as compared with the average person of his/her age in:													
Ability to see the world from someone else's perspective	65.4	62.4	70.1	62.1	62.3	62.6	64.2	62.7	60.6	69.1	73.7	59.3	67.2
Tolerance of others with different beliefs	72.3	69.1	77.4	64.6	68.9	69.2	71.3	70.3	66.0	76.6	80.2	61.5	70.1
Openness to having my own views challenged	60.7	59.0	63.3	63.0	58.9	59.2	61.6	58.3	56.7	62.7	66.0	60.5	67.3
Ability to discuss and negotiate controversial issues	69.4	67.1	73.0	66.8	67.4	66.7	68.6	66.9	64.1	72.0	77.0	64.6	70.8
Ability to work cooperatively with diverse people	78.6	76.8	81.5	76.8	76.9	76.6	77.7	77.8	74.5	81.0	83.6	74.8	80.6
WHAT IS THE HIGHEST LEVEL OF FORMAL EDUCATION OBTAINED BY YOUR PARENTS?													
Father													
Grammar school or less	3.5	3.9	2.9	6.1	4.3	3.4	3.3	3.5	3.4	3.1	2.0	5.5	7.2
Some high school	4.3	5.0	3.2	9.3	5.5	4.4	4.3	4.2	4.5	3.4	2.3	10.3	7.4
High school graduate	18.2	21.7	13.0	33.2	22.4	20.6	19.7	20.6	21.7	13.9	9.7	36.3	27.8
Postsecondary school other than college	3.1	3.4	2.6	3.5	3.3	3.5	3.2	4.2	3.6	2.7	2.0	3.7	3.2
Some college	14.5	15.8	12.5	18.7	16.8	14.5	14.2	15.2	14.7	13.2	9.7	18.6	18.9
College degree	29.1	27.7	31.4	17.5	27.5	27.9	27.3	28.6	28.2	31.8	29.7	16.7	18.8
Some graduate school	2.2	1.8	2.7	1.4	1.6	2.1	2.1	2.1	2.1	2.6	3.1	1.1	1.8
Graduate degree	25.1	20.7	31.8	10.4	18.6	23.7	25.9	21.7	21.8	29.3	41.5	7.8	15.0
Mother													
Grammar school or less	3.2	3.5	2.6	5.5	3.9	2.9	3.0	2.8	2.9	2.9	1.8	5.5	5.7
Some high school	3.3	3.7	2.6	5.3	4.1	3.2	3.6	3.0	2.8	2.8	1.7	5.4	5.1
High school graduate	17.2	19.6	13.7	23.8	20.2	18.6	17.7	19.0	19.6	14.6	10.1	26.0	19.8
Postsecondary school other than college	3.3	3.7	2.8	3.4	3.7	3.6	3.3	4.4	3.6	2.9	2.4	3.3	3.8
Some college	16.6	18.0	14.5	19.6	19.5	16.0	14.9	15.7	17.5	15.3	11.2	20.7	17.7
College degree	34.1	31.9	37.4	25.9	31.2	32.8	32.2	34.0	33.2	37.3	38.0	25.5	26.6
Some graduate school	2.8	2.5	3.3	1.4	2.2	2.9	2.9	2.7	3.0	3.1	4.0	0.9	2.2
Graduate degree	19.5	17.1	23.1	15.0	15.1	19.9	22.4	18.5	17.4	21.1	30.9	12.7	19.2
During the past year, did you "frequently":													
Ask questions in class	49.9	48.5	51.9	49.5	47.0	50.7	52.2	51.2	48.6	50.2	58.4	46.6	54.7
Support your opinions with a logical argument	60.7	56.8	66.8	51.1	56.4	57.3	59.6	57.4	54.3	64.8	74.6	47.1	58.5
Seek solutions to problems and explain them to others	50.9	47.0	57.0	46.1	47.0	46.9	48.8	46.8	44.4	55.0	65.0	44.2	49.5
Revise your papers to improve your writing	36.9	35.3	39.2	43.1	33.6	37.7	38.2	39.2	36.2	37.7	45.1	42.3	44.5
Evaluate the quality or reliability of information you received	36.9	34.0	41.3	36.3	33.9	34.3	35.6	35.0	32.3	39.6	47.9	34.5	39.5
Take a risk because you feel you have more to gain	43.6	43.7	43.4	44.4	43.4	44.0	45.3	43.6	42.6	42.8	45.7	43.7	45.8
Seek alternative solutions to a problem	45.7	43.9	48.4	44.9	44.1	43.6	45.2	44.3	41.3	47.2	52.7	43.1	48.3
Look up scientific research articles and resources	24.0	21.6	27.7	21.5	21.7	21.5	22.5	22.6	19.6	26.6	31.6	18.3	27.4
Explore topics on your own, even though it was not required for a class	34.8	32.7	38.2	27.8	32.9	32.3	35.3	31.3	28.9	36.6	44.3	25.1	32.7
Accept mistakes as part of the learning process	50.3	49.1	52.0	53.9	49.2	48.9	50.8	48.6	46.6	51.6	53.7	51.7	58.0
Seek feedback on your academic work	41.1	39.9	42.8	48.7	38.8	41.4	43.5	41.5	38.7	41.6	47.8	46.8	52.1
Take notes during class	51.0	50.3	52.0	66.1	47.3	54.5	56.3	57.8	50.8	50.6	57.4	67.2	64.2

WEIGHTED NATIONAL NORMS FOR FRESHMAN MEN, FALL 2008

	ALL BACC. INSTS.	ALL 4-YR. COLLEGES	ALL UNI-VERSITIES	ALL BLACK COLLEGES	FOUR-YEAR COLLEGES PUBLIC	ALL PRIV.	NONSECT.	CATHOLIC	OTH. REL.	UNIVERSITIES PUBLIC	PRIVATE	BLACK COLLEGES PUBLIC	PRIVATE
Your probable career occupation													
Accountant or actuary	2.9	3.1	2.6	2.8	2.7	3.6	3.6	4.9	3.0	2.7	2.2	3.2	2.1
Actor or entertainer	1.3	1.7	0.8	1.7	1.7	1.8	2.5	0.8	1.3	0.7	1.2	2.0	1.2
Architect or urban planner	1.0	0.7	1.5	1.3	0.7	0.6	0.7	0.3	0.7	1.5	1.5	1.4	1.2
Artist	2.1	2.9	1.0	2.3	2.2	3.8	6.8	0.9	1.6	1.1	0.9	2.9	1.2
Business (clerical)	0.8	0.9	0.7	0.9	0.8	1.1	1.1	1.2	0.9	0.7	0.6	0.9	0.9
Business executive (management, administrator)	9.9	9.5	10.5	10.5	8.2	11.3	12.4	12.5	9.4	9.7	13.4	10.6	10.2
Business owner or proprietor	4.8	5.2	4.0	6.7	5.1	5.5	5.6	5.5	5.3	3.9	4.6	6.2	7.5
Business salesperson or buyer	1.0	1.2	0.9	1.0	1.2	1.1	1.2	1.3	1.0	0.9	0.7	1.1	0.8
Clergy (minister, priest)	0.3	0.4	0.1	0.1	0.1	0.8	0.1	0.4	1.9	0.1	0.3	0.0	0.2
Clergy (other religious)	0.1	0.1	0.0	0.0	0.0	0.2	0.0	0.0	0.4	0.0	0.0	0.0	0.1
Clinical psychologist	0.6	0.7	0.5	0.9	0.8	0.6	0.5	0.6	0.5	0.6	0.4	1.2	0.6
College administrator/staff	0.1	0.1	0.0	0.1	0.1	0.1	0.0	0.1	0.1	0.0	0.0	0.0	0.3
College teacher	0.6	0.6	0.5	0.4	0.6	0.8	0.8	0.4	0.9	0.5	0.9	0.5	0.1
Computer programmer or analyst	3.4	3.2	3.7	6.6	3.7	2.4	2.3	2.5	2.4	3.8	3.4	8.1	3.9
Conservationist or forester	0.3	0.3	0.4	0.1	0.3	0.3	0.2	0.2	0.4	0.5	0.1	0.1	0.0
Dentist (including orthodontist)	1.1	1.1	1.3	1.8	1.2	0.9	0.6	1.6	1.0	1.3	1.1	0.9	3.3
Dietitian or nutritionist	0.2	0.2	0.2	0.0	0.2	0.1	0.1	0.1	0.2	0.2	0.1	0.0	0.1
Engineer	13.4	8.4	20.7	10.1	10.5	5.5	5.4	6.9	4.9	21.8	16.7	11.8	7.0
Farmer or rancher	0.3	0.3	0.5	0.2	0.3	0.3	0.2	0.1	0.5	0.5	0.1	0.2	0.1
Foreign service worker (including diplomat)	0.5	0.5	0.6	0.2	0.4	0.6	0.8	0.4	0.5	0.5	1.2	0.0	0.5
Homemaker (full-time)	0.0	0.0	0.0	0.0	0.0	0.1	0.1	0.0	0.1	0.0	0.0	0.0	0.1
Interior decorator (including designer)	0.0	0.1	0.0	0.0	0.0	0.1	0.1	0.0	0.0	0.0	0.0	0.0	0.0
Lab technician or hygienist	0.1	0.1	0.1	0.2	0.2	0.1	0.1	0.2	0.1	0.1	0.1	0.3	0.0
Law enforcement officer	2.0	2.8	0.7	1.7	3.0	2.4	2.1	2.8	2.5	0.8	0.6	2.0	1.1
Lawyer (attorney) or judge	3.2	2.8	3.8	4.2	2.5	3.4	3.5	4.1	3.0	3.4	5.5	2.9	6.4
Military service (career)	3.0	4.4	0.9	1.2	7.0	0.8	0.6	1.1	0.7	1.0	0.6	1.1	1.3
Musician (performer, composer)	2.3	2.7	1.8	2.8	2.9	2.4	1.8	1.2	3.8	1.6	2.4	2.5	3.3
Nurse	0.9	1.2	0.4	1.2	1.4	1.1	0.6	1.9	1.3	0.4	0.3	1.4	0.7
Optometrist	0.3	0.2	0.3	0.2	0.3	0.2	0.2	0.3	0.2	0.3	0.1	0.1	0.4
Pharmacist	1.7	1.6	2.0	3.5	1.5	1.6	1.2	2.8	1.5	2.2	1.5	1.3	7.6
Physician	5.7	4.1	8.1	5.6	3.4	5.0	4.1	6.7	5.3	7.5	10.6	2.3	11.5
Policymaker/Government	1.2	1.1	1.3	0.7	1.0	1.3	1.4	1.4	1.1	1.1	1.9	0.4	1.3
School counselor	0.1	0.1	0.0	0.4	0.1	0.2	0.1	0.2	0.2	0.6	0.0	0.5	0.3
School principal or superintendent	0.0	0.0	0.0	0.2	0.0	0.1	0.1	0.0	0.0	0.0	0.0	0.1	0.2
Scientific researcher	2.2	1.6	3.0	0.8	1.5	1.7	1.9	1.4	1.7	2.8	3.5	0.8	0.8
Social, welfare, or recreation worker	0.3	0.4	0.2	1.1	0.4	0.4	0.2	0.4	0.5	0.2	0.2	1.4	0.6
Therapist (physical, occupational, speech)	1.8	2.2	1.1	2.3	2.2	2.2	1.3	2.7	3.0	1.2	0.7	3.3	0.5
Teacher or administrator (elementary)	0.8	1.2	0.3	1.6	1.1	1.2	0.8	1.1	1.7	0.4	0.2	2.3	0.4
Teacher or administrator (secondary)	4.0	5.4	2.0	3.6	5.5	5.1	3.6	4.8	7.0	2.2	1.1	4.8	1.4
Veterinarian	0.4	0.4	0.5	0.4	0.3	0.5	0.7	0.4	0.4	0.6	0.2	0.2	0.7
Writer or journalist	1.8	1.9	1.7	1.5	1.7	2.3	2.4	2.4	2.2	1.5	2.1	1.5	1.5
Skilled trades	0.4	0.6	0.3	0.3	0.6	0.4	0.5	0.4	0.4	0.3	0.2	0.4	0.2
Laborer (unskilled)	0.5	0.5	0.4	0.2	0.6	0.5	0.5	0.5	0.5	0.5	0.2	0.1	0.2
Semi-skilled worker	0.4	0.4	0.3	0.2	0.4	0.3	0.4	0.3	0.3	0.3	0.2	0.3	0.1
Unemployed	1.3	1.3	1.1	2.2	1.3	1.3	1.2	1.3	1.6	1.2	1.0	1.9	2.7
Other	7.2	8.2	5.7	7.5	7.9	8.7	9.0	7.5	8.9	6.0	4.5	7.1	8.3
Undecided	13.5	13.7	13.2	8.8	12.6	15.4	16.4	13.2	15.1	13.3	12.8	9.7	7.1

WEIGHTED NATIONAL NORMS FOR FRESHMAN MEN, FALL 2008

	ALL BACC. INSTS.	ALL 4-YR. COLLEGES	ALL UNI-VERSITIES	ALL BLACK COLLEGES	FOUR-YEAR COLLEGES					UNIVERSITIES		BLACK COLLEGES	
					PUBLIC	ALL PRIV.	NONSECT.	CATHOLIC	OTH. REL.	PUBLIC	PRIVATE	PUBLIC	PRIVATE
Your father's occupation [3]													
Artist	1.2	1.3	1.2	1.2	1.0	1.6	2.0	1.0	1.2	1.2	1.4	1.0	1.5
Business	28.4	26.9	30.7	15.9	25.5	29.0	30.5	30.0	26.7	29.5	35.0	15.4	16.9
Business (clerical)	1.4	1.4	0.6	1.6	1.4	1.5	1.5	1.5	1.4	1.4	1.4	1.8	1.2
Clergy	0.9	1.0	0.6	1.5	0.8	1.4	0.5	0.4	2.9	0.6	0.6	1.3	1.8
College teacher	0.8	0.7	1.0	0.4	0.6	1.0	1.1	0.7	1.0	0.8	1.5	0.1	0.9
Doctor (MD or DDS)	3.2	2.3	4.5	0.9	1.8	3.1	3.3	2.9	2.9	3.8	7.0	0.2	2.2
Education (secondary)	2.3	2.5	2.1	1.5	2.4	2.7	2.4	2.2	3.3	2.2	1.9	1.3	1.7
Education (elementary)	0.7	0.7	0.7	0.6	0.6	0.8	0.8	0.7	0.9	0.7	0.6	0.4	1.0
Engineer	9.0	7.5	11.2	5.4	8.2	6.6	6.6	7.3	6.4	11.7	9.4	5.5	5.2
Farmer or forester	1.3	1.2	1.5	0.9	1.2	1.2	0.7	0.8	1.8	1.7	0.6	1.2	0.5
Health professional	1.5	1.4	1.6	1.8	1.4	1.5	1.4	1.6	1.4	1.7	1.5	2.0	1.3
Homemaker (full-time)	0.4	0.4	0.3	0.1	0.4	0.4	0.4	0.4	0.3	0.3	0.3	0.0	0.3
Lawyer	2.6	2.1	3.3	1.2	1.6	2.7	3.1	2.4	2.2	2.8	5.4	0.8	1.8
Military (career)	1.8	2.3	1.1	4.8	2.9	1.3	1.1	1.2	1.5	1.2	0.8	5.1	4.3
Nurse	0.6	0.6	0.5	0.8	0.7	0.5	0.5	0.6	0.6	0.5	0.3	0.9	0.7
Research scientist	0.8	0.6	1.2	0.1	0.5	0.6	0.8	0.5	0.5	1.1	1.7	0.2	0.1
Social/welfare/rec worker	0.6	0.7	0.6	1.1	0.7	0.6	0.5	0.7	0.5	0.6	0.5	1.1	1.1
Skilled worker	7.6	8.7	6.0	8.3	9.5	7.5	7.0	8.7	7.7	6.4	4.5	8.9	7.1
Semi-skilled worker	3.0	3.3	2.6	3.7	3.5	2.9	2.6	3.4	3.0	2.8	1.7	3.7	3.8
Unskilled worker	3.0	3.3	2.4	5.1	3.7	2.9	2.6	3.4	3.0	2.7	1.3	5.3	4.6
Unemployed	2.5	2.7	2.2	7.8	2.7	2.8	2.8	3.0	2.8	2.3	1.8	8.4	6.9
Other	26.4	28.4	23.3	35.2	29.0	27.5	27.7	26.5	27.8	24.0	20.7	35.4	34.9
Your mother's occupation [3]													
Artist	2.1	2.0	2.3	0.7	1.7	2.4	3.0	1.5	2.1	2.1	2.9	0.2	1.5
Business	16.4	16.1	16.8	17.7	16.4	15.6	15.8	16.1	15.2	16.7	17.0	17.6	17.8
Business (clerical)	4.2	4.2	4.1	3.3	4.1	4.4	4.6	4.5	4.2	4.2	3.7	2.6	4.5
Clergy	0.3	0.3	0.3	0.3	0.2	0.5	0.3	0.1	0.8	0.2	0.3	0.3	0.4
College teacher	0.6	0.5	0.6	0.9	0.4	0.7	0.7	0.5	0.7	0.5	0.9	1.2	0.3
Doctor (MD or DDS)	1.6	1.3	2.0	1.0	1.0	1.6	1.8	1.6	1.4	1.7	3.0	0.7	1.6
Education (secondary)	4.9	5.0	4.7	5.5	4.8	5.2	5.1	4.7	5.6	4.7	4.7	5.7	5.1
Education (elementary)	8.4	8.4	8.3	6.2	8.3	8.5	7.6	8.9	9.5	8.6	7.1	5.3	7.7
Engineer	1.0	0.7	1.4	0.9	0.8	0.6	0.7	0.6	0.4	1.3	1.5	0.9	0.8
Farmer or forester	0.3	0.3	0.3	0.0	0.3	0.3	0.2	0.1	0.3	0.3	0.2	0.0	0.0
Health professional	3.5	3.1	4.0	3.2	2.9	3.5	3.6	3.5	3.2	3.9	4.1	3.6	2.5
Homemaker (full-time)	7.9	6.6	9.8	1.2	5.9	7.6	7.5	7.5	7.7	9.0	12.6	0.7	2.1
Lawyer	1.2	0.9	1.5	0.8	0.7	1.3	1.7	0.7	0.9	1.3	2.6	0.4	1.5
Military (career)	0.2	0.3	0.1	0.8	0.3	0.2	0.2	0.2	0.3	0.2	0.1	1.0	0.6
Nurse	8.5	9.1	7.6	10.5	9.5	8.6	8.1	9.6	8.9	7.7	6.9	10.8	10.0
Research scientist	0.5	0.3	0.7	0.3	0.3	0.3	0.4	0.3	0.3	0.6	1.1	0.2	0.5
Social/welfare/rec worker	1.8	1.9	1.6	4.7	1.8	2.0	1.9	2.2	1.9	1.6	1.6	5.2	4.0
Skilled worker	1.8	2.0	1.5	2.0	2.2	1.7	1.7	1.8	1.7	1.6	1.1	2.3	1.5
Semi-skilled worker	2.1	2.1	2.0	1.4	2.4	1.7	1.5	1.7	1.9	2.1	1.6	1.4	1.4
Unskilled worker	1.8	1.9	1.6	2.2	2.2	1.5	1.4	1.4	1.6	1.8	0.9	2.7	1.3
Unemployed	7.0	7.0	6.9	7.7	7.5	6.3	6.2	7.2	6.1	7.0	6.8	8.1	6.8
Other	24.3	25.9	22.0	29.0	26.2	25.5	25.9	25.3	25.2	22.7	19.2	29.4	28.2
How would you characterize your political views?													
Far left	3.6	3.5	3.7	4.6	3.1	4.0	5.0	3.1	3.2	3.6	4.3	5.1	3.6
Liberal	26.7	24.2	30.5	31.7	22.9	26.1	31.4	24.7	19.9	29.8	33.4	28.3	37.6
Middle-of-the-road	44.2	45.8	41.8	43.6	46.7	44.5	44.5	46.3	43.8	42.6	38.9	44.5	42.1
Conservative	22.9	23.6	21.8	17.4	24.2	22.8	17.0	23.6	29.8	21.9	21.3	19.0	14.5
Far right	2.6	2.9	2.1	2.8	3.1	2.6	2.2	2.3	3.3	2.1	2.1	3.1	2.2

WEIGHTED NATIONAL NORMS FOR FRESHMAN MEN, FALL 2008

	ALL BACC. INSTS.	ALL 4-YR. COLLEGES	ALL UNI-VERSITIES	ALL BLACK COLLEGES	FOUR-YEAR COLLEGES					UNIVERSITIES		BLACK COLLEGES	
					PUBLIC	ALL PRIV.	NONSECT.	CATHOLIC	OTH. REL.	PUBLIC	PRIVATE	PUBLIC	PRIVATE
Student agrees "strongly" or "somewhat":													
There is too much concern in the courts for the rights of criminals	60.3	62.0	57.7	52.1	63.8	59.5	56.2	61.3	62.8	58.6	54.2	53.4	49.7
Abortion should be legal	59.1	56.0	63.7	50.7	56.2	55.9	65.7	52.0	45.4	62.9	66.7	50.8	50.6
The death penalty should be abolished	31.2	29.8	33.4	43.2	26.6	34.2	37.3	35.0	30.1	31.5	40.9	42.3	44.8
Marijuana should be legalized	46.7	46.1	47.7	49.5	45.1	47.4	53.7	45.6	40.5	47.5	48.6	49.8	49.1
It is important to have laws prohibiting homosexual relationships	30.1	33.2	25.2	48.1	33.3	33.2	25.7	32.4	42.8	26.2	21.5	50.3	44.1
Racial discrimination is no longer a major problem in America	25.1	26.0	23.7	18.3	26.5	25.2	23.5	24.5	27.6	23.8	23.0	18.2	18.4
Realistically, an individual can do little to bring about changes in our society	31.3	32.6	29.2	37.7	33.3	31.6	31.5	31.6	31.8	29.5	27.8	39.9	33.7
Wealthy people should pay a larger share of taxes than they do now	59.5	59.8	58.9	65.9	59.2	60.7	63.3	60.6	57.5	59.1	58.0	66.1	65.5
Same-sex couples should have the right to legal marital status	58.8	55.3	64.1	41.9	55.0	55.8	64.9	55.8	44.5	63.0	68.5	40.2	44.8
Affirmative action in college admissions should be abolished	53.3	50.2	58.1	36.3	50.6	49.7	50.1	51.5	48.3	57.4	60.5	37.7	33.8
Federal military spending should be increased	32.2	35.4	27.5	34.3	37.9	31.7	28.3	32.7	35.5	27.5	27.1	36.9	29.9
The federal government should do more to control the sale of handguns	63.7	62.6	65.4	73.4	60.2	66.0	70.5	67.1	59.9	64.1	70.6	72.6	75.0
Only volunteers should serve in the armed forces	65.6	64.2	67.8	65.4	63.4	65.2	68.5	65.0	61.2	66.8	71.7	63.6	68.7
The federal government is not doing enough to control environmental pollution	75.6	74.3	77.6	77.9	73.1	75.9	80.2	75.7	70.7	77.0	79.6	77.3	79.0
A national health care plan is needed to cover everybody's medical costs	65.2	66.6	63.1	82.4	65.2	68.6	72.8	69.8	62.8	63.0	63.3	83.2	80.8
Undocumented immigrants should be denied access to public education	52.6	54.1	50.2	43.9	55.9	51.7	49.1	53.4	54.0	51.2	46.2	44.6	42.9
Through hard work, everybody can succeed in American society	79.6	80.2	78.6	75.1	81.8	77.8	76.2	79.6	78.9	79.5	75.1	75.5	74.4
Dissent is a critical component of the political process	66.0	63.1	70.5	58.3	62.6	63.8	65.2	63.2	62.3	68.8	76.7	58.9	57.2
Colleges have the right to ban extreme speakers from campus	43.9	45.1	41.9	43.8	45.0	45.3	41.9	46.5	48.9	41.1	44.9	44.2	43.0
Students from disadvantaged social backgrounds should be given preferential treatment in college admissions	41.1	42.7	38.7	62.2	41.9	44.0	44.6	42.1	44.1	38.6	38.9	63.3	60.1
The federal government should raise taxes to reduce the deficit	33.0	30.3	37.0	28.7	29.2	31.9	34.1	30.2	30.0	36.4	39.3	25.8	32.1
Addressing global warming should be a federal priority	70.5	69.2	72.4	79.7	67.9	71.1	76.6	72.3	63.7	71.6	75.7	79.0	80.9

WEIGHTED NATIONAL NORMS FOR FRESHMAN MEN, FALL 2008

	ALL BACC. INSTS.	ALL 4-YR. COLLEGES	ALL UNI-VERSITIES	ALL BLACK COLLEGES	FOUR-YEAR COLLEGES					UNIVERSITIES		BLACK COLLEGES	
					PUBLIC	ALL PRIV.	NONSECT.	CATHOLIC	OTH. REL.	PUBLIC	PRIVATE	PUBLIC	PRIVATE
DURING YOUR LAST YEAR IN HIGH SCHOOL, HOW MUCH TIME DID YOU SPEND DURING A TYPICAL WEEK DOING THE FOLLOWING?													
Studying/homework													
None	3.2	3.7	2.4	4.5	4.1	3.2	3.1	2.5	3.5	2.5	2.1	5.6	2.5
Less than one hour	14.1	16.1	11.0	14.2	17.6	13.9	13.5	12.5	15.1	11.7	8.2	16.7	9.8
1 to 2 hours	24.6	27.0	20.8	30.3	28.7	24.5	23.3	24.4	26.1	22.1	15.9	32.0	27.4
3 to 5 hours	27.7	27.3	28.2	26.2	26.7	28.1	27.8	28.9	28.2	29.1	24.8	26.9	24.9
6 to 10 hours	17.4	15.5	20.2	14.4	14.2	17.4	17.7	18.8	16.3	19.6	22.7	11.8	19.2
11 to 15 hours	7.3	5.9	9.4	5.2	5.0	7.0	7.7	7.4	6.1	8.4	13.3	3.6	8.1
16 to 20 hours	3.2	2.5	4.4	2.4	2.0	3.2	3.7	3.2	2.6	3.7	6.9	1.6	3.8
Over 20 hours	2.6	2.0	3.6	2.8	1.6	2.6	3.1	2.3	2.1	2.9	6.0	1.9	4.5
Socializing with friends													
None	0.4	0.4	0.4	0.8	0.4	0.4	0.5	0.4	0.4	0.4	0.5	0.7	1.0
Less than one hour	1.5	1.6	1.2	2.3	1.7	1.5	1.6	1.0	1.6	1.2	1.2	2.4	2.1
1 to 2 hours	6.0	6.2	5.8	9.6	6.7	5.4	5.1	5.4	5.9	5.9	5.4	10.0	9.0
3 to 5 hours	18.3	18.1	18.6	22.3	18.6	17.5	17.2	16.9	18.2	18.9	17.7	23.0	21.2
6 to 10 hours	25.9	24.7	27.8	22.3	24.5	25.0	24.2	25.9	25.8	27.6	28.2	22.4	22.2
11 to 15 hours	18.7	18.2	19.4	13.9	17.6	19.0	19.0	19.4	18.9	19.2	20.1	12.4	16.5
16 to 20 hours	11.4	11.6	11.1	8.2	11.2	12.2	12.8	12.5	11.2	11.0	11.6	8.0	8.5
Over 20 hours	17.7	19.1	15.6	20.6	19.3	18.8	19.6	18.7	17.9	15.7	15.3	21.2	19.5
Talking with teachers outside of class													
None	11.4	11.9	10.7	11.9	12.8	10.6	10.6	9.7	11.1	11.3	8.3	13.7	8.8
Less than one hour	43.1	42.4	44.2	34.6	43.7	40.5	39.3	42.7	41.1	45.5	39.3	36.4	31.4
1 to 2 hours	30.5	30.1	31.2	30.0	29.1	31.5	31.7	31.0	31.4	30.3	35.0	29.8	30.5
3 to 5 hours	10.3	10.5	10.1	13.5	9.7	11.6	12.3	11.3	10.9	9.4	12.5	11.2	17.5
6 to 10 hours	2.9	3.2	2.5	5.8	3.0	3.4	3.4	3.2	3.3	2.3	3.3	5.8	5.7
11 to 15 hours	0.9	1.0	0.7	0.8	0.9	1.2	1.5	0.8	1.1	0.7	0.8	1.8	2.6
16 to 20 hours	0.3	0.3	0.2	0.5	0.2	0.4	0.4	0.5	0.4	0.2	0.3	0.1	1.2
Over 20 hours	0.6	0.6	0.4	1.6	0.6	0.8	0.8	0.7	0.7	0.4	0.5	1.3	2.3
Exercise or sports													
None	3.0	3.2	2.7	4.0	3.3	3.0	3.4	2.1	2.7	2.8	2.5	3.9	4.1
Less than one hour	6.0	5.8	6.3	6.4	6.2	5.2	5.6	4.1	5.1	6.4	5.8	6.7	5.8
1 to 2 hours	12.4	11.8	13.2	15.3	12.6	10.7	11.0	10.8	10.3	13.3	12.7	16.0	14.2
3 to 5 hours	18.0	16.9	19.9	21.0	17.7	15.7	16.2	17.1	14.5	19.7	20.6	21.1	20.9
6 to 10 hours	19.9	18.8	21.6	17.0	19.4	18.0	18.4	18.3	17.3	21.7	21.4	16.9	17.2
11 to 15 hours	15.7	15.7	15.7	10.7	15.2	16.3	16.2	16.9	16.2	15.7	16.0	10.5	11.2
16 to 20 hours	10.1	10.7	9.1	8.3	10.0	11.8	11.4	11.4	12.5	9.1	9.2	8.8	7.4
Over 20 hours	14.9	17.2	11.4	17.3	15.6	19.3	17.8	19.3	21.4	11.4	11.8	16.1	19.2
Partying													
None	24.8	24.3	25.5	16.8	25.1	23.3	20.5	19.7	28.7	25.9	23.8	19.2	12.5
Less than one hour	15.0	14.2	16.2	11.8	14.3	14.0	13.2	13.6	15.1	16.3	15.9	11.0	13.2
1 to 2 hours	18.5	17.9	19.6	20.3	18.1	17.6	17.3	18.9	17.3	19.7	19.0	19.9	21.2
3 to 5 hours	19.6	19.5	19.7	25.7	19.1	20.0	21.3	22.0	17.5	19.4	20.9	25.3	26.4
6 to 10 hours	11.8	12.4	10.9	13.5	12.0	13.0	14.3	13.8	11.0	10.6	12.0	12.8	14.7
11 to 15 hours	5.1	5.7	4.3	5.1	5.5	5.9	6.5	6.3	5.0	4.3	4.2	4.8	5.6
16 to 20 hours	2.2	2.5	1.7	2.1	2.4	2.7	3.1	2.3	2.3	1.7	1.8	2.0	2.2
Over 20 hours	3.0	3.5	2.1	4.6	3.6	3.4	3.8	3.3	3.1	2.1	2.3	4.9	4.2

WEIGHTED NATIONAL NORMS FOR FRESHMAN MEN, FALL 2008

DURING YOUR LAST YEAR IN HIGH SCHOOL, HOW MUCH TIME DID YOU SPEND DURING A TYPICAL WEEK DOING THE FOLLOWING?

	ALL BACC. INSTS.	ALL 4-YR. COLLEGES	ALL UNI-VERSITIES	ALL BLACK COLLEGES	FOUR-YEAR COLLEGES PUBLIC	ALL PRIV.	NONSECT.	CATHOLIC	OTH. REL.	UNIVERSITIES PUBLIC	PRIVATE	BLACK COLLEGES PUBLIC	PRIVATE
Working (for pay)													
None	35.6	32.6	40.2	31.5	31.7	33.9	35.1	31.4	33.5	38.4	47.0	30.0	34.1
Less than one hour	3.6	3.4	3.8	3.0	3.1	3.8	3.7	3.6	4.1	3.7	4.4	3.2	2.6
1 to 2 hours	4.7	4.5	5.0	4.8	4.3	4.8	4.6	4.1	5.4	4.8	5.8	4.9	4.8
3 to 5 hours	7.9	7.9	7.9	8.1	7.6	8.3	8.0	8.3	8.7	7.7	8.7	7.7	8.8
6 to 10 hours	11.4	11.7	10.8	13.1	11.2	12.5	12.2	13.1	12.6	11.1	9.8	14.0	11.3
11 to 15 hours	11.0	11.2	10.6	8.4	11.2	11.3	11.4	12.3	10.7	11.1	8.6	7.4	10.2
16 to 20 hours	11.6	12.3	10.4	11.7	13.3	11.1	11.4	12.0	10.2	11.1	7.6	12.3	10.6
Over 20 hours	14.3	16.2	11.3	19.5	17.6	14.4	13.7	15.3	14.8	12.1	8.1	20.5	17.6
Volunteer work													
None	33.5	36.2	29.2	32.5	38.6	32.9	34.8	29.6	31.9	30.5	24.4	37.2	24.3
Less than one hour	23.4	22.7	24.3	16.0	22.8	22.7	21.5	23.0	24.1	24.8	22.5	15.9	16.1
1 to 2 hours	22.7	21.1	25.3	22.0	20.2	22.5	21.9	24.2	22.4	24.7	27.6	20.1	25.5
3 to 5 hours	11.5	11.0	12.4	14.8	10.3	11.9	11.7	12.5	11.9	11.7	15.3	13.7	16.7
6 to 10 hours	4.7	4.5	5.0	7.1	4.1	4.9	4.7	5.5	5.0	4.8	5.9	6.1	8.8
11 to 15 hours	1.7	1.8	1.6	3.5	1.6	2.0	2.0	2.1	1.9	1.5	2.0	3.5	3.6
16 to 20 hours	0.9	1.0	0.7	1.1	0.8	1.2	1.3	1.3	1.0	0.7	0.7	1.1	1.1
Over 20 hours	1.6	1.7	1.4	3.0	1.5	2.0	2.2	1.9	1.8	1.3	1.7	2.4	3.9
Student clubs/groups													
None	35.4	39.9	28.4	35.2	42.0	36.9	36.9	34.0	38.1	30.9	18.8	41.5	24.1
Less than one hour	15.0	14.8	15.3	11.1	14.9	14.8	13.8	15.6	15.8	15.9	13.0	10.6	11.9
1 to 2 hours	22.7	20.6	26.1	21.1	20.0	21.4	21.7	22.4	20.7	25.5	28.3	20.7	21.9
3 to 5 hours	14.3	12.8	16.8	14.3	11.9	14.0	14.3	14.4	13.4	15.5	21.8	12.1	18.2
6 to 10 hours	6.4	5.9	7.2	8.0	5.5	6.4	6.5	6.9	6.1	6.5	9.5	6.8	10.1
11 to 15 hours	2.7	2.6	2.9	3.6	2.5	2.8	2.8	3.1	2.7	2.6	4.1	3.1	4.5
16 to 20 hours	1.3	1.3	1.4	1.8	1.2	1.4	1.7	1.2	1.2	1.2	1.9	1.7	2.1
Over 20 hours	2.1	2.2	2.0	4.8	2.1	2.2	2.4	2.5	2.0	1.9	2.7	3.5	7.2
Watching TV													
None	6.6	6.2	7.3	4.8	5.9	6.6	7.4	5.1	6.3	7.1	8.0	4.4	5.3
Less than one hour	12.9	12.7	13.1	9.9	13.2	12.1	12.1	12.1	12.1	13.3	12.5	9.7	10.4
1 to 2 hours	23.0	22.7	23.4	20.8	23.0	22.1	22.7	21.4	21.8	23.7	22.6	21.4	19.8
3 to 5 hours	27.1	26.8	27.4	25.1	26.7	27.0	26.9	27.7	26.8	27.5	27.3	25.5	24.4
6 to 10 hours	17.0	17.2	16.7	16.5	17.1	17.4	16.7	18.5	17.7	16.5	17.6	16.5	16.4
11 to 15 hours	6.9	7.2	6.4	9.6	7.0	7.5	7.1	7.7	7.8	6.4	6.6	9.2	10.2
16 to 20 hours	2.8	3.0	2.5	4.9	3.0	2.9	2.8	3.1	3.1	2.5	2.5	4.7	5.2
Over 20 hours	3.7	4.2	3.0	8.5	4.0	4.4	4.4	4.4	4.5	3.1	2.9	8.6	8.3
Household/childcare duties													
None	24.8	26.0	22.8	22.0	25.7	26.5	27.7	22.3	26.7	22.6	23.5	23.0	20.4
Less than one hour	20.3	19.5	21.6	15.3	19.7	19.4	19.1	19.1	19.9	21.7	20.9	16.3	13.7
1 to 2 hours	29.3	28.0	31.2	24.7	28.1	27.7	27.1	29.5	27.8	31.3	31.1	25.3	23.7
3 to 5 hours	16.8	16.8	16.8	19.6	16.9	16.8	16.5	18.1	16.4	16.8	16.9	19.0	20.5
6 to 10 hours	5.4	5.7	4.9	9.0	5.8	5.6	5.5	6.5	5.2	4.9	5.0	7.9	11.2
11 to 15 hours	1.7	1.9	1.3	3.8	1.8	2.1	2.1	2.5	1.9	1.3	1.4	3.5	4.5
16 to 20 hours	0.7	0.8	0.5	1.5	0.8	0.7	0.7	0.7	0.7	0.5	0.4	1.6	1.7
Over 20 hours	1.1	1.2	0.8	3.8	1.2	1.3	1.3	1.3	1.3	0.9	0.8	3.5	4.4

WEIGHTED NATIONAL NORMS FOR FRESHMAN MEN, FALL 2008

	ALL BACC. INSTS.	ALL 4-YR. COLLEGES	ALL UNI-VERSITIES	ALL BLACK COLLEGES	FOUR-YEAR COLLEGES					UNIVERSITIES		BLACK COLLEGES	
					PUBLIC	ALL PRIV.	NONSECT.	CATHOLIC	OTH. REL.	PUBLIC	PRIVATE	PUBLIC	PRIVATE
DURING YOUR LAST YEAR IN HIGH SCHOOL, HOW MUCH TIME DID YOU SPEND DURING A TYPICAL WEEK DOING THE FOLLOWING?													
Reading for pleasure													
None	31.7	34.7	27.1	35.0	35.3	33.9	32.4	34.0	35.9	28.4	22.0	38.9	28.0
Less than one hour	24.9	24.1	26.2	25.7	24.2	23.9	23.6	25.1	23.6	26.4	25.4	26.0	25.1
1 to 2 hours	21.7	20.3	24.0	21.6	20.1	20.6	21.1	21.9	19.2	23.4	26.2	19.8	25.0
3 to 5 hours	12.7	12.0	13.9	8.8	11.7	12.3	13.2	11.1	11.8	13.4	15.9	7.9	10.3
6 to 10 hours	5.3	5.2	5.5	4.3	5.1	5.3	5.4	4.4	5.6	5.3	6.6	3.5	5.7
11 to 15 hours	1.9	1.9	1.9	2.2	1.9	2.1	2.2	1.9	2.0	1.8	2.2	2.0	2.3
16 to 20 hours	0.7	0.8	0.6	1.4	0.8	0.9	0.9	0.9	0.8	0.6	0.7	1.0	2.1
Over 20 hours	0.9	1.0	0.8	1.0	0.9	1.0	1.1	0.6	1.1	0.8	1.1	0.8	1.5
Playing video/computer games													
None	16.8	17.2	16.1	20.4	16.6	18.1	19.3	17.0	17.1	15.7	17.7	19.4	21.7
Less than one hour	18.3	18.5	18.1	17.4	18.8	18.0	17.9	18.3	18.0	18.2	17.8	17.7	16.9
1 to 2 hours	21.7	21.7	21.7	20.7	21.6	21.9	21.8	22.2	21.8	21.7	21.8	20.6	20.9
3 to 5 hours	20.0	19.5	20.8	19.0	19.1	20.0	20.0	20.4	19.8	20.9	20.6	19.8	17.7
6 to 10 hours	11.7	11.6	11.9	10.7	11.8	11.2	10.5	11.8	11.8	12.0	11.8	11.0	10.0
11 to 15 hours	5.4	5.3	5.4	4.2	5.5	5.1	4.8	5.2	5.5	5.6	5.0	4.0	4.7
16 to 20 hours	2.4	2.5	2.3	3.1	2.7	2.2	2.1	2.3	2.2	2.4	2.1	3.2	3.1
Over 20 hours	3.6	3.8	3.4	4.5	4.0	3.4	3.6	2.8	3.6	3.5	3.0	4.2	5.0
Online social networks (MySpace, Facebook, etc.)													
None	13.6	13.8	13.2	10.3	15.4	11.6	10.9	12.5	12.1	14.0	10.1	10.6	9.6
Less than one hour	20.5	20.3	21.0	15.9	21.4	18.7	18.8	19.8	18.2	21.6	18.7	16.2	15.4
1 to 2 hours	27.3	26.7	28.3	25.1	26.3	27.2	27.1	27.4	27.1	28.1	29.2	26.6	22.5
3 to 5 hours	20.9	20.5	21.6	20.1	19.2	22.3	23.0	21.7	21.7	21.0	23.7	19.6	20.9
6 to 10 hours	9.5	9.8	9.1	11.6	9.3	10.4	10.4	9.6	10.8	8.7	10.5	11.4	11.9
11 to 15 hours	3.9	4.2	3.4	6.6	3.9	4.6	4.5	4.3	4.7	3.3	3.8	5.9	7.9
16 to 20 hours	1.7	1.9	1.3	3.9	1.7	2.2	2.2	2.2	2.1	1.3	1.5	3.6	4.5
Over 20 hours	2.6	2.9	2.2	6.5	2.7	3.1	3.2	2.5	3.3	2.1	2.4	6.0	7.3
Are you: [4]													
White/Caucasian	73.2	74.0	72.1	4.2	72.7	75.7	72.9	75.0	79.6	72.0	72.1	4.5	3.7
African American/Black	9.9	13.1	5.0	92.1	12.1	14.5	15.1	13.4	14.2	4.9	5.2	92.3	91.7
American Indian/Alaska Native	2.4	2.9	1.7	3.7	3.3	2.2	2.0	1.6	2.6	1.7	1.5	3.5	3.9
Asian American/Asian	9.5	5.1	16.3	2.6	5.1	5.1	6.6	5.3	3.2	15.9	17.5	0.9	5.6
Native Hawaiian/Pacific Islander	1.4	1.3	1.4	0.6	1.6	0.9	0.9	1.4	0.6	1.5	0.9	0.5	0.9
Mexican American/Chicano	5.3	5.4	5.3	0.7	7.3	2.6	2.1	4.0	2.7	5.8	3.3	0.7	0.9
Puerto Rican	1.3	1.5	1.0	2.1	1.1	2.1	2.9	1.9	1.1	0.8	1.7	2.2	1.8
Other Latino	3.8	3.9	3.7	2.1	4.1	3.5	4.3	3.5	2.5	3.3	5.1	1.6	3.1
Other	3.9	3.9	3.8	3.9	4.0	3.8	4.5	3.2	3.3	3.7	4.0	4.0	3.8

WEIGHTED NATIONAL NORMS FOR FRESHMAN MEN, FALL 2008

	ALL BACC. INSTS.	ALL 4-YR. COLLEGES	ALL UNI-VERSITIES	ALL BLACK COLLEGES	FOUR-YEAR COLLEGES					UNIVERSITIES		BLACK COLLEGES	
					PUBLIC	ALL PRIV.	NONSECT.	CATHOLIC	OTH. REL.	PUBLIC	PRIVATE	PUBLIC	PRIVATE
Reasons noted as "very important" in influencing student's decision to attend this particular college													
My parents wanted me to come here	13.4	14.6	11.6	25.6	14.5	14.8	14.1	14.8	15.7	11.2	13.1	25.3	26.2
My relatives wanted me to come here	6.1	6.9	4.8	17.1	7.0	6.7	6.3	6.6	7.2	4.6	5.3	16.6	18.0
My teacher advised me	6.7	7.4	5.6	12.2	7.2	7.7	9.0	7.4	6.3	5.3	6.7	11.9	12.8
This college has a very good academic reputation	59.5	55.0	66.7	51.0	52.1	59.0	60.1	63.3	55.7	63.5	78.6	39.4	71.2
This college has a good reputation for its social activities	36.2	33.8	40.0	36.6	32.3	36.0	35.9	38.1	35.1	40.4	38.8	32.4	44.1
I was offered financial assistance	38.1	41.9	32.2	48.1	32.5	54.9	50.6	59.9	58.0	28.8	44.5	49.0	46.6
The cost of attending this college	35.8	38.8	31.1	46.8	44.8	30.4	31.6	32.2	28.0	33.1	23.7	54.4	33.5
High school counselor advised me	9.5	10.4	8.1	16.8	10.1	10.9	12.6	11.9	8.3	7.4	10.4	16.6	17.2
Private college counselor advised me	3.7	4.2	2.8	8.2	3.1	5.7	6.1	5.1	5.5	2.3	4.9	6.8	10.6
I wanted to live near home	16.4	19.2	11.8	18.9	21.0	16.7	16.5	21.4	14.9	12.2	10.2	19.6	17.6
Not offered aid by first choice	7.3	7.5	7.1	13.6	6.6	8.8	8.6	9.8	8.6	7.0	7.5	13.2	14.2
Could not afford first choice	9.5	10.0	8.6	17.6	10.6	9.2	9.4	10.2	8.5	9.2	6.7	18.6	15.9
This college's graduates gain admission to top graduate/professional schools	30.8	27.6	35.9	34.0	24.6	31.8	34.6	32.8	27.9	32.6	47.8	22.2	54.7
This college's graduates get good jobs	50.5	47.9	54.6	51.4	45.1	51.7	54.4	55.5	46.5	51.2	66.9	42.4	67.1
I was attracted by the religious affiliation/orientation of the college	6.1	7.5	3.9	10.1	3.9	12.5	4.8	13.1	22.2	2.6	8.6	7.3	14.8
I wanted to go to a school about the size of this college	31.2	33.0	28.3	28.6	26.8	41.5	40.1	42.4	42.9	26.4	35.4	28.5	28.8
Rankings in national magazines	17.3	12.8	24.4	19.2	11.3	14.9	16.8	15.6	12.3	22.6	30.9	11.8	32.1
Information from a website	15.3	14.7	16.2	22.9	13.7	16.1	18.4	14.8	13.6	15.0	20.5	19.4	29.1
I was admitted through an Early Action or Early Decision program	10.4	9.7	11.5	9.7	7.9	12.2	14.4	10.6	10.0	9.0	20.5	8.2	12.3
The athletic department recruited me	11.2	15.6	4.4	13.2	9.4	24.1	20.8	19.1	30.5	3.7	6.9	14.1	11.6
A visit to campus	35.7	36.8	33.8	32.1	31.2	44.5	46.0	41.6	43.9	31.4	43.1	31.3	33.6

WEIGHTED NATIONAL NORMS FOR FRESHMAN MEN, FALL 2008

YOUR PROBABLE MAJOR	ALL BACC. INSTS.	ALL 4-YR. COLLEGES	ALL UNI-VERSITIES	ALL BLACK COLLEGES	FOUR-YEAR COLLEGES					UNIVERSITIES		BLACK COLLEGES	
					PUBLIC	ALL PRIV.	NONSECT.	CATHOLIC	OTH. REL.	PUBLIC	PRIVATE	PUBLIC	PRIVATE
Arts and Humanities													
Art, fine and applied	2.4	3.3	1.1	1.8	2.4	4.5	7.8	1.1	1.8	1.2	0.8	2.5	0.6
English (language & literature)	1.2	1.2	1.2	0.9	1.0	1.6	1.7	1.4	1.5	1.1	1.4	0.5	1.5
History	1.9	2.2	1.4	0.3	2.4	2.0	1.9	2.1	2.2	1.4	1.5	0.7	0.6
Journalism	1.0	1.1	0.9	0.7	1.0	1.3	1.3	1.8	1.1	0.9	1.1	0.7	0.7
Language and Literature (except English)	0.4	0.4	0.4	0.1	0.4	0.4	0.4	0.3	0.4	0.4	0.5	0.0	0.2
Music	2.1	2.4	1.5	2.9	2.6	2.2	1.5	1.0	3.6	1.3	2.4	2.8	3.2
Philosophy	0.5	0.5	0.5	0.4	0.4	0.6	0.5	0.8	0.6	0.4	0.6	0.1	0.9
Speech	0.0	0.0	0.0	0.0	0.0	0.0	0.1	0.0	0.0	0.0	0.1	0.0	0.1
Theater or Drama	1.1	1.4	0.6	0.5	1.4	1.4	1.9	0.5	1.1	0.5	0.9	0.4	0.8
Theology or Religion	0.3	0.4	0.1	0.0	0.1	0.9	0.2	0.3	2.1	0.0	0.2	0.0	0.1
Other Arts and Humanities	1.0	1.1	0.8	0.3	1.0	1.3	1.8	0.5	0.9	0.7	1.2	0.4	0.1
Biological Science													
Biology (general)	4.3	3.6	5.3	6.1	3.2	4.2	3.5	6.3	4.0	5.2	5.7	3.4	11.0
Biochemistry or Biophysics	1.4	1.0	2.1	0.4	0.9	1.1	0.9	0.9	1.3	2.2	1.8	0.4	0.4
Botany	0.1	0.0	0.1	0.2	0.1	0.0	0.0	0.0	0.0	0.1	0.1	0.4	0.0
Environmental Science	0.8	0.8	0.8	0.1	0.7	1.0	1.0	0.7	1.2	0.9	0.4	0.2	0.0
Marine (Life) Science	0.3	0.4	0.2	0.5	0.5	0.3	0.3	0.3	0.4	0.2	0.2	0.7	0.0
Microbiology or Bacteriology	0.3	0.2	0.5	0.1	0.2	0.1	0.1	0.1	0.2	0.6	0.3	0.1	0.0
Zoology	0.3	0.3	0.3	0.1	0.4	0.2	0.3	0.1	0.3	0.3	0.1	0.0	0.3
Other Biological Science	0.6	0.4	1.0	0.4	0.4	0.4	0.5	0.4	0.3	1.1	0.8	0.2	0.7
Business													
Accounting	3.1	3.4	2.6	3.6	3.1	3.7	3.8	4.9	3.0	2.7	2.0	3.7	3.4
Business Admin. (general)	5.3	5.9	4.3	6.6	5.6	6.3	6.3	5.8	6.6	4.4	4.3	7.1	5.7
Finance	2.9	2.3	3.8	1.8	1.9	2.9	3.4	4.2	1.7	3.2	6.0	1.0	3.4
International Business	1.7	1.7	1.6	1.0	1.3	2.1	2.6	2.4	1.5	1.4	2.4	0.6	1.7
Marketing	2.8	3.1	2.3	4.7	3.1	3.0	2.9	4.1	2.7	2.4	1.9	4.3	5.5
Management	5.2	6.1	3.8	7.4	5.5	6.9	7.3	6.8	6.3	3.9	3.4	8.3	5.6
Secretarial Studies	0.0	0.0	0.0	0.0	0.0	0.0	0.0	0.0	0.0	0.0	0.0	0.0	0.0
Other Business	1.2	1.2	1.2	0.8	1.0	1.5	1.8	1.5	1.3	1.1	1.5	1.0	0.5
Education													
Business Education	0.2	0.2	0.1	0.1	0.2	0.2	0.2	0.1	0.2	0.1	0.1	0.1	0.2
Elementary Education	0.5	0.8	0.2	1.5	0.8	0.8	0.4	1.0	1.2	0.2	0.1	2.1	0.2
Music or Art Education	0.6	0.8	0.3	1.1	1.0	0.6	0.5	0.3	1.0	0.3	0.2	1.3	0.8
Physical Education or Recreation	1.3	1.9	0.3	3.3	1.9	2.0	1.6	0.8	2.9	0.4	0.1	4.4	1.4
Secondary Education	1.8	2.5	0.7	2.1	2.3	2.7	1.9	2.9	3.7	0.8	0.4	2.7	0.9
Special Education	0.1	0.2	0.0	0.2	0.2	0.2	0.1	0.1	0.3	0.0	0.0	0.3	0.1
Other Education	0.1	0.2	0.1	0.3	0.2	0.2	0.1	0.0	0.3	0.1	0.0	0.5	0.0
Engineering													
Aeronautical or Astronautical Engineering	1.8	1.4	2.5	0.4	2.1	0.3	0.4	0.4	0.2	2.8	1.4	0.4	0.4
Civil Engineering	2.2	1.8	2.9	1.4	2.5	0.8	0.4	1.7	1.0	3.0	2.3	1.5	1.2
Chemical Engineering	1.2	0.4	2.5	0.2	0.5	0.3	0.3	0.5	0.3	2.5	2.6	0.0	0.5
Computer Engineering	2.2	1.5	3.2	4.1	2.0	0.9	0.9	1.0	0.8	3.5	2.3	4.4	3.6
Electrical or Electronic Engineering	2.0	1.4	2.9	2.5	1.8	0.8	0.8	1.2	0.6	3.0	2.4	3.2	1.4
Industrial Engineering	0.3	0.2	0.5	0.4	0.2	0.1	0.2	0.0	0.0	0.5	0.4	0.6	0.1
Mechanical Engineering	4.8	3.4	7.0	2.4	4.3	2.1	2.2	3.1	1.6	7.3	5.8	2.5	2.2
Other Engineering	2.5	1.5	4.1	0.6	2.0	0.8	0.9	0.6	0.8	4.0	4.3	0.7	0.2

WEIGHTED NATIONAL NORMS FOR FRESHMAN MEN, FALL 2008

YOUR PROBABLE MAJOR	ALL BACC. INSTS.	ALL 4-YR. COLLEGES	ALL UNI-VERSITIES	ALL BLACK COLLEGES	FOUR-YEAR COLLEGES PUBLIC	ALL PRIV.	NONSECT.	CATHOLIC	OTH. REL.	UNIVERSITIES PUBLIC	PRIVATE	BLACK COLLEGES PUBLIC	PRIVATE
Physical Science													
Astronomy	0.2	0.1	0.2	0.0	0.2	0.1	0.1	0.0	0.1	0.3	0.1	0.0	0.0
Atmospheric Science (incl. Meteorology)	0.1	0.1	0.1	0.1	0.1	0.1	0.0	0.0	0.2	0.2	0.1	0.1	0.0
Chemistry	1.3	1.2	1.5	1.6	1.2	1.2	1.1	1.6	1.1	1.4	1.7	0.9	2.9
Earth Science	0.2	0.2	0.2	0.0	0.2	0.2	0.3	0.1	0.1	0.2	0.1	0.0	0.0
Marine Science (incl. Oceanography)	0.1	0.2	0.1	0.1	0.2	0.1	0.1	0.1	0.1	0.1	0.1	0.1	0.0
Mathematics	1.0	0.8	1.2	0.3	0.7	1.0	0.9	0.9	1.1	1.1	1.4	0.4	0.3
Physics	1.0	0.8	1.4	0.4	0.8	0.8	0.8	0.4	0.9	1.2	1.9	0.3	0.6
Other Physical Science	0.2	0.3	0.2	0.0	0.3	0.3	0.3	0.2	0.3	0.2	0.2	0.0	0.1
Professional													
Architecture or Urban Planning	0.7	0.4	1.3	0.4	0.3	0.4	0.5	0.2	0.4	1.2	1.4	0.4	0.5
Family & Consumer Sciences	0.0	0.0	0.0	0.1	0.0	0.0	0.0	0.0	0.0	0.0	0.0	0.1	0.0
Health Technology (medical, dental, laboratory)	0.4	0.5	0.4	0.5	0.6	0.3	0.3	0.5	0.4	0.4	0.3	0.4	0.6
Library or Archival Science	0.0	0.0	0.1	0.1	0.0	0.1	0.0	0.1	0.0	0.1	0.0	0.0	0.2
Medicine, Dentistry, Veterinary Medicine	2.9	2.4	3.5	3.0	2.1	2.8	2.2	3.8	3.1	3.3	4.5	1.1	6.5
Nursing	0.9	1.2	0.3	1.0	1.3	1.1	0.6	2.0	1.2	0.4	0.3	1.2	0.5
Pharmacy	1.2	1.0	1.4	2.5	0.9	1.2	1.0	2.1	0.9	1.4	1.4	0.9	5.6
Therapy (occupational, physical, speech)	1.4	1.8	0.8	1.2	1.8	2.0	1.3	2.3	2.7	0.9	0.5	1.8	0.1
Other Professional	0.6	0.7	0.4	0.4	0.6	0.7	0.7	1.0	0.7	0.4	0.6	0.3	0.6
Social Science													
Anthropology	0.3	0.3	0.3	0.0	0.3	0.3	0.4	0.1	0.2	0.4	0.2	0.0	0.1
Economics	1.2	0.9	1.6	0.2	0.5	1.5	2.5	0.7	0.7	1.2	3.0	0.0	0.7
Ethnic Studies	0.0	0.0	0.1	0.0	0.0	0.0	0.0	0.1	0.0	0.1	0.0	0.0	0.0
Geography	0.1	0.1	0.1	0.0	0.1	0.1	0.1	0.0	0.1	0.1	0.0	0.0	0.1
Political Science (gov't., international relations)	3.2	3.2	3.4	2.6	3.1	3.3	3.4	3.4	3.1	2.9	5.1	1.4	4.7
Psychology	2.5	2.6	2.3	3.6	2.7	2.6	2.7	2.7	2.4	2.4	1.8	3.6	3.7
Public Policy	0.1	0.1	0.1	0.0	0.0	0.1	0.2	0.0	0.0	0.1	0.3	0.0	0.1
Social Work	0.1	0.2	0.1	0.6	0.2	0.2	0.1	0.2	0.2	0.1	0.1	1.0	0.0
Sociology	0.5	0.5	0.5	0.7	0.4	0.5	0.3	0.6	0.6	0.5	0.3	0.4	1.4
Women's Studies	0.0	0.0	0.0	0.0	0.0	0.0	0.0	0.0	0.0	0.0	0.0	0.0	0.0
Other Social Science	0.3	0.3	0.2	0.2	0.3	0.3	0.3	0.2	0.2	0.2	0.2	0.0	0.5
Technical													
Building Trades	0.1	0.1	0.1	0.0	0.0	0.1	0.1	0.0	0.1	0.1	0.0	0.0	0.1
Data Processing or Computer Programming	1.0	1.1	1.0	1.6	1.2	0.9	1.0	0.8	0.8	1.0	1.0	2.4	0.3
Drafting or Design	0.3	0.3	0.1	0.9	0.3	0.3	0.4	0.1	0.3	0.2	0.1	1.1	0.4
Electronics	0.1	0.1	0.1	0.5	0.1	0.1	0.1	0.0	0.1	0.1	0.0	0.8	0.0
Mechanics	0.1	0.1	0.1	0.1	0.0	0.1	0.0	0.2	0.1	0.1	0.0	0.1	0.6
Other Technical	0.2	0.2	0.2	0.0	0.2	0.2	0.2	0.1	0.3	0.2	0.1	0.0	0.1
Other Fields													
Agriculture	0.5	0.3	0.7	0.4	0.4	0.2	0.2	0.0	0.2	0.8	0.1	0.6	0.0
Communications	1.2	1.4	0.8	1.8	1.3	1.6	1.6	1.5	1.8	0.7	1.2	2.1	1.3
Computer Science	2.0	1.9	2.0	4.5	2.3	1.4	1.2	1.5	1.6	1.9	2.3	5.5	2.8
Forestry	0.2	0.1	0.2	0.3	0.2	0.1	0.0	0.0	0.1	0.3	0.0	0.5	0.0
Kinesiology	0.7	0.9	0.5	0.3	1.2	0.5	0.2	0.2	1.1	0.6	0.6	0.1	0.6
Law Enforcement	2.1	3.1	0.6	2.6	3.3	2.7	2.6	3.1	2.7	0.6	0.6	3.1	1.7
Military Science	0.2	0.3	0.1	0.3	0.5	0.1	0.1	0.2	0.1	0.1	0.1	0.4	0.1
Other Field	1.3	1.6	0.9	1.6	1.4	1.8	1.9	1.6	1.9	0.9	0.7	1.9	0.9
Undecided	5.6	6.0	4.9	2.8	6.0	5.9	5.9	5.4	6.3	5.1	4.3	3.3	1.8

WEIGHTED NATIONAL NORMS FOR FRESHMAN MEN, FALL 2008

Objectives considered to be "essential" or "very important":	ALL BACC. INSTS.	ALL 4-YR. COLLEGES	ALL UNI-VERSITIES	ALL BLACK COLLEGES	FOUR-YEAR COLLEGES					UNIVERSITIES		BLACK COLLEGES	
					PUBLIC	ALL PRIV.	NONSECT.	CATHOLIC	OTH. REL.	PUBLIC	PRIVATE	PUBLIC	PRIVATE
Becoming accomplished in one of the performing arts (acting, dancing, etc.)	16.0	17.2	14.1	25.9	16.9	17.6	18.8	12.7	18.3	13.3	16.8	25.7	26.3
Becoming an authority in my field	62.2	62.3	62.2	75.3	62.2	62.4	63.5	62.7	60.8	60.9	66.9	76.0	73.9
Obtaining recognition from my colleagues for contributions to my special field	58.1	57.4	59.3	68.5	57.0	57.8	60.4	58.2	54.3	58.4	62.4	69.2	67.3
Influencing the political structure	24.9	25.6	23.9	42.1	25.1	26.2	26.9	27.0	25.0	23.1	26.8	40.9	44.1
Influencing social values	41.5	43.2	38.6	59.9	41.8	45.2	44.7	45.3	45.8	37.8	41.6	59.8	59.9
Raising a family	75.7	75.7	75.6	79.9	75.5	76.0	73.5	78.7	78.1	75.7	75.4	79.7	80.3
Being very well off financially	77.8	77.3	78.6	87.2	78.6	75.4	77.0	79.8	71.5	79.2	76.4	88.6	84.7
Helping others who are in difficulty	62.1	62.4	61.7	73.6	61.0	64.3	62.9	65.2	65.6	60.8	65.0	72.3	76.0
Making a theoretical contribution to science	24.1	21.0	29.0	31.7	21.2	20.7	20.4	22.6	20.2	28.9	29.5	29.8	35.2
Writing original works (poems, novels, short stories, etc.)	16.4	17.5	14.7	27.4	16.5	18.9	20.7	15.6	18.0	13.8	17.9	27.7	26.9
Creating artistic works (painting, sculpture, decorating, etc.)	15.2	16.5	13.2	23.1	15.4	17.9	21.1	12.8	16.2	12.7	14.9	23.9	21.5
Becoming successful in a business of my own	47.6	48.3	46.6	71.1	47.0	50.2	52.3	51.8	46.7	46.3	47.4	71.4	70.6
Becoming involved in programs to clean up the environment	26.6	25.6	28.3	43.7	24.3	27.3	29.1	26.8	25.3	27.9	29.7	44.6	42.0
Developing a meaningful philosophy of life	51.7	50.6	53.5	55.9	48.9	53.1	54.3	51.3	52.3	51.9	59.1	54.7	58.1
Participating in a community action program	24.8	24.9	24.8	46.3	23.1	27.2	26.7	27.3	27.9	23.5	29.5	45.9	47.0
Helping to promote racial understanding	34.0	34.6	33.0	60.2	33.6	36.1	37.4	36.4	34.3	32.2	35.8	58.2	63.7
Keeping up to date with political affairs	42.0	40.5	44.4	52.9	39.8	41.5	43.3	41.7	39.1	42.7	50.5	51.0	56.4
Becoming a community leader	36.0	36.8	34.7	55.5	35.8	38.2	37.6	38.2	38.9	33.2	40.4	54.8	56.7
Improving my understanding of other countries and cultures	47.9	46.6	50.0	56.8	45.3	48.4	51.4	47.9	45.0	48.2	56.6	54.7	60.6
Adopting "green" practices to protect the environment	40.0	37.6	43.7	45.2	36.0	39.8	43.5	39.8	35.2	43.0	46.4	45.3	44.9

WEIGHTED NATIONAL NORMS FOR FRESHMAN MEN, FALL 2008

	ALL BACC. INSTS.	ALL 4-YR. COLLEGES	ALL UNI-VERSITIES	ALL BLACK COLLEGES	FOUR-YEAR COLLEGES					UNIVERSITIES		BLACK COLLEGES	
					PUBLIC	ALL PR.V.	NONSECT.	CATHOLIC	OTH. REL.	PUBLIC	PRIVATE	PUBLIC	PRIVATE
Student estimates chances are "very good" that he/she will:													
Change major field	12.2	11.6	13.1	11.8	11.7	11.4	12.0	10.4	11.0	13.3	12.4	12.8	10.0
Change career choice	11.4	10.6	12.7	8.6	10.1	11.4	12.1	10.2	11.1	12.6	13.2	9.9	6.2
Participate in student government	5.8	5.9	5.7	12.0	5.6	6.3	6.5	6.3	6.0	5.1	7.9	10.5	14.6
Get a job to help pay for college expenses	41.6	41.3	42.1	37.8	41.1	41.5	41.9	43.4	40.0	43.0	38.5	37.6	38.2
Work full-time while attending college	6.2	7.5	4.2	10.4	9.0	5.3	6.0	5.5	4.4	4.4	3.7	10.5	10.1
Join a social fraternity or sorority	7.7	7.4	8.1	29.7	7.2	7.6	8.1	5.9	7.8	8.0	8.5	28.6	31.7
Play varsity/intercollegiate athletics	21.4	26.7	12.9	28.5	20.9	34.6	32.2	29.2	40.2	12.0	16.4	32.4	21.6
Make at least a "B" average	61.0	57.6	66.3	60.9	54.5	61.9	63.2	64.4	59.2	64.6	72.9	57.0	67.9
Need extra time to complete your degree requirements	6.0	6.5	5.4	11.0	6.9	5.9	5.8	5.8	6.2	5.7	4.0	11.5	10.1
Participate in student protests or demonstrations	5.5	5.4	5.6	8.8	4.9	6.1	6.7	5.6	5.5	5.3	6.6	8.1	10.0
Transfer to another college before graduating	7.4	9.3	4.5	11.9	10.8	7.2	6.8	5.7	8.4	4.9	3.1	13.6	9.0
Be satisfied with your college	50.8	47.0	56.8	37.8	44.3	50.7	51.7	52.3	48.9	54.9	63.8	31.5	49.1
Participate in volunteer or community service work	18.1	16.8	20.3	31.3	14.3	20.2	18.9	21.4	21.4	17.7	30.0	31.1	31.7
Seek personal counseling	7.3	7.1	7.7	11.7	7.1	7.2	7.4	7.3	6.9	7.7	7.4	10.7	13.3
Communicate regularly with your professors	31.9	31.1	33.2	31.8	28.7	34.5	36.5	33.5	32.3	30.5	42.9	28.6	37.8
Socialize with someone of another racial/ethnic group	60.3	57.4	65.1	49.8	55.8	59.5	61.3	58.1	57.7	63.5	70.9	48.4	52.5
Participate in student clubs/groups	37.0	32.8	43.5	34.3	31.6	34.5	36.5	35.7	31.3	40.6	54.1	31.7	38.9
Participate in a study abroad program	20.6	19.0	23.2	19.7	14.9	24.7	27.6	23.1	21.7	20.9	31.6	18.0	22.6
Have a roommate of different race/ethnicity	26.0	23.8	29.3	17.5	23.3	24.6	27.2	19.5	23.6	27.5	36.0	18.7	15.2
Discuss course content with students outside of class	40.6	35.7	48.3	33.5	34.0	38.0	39.7	36.6	36.3	46.1	56.4	30.6	38.7
Work on a professor's research project	27.0	27.5	26.3	39.7	27.3	27.8	29.4	26.0	26.5	25.2	30.2	40.3	38.7
Get tutoring help in specific courses	24.8	25.4	23.8	40.1	25.9	24.7	24.5	24.4	25.0	24.4	21.5	38.2	43.7
Do you give the Higher Education Research Institute (HERI) permission to include your ID number should your college request the data for additional research analyses?													
Yes	67.5	70.1	63.5	60.0	73.5	65.3	63.8	64.5	67.5	64.5	59.6	63.8	53.0
No	32.5	29.9	36.5	40.0	26.5	34.7	36.2	35.5	32.5	35.5	40.4	36.2	47.0

2008 National Norms

Type of Institution and Control for Women

NOTES

These notes refer to report items that are followed by numbers in [brackets].

[1] Based on the recommendations of the National Commission on Excellence In Education.

[2] Percentage responding "frequently" <u>only</u>.

[3] Recategorization of this item from a longer list is shown in Appendix C.

[4] Percentages will add to more than 100.0 if any student marked more than one category.

WEIGHTED NATIONAL NORMS FOR FRESHMAN WOMEN, FALL 2008

	ALL BACC. INSTS.	ALL 4-YR. COLLEGES	ALL UNI-VERSITIES	ALL BLACK COLLEGES	FOUR-YEAR COLLEGES PUBLIC	ALL PRIV.	NONSECT.	CATHOLIC	OTH. REL.	UNIVERSITIES PUBLIC	PRIVATE	BLACK COLLEGES PUBLIC	PRIVATE
How old will you be on December 31 of this year?													
16 or younger	0.1	0.1	0.0	0.0	0.0	0.1	0.1	0.0	0.2	0.0	0.1	0.0	0.0
17	1.8	1.8	1.9	2.1	1.7	1.9	2.1	2.1	1.6	1.9	2.2	1.3	3.5
18	73.0	72.8	73.3	71.5	73.9	71.4	73.7	72.8	67.7	72.8	74.9	70.2	73.5
19	24.0	23.9	24.2	24.0	23.0	25.1	22.4	24.1	29.2	24.8	22.3	25.4	21.6
20	0.7	0.8	0.4	1.4	0.7	1.0	1.2	0.5	1.0	0.4	0.5	1.8	0.8
21 to 24	0.3	0.4	0.1	0.9	0.4	0.4	0.5	0.2	0.3	0.1	0.1	1.0	0.6
25 to 29	0.1	0.1	0.0	0.1	0.1	0.0	0.1	0.1	0.0	0.0	0.0	0.2	0.1
30 to 39	0.0	0.0	0.0	0.0	0.1	0.0	0.0	0.1	0.0	0.0	0.0	0.1	0.0
40 to 54	0.0	0.0	0.0	0.0	0.0	0.0	0.0	0.0	0.0	0.0	0.0	0.0	0.1
55 or older	0.0	0.0	0.0	0.0	0.0	0.0	0.0	0.0	0.0	0.0	0.0	0.1	0.0
Is English your native language?													
Yes	90.8	92.7	87.7	98.4	92.3	93.1	91.0	92.6	95.9	87.7	87.8	98.3	98.6
No	9.2	7.3	12.3	1.6	7.7	6.9	9.0	7.4	4.1	12.3	12.2	1.7	1.4
In what year did you graduate from high school?													
2008	98.4	98.0	99.2	96.4	98.1	97.8	97.3	98.6	98.0	99.3	98.9	95.6	97.8
2007	1.0	1.2	0.6	2.4	1.1	1.4	1.8	0.8	1.2	0.5	0.9	3.0	1.3
2006	0.2	0.2	0.1	0.4	0.3	0.2	0.3	0.1	0.2	0.1	0.1	0.6	0.2
2005 or earlier	0.2	0.3	0.1	0.6	0.4	0.3	0.4	0.3	0.2	0.1	0.0	0.7	0.4
Did not graduate but passed G.E.D. test	0.1	0.2	0.0	0.2	0.2	0.2	0.1	0.1	0.2	0.0	0.0	0.1	0.3
Never completed high school	0.0	0.0	0.0	0.0	0.0	0.1	0.0	0.0	0.2	0.0	0.0	0.0	0.0
How many miles is this college from your permanent home?													
5 or less	5.3	6.8	2.8	7.2	8.0	5.3	5.5	7.0	4.1	2.6	3.5	9.6	3.2
6 to 10	6.3	8.1	3.2	5.3	9.2	6.7	7.0	9.1	4.9	2.8	4.5	6.1	4.2
11 to 50	24.3	28.4	17.5	13.5	31.4	24.4	23.5	33.0	20.8	17.7	16.7	13.5	13.4
51 to 100	17.9	17.9	18.0	16.6	19.0	16.3	14.6	15.7	18.9	20.3	9.5	20.0	11.1
101 to 500	32.4	26.3	42.7	34.4	24.8	28.3	25.9	23.8	33.7	45.5	32.1	37.0	30.1
Over 500	13.8	12.6	15.8	23.1	7.6	19.0	23.5	11.4	17.6	11.1	33.6	13.8	38.0
What was your average grade in high school?													
A or A+	24.6	19.8	32.8	12.5	16.6	24.1	21.9	22.1	27.9	30.1	43.1	9.4	17.5
A-	26.4	23.2	31.9	14.8	21.6	25.4	24.4	26.1	26.4	31.4	33.7	13.1	17.6
B+	21.3	22.7	18.9	24.1	23.9	21.2	22.2	22.6	19.0	20.1	14.7	25.9	21.1
B	18.6	22.1	12.7	22.6	24.9	18.4	19.0	19.5	17.0	14.3	6.9	22.9	22.2
B-	5.6	7.4	2.6	12.1	8.1	6.6	7.4	6.2	5.8	2.9	1.2	12.8	10.9
C+	2.5	3.5	0.8	10.4	3.8	3.2	3.6	2.6	2.9	0.9	0.3	12.4	7.3
C	0.8	1.1	0.3	3.3	1.1	1.1	1.3	1.0	0.9	0.3	0.1	3.3	3.3
D	0.0	0.0	0.0	0.1	0.0	0.0	0.1	0.0	0.0	0.0	0.0	0.1	0.1
From what kind of high school did you graduate?													
Public school (not charter or magnet)	78.9	78.8	78.9	79.6	83.9	72.2	71.2	68.6	75.5	82.8	64.2	85.3	70.4
Public charter school	2.0	2.2	1.5	3.1	2.5	2.0	2.1	2.2	1.7	1.6	1.2	1.8	5.4
Public magnet school	3.6	3.3	4.0	10.1	3.5	3.1	3.5	2.5	2.9	3.9	4.1	8.4	12.8
Private religious/parochial school	9.8	9.8	9.7	4.2	6.8	13.7	11.8	20.3	12.5	7.8	16.9	2.5	7.1
Private independent college-prep school	5.2	5.0	5.6	2.6	2.8	7.8	10.9	5.8	5.1	3.6	13.2	1.5	4.3
Home school	0.6	0.8	0.3	0.3	0.5	1.2	0.5	0.7	2.3	0.3	0.3	0.5	0.1
Prior to this term, have you ever taken courses for credit at this institution?													
No	95.5	95.1	96.2	92.1	94.6	95.8	95.8	95.6	95.8	96.1	96.4	93.8	89.3
Yes	4.5	4.9	3.8	7.9	5.4	4.2	4.2	4.4	4.2	3.9	3.6	6.2	10.7

WEIGHTED NATIONAL NORMS FOR FRESHMAN WOMEN, FALL 2008

	ALL BACC. INSTS.	ALL 4-YR. COLLEGES	ALL UNI-VERSITIES	ALL BLACK COLLEGES	FOUR-YEAR COLLEGES PUBLIC	ALL PRIV.	NONSECT.	CATHOLIC	OTH. REL.	UNIVERSITIES PUBLIC	PRIVATE	BLACK COLLEGES PUBLIC	PRIVATE
Since leaving high school, have you ever taken courses, whether for credit or not for credit, at any other institution (university, 4- or 2-year college, technical, vocational, or business school)?													
No	87.3	87.6	86.8	85.5	87.6	87.7	88.5	88.3	86.5	86.5	88.1	84.9	86.4
Yes	12.7	12.4	13.2	14.5	12.4	12.3	11.5	11.7	13.5	13.5	11.9	15.1	13.6
Where do you plan to live during the fall term?													
With my family or other relatives	14.6	19.7	6.0	10.8	25.1	12.7	15.4	16.4	7.1	5.4	8.0	12.9	7.4
Other private home, apartment, or room	4.2	4.6	3.4	3.1	7.2	1.3	1.8	1.1	0.8	4.2	0.4	3.5	2.4
College residence hall	78.0	72.8	87.0	82.8	63.6	84.6	81.3	81.6	90.5	86.2	90.3	79.9	87.5
Fraternity or sorority house	0.3	0.1	0.7	0.0	0.1	0.1	0.1	0.0	0.0	0.9	0.0	0.0	0.0
Other campus student housing	2.6	2.5	2.8	2.9	3.6	1.2	1.2	0.8	1.4	3.1	1.3	3.1	2.5
Other	0.3	0.3	0.2	0.4	0.4	0.2	0.1	0.1	0.2	0.2	0.0	0.6	0.1
To how many colleges other than this one did you apply for admission this year?													
None	14.5	15.9	12.2	11.0	18.2	13.0	11.5	10.1	16.4	13.4	7.8	12.4	8.6
One	10.8	11.6	9.5	9.7	13.1	9.7	7.8	9.0	12.5	10.6	5.4	10.1	9.0
Two	13.7	15.1	11.4	16.4	16.5	13.2	10.9	13.4	16.0	12.6	7.0	17.8	14.1
Three	15.3	16.5	13.1	19.5	17.2	15.6	14.1	16.1	17.3	13.9	10.2	20.2	18.4
Four	13.0	13.6	12.0	16.8	13.1	14.3	14.6	15.5	13.3	12.3	10.7	16.6	17.2
Five	9.7	9.4	10.2	10.3	8.6	10.4	11.3	11.3	8.8	9.8	11.4	9.4	11.6
Six	7.5	6.8	8.8	6.3	6.1	7.7	8.9	8.4	5.6	8.2	11.1	5.6	7.5
Seven to ten	12.3	8.9	18.2	7.3	6.0	12.6	16.0	13.3	7.9	15.8	27.1	5.7	9.8
Eleven or more	3.1	2.1	4.6	2.8	1.1	3.5	4.9	2.9	2.1	3.4	9.4	2.1	3.8
Were you accepted by your first choice college?													
Yes	79.5	82.2	75.0	80.5	82.7	81.6	76.6	82.4	87.5	75.7	72.2	80.1	81.1
No	20.5	17.8	25.0	19.5	17.3	18.4	23.4	17.6	12.5	24.3	27.8	19.9	18.9
Is this college your:													
First choice?	60.4	60.5	60.2	46.8	59.2	62.1	58.6	60.6	67.5	60.4	59.6	41.9	54.8
Second choice?	26.6	27.4	25.1	31.2	28.8	25.7	27.0	28.3	22.5	25.1	25.2	33.7	27.1
Third choice?	8.5	8.2	9.0	14.0	8.3	8.2	9.5	7.8	6.7	8.7	9.8	15.2	12.0
Less than third choice?	4.5	3.9	5.7	8.0	3.7	4.0	4.8	3.3	3.3	5.7	5.4	9.1	6.1
Citizenship status													
U.S. citizen	96.5	97.0	95.7	98.7	97.7	96.1	94.3	97.5	97.6	96.3	93.4	98.6	98.8
Permanent resident (green card)	2.0	1.6	2.7	1.1	1.5	1.7	2.3	1.6	0.9	2.6	2.8	1.3	0.7
Neither	1.5	1.4	1.6	0.3	0.7	2.2	3.4	0.9	1.4	1.1	3.7	0.1	0.5
Are your parents:													
Both alive and living with each other?	68.0	64.9	73.4	34.4	63.0	67.4	64.6	69.2	70.0	72.3	77.5	33.8	35.3
Both alive, divorced or living apart?	28.0	30.8	23.4	57.2	32.5	28.5	31.2	26.5	26.1	24.4	19.6	57.2	57.1
One or both deceased?	3.9	4.3	3.2	8.4	4.5	4.1	4.2	4.3	4.0	3.3	3.0	8.9	7.6

WEIGHTED NATIONAL NORMS FOR FRESHMAN WOMEN, FALL 2008

	ALL BACC. INSTS.	ALL 4-YR. COLLEGES	ALL UNI-VERSITIES	ALL BLACK COLLEGES	FOUR-YEAR COLLEGES					UNIVERSITIES		BLACK COLLEGES	
					PUBLIC	ALL PRIV.	NONSECT.	CATHOLIC	OTH. REL.	PUBLIC	PRIVATE	PUBLIC	PRIVATE
During high school (grades 9-12) how many years did you study each of the following subjects? [1]													
English (4 years)	98.2	97.9	98.7	96.7	98.0	97.8	97.9	98.5	97.2	98.6	99.0	96.4	97.2
Mathematics (3 years)	98.5	98.2	99.1	97.2	98.0	98.5	98.8	99.1	97.8	98.9	99.6	96.7	98.2
Foreign Language (2 years)	93.8	92.4	96.2	87.0	91.4	93.6	93.8	95.4	92.5	95.7	97.9	84.9	90.5
Physical Science (2 years)	58.4	55.3	63.8	36.7	52.6	58.7	61.4	58.5	55.3	62.5	68.3	32.2	44.0
Biological Science (2 years)	50.9	48.3	55.4	38.0	46.3	50.8	50.7	52.1	50.2	55.1	56.6	34.2	44.2
History/Am. Govt. (1 year)	98.9	98.7	99.1	96.5	98.7	98.8	99.0	99.0	98.4	99.0	99.3	96.5	96.4
Computer Science (1/2 year)	56.6	59.8	51.2	60.3	62.6	56.2	53.3	58.7	58.5	51.9	48.6	61.7	57.9
Arts and/or Music (1 year)	85.8	84.6	87.8	74.5	83.4	86.1	87.8	83.0	85.8	87.5	88.7	72.5	77.9
WHAT IS THE HIGHEST ACADEMIC DEGREE THAT YOU INTEND TO OBTAIN?													
Highest planned													
None	0.8	0.9	0.5	1.4	0.9	1.0	1.1	1.0	0.9	0.6	0.4	1.5	1.3
Vocational certificate	0.1	0.2	0.1	0.1	0.1	0.2	0.3	0.1	0.2	0.1	0.0	0.1	0.2
Associate (A.A. or equivalent)	0.5	0.7	0.2	0.6	0.8	0.7	0.6	0.7	0.7	0.3	0.1	0.8	0.2
Bachelor's degree (B.A., B.S., etc.)	21.3	23.9	16.9	11.8	25.8	21.4	20.1	19.4	24.1	18.4	11.5	14.8	7.1
Master's degree (M.A., M.S., etc.)	42.5	43.7	40.6	34.8	44.4	42.9	43.5	44.8	41.1	40.9	39.3	39.6	27.1
Ph.D. or Ed.D.	18.4	17.3	20.2	29.3	16.5	18.2	18.1	18.4	18.3	20.0	21.0	27.3	32.5
M.D., D.O., D.D.S., D.V.M.	10.5	7.8	14.9	12.8	6.7	9.2	8.9	9.9	9.2	14.0	18.0	8.7	19.6
J.D. (Law)	3.9	3.3	5.0	5.7	2.7	4.0	4.7	3.7	3.3	4.3	7.8	3.7	9.0
B.D. or M.DIV. (Divinity)	0.3	0.3	0.2	0.8	0.3	0.4	0.4	0.3	0.4	0.2	0.2	0.9	0.8
Other	1.7	1.9	1.4	2.6	1.8	2.0	2.3	1.7	1.8	1.3	1.6	2.7	2.3
Highest planned at this college													
None	1.2	1.5	0.7	3.1	1.8	1.1	1.0	1.0	1.3	0.8	0.5	4.0	1.6
Vocational certificate	0.2	0.2	0.1	0.3	0.2	0.2	0.2	0.1	0.3	0.1	0.1	0.3	0.3
Associate (A.A. or equivalent)	2.3	3.1	1.1	3.6	3.7	2.4	2.1	2.5	2.7	1.2	0.7	4.2	2.5
Bachelor's degree (B.A., B.S., etc.)	70.1	71.1	68.5	65.3	67.6	75.1	76.7	67.0	77.5	68.3	69.2	62.9	69.0
Master's degree (M.A., M.S., etc.)	19.2	18.9	19.6	18.2	21.2	16.1	15.4	22.1	13.6	19.9	18.7	19.8	15.9
Ph.D. or Ed.D.	3.3	2.6	4.4	5.7	2.7	2.4	1.9	4.2	1.9	4.4	4.4	5.5	6.1
M.D., D.O., D.D.S., D.V.M.	1.9	0.7	3.7	1.0	0.7	0.7	0.7	1.1	0.6	3.7	3.7	0.4	1.9
J.D. (Law)	0.5	0.4	0.8	0.5	0.3	0.4	0.4	0.5	0.5	0.6	1.4	0.4	0.7
B.D. or M.DIV. (Divinity)	0.2	0.2	0.1	0.4	0.2	0.2	0.2	0.1	0.2	0.1	0.1	0.3	0.6
Other	1.2	1.4	1.0	1.9	1.4	1.3	1.4	1.3	1.3	0.9	1.3	2.2	1.4
HOW WOULD YOU DESCRIBE THE RACIAL COMPOSITION OF THE:													
High school I last attended													
Completely non-White	3.6	3.9	3.1	14.9	4.2	3.4	4.0	4.3	2.2	3.3	2.5	14.9	15.0
Mostly non-White	13.5	13.0	14.4	34.0	14.2	11.5	12.5	11.8	9.9	15.3	11.3	35.9	30.8
Roughly half non-White	25.9	26.0	25.7	26.7	27.4	24.2	24.7	20.1	25.7	26.2	23.6	28.2	24.3
Mostly White	49.8	49.7	49.9	22.5	47.3	52.8	51.5	54.5	53.6	48.6	54.8	19.8	26.8
Completely White	7.2	7.4	6.9	1.9	6.8	8.1	7.3	9.2	8.6	6.6	7.9	1.2	3.1
Neighborhood where I grew up													
Completely non-White	6.3	7.0	5.2	26.5	7.6	6.3	7.2	7.0	4.7	5.3	4.6	27.3	25.2
Mostly non-White	11.8	11.9	11.7	33.8	12.8	10.7	12.1	10.7	9.0	12.1	10.1	34.0	33.6
Roughly half non-White	13.9	13.8	14.1	19.7	14.4	13.1	13.6	12.6	12.6	14.1	14.0	20.1	19.0
Mostly White	48.7	47.4	50.9	16.9	46.3	48.8	48.2	46.6	50.9	50.3	53.2	16.0	18.4
Completely White	19.2	19.9	18.1	3.1	18.9	21.1	19.0	23.1	22.8	18.1	18.1	2.6	3.8

	ALL BACC. INSTS.	ALL 4-YR. COLLEGES	ALL UNI-VERSITIES	ALL BLACK COLLEGES	FOUR-YEAR COLLEGES					UNIVERSITIES		BLACK COLLEGES	
					PUBLIC	ALL PRIV.	NONSECT.	CATHOLIC	OTH. REL.	PUBLIC	PRIVATE	PUBLIC	PRIVATE
Do you have a disability?													
Hearing	0.5	0.6	0.4	0.2	0.5	0.6	0.6	0.6	0.7	0.4	0.4	0.2	0.2
Speech	0.2	0.2	0.1	0.2	0.2	0.2	0.2	0.2	0.2	0.1	0.1	0.2	0.1
Orthopedic	0.5	0.6	0.4	0.5	0.6	0.6	0.6	0.5	0.6	0.4	0.4	0.5	0.4
Learning disability	2.8	3.4	1.9	1.5	2.7	4.3	4.9	3.4	4.0	1.7	2.4	1.2	2.0
Partially sighted or blind	1.2	1.2	1.2	1.3	1.3	1.2	1.2	1.1	1.4	1.3	1.2	1.1	1.7
Health-related	1.6	1.7	1.3	2.0	1.6	1.9	1.8	1.9	2.0	1.3	1.2	1.8	2.2
Other	1.2	1.3	0.9	1.2	1.3	1.4	1.4	1.2	1.6	0.9	0.8	1.1	1.3
HOW MUCH OF YOUR FIRST YEAR'S EDUCATIONAL EXPENSES (ROOM, BOARD TUITION, AND FEES) DO YOU EXPECT TO COVER FROM:													
Family resources (parents, relatives, spouse, etc.)													
None	19.7	22.1	15.7	39.5	24.5	18.9	18.8	18.5	19.2	16.9	11.3	44.4	31.3
Less than $1,000	12.7	14.5	9.4	21.3	16.9	11.5	10.6	11.7	12.7	10.4	5.7	24.6	15.8
$1,000 to 2,999	14.2	15.6	12.0	16.5	17.6	13.0	11.8	13.7	14.1	13.1	7.6	15.4	18.4
$3,000 to 5,999	12.7	13.1	12.1	9.9	13.6	12.4	11.1	13.5	13.6	13.2	8.3	8.2	12.6
$6,000 to 9,999	10.6	10.3	11.0	4.8	9.9	10.9	10.2	11.5	11.4	11.5	9.1	3.6	6.8
$10,000 +	30.1	24.4	39.7	8.1	17.6	33.3	37.6	31.2	29.0	34.9	57.9	3.8	15.1
My own resources (savings from work, work-study, other income)													
None	33.9	34.4	32.9	55.3	35.6	32.9	34.8	28.4	32.9	31.9	37.0	58.0	50.9
Less than $1,000	29.4	30.4	27.6	26.9	32.8	27.4	26.8	27.4	28.1	28.4	24.3	26.7	27.2
$1,000 to 2,999	23.8	22.7	25.5	13.1	21.3	24.7	24.1	26.8	24.1	25.9	24.3	11.7	15.4
$3,000 to 5,999	8.4	8.0	9.2	2.9	7.0	9.2	8.6	10.8	9.1	9.4	8.3	2.3	3.8
$6,000 to 9,999	2.4	2.3	2.5	0.9	1.9	2.9	2.5	3.4	3.0	2.5	2.8	0.7	1.4
$10,000 +	2.2	2.1	2.3	0.9	1.5	3.0	3.1	3.2	2.7	2.0	3.3	0.6	1.3
Aid which not be repaid (grants, scholarships, military funding, etc.)													
None	28.3	27.0	30.4	22.9	33.6	18.5	23.8	14.6	13.9	31.7	25.8	22.5	23.5
Less than $1,000	7.4	7.2	7.6	6.4	9.8	4.0	4.5	3.7	3.4	8.6	3.6	6.7	6.0
$1,000 to 2,999	14.4	14.8	13.5	16.5	19.0	9.4	9.8	9.1	9.1	15.0	7.7	17.7	14.5
$3,000 to 5,999	14.3	15.2	12.8	21.1	17.4	12.2	12.0	12.6	12.3	14.3	7.2	23.7	17.0
$6,000 to 9,999	11.6	12.0	10.8	13.9	9.6	15.2	14.2	16.3	15.8	11.2	9.2	13.6	14.6
$10,000 +	24.1	23.7	24.9	19.1	10.6	40.6	35.6	43.6	45.5	19.2	46.4	15.9	24.4
Aid which must be repaid (loans, etc.)													
None	48.5	46.1	52.7	39.2	52.7	37.5	40.8	32.2	36.3	53.2	50.7	44.0	31.2
Less than $1,000	4.0	4.3	3.5	5.8	5.1	3.2	2.9	3.8	3.3	3.8	2.2	6.7	4.3
$1,000 to 2,999	9.8	10.8	8.3	12.4	11.5	9.8	8.8	11.0	10.4	8.4	7.7	14.5	8.9
$3,000 to 5,999	16.0	16.7	14.8	17.2	15.2	18.8	16.3	21.3	20.5	14.8	14.9	18.0	15.9
$6,000 to 9,999	9.4	10.1	8.2	11.2	8.0	12.9	11.9	13.4	14.0	8.3	8.0	10.6	12.2
$10,000 +	12.2	12.0	12.6	14.3	7.4	17.8	19.3	18.3	15.5	11.5	16.6	6.3	27.4
Other than above													
None	94.1	93.9	94.3	92.9	94.5	93.1	93.8	91.8	92.9	94.4	94.1	93.3	92.3
Less than $1,000	2.3	2.4	2.1	2.7	2.4	2.4	2.0	2.9	2.5	2.2	1.7	2.6	2.8
$1,000 to 2,999	1.4	1.4	1.4	1.8	1.4	1.4	1.2	1.7	1.5	1.5	1.1	1.8	1.9
$3,000 to 5,999	0.9	0.9	0.7	0.9	0.8	1.1	1.1	1.1	1.1	0.7	0.8	0.9	0.9
$6,000 to 9,999	0.5	0.5	0.5	0.6	0.3	0.7	0.7	0.8	0.6	0.5	0.5	0.6	0.6
$10,000 +	0.9	0.9	1.0	1.1	0.6	1.3	1.2	1.7	1.3	0.8	1.8	0.8	1.5

WEIGHTED NATIONAL NORMS FOR FRESHMAN WOMEN, FALL 2008

	ALL BACC. INSTS.	ALL 4-YR. COLLEGES	ALL UNI-VERSITIES	ALL BLACK COLLEGES	FOUR-YEAR COLLEGES					UNIVERSITIES		BLACK COLLEGES	
					PUBLIC	ALL PRIV.	NONSECT.	CATHOLIC	OTH. REL.	PUBLIC	PRIVATE	PUBLIC	PRIVATE
What is your best estimate of your parents' total income last year? Consider income from all sources before taxes													
Less than $10,000	4.3	5.1	3.0	14.2	5.5	4.6	4.8	4.7	4.2	3.2	2.2	15.6	12.0
$10,000 to 14,999	3.4	4.0	2.5	7.8	4.5	3.3	3.3	3.4	3.3	2.7	1.6	8.0	7.5
$15,000 to 19,999	2.8	3.2	2.2	6.2	3.4	2.9	3.1	3.1	2.6	2.4	1.6	6.7	5.4
$20,000 to 24,999	3.9	4.4	3.1	8.1	4.8	3.8	3.7	3.9	4.0	3.4	2.0	8.6	7.4
$25,000 to 29,999	3.7	4.1	3.0	7.0	4.4	3.7	3.6	3.5	4.1	3.2	2.0	7.6	6.0
$30,000 to 39,999	7.0	7.7	6.0	10.9	8.0	7.3	7.0	7.5	7.5	6.3	4.6	11.0	10.9
$40,000 to 49,999	8.2	9.1	6.5	10.4	9.4	8.8	8.3	8.7	9.5	7.0	5.0	10.5	10.1
$50,000 to 59,999	8.6	9.3	7.5	8.3	9.3	9.4	9.1	9.1	9.9	8.0	5.7	8.4	8.1
$60,000 to 74,999	11.3	11.9	10.3	8.8	12.2	11.5	10.5	12.1	12.4	10.8	8.6	8.2	9.7
$75,000 to 99,999	13.4	13.0	14.0	7.1	13.0	13.1	12.6	13.7	13.4	14.4	12.5	6.6	7.9
$100,000 to 149,999	15.5	13.8	18.4	6.1	13.4	14.2	14.1	14.9	13.9	18.1	19.3	6.0	6.4
$150,000 to 199,999	7.3	6.3	9.1	2.4	5.9	6.8	7.3	7.0	6.1	8.6	10.8	1.6	3.7
$200,000 to 249,999	3.7	2.9	5.1	1.0	2.2	3.7	4.1	3.2	3.5	4.5	7.5	0.5	1.9
$250,000 or more	6.7	5.1	9.3	1.6	3.9	6.7	8.5	5.1	5.5	7.4	16.6	0.7	3.0
Do you have any concern about your ability to finance your college education?													
None (I am confident that I will have sufficient funds)	30.2	29.7	31.0	26.4	30.2	29.2	29.7	26.9	29.7	30.2	34.2	27.7	24.1
Some (but I probably will have enough funds)	56.9	57.0	56.6	51.5	56.8	57.3	55.9	59.2	57.9	57.1	54.7	51.5	51.4
Major (not sure I will have enough funds to complete college)	12.9	13.3	12.4	22.2	13.1	13.6	14.4	13.8	12.4	12.7	11.1	20.7	24.5
Your current religious preference													
Baptist	11.2	14.1	6.3	51.0	15.6	12.1	9.2	7.1	18.5	6.4	5.8	52.2	48.9
Buddhist	1.2	0.7	1.9	0.0	0.7	0.8	1.2	0.6	0.4	2.0	1.5	0.0	0.1
Church of Christ	4.0	4.6	2.9	8.8	5.0	4.1	4.3	3.0	4.5	3.2	1.7	9.0	8.5
Eastern Orthodox	0.6	0.5	0.8	0.0	0.4	0.6	0.8	0.7	0.4	0.7	1.2	0.0	0.1
Episcopalian	1.4	1.4	1.5	0.7	1.2	1.8	2.2	1.0	1.6	1.3	1.9	0.6	0.9
Hindu	0.7	0.4	1.4	0.0	0.2	0.5	0.8	0.2	0.3	1.3	1.8	0.0	0.0
Jewish	2.5	1.6	3.9	0.0	1.4	1.9	3.4	0.3	1.0	3.4	6.0	0.0	0.1
LDS (Mormon)	2.4	2.1	2.9	0.1	3.6	0.2	0.2	0.1	0.2	3.6	0.1	0.1	0.1
Lutheran	3.6	3.3	4.2	0.3	2.7	4.1	2.4	3.6	6.4	4.7	2.5	0.3	0.2
Methodist	4.8	5.0	4.3	5.9	5.1	4.8	3.7	3.0	7.3	4.6	3.4	6.1	5.5
Muslim	0.9	0.8	1.0	0.6	0.9	0.8	1.2	0.6	0.4	0.9	1.5	0.4	0.9
Presbyterian	3.2	2.8	3.7	0.6	2.6	3.1	2.6	1.7	4.5	3.8	3.4	0.6	0.6
Quaker	0.2	0.2	0.2	0.1	0.1	0.3	0.2	0.2	0.4	0.1	0.2	0.1	0.0
Roman Catholic	25.4	24.6	26.8	4.9	23.4	26.1	24.9	52.8	13.0	25.2	33.1	3.8	6.6
Seventh Day Adventist	0.5	0.6	0.4	1.1	0.4	0.8	0.5	0.3	1.3	0.4	0.2	1.3	0.9
United Church of Christ/Congregational	0.8	0.9	0.6	0.9	0.8	1.1	1.2	0.8	1.0	0.6	0.6	1.0	0.7
Other Christian	13.9	15.1	11.8	15.9	14.6	15.9	11.6	10.1	24.3	12.4	9.4	15.1	17.1
Other Religion	3.1	3.3	2.9	3.4	3.4	3.2	3.8	2.3	2.9	2.9	2.7	3.7	2.9
None	19.6	17.9	22.6	5.7	17.9	17.9	25.8	11.5	11.5	22.6	22.9	5.7	5.8

WEIGHTED NATIONAL NORMS FOR FRESHMAN WOMEN, FALL 2008

	ALL BACC. INSTS.	ALL 4-YR. COLLEGES	ALL UNI-VERSITIES	ALL BLACK COLLEGES	FOUR-YEAR COLLEGES					UNIVERSITIES		BLACK COLLEGES	
					PUBLIC	ALL PRIV.	NONSECT.	CATHOLIC	OTH. REL.	PUBLIC	PRIVATE	PUBLIC	PRIVATE
Father's current religious preference													
Baptist	10.8	13.5	6.4	46.9	15.1	11.3	8.7	6.5	17.2	6.6	5.8	48.1	44.9
Buddhist	1.6	0.9	2.9	0.2	0.8	1.0	1.5	0.7	0.5	3.0	2.3	0.2	0.2
Church of Christ	3.8	4.4	2.9	7.3	4.7	4.0	4.3	3.0	4.2	3.1	1.9	7.3	7.2
Eastern Orthodox	0.7	0.6	0.9	0.0	0.5	0.8	1.0	1.0	0.4	0.8	1.4	0.0	0.1
Episcopalian	1.7	1.7	1.8	0.8	1.4	2.0	2.6	1.2	1.7	1.6	2.5	0.8	0.8
Hindu	0.9	0.4	1.6	0.0	0.3	0.6	0.9	0.3	0.3	1.4	2.2	0.0	0.0
Jewish	3.2	2.3	4.7	0.1	1.9	2.8	4.8	0.8	1.4	4.1	6.9	0.1	0.1
LDS (Mormon)	2.4	2.2	2.9	0.1	3.7	0.2	0.2	0.1	0.3	3.7	0.1	0.2	0.1
Lutheran	4.3	3.9	4.9	0.5	3.2	4.8	3.1	4.4	7.1	5.4	3.1	0.5	0.4
Methodist	4.9	5.1	4.6	5.2	5.1	5.0	4.1	3.2	7.1	4.8	3.8	5.6	4.5
Muslim	1.3	1.3	1.4	1.9	1.3	1.2	1.8	1.0	0.7	1.3	2.0	1.6	2.4
Presbyterian	3.7	3.4	4.1	0.7	3.1	3.6	3.4	2.2	4.8	4.2	4.1	0.9	0.4
Quaker	0.2	0.2	0.2	0.0	0.2	0.3	0.2	0.1	0.4	0.2	0.2	0.0	0.0
Roman Catholic	28.4	27.6	29.7	5.7	26.6	29.0	29.0	52.8	15.7	28.0	35.8	4.4	7.7
Seventh Day Adventist	0.5	0.6	0.4	1.3	0.5	0.8	0.5	0.4	1.4	0.5	0.3	1.5	1.1
United Church of Christ/Congregational	0.8	0.9	0.7	0.8	0.7	1.1	1.3	0.7	1.1	0.7	0.6	0.9	0.7
Other Christian	12.3	13.3	10.5	13.6	12.9	13.9	10.6	8.6	21.0	11.0	8.3	12.8	15.0
Other Religion	2.3	2.5	2.1	3.2	2.6	2.2	2.5	1.9	2.1	2.2	1.8	3.3	2.8
None	16.1	15.4	17.3	11.6	15.4	15.5	19.5	11.3	12.7	17.4	16.8	11.7	11.5
Mother's current religious preference													
Baptist	11.7	14.6	6.8	51.6	16.2	12.6	10.0	7.5	18.7	6.9	6.2	52.2	50.4
Buddhist	1.7	0.9	3.1	0.2	0.9	1.0	1.5	0.7	0.5	3.2	2.6	0.2	0.2
Church of Christ	4.3	5.0	3.3	8.7	5.4	4.4	4.9	3.2	4.4	3.6	2.2	9.5	7.4
Eastern Orthodox	0.7	0.6	1.0	0.0	0.5	0.7	1.0	0.7	0.4	0.9	1.4	0.0	0.1
Episcopalian	1.9	1.9	2.0	1.1	1.5	2.3	3.1	1.2	2.0	1.9	2.6	0.9	1.3
Hindu	0.8	0.4	1.5	0.0	0.3	0.5	0.9	0.2	0.3	1.4	2.1	0.0	0.0
Jewish	3.0	2.1	4.4	0.1	1.8	2.4	4.1	0.5	1.2	3.9	6.6	0.0	0.1
LDS (Mormon)	2.5	2.3	3.0	0.1	3.9	0.2	0.2	0.2	0.3	3.7	0.2	0.1	0.1
Lutheran	4.4	4.1	5.0	0.4	3.3	5.1	3.5	4.3	7.5	5.5	3.3	0.4	0.5
Methodist	5.6	5.8	5.3	6.3	5.9	5.8	4.7	3.4	8.4	5.6	4.2	6.6	5.7
Muslim	1.0	1.0	1.2	0.7	1.0	0.9	1.4	0.7	0.4	1.1	1.7	0.5	0.9
Presbyterian	3.9	3.6	4.5	0.6	3.3	3.9	3.7	2.2	5.2	4.5	4.2	0.6	0.7
Quaker	0.2	0.2	0.2	0.1	0.2	0.3	0.3	0.2	0.4	0.2	0.2	0.1	0.1
Roman Catholic	30.2	29.1	31.8	5.2	28.2	30.4	30.6	55.9	16.1	30.1	38.4	4.3	6.7
Seventh Day Adventist	0.6	0.7	0.5	1.3	0.5	0.9	0.6	0.5	1.4	0.5	0.3	1.5	0.9
United Church of Christ/Congregational	1.0	1.1	0.8	0.8	0.9	1.3	1.6	0.9	1.3	0.8	0.8	0.8	0.8
Other Christian	13.6	14.7	11.8	15.2	14.1	15.4	12.5	9.7	22.3	12.4	9.3	14.2	16.7
Other Religion	2.5	2.7	2.3	3.4	2.8	2.5	2.9	1.9	2.3	2.4	2.0	3.7	2.9
None	10.2	9.4	11.6	4.2	9.4	9.3	12.7	6.2	6.8	11.6	11.6	4.2	4.3

WEIGHTED NATIONAL NORMS FOR FRESHMAN WOMEN, FALL 2008

	ALL BACC. INSTS.	ALL 4-YR. COLLEGES	ALL UNI-VERSITIES	ALL BLACK COLLEGES	FOUR-YEAR COLLEGES					UNIVERSITIES		BLACK COLLEGES	
					PUBLIC	ALL PRIV.	NONSECT.	CATHOLIC	OTH. REL.	PUBLIC	PRIVATE	PUBLIC	PRIVATE
During the past year, student "frequently" or "occasionally":													
Attended a religious service	77.7	78.7	76.1	92.4	77.9	79.6	71.2	84.4	87.7	76.0	76.7	91.9	93.3
Was bored in class [2]	37.9	37.5	38.5	34.5	39.6	34.7	35.5	32.8	34.7	38.9	36.9	37.0	30.2
Participated in political demonstrations	25.8	25.2	26.8	35.9	24.4	26.4	27.2	26.4	25.4	26.7	26.8	35.3	37.0
Tutored another student	58.1	53.5	65.8	59.3	52.7	54.5	53.5	56.0	55.1	64.3	71.5	55.6	65.2
Studied with other students	90.1	88.7	92.5	87.8	88.2	89.3	88.5	91.0	89.3	92.4	92.9	87.2	88.9
Was a guest in a teacher's home	21.0	21.0	21.0	18.1	19.5	22.9	21.7	18.0	27.2	20.4	23.2	17.0	20.0
Smoked cigarettes [2]	4.2	5.0	2.9	1.3	5.4	4.6	6.0	3.6	3.3	3.0	2.7	1.6	0.9
Drank beer	32.8	32.1	34.1	7.5	31.7	32.5	38.9	33.1	24.0	33.4	37.0	9.6	4.0
Drank wine or liquor	43.2	42.9	43.7	31.6	42.6	43.3	50.8	43.1	33.8	42.9	46.7	34.6	26.6
Felt overwhelmed by all I had to do [2]	37.3	37.7	36.8	33.8	37.4	38.0	38.0	37.2	38.4	36.6	37.6	34.9	31.9
Felt depressed [2]	8.2	9.0	6.7	12.9	9.2	8.9	9.6	7.8	8.6	6.7	6.7	14.7	10.0
Performed volunteer work	87.3	85.0	91.3	84.5	82.7	88.1	86.3	89.2	89.7	90.7	93.7	82.9	87.0
Played a musical instrument	41.5	39.5	44.9	36.0	37.5	42.2	41.1	36.7	46.7	44.2	47.8	36.1	35.8
Asked a teacher for advice after class [2]	30.5	29.8	31.7	30.9	28.3	31.8	31.7	31.9	31.8	31.3	33.5	26.4	38.3
Voted in a student election [2]	24.1	23.4	25.3	33.2	22.8	24.2	23.4	25.5	24.4	24.6	27.9	30.0	38.4
Socialized with someone of another racial/ethnic group [2]	70.5	69.2	72.7	71.8	69.3	68.9	71.4	65.8	67.5	72.1	74.8	68.7	76.8
Came late to class	58.9	58.5	59.5	67.3	60.1	56.5	58.8	52.8	55.6	59.9	57.8	66.9	67.9
Used the Internet: [2]													
For research or homework	80.7	78.3	84.9	80.9	76.1	81.3	81.8	83.2	79.5	84.0	88.2	79.1	83.9
To read news sites	40.1	38.2	43.4	43.4	36.4	40.5	42.5	42.3	36.9	41.4	50.7	41.2	47.0
To read blogs	27.0	26.6	27.7	28.0	26.2	27.2	27.6	26.7	26.9	27.5	28.4	27.0	29.7
To blog	16.5	16.6	16.4	17.4	16.5	16.7	15.7	17.1	17.7	16.8	15.0	17.5	17.3
Performed community service as part of a class	61.4	60.5	62.9	59.5	58.8	62.8	61.0	67.6	62.4	62.4	64.9	56.5	64.5
Discussed religion [2]	32.8	32.3	33.7	34.2	30.0	35.4	30.6	33.8	42.5	32.6	37.7	30.4	40.4
Discussed politics [2]	33.7	30.9	38.4	32.0	28.5	33.9	35.4	32.5	32.8	37.2	43.3	27.9	38.7
Worked on a local, state or national political campaign	11.3	10.4	13.0	14.9	9.9	11.0	11.0	11.2	11.0	12.6	14.4	13.5	17.2
Student rated self "above average" or "highest 10%" as compared with the average person of his/her age in:													
Academic ability	66.2	59.5	77.8	56.6	56.5	63.2	61.9	62.5	65.3	75.7	85.8	50.1	67.3
Artistic ability	31.5	30.5	33.3	24.0	28.6	32.9	37.9	25.2	30.7	32.2	37.2	21.3	28.4
Computer skills	30.1	30.1	30.1	41.1	30.8	29.3	30.0	31.1	27.3	29.9	30.5	40.2	42.6
Cooperativeness	74.4	72.9	77.0	73.4	72.2	73.7	72.9	75.1	74.0	76.9	77.5	70.9	77.4
Creativity	56.3	55.6	57.5	59.8	54.0	57.7	61.5	52.5	55.7	56.7	60.5	57.8	63.1
Drive to achieve	77.3	74.3	82.5	82.2	72.5	76.7	77.0	77.6	75.8	81.5	86.4	79.2	87.1
Emotional health	48.3	45.3	53.4	52.1	44.6	46.2	44.7	47.6	47.2	53.1	54.6	48.6	57.6
Leadership ability	58.7	55.9	63.3	67.7	55.2	56.9	55.7	58.1	57.8	62.6	65.9	64.7	72.7
Mathematical ability	36.5	31.5	45.0	32.1	30.4	33.0	32.2	33.7	33.6	42.8	53.2	29.7	36.1
Physical health	45.9	43.3	50.4	43.1	41.9	45.0	43.8	47.0	45.4	49.8	52.5	39.8	48.5
Popularity	32.6	31.3	34.9	45.3	31.8	30.6	30.8	32.0	29.7	34.3	37.2	44.6	46.5
Public speaking ability	34.3	32.0	38.4	39.0	31.2	33.0	33.3	32.2	33.0	37.0	43.8	36.2	43.5
Self-confidence (intellectual)	53.4	50.4	58.4	72.6	49.3	51.8	51.7	51.2	52.4	57.1	63.7	70.9	75.4
Self-confidence (social)	48.1	46.7	50.6	70.1	47.3	46.0	45.7	47.2	45.7	50.6	50.5	69.7	70.7
Self-understanding	54.3	52.1	58.1	69.4	50.9	53.6	54.3	52.1	53.6	57.4	60.7	67.5	72.6
Spirituality	40.4	40.5	40.2	60.7	39.9	41.4	36.0	40.4	48.8	40.4	39.8	59.6	62.4
Understanding of others	68.8	67.2	71.4	67.1	66.6	68.0	68.2	68.3	67.7	71.0	72.8	65.2	70.1
Writing ability	49.2	46.3	54.1	49.7	44.3	49.0	50.4	47.0	48.4	52.5	60.5	46.9	54.2

WEIGHTED NATIONAL NORMS FOR FRESHMAN WOMEN, FALL 2008

	ALL BACC. INSTS.	ALL 4-YR. COLLEGES	ALL UNI-VERSITIES	ALL BLACK COLLEGES	FOUR-YEAR COLLEGES					UNIVERSITIES		BLACK COLLEGES	
					PUBLIC	ALL PRIV.	NONSECT.	CATHOLIC	OTH. REL.	PUBLIC	PRIVATE	PUBLIC	PRIVATE
Student rated self "above average" or "highest 10%" as compared with the average person of his/her age in:													
Ability to see the world from someone else's perspective	65.2	62.3	70.3	57.5	61.3	63.7	65.6	62.1	62.0	69.2	74.5	53.6	63.8
Tolerance of others with different beliefs	73.9	70.7	79.5	62.0	69.7	71.9	74.6	71.5	68.6	78.6	82.6	57.6	68.9
Openness to having my own views challenged	56.6	54.8	59.6	58.3	54.2	55.5	58.6	54.7	51.8	58.7	63.2	54.5	64.4
Ability to discuss and negotiate controversial issues	58.5	55.8	63.0	60.8	55.3	56.5	58.9	55.7	54.0	61.9	67.3	57.0	66.9
Ability to work cooperatively with diverse people	78.7	76.5	82.5	76.3	76.0	77.1	78.4	77.3	75.4	82.0	84.7	73.1	81.4
WHAT IS THE HIGHEST LEVEL OF FORMAL EDUCATION OBTAINED BY YOUR PARENTS?													
Father													
Grammar school or less	4.6	4.9	4.0	5.7	5.9	3.7	4.2	4.5	2.8	4.5	2.2	5.6	5.9
Some high school	5.7	6.6	4.1	11.3	7.3	5.7	6.2	5.7	5.2	4.4	3.0	12.4	9.4
High school graduate	21.0	24.5	15.0	35.9	26.3	22.1	21.3	23.8	22.1	16.2	10.5	38.6	31.4
Postsecondary school other than college	3.6	4.0	3.1	4.6	4.0	3.9	3.3	4.9	4.1	3.3	2.3	4.8	4.5
Some college	15.4	16.2	13.9	18.5	17.2	14.9	14.1	15.6	15.7	14.7	10.8	17.7	19.8
College degree	26.0	24.5	28.7	14.5	23.4	26.0	25.0	25.8	27.3	28.7	28.6	13.8	15.5
Some graduate school	2.1	1.9	2.6	0.8	1.6	2.3	2.2	2.0	2.5	2.4	3.3	0.6	1.3
Graduate degree	21.6	17.4	28.6	8.7	14.4	21.4	23.8	17.6	20.4	25.8	39.2	6.5	12.2
Mother													
Grammar school or less	4.2	4.5	3.8	5.7	5.4	3.4	3.6	4.2	2.7	4.2	2.0	5.2	6.7
Some high school	4.1	4.5	3.5	6.8	5.2	3.6	3.9	3.8	3.0	3.8	2.3	7.5	5.7
High school graduate	18.4	20.8	14.3	22.4	22.2	19.0	18.2	21.4	18.6	15.3	10.4	24.2	19.4
Postsecondary school other than college	3.8	4.1	3.2	4.2	4.2	4.1	3.7	4.7	4.1	3.3	2.8	4.1	4.3
Some college	18.3	19.2	16.7	24.6	20.4	17.6	16.2	17.9	19.2	17.8	12.5	25.3	23.4
College degree	31.1	29.3	34.2	22.9	27.5	31.6	31.0	30.5	32.8	33.6	36.7	23.2	22.3
Some graduate school	2.7	2.3	3.3	1.6	1.9	2.9	3.2	2.3	2.7	3.0	4.2	1.3	2.1
Graduate degree	17.4	15.3	21.0	11.9	13.1	18.0	20.1	15.1	16.9	18.9	29.2	9.2	16.2
During the past year, did you "frequently":													
Ask questions in class	57.2	56.0	59.1	60.9	54.6	57.9	58.1	57.6	57.6	57.8	64.1	56.4	68.4
Support your opinions with a logical argument	55.6	52.6	60.7	51.8	50.8	54.9	57.7	53.0	52.3	58.5	69.2	47.9	58.1
Seek solutions to problems and explain them to others	52.3	49.4	57.1	50.6	47.6	51.9	53.6	51.3	50.0	54.9	65.7	46.2	57.7
Revise your papers to improve your writing	54.7	53.3	57.1	54.4	50.4	57.1	56.2	57.4	58.0	55.7	62.3	52.7	57.1
Evaluate the quality or reliability of information you received	37.1	35.0	40.8	39.3	33.2	37.3	38.6	36.8	35.9	39.0	47.7	36.7	43.4
Take a risk because you feel you have more to gain	37.0	37.0	36.9	38.9	37.0	37.1	38.9	36.9	34.9	36.3	39.0	39.4	38.0
Seek alternative solutions to a problem	43.1	42.1	44.8	45.2	40.8	43.7	45.4	43.1	42.0	43.6	49.5	42.0	50.4
Look up scientific research articles and resources	20.6	19.3	22.8	21.0	18.2	20.7	21.2	21.7	19.4	21.5	27.7	18.3	25.4
Explore topics on your own, even though it was not required for a class	28.5	27.5	30.4	27.6	26.1	29.2	32.0	26.5	27.1	28.9	35.8	25.3	31.3
Accept mistakes as part of the learning process	52.7	52.2	53.6	59.9	52.3	52.1	53.5	52.0	50.4	53.5	54.1	58.6	62.0
Seek feedback on your academic work	53.2	52.0	55.5	60.7	50.1	54.4	55.7	54.8	52.5	54.4	59.6	57.9	65.1
Take notes during class	78.0	77.3	79.3	82.9	75.2	80.1	79.7	82.1	79.5	78.3	82.9	83.1	82.6

WEIGHTED NATIONAL NORMS FOR FRESHMAN WOMEN, FALL 2008

	ALL BACC. INSTS.	ALL 4-YR. COLLEGES	AL. UNI- VERSITIES	ALL BLACK COLLEGES	FOUR-YEAR COLLEGES					UNIVERSITIES		BLACK COLLEGES	
					PUBLIC	ALL PRIV.	NONSECT.	CATHOLIC	OTH. REL.	PUBLIC	PRIVATE	PUBLIC	PRIVATE
Your probable career occupation													
Accountant or actuary	2.0	2.1	1.9	2.9	2.1	2.1	2.1	2.2	2.0	2.0	1.7	3.3	2.2
Actor or entertainer	1.4	1.6	1.0	1.3	1.5	1.6	2.1	0.8	1.5	0.9	1.6	1.1	1.5
Architect or urban planner	0.6	0.3	1.2	0.3	0.2	0.3	0.6	0.2	0.2	1.1	1.5	0.5	0.1
Artist	3.1	3.8	1.9	0.5	2.8	5.1	9.1	1.2	2.3	1.9	1.8	0.7	0.3
Business (clerical)	0.6	0.6	0.6	0.5	0.6	0.6	0.6	0.6	0.5	0.7	0.5	0.6	0.5
Business executive (management, administrator)	5.5	4.8	6.7	4.1	4.5	5.1	5.4	5.6	4.6	6.4	7.7	3.8	4.7
Business owner or proprietor	2.0	2.1	2.0	2.7	2.0	2.2	2.7	1.7	1.9	2.0	1.9	2.4	3.1
Business salesperson or buyer	0.8	0.8	0.8	0.3	0.8	0.8	1.0	0.8	0.6	0.9	0.6	0.2	0.5
Clergy (minister, priest)	0.1	0.1	0.0	0.0	0.0	0.1	0.0	0.0	0.4	0.0	0.0	0.0	0.0
Clergy (other religious)	0.1	0.1	0.0	0.0	0.0	0.2	0.0	0.0	0.4	0.0	0.1	0.1	0.0
Clinical psychologist	2.0	2.1	1.8	3.3	2.1	2.2	2.1	2.3	2.2	1.8	1.7	3.3	3.4
College administrator/staff	0.0	0.0	0.0	0.0	0.0	0.0	0.0	0.0	0.0	0.1	0.0	0.0	0.1
College teacher	0.4	0.4	0.5	0.3	0.3	0.5	0.6	0.3	0.6	0.4	0.7	0.2	0.4
Computer programmer or analyst	0.4	0.4	0.4	1.7	0.4	0.4	0.4	0.2	0.4	0.4	0.4	2.1	1.1
Conservationist or forester	0.3	0.2	0.4	0.1	0.1	0.3	0.3	0.1	0.3	0.4	0.2	0.2	0.1
Dentist (including orthodontist)	1.2	1.1	1.5	1.5	1.2	0.9	0.8	1.0	0.9	1.5	1.3	1.3	1.9
Dietitian or nutritionist	0.8	0.6	1.0	0.1	0.8	0.4	0.2	0.8	0.5	1.2	0.4	0.2	0.0
Engineer	2.5	1.2	4.8	1.9	1.4	1.0	1.1	1.2	0.7	4.6	5.5	1.9	1.9
Farmer or rancher	0.2	0.1	0.2	0.1	0.1	0.2	0.2	0.0	0.2	0.2	0.1	0.0	0.1
Foreign service worker (including diplomat)	1.0	0.8	1.4	0.1	0.5	1.2	1.3	0.8	1.2	1.1	2.6	0.0	0.3
Homemaker (full-time)	0.1	0.1	0.1	0.0	0.1	0.1	0.1	0.1	0.3	0.2	0.1	0.0	0.0
Interior decorator (including designer)	0.7	0.7	0.7	0.0	0.6	0.7	1.1	0.3	0.5	0.8	0.4	0.1	0.0
Lab technician or hygienist	0.5	0.3	0.2	0.2	0.3	0.2	0.3	0.3	0.3	0.2	0.1	0.2	0.2
Law enforcement officer	0.5	0.7	0.3	1.2	0.9	0.5	0.4	0.6	0.6	0.3	0.2	1.5	0.9
Lawyer (attorney) or judge	3.6	3.1	4.3	6.1	2.7	3.6	4.0	3.7	3.1	3.9	5.9	4.4	8.8
Military service (career)	0.6	0.8	0.1	0.4	1.3	0.2	0.1	0.2	0.2	0.1	0.2	0.5	0.3
Musician (performer, composer)	1.2	1.2	1.0	1.1	1.2	1.3	0.9	0.6	2.3	1.0	1.3	0.9	1.3
Nurse	7.4	9.5	3.9	13.5	11.3	7.2	3.9	13.8	7.5	4.2	3.0	17.8	6.4
Optometrist	0.4	0.4	0.5	0.6	0.5	0.3	0.2	0.5	0.4	0.5	0.4	0.6	0.5
Pharmacist	2.3	1.9	2.9	3.8	1.9	1.8	1.4	2.9	1.8	2.9	2.5	2.0	6.6
Physician	6.8	4.7	10.3	9.2	3.7	6.1	5.4	7.6	6.1	9.3	14.0	5.0	15.9
Policymaker/Government	0.7	0.5	1.0	0.4	0.4	0.7	0.8	0.6	0.7	0.8	1.6	0.3	0.6
School counselor	0.5	0.6	0.4	0.6	0.7	0.5	0.3	0.6	0.7	0.4	0.2	0.4	0.8
School principal or superintendent	0.0	0.0	0.0	0.0	0.0	0.0	0.0	0.0	0.0	0.0	0.1	0.1	0.0
Scientific researcher	1.8	1.4	2.5	0.7	1.1	1.7	2.0	1.1	1.7	2.3	3.1	0.7	0.6
Social, welfare, or recreation worker	1.7	2.0	1.2	3.9	2.2	1.7	1.3	1.6	2.2	1.3	0.9	4.6	2.9
Therapist (physical, occupational, speech)	3.9	4.3	3.3	3.0	4.7	3.7	2.5	4.7	4.7	3.5	2.4	3.4	2.4
Teacher or administrator (elementary)	6.7	8.6	3.5	6.7	9.8	7.1	5.3	7.7	9.1	3.9	1.9	8.6	3.5
Teacher or administrator (secondary)	4.3	5.1	2.9	2.8	5.8	4.2	2.9	4.5	5.7	3.2	1.8	3.6	1.6
Veterinarian	1.8	1.6	2.1	0.7	1.2	2.1	2.8	0.9	2.0	2.5	0.8	0.3	1.2
Writer or journalist	3.5	3.3	3.9	2.8	2.8	4.0	4.6	3.3	3.8	3.6	5.0	2.4	3.4
Skilled trades	0.1	0.1	0.1	0.0	0.1	0.2	0.1	0.1	0.2	0.1	0.1	0.1	0.0
Laborer (unskilled)	0.2	0.2	0.1	0.2	0.2	0.1	0.2	0.2	0.1	0.2	0.1	0.2	0.1
Semi-skilled worker	0.1	0.1	0.1	0.1	0.2	0.1	0.1	0.1	0.1	0.1	0.1	0.1	0.1
Unemployed	1.3	1.4	1.2	3.1	1.5	1.2	1.3	1.2	1.2	1.3	0.9	3.9	2.0
Other	9.9	10.4	9.0	11.3	10.1	10.9	11.6	10.2	10.5	9.5	7.2	10.9	11.9
Undecided	14.5	13.6	16.2	5.8	13.2	14.1	15.6	12.4	13.1	16.3	15.6	5.6	6.0

WEIGHTED NATIONAL NORMS FOR FRESHMAN WOMEN, FALL 2008

	ALL BACC. INSTS.	ALL 4-YR. COLLEGES	ALL UNI-VERSITIES	ALL BLACK COLLEGES	FOUR-YEAR COLLEGES PUBLIC	ALL PRIV.	NONSECT.	CATHOLIC	OTH. REL.	UNIVERSITIES PUBLIC	PRIVATE	BLACK COLLEGES PUBLIC	PRIVATE
Your father's occupation [3]													
Artist	1.2	1.2	1.1	1.1	1.0	1.5	2.0	0.9	1.3	1.1	1.2	1.1	1.1
Business	26.0	24.3	28.7	13.2	23.3	25.7	25.9	26.5	24.9	27.6	32.7	12.2	14.8
Business (clerical)	1.2	1.2	1.2	1.0	1.2	1.2	1.2	1.2	1.2	1.2	1.1	0.6	1.5
Clergy	0.8	0.9	0.5	1.8	0.6	1.4	0.6	0.5	2.7	0.5	0.7	1.8	1.8
College teacher	0.6	0.6	0.8	0.4	0.3	0.9	1.2	0.4	0.9	0.6	1.4	0.2	0.6
Doctor (MD or DDS)	2.6	1.8	3.8	0.6	1.1	2.7	3.1	1.9	2.6	3.1	6.6	0.1	1.3
Education (secondary)	2.0	2.1	1.9	1.8	2.1	2.2	1.9	1.9	2.7	1.9	1.7	1.6	2.2
Education (elementary)	0.6	0.7	0.6	0.6	0.7	0.7	0.6	0.7	0.8	0.6	0.4	0.6	0.5
Engineer	8.4	7.2	10.4	4.4	7.3	7.0	6.8	7.2	7.1	10.6	9.6	4.0	5.0
Farmer or forester	1.4	1.3	1.5	0.4	1.2	1.4	0.7	1.0	2.4	1.8	0.7	0.4	0.3
Health professional	1.3	1.2	1.6	0.8	1.2	1.3	1.4	1.1	1.3	1.5	1.6	0.7	0.9
Homemaker (full-time)	0.2	0.2	0.2	0.1	0.2	0.2	0.3	0.2	0.2	0.2	0.2	0.2	0.1
Lawyer	2.3	1.8	3.1	0.7	1.2	2.5	3.3	2.0	1.9	2.6	5.2	0.3	1.5
Military (career)	1.6	1.8	1.2	4.1	2.3	1.3	1.1	1.2	1.5	1.3	0.8	4.5	3.5
Nurse	0.5	0.5	0.4	0.6	0.5	0.5	0.5	0.6	0.5	0.4	0.4	0.7	0.4
Research scientist	0.7	0.5	1.1	0.2	0.4	0.6	0.8	0.4	0.5	1.0	1.5	0.3	0.2
Social/welfare/rec worker	0.5	0.6	0.4	1.1	0.6	0.6	0.5	0.6	0.6	0.4	0.4	0.9	1.3
Skilled worker	6.4	7.0	5.4	6.3	7.3	6.7	6.5	7.4	6.7	5.7	4.5	6.1	6.7
Semi-skilled worker	2.7	2.8	2.5	3.3	3.1	2.4	2.2	2.6	2.5	2.7	1.6	3.7	2.5
Unskilled worker	3.3	3.6	2.7	3.8	4.1	2.9	2.6	3.7	2.7	3.0	1.5	4.3	3.1
Unemployed	3.8	4.1	3.3	9.9	4.3	3.8	4.4	3.9	3.1	3.5	2.5	11.0	8.0
Other	31.9	34.6	27.3	43.9	36.2	32.6	32.5	34.3	31.7	28.3	23.6	44.6	42.6
Your mother's occupation [3]													
Artist	1.8	1.7	2.0	0.7	1.4	2.2	3.0	1.3	1.9	1.9	2.5	0.7	0.8
Business	16.4	16.0	16.9	15.2	16.1	15.9	16.1	16.2	15.5	16.8	17.4	14.1	16.8
Business (clerical)	4.1	4.2	3.9	3.9	4.3	4.1	3.9	4.2	4.2	4.1	3.4	3.7	4.2
Clergy	0.2	0.3	0.2	0.3	0.2	0.4	0.2	0.3	0.6	0.2	0.3	0.4	0.2
College teacher	0.5	0.4	0.5	0.2	0.2	0.6	0.7	0.3	0.6	0.4	1.0	0.1	0.3
Doctor (MD or DDS)	1.3	1.1	1.6	0.9	0.8	1.4	1.8	0.9	1.2	1.3	2.9	0.3	1.9
Education (secondary)	4.2	4.2	4.3	4.1	4.1	4.3	4.0	3.7	4.9	4.3	4.3	3.5	5.2
Education (elementary)	7.5	7.4	7.6	6.1	7.2	7.6	6.8	7.4	8.7	7.7	6.9	6.5	5.4
Engineer	0.8	0.6	1.3	0.5	0.6	0.6	0.6	0.4	0.6	1.2	1.4	0.5	0.6
Farmer or forester	0.2	0.2	0.2	0.1	0.2	0.2	0.2	0.2	0.3	0.3	0.2	0.1	0.2
Health professional	3.4	3.2	3.7	2.4	3.1	3.2	3.2	3.3	3.2	3.8	3.6	2.6	2.2
Homemaker (full-time)	9.4	8.2	11.5	1.9	7.4	9.4	8.9	8.8	10.1	10.8	14.0	1.8	2.1
Lawyer	0.9	0.7	1.3	0.6	0.4	1.0	1.4	0.6	0.7	1.0	2.3	0.5	0.7
Military (career)	0.2	0.2	0.2	0.7	0.3	0.2	0.2	0.1	0.2	0.2	0.1	0.6	0.9
Nurse	8.0	8.4	7.3	8.7	8.5	8.2	7.4	9.5	8.5	7.4	7.0	9.1	8.1
Research scientist	0.4	0.3	0.6	0.1	0.2	0.3	0.4	0.2	0.3	0.6	0.8	0.1	0.2
Social/welfare/rec worker	1.8	1.9	1.6	3.2	1.5	1.9	1.9	1.9	1.9	1.6	1.5	3.6	2.7
Skilled worker	1.3	1.3	1.3	1.9	1.5	1.2	1.1	1.3	1.2	1.4	0.9	2.2	1.5
Semi-skilled worker	1.6	1.6	1.6	1.8	1.7	1.5	1.5	1.8	1.4	1.7	1.1	1.8	1.8
Unskilled worker	1.7	1.7	1.6	2.0	2.1	1.3	1.1	1.7	1.3	1.8	0.9	2.5	1.2
Unemployed	6.7	6.9	6.4	8.3	7.3	6.4	6.8	6.2	6.1	6.5	5.9	8.6	7.7
Other	27.6	29.5	24.4	36.2	30.6	28.0	28.5	29.7	26.6	25.1	21.6	36.6	35.5
How would you characterize your political views?													
Far left	2.9	2.9	3.0	3.8	2.5	3.4	4.7	2.1	2.5	2.7	3.9	4.1	3.2
Liberal	34.5	31.8	39.0	38.3	30.4	33.6	41.4	32.4	24.5	38.0	42.6	36.8	40.7
Middle-of-the-road	42.5	44.5	39.2	38.2	47.0	41.3	39.9	45.3	40.9	39.9	36.5	36.9	40.1
Conservative	18.9	19.5	18.0	17.3	18.8	20.3	13.2	18.9	29.9	18.4	16.3	19.4	14.0
Far right	1.1	1.3	0.9	2.5	1.2	1.4	0.7	1.3	2.3	0.9	0.7	2.7	2.0

WEIGHTED NATIONAL NORMS FOR FRESHMAN WOMEN, FALL 2008

	ALL BACC. INSTS.	ALL 4-YR. COLLEGES	ALL UNI-VERSITIES	ALL BLACK COLLEGES	FOUR-YEAR COLLEGES PUBLIC	ALL. PRIV.	NONSECT.	CATHOLIC	OTH. REL.	UNIVERSITIES PUBLIC	PRIVATE	BLACK COLLEGES PUBLIC	PRIVATE
Student agrees "strongly" or "somewhat":													
There is too much concern in the courts for the rights of criminals	55.0	56.3	52.8	48.0	58.7	53.2	49.4	55.8	56.4	53.6	49.7	51.6	42.4
Abortion should be legal	57.6	54.5	62.8	49.7	54.2	54.9	66.7	51.4	42.4	61.9	66.4	47.5	53.1
The death penalty should be abolished	38.0	36.6	40.5	45.6	33.3	40.8	44.3	41.4	36.3	38.3	48.6	46.0	45.0
Marijuana should be legalized	36.8	36.4	37.6	36.4	36.4	36.3	43.9	33.4	28.7	37.0	39.7	38.4	33.2
It is important to have laws prohibiting homosexual relationships	17.9	19.3	15.4	27.4	18.9	20.0	12.7	16.7	30.7	15.9	13.5	28.1	26.2
Racial discrimination is no longer a major problem in America	16.0	16.6	15.1	12.3	17.3	15.6	13.7	15.7	17.8	15.2	14.7	12.7	11.6
Realistically, an individual can do little to bring about changes in our society	24.0	25.7	21.1	34.0	27.1	23.9	24.1	24.4	23.5	21.6	19.5	37.2	29.1
Wealthy people should pay a larger share of taxes than they do now	61.2	62.0	59.8	63.2	61.2	63.0	66.2	62.6	59.3	60.1	58.6	62.6	64.3
Same-sex couples should have the right to legal marital status	72.4	70.6	75.4	57.8	71.3	69.7	80.3	73.3	54.7	74.7	78.2	56.9	59.2
Affirmative action in college admissions should be abolished	42.7	39.4	48.4	31.7	38.4	40.6	40.8	40.9	40.2	47.3	52.4	34.7	27.2
Federal military spending should be increased	24.4	26.7	20.3	32.8	28.2	24.8	20.9	26.0	28.9	20.6	19.3	36.2	27.7
The federal government should do more to control the sale of handguns	79.3	78.7	80.2	84.2	77.7	80.1	83.4	81.4	75.2	79.5	83.1	84.4	83.8
Only volunteers should serve in the armed forces	67.5	66.3	69.6	62.4	65.0	68.0	71.8	66.8	64.0	68.9	72.4	59.3	67.1
The federal government is not doing enough to control environmental pollution	81.9	80.8	83.9	80.2	80.4	81.4	85.6	81.3	76.3	83.4	85.5	80.2	80.1
A national health care plan is needed to cover everybody's medical costs	74.4	75.8	72.1	87.0	75.6	76.1	81.1	77.4	69.3	71.9	72.7	88.2	85.2
Undocumented immigrants should be denied access to public education	42.7	43.9	40.5	40.5	46.0	41.2	36.9	43.2	45.4	41.5	36.8	43.3	36.1
Through hard work, everybody can succeed in American society	77.9	78.3	77.2	78.4	80.4	75.5	71.8	79.3	77.8	78.5	72.5	80.8	74.8
Dissent is a critical component of the political process	58.8	56.0	63.7	54.8	54.7	57.7	59.0	55.8	57.1	61.5	71.1	55.8	53.1
Colleges have the right to ban extreme speakers from campus	37.6	38.6	35.9	41.2	38.0	39.4	34.0	40.5	45.2	35.6	37.0	41.5	40.6
Students from disadvantaged social backgrounds should be given preferential treatment in college admissions	38.1	39.4	35.8	53.3	39.4	39.4	39.9	37.6	39.7	36.2	34.6	53.8	52.4
The federal government should raise taxes to reduce the deficit	24.4	22.4	28.0	19.5	21.6	23.4	25.1	22.1	22.1	27.4	30.2	18.1	21.6
Addressing global warming should be a federal priority	77.4	76.1	79.7	77.4	75.4	77.0	83.3	78.1	68.8	79.0	82.2	76.1	79.4

WEIGHTED NATIONAL NORMS FOR FRESHMAN WOMEN, FALL 2008

	ALL BACC. INSTS.	ALL 4-YR. COLLEGES	ALL UNI-VERSITIES	ALL BLACK COLLEGES	FOUR-YEAR COLLEGES					UNIVERSITIES		BLACK COLLEGES	
					PUBLIC	ALL PRIV.	NONSECT.	CATHOLIC	OTH. REL.	PUBLIC	PRIVATE	PUBLIC	PRIVATE
DURING YOUR LAST YEAR IN HIGH SCHOOL, HOW MUCH TIME DID YOU SPEND DURING A TYPICAL WEEK DOING THE FOLLOWING?													
Studying/homework													
None	0.9	1.2	0.6	1.5	1.4	0.8	0.9	0.8	0.8	0.6	0.5	1.4	1.8
Less than one hour	8.1	9.6	5.4	10.2	11.3	7.4	7.9	6.9	7.1	5.9	3.6	11.2	8.6
1 to 2 hours	20.0	22.8	15.1	30.1	25.5	19.2	19.4	19.1	19.1	16.2	11.0	31.9	27.3
3 to 5 hours	29.6	30.5	28.0	29.6	31.6	29.0	27.7	29.5	30.5	29.7	21.7	32.0	26.0
6 to 10 hours	21.3	19.5	24.5	15.8	17.7	21.8	21.0	23.2	22.0	24.5	24.7	14.0	18.7
11 to 15 hours	10.6	8.9	13.5	6.9	7.0	11.3	11.5	11.2	11.1	12.5	17.2	5.4	9.3
16 to 20 hours	5.6	4.5	7.4	3.2	3.3	6.1	6.7	5.4	5.6	6.3	11.7	2.4	4.4
Over 20 hours	3.9	3.1	5.5	2.6	2.1	4.3	4.9	3.9	3.7	4.4	9.7	1.8	3.9
Socializing with friends													
None	0.2	0.3	0.2	0.6	0.3	0.2	0.2	0.3	0.3	0.2	0.2	0.6	0.7
Less than one hour	1.5	1.7	1.2	2.6	1.8	1.5	1.5	1.5	1.7	1.3	0.9	2.7	2.6
1 to 2 hours	6.9	7.2	6.5	9.0	7.5	6.7	6.5	6.7	6.9	6.8	5.5	9.1	8.8
3 to 5 hours	20.4	20.2	20.7	23.3	20.4	20.0	19.4	19.0	21.2	20.9	19.9	24.1	22.1
6 to 10 hours	27.3	26.3	28.9	23.1	25.9	26.9	26.3	27.1	27.5	28.6	29.9	22.8	23.6
11 to 15 hours	18.5	18.1	19.3	14.5	17.7	18.6	18.5	19.0	18.5	19.1	20.1	14.1	15.1
16 to 20 hours	11.3	11.3	11.1	9.7	10.9	11.9	12.2	12.3	11.2	11.0	11.5	9.9	9.3
Over 20 hours	13.9	14.9	12.1	17.1	15.4	14.3	15.4	14.2	12.9	12.2	12.0	16.7	17.9
Talking with teachers outside of class													
None	7.6	8.2	6.7	9.3	9.2	6.9	6.9	7.4	6.7	7.0	5.2	10.9	6.9
Less than one hour	40.6	40.4	41.1	35.1	41.9	38.3	36.9	39.7	39.4	42.3	36.6	36.9	32.2
1 to 2 hours	33.2	32.6	34.3	30.7	31.5	33.9	33.9	33.4	34.2	33.5	37.2	29.6	32.5
3 to 5 hours	13.0	13.0	13.0	16.0	11.9	14.3	15.2	13.7	13.6	12.4	15.4	14.9	17.7
6 to 10 hours	3.4	3.6	3.2	5.2	3.2	4.1	4.5	3.6	3.7	3.1	3.7	4.4	6.4
11 to 15 hours	1.2	1.3	1.0	2.0	1.3	1.3	1.5	1.2	1.3	1.0	1.1	1.5	2.7
16 to 20 hours	0.5	0.5	0.4	0.9	0.5	0.5	0.6	0.5	0.4	0.4	0.4	0.9	0.9
Over 20 hours	0.4	0.5	0.3	0.8	0.4	0.5	0.5	0.5	0.5	0.3	0.3	0.9	0.8
Exercise or sports													
None	6.0	6.8	4.7	13.6	7.1	6.4	7.2	5.5	5.9	4.8	4.0	14.5	12.1
Less than one hour	11.3	11.9	10.4	16.2	12.7	10.8	11.5	9.9	10.4	10.7	9.3	17.7	13.9
1 to 2 hours	17.6	18.0	17.0	19.7	18.5	17.2	17.9	16.8	16.6	17.3	15.9	20.1	19.1
3 to 5 hours	20.3	19.7	21.4	17.5	19.9	19.4	19.6	19.4	19.0	21.1	22.3	17.1	18.2
6 to 10 hours	17.9	16.8	19.7	13.1	16.3	17.4	17.1	18.0	17.6	19.5	20.3	12.8	13.7
11 to 15 hours	12.7	12.3	13.3	7.2	11.7	13.1	12.1	14.4	13.5	13.1	13.8	6.1	8.8
16 to 20 hours	7.2	7.1	7.2	4.1	6.5	7.9	7.5	7.9	8.5	7.1	7.6	3.4	5.2
Over 20 hours	7.1	7.4	6.5	8.6	7.1	7.8	7.1	8.1	8.5	6.4	6.9	8.3	9.0
Partying													
None	32.3	32.5	32.0	23.2	30.8	34.7	29.6	29.4	44.0	32.7	29.8	23.1	23.4
Less than one hour	15.2	14.8	15.8	11.7	14.7	15.0	14.8	14.8	15.3	15.8	15.9	11.0	12.9
1 to 2 hours	17.9	17.5	18.7	19.7	17.8	17.1	17.8	18.6	15.5	18.7	18.7	19.6	19.7
3 to 5 hours	18.4	18.2	18.9	25.1	18.7	17.5	17.3	19.8	14.1	18.5	20.2	25.7	24.2
6 to 10 hours	9.6	9.7	9.5	10.7	10.1	9.2	10.8	10.8	6.3	9.3	10.2	11.3	9.8
11 to 15 hours	3.6	4.0	3.0	4.3	4.3	3.6	4.3	3.8	2.7	3.0	3.1	3.5	5.4
16 to 20 hours	1.5	1.7	1.2	2.0	1.8	1.5	1.9	1.5	1.0	1.1	1.3	2.2	1.5
Over 20 hours	1.3	1.6	0.8	3.4	1.8	1.3	1.6	1.3	1.0	0.8	0.9	3.6	3.1

WEIGHTED NATIONAL NORMS FOR FRESHMAN WOMEN, FALL 2008

	ALL BACC. INSTS.	ALL 4-YR. COLLEGES	ALL UNI-VERSITIES	ALL BLACK COLLEGES	FOUR-YEAR COLLEGES PUBLIC	ALL PRIV.	NONSECT.	CATHOLIC	OTH. REL.	UNIVERSITIES PUBLIC	PRIVATE	BLACK COLLEGES PUBLIC	PRIVATE
DURING YOUR LAST YEAR IN HIGH SCHOOL, HOW MUCH TIME DID YOU SPEND DURING A TYPICAL WEEK DOING THE FOLLOWING?													
Working (for pay)													
None	31.9	29.8	35.6	33.9	28.0	32.0	33.7	27.6	32.4	34.1	41.2	31.9	37.1
Less than one hour	2.4	2.2	2.7	1.8	2.0	2.5	2.6	2.1	2.5	2.5	3.3	1.9	1.7
1 to 2 hours	3.8	3.4	4.4	2.2	3.0	3.9	3.9	3.6	4.1	4.1	5.6	2.0	2.5
3 to 5 hours	7.7	7.4	8.3	6.1	7.0	7.9	7.5	8.3	8.3	8.0	9.4	6.6	5.3
6 to 10 hours	13.1	12.9	13.6	12.2	12.4	13.5	12.8	15.0	13.4	13.7	12.9	12.9	11.2
11 to 15 hours	13.8	13.9	13.7	9.5	14.4	13.2	12.4	15.1	13.3	14.3	11.4	9.7	9.2
16 to 20 hours	13.9	15.0	12.0	12.7	16.3	13.3	13.1	14.2	12.9	12.8	9.1	12.8	12.5
Over 20 hours	13.4	15.6	9.7	21.5	17.0	13.8	14.1	14.2	13.1	10.4	7.1	22.3	20.3
Volunteer work													
None	22.8	25.3	18.4	24.6	28.1	21.7	23.7	20.3	20.0	19.3	15.1	28.4	18.7
Less than one hour	20.8	20.7	21.1	12.9	21.2	20.0	18.9	19.6	21.6	21.7	18.9	14.1	11.2
1 to 2 hours	27.1	25.8	29.5	23.7	24.6	27.3	26.5	28.0	28.0	29.1	30.9	23.1	24.5
3 to 5 hours	16.6	15.5	18.6	19.4	14.2	17.2	17.0	18.4	16.9	17.9	21.1	17.9	21.7
6 to 10 hours	6.7	6.5	7.1	8.4	6.0	7.1	7.1	7.3	7.1	6.8	8.2	6.6	11.1
11 to 15 hours	2.5	2.5	2.5	3.9	2.3	2.9	3.0	2.6	2.9	2.4	2.8	3.8	4.2
16 to 20 hours	1.3	1.3	1.2	2.5	1.3	1.4	1.5	1.3	1.4	1.2	1.3	2.5	2.7
Over 20 hours	2.1	2.3	1.6	4.6	2.3	2.3	2.4	2.6	2.1	1.6	1.7	3.7	5.9
Student clubs/groups													
None	22.6	26.1	16.5	24.1	28.9	22.5	23.6	21.4	21.8	18.1	10.7	27.6	18.6
Less than one hour	13.3	13.5	13.1	10.2	14.0	12.7	11.9	13.4	13.4	13.8	10.8	10.3	10.2
1 to 2 hours	26.8	25.6	28.9	25.4	24.7	26.8	26.2	27.7	27.1	28.9	29.2	26.4	24.0
3 to 5 hours	19.6	18.2	22.1	21.1	16.5	20.3	20.2	20.8	20.2	21.2	25.6	20.2	22.4
6 to 10 hours	9.2	8.5	10.5	9.3	7.9	9.4	9.6	9.1	9.3	9.8	13.1	8.0	11.4
11 to 15 hours	4.0	3.8	4.3	4.4	3.5	4.1	4.2	3.8	4.1	4.1	5.2	3.0	6.5
16 to 20 hours	2.0	1.9	2.1	2.2	1.8	1.9	2.1	1.9	1.8	2.0	2.6	1.7	2.9
Over 20 hours	2.4	2.5	2.4	3.3	2.7	2.2	2.2	2.0	2.2	2.2	2.8	2.9	4.1
Watching TV													
None	6.6	6.3	7.0	4.7	6.0	6.8	7.4	5.1	6.8	6.9	7.3	4.8	4.6
Less than one hour	16.3	16.5	16.0	12.7	17.1	15.6	15.4	16.1	15.6	16.4	14.7	13.0	12.3
1 to 2 hours	26.3	26.1	26.7	21.3	26.6	25.6	25.3	26.1	25.8	27.0	25.6	21.6	20.9
3 to 5 hours	27.9	27.5	28.7	26.2	27.1	27.9	27.5	28.6	28.1	28.4	29.8	26.5	25.8
6 to 10 hours	14.0	14.0	14.0	16.2	13.5	14.6	14.3	15.0	14.9	13.7	14.8	15.3	17.5
11 to 15 hours	4.7	4.9	4.3	8.8	4.8	5.1	5.5	4.9	4.7	4.3	4.4	9.2	8.2
16 to 20 hours	1.9	2.1	1.6	3.7	2.2	1.9	1.9	1.8	2.0	1.5	1.8	3.9	3.5
Over 20 hours	2.3	2.6	1.7	6.3	2.6	2.5	2.7	2.4	2.3	1.7	1.6	5.7	7.3
Household/childcare duties													
None	12.9	12.9	12.9	14.3	12.3	13.6	15.5	11.2	12.6	12.3	14.8	14.3	14.3
Less than one hour	19.0	18.0	20.8	13.4	17.7	18.4	18.8	17.6	18.4	20.7	21.4	14.0	12.4
1 to 2 hours	32.5	31.7	33.8	27.8	31.4	32.0	31.1	32.7	32.8	33.9	33.7	28.5	26.8
3 to 5 hours	21.6	21.8	21.1	21.2	22.3	21.3	20.1	23.2	21.7	21.4	20.0	20.9	21.7
6 to 10 hours	7.9	8.5	6.8	11.0	8.3	8.1	8.2	8.5	7.8	7.0	6.3	11.0	11.0
11 to 15 hours	2.8	3.2	2.2	4.2	3.4	3.0	2.9	3.1	3.1	2.2	2.0	3.2	5.6
16 to 20 hours	1.3	1.4	1.0	3.1	1.5	1.4	1.4	1.4	1.4	1.1	0.8	3.4	2.7
Over 20 hours	2.0	2.4	1.3	5.0	2.7	2.2	2.2	2.3	2.1	1.4	0.9	4.8	5.4

WEIGHTED NATIONAL NORMS FOR FRESHMAN WOMEN, FALL 2008

	ALL BACC. INSTS.	ALL 4-YR. COLLEGES	ALL UNI-VERSITIES	ALL BLACK COLLEGES	FOUR-YEAR COLLEGES					UNIVERSITIES		BLACK COLLEGES	
					PUBLIC	ALL PRIV.	NONSECT.	CATHOLIC	OTH. REL.	PUBLIC	PRIVATE	PUBLIC	PRIVATE
DURING YOUR LAST YEAR IN HIGH SCHOOL, HOW MUCH TIME DID YOU SPEND DURING A TYPICAL WEEK DOING THE FOLLOWING?													
Reading for pleasure													
None	18.8	20.3	16.3	20.0	22.1	17.9	16.7	19.8	18.3	16.8	14.2	21.9	17.1
Less than one hour	23.1	22.7	23.8	21.6	23.2	21.9	21.3	24.0	21.7	24.1	22.8	22.3	20.5
1 to 2 hours	25.6	24.5	27.6	25.7	23.8	25.3	25.6	25.7	24.8	27.3	28.4	26.1	25.2
3 to 5 hours	17.9	17.2	19.0	16.7	16.1	18.7	19.5	16.8	18.7	18.7	20.3	16.2	17.5
6 to 10 hours	8.4	8.5	8.2	8.1	8.1	9.1	9.4	7.7	9.4	8.0	8.9	7.1	9.6
11 to 15 hours	3.3	3.5	3.0	3.3	3.3	3.7	3.9	3.2	3.8	2.9	3.1	2.5	4.5
16 to 20 hours	1.4	1.5	1.1	1.6	1.6	1.5	1.6	1.2	1.5	1.0	1.2	1.4	1.7
Over 20 hours	1.5	1.8	1.1	2.9	1.8	1.8	2.0	1.6	1.7	1.1	1.1	2.4	3.8
Playing video/computer games													
None	58.7	57.6	60.8	55.7	57.4	57.9	57.6	58.9	57.6	60.3	62.4	54.1	58.1
Less than one hour	21.2	21.4	20.7	19.5	21.5	21.4	20.8	21.6	22.1	21.0	19.5	20.0	18.8
1 to 2 hours	11.0	11.3	10.4	13.1	11.7	10.9	10.7	10.9	11.3	10.4	10.1	14.0	11.7
3 to 5 hours	5.4	5.6	5.0	6.1	5.5	5.7	6.3	5.3	5.1	5.0	4.9	6.4	5.6
6 to 10 hours	2.1	2.2	1.9	2.7	2.2	2.2	2.4	1.9	2.2	1.9	1.9	2.7	2.7
11 to 15 hours	0.8	0.9	0.7	1.5	0.9	1.0	1.1	0.8	0.9	0.7	0.7	1.5	1.5
16 to 20 hours	0.4	0.4	0.3	0.3	0.4	0.4	0.4	0.3	0.3	0.3	0.2	0.2	0.5
Over 20 hours	0.5	0.5	0.3	1.0	0.5	0.5	0.6	0.3	0.5	0.4	0.3	1.0	1.1
Online social networks (MySpace, Facebook, etc.)													
None	9.0	9.5	8.2	8.6	10.4	8.3	7.9	8.6	8.7	8.8	6.0	8.6	8.6
Less than one hour	16.7	16.8	16.7	15.9	18.1	15.0	15.3	16.0	14.1	17.5	13.9	15.7	16.0
1 to 2 hours	27.3	26.7	28.4	24.4	27.0	26.4	26.2	27.1	26.3	28.5	28.1	25.5	22.7
3 to 5 hours	25.8	25.0	27.2	22.1	23.6	26.8	26.6	26.3	27.4	26.4	30.1	23.2	20.3
6 to 10 hours	11.7	11.8	11.5	13.5	11.2	12.7	12.6	12.0	13.2	11.1	13.1	13.0	14.3
11 to 15 hours	4.5	4.7	4.1	6.1	4.4	5.2	5.3	5.0	5.0	4.0	4.5	5.1	7.5
16 to 20 hours	2.1	2.2	1.8	3.7	2.1	2.4	2.7	2.2	2.3	1.7	2.1	3.4	4.1
Over 20 hours	2.8	3.2	2.1	5.8	3.2	3.1	3.4	2.9	2.9	2.1	2.3	5.4	6.4
Are you: [4]													
White/Caucasian	70.8	71.5	69.6	4.2	69.6	73.9	69.6	73.3	79.9	69.7	69.3	4.5	3.7
African American/Black	12.5	15.5	7.3	94.8	15.7	15.1	16.7	14.1	13.7	7.1	7.8	93.8	96.5
American Indian/Alaska Native	2.7	3.1	2.1	3.4	3.6	2.5	2.7	1.8	2.6	2.2	1.8	3.5	3.3
Asian American/Asian	8.3	4.7	14.6	0.9	3.9	5.6	7.8	4.9	3.3	13.9	17.0	0.6	1.5
Native Hawaiian/Pacific Islander	1.3	1.2	1.4	0.4	1.4	1.0	0.9	1.8	0.7	1.5	1.0	0.3	0.5
Mexican American/Chicano	6.0	5.3	7.1	0.5	7.4	2.7	1.5	4.8	2.9	8.1	3.5	0.6	0.2
Puerto Rican	1.5	1.7	1.1	2.1	1.2	2.4	3.4	2.1	1.1	0.9	1.8	2.6	1.2
Other Latino	4.5	4.4	4.7	1.5	4.7	4.0	5.1	4.3	2.5	4.4	5.8	1.4	1.7
Other	4.1	4.2	3.9	4.4	4.2	4.3	5.2	3.7	3.5	3.7	4.6	4.0	4.9

WEIGHTED NATIONAL NORMS FOR FRESHMAN WOMEN, FALL 2008

	ALL BACC. INSTS.	ALL 4-YR. COLLEGES	ALL UNI-VERSITIES	ALL BLACK COLLEGES	FOUR-YEAR COLLEGES					UNIVERSITIES		BLACK COLLEGES	
					PUBLIC	ALL PRIV.	NONSECT.	CATHOLIC	OTH. REL.	PUBLIC	PRIVATE	PUBLIC	PRIVATE
Reasons noted as "very important" in influencing student's decision to attend this particular college													
My parents wanted me to come here	15.7	16.2	14.8	20.3	16.6	15.7	13.6	18.2	16.8	14.7	15.2	19.6	21.5
My relatives wanted me to come here	5.6	5.9	5.0	12.4	6.3	5.5	4.7	6.7	5.8	5.1	4.7	12.7	12.0
My teacher advised me	7.0	7.5	6.1	8.6	7.6	7.4	8.4	7.5	6.2	6.0	6.4	8.8	8.4
This college has a very good academic reputation	68.9	66.7	72.7	63.4	62.6	71.9	71.8	76.1	69.6	70.1	82.1	55.5	75.4
This college has a good reputation for its social activities	40.2	38.7	42.7	39.8	37.9	39.8	38.5	40.6	41.2	43.3	40.4	35.1	46.9
I was offered financial assistance	47.0	50.6	40.8	54.6	41.2	62.5	57.1	67.4	66.7	38.1	50.6	60.1	46.1
The cost of attending this college	43.3	46.1	38.3	53.2	53.3	36.6	36.3	40.2	35.0	40.6	30.0	62.1	39.3
High school counselor advised me	10.7	11.7	9.0	14.1	12.2	11.1	12.9	12.4	8.0	8.6	10.3	14.6	13.2
Private college counselor advised me	3.6	4.1	2.7	5.2	2.9	5.6	5.7	5.2	5.7	2.3	4.2	4.5	6.3
I wanted to live near home	23.1	26.7	16.7	21.8	29.0	23.9	22.1	29.8	22.8	17.5	13.8	25.1	16.8
Not offered aid by first choice	9.4	9.7	9.0	15.6	9.3	10.1	10.1	11.5	9.4	8.9	9.2	17.4	12.9
Could not afford first choice	12.6	13.1	11.8	17.8	14.8	10.8	10.9	12.8	9.5	12.5	9.0	20.9	13.0
This college's graduates gain admission to top graduate/professional schools	38.6	35.4	44.2	45.5	31.3	40.7	42.8	43.6	36.5	41.3	54.8	36.0	59.8
This college's graduates get good jobs	57.3	55.6	60.4	59.9	51.0	61.5	63.2	66.2	56.8	57.3	71.3	53.4	69.7
I was attracted by the religious affiliation/orientation of the college	8.6	10.4	5.5	14.9	4.4	18.0	5.8	18.8	32.8	3.7	11.8	9.5	23.0
I wanted to go to a school about the size of this college	44.5	48.5	37.5	40.6	40.7	58.4	55.0	58.5	62.6	34.8	47.1	37.7	45.0
Rankings in national magazines	17.8	13.6	25.2	24.0	11.2	16.7	19.2	16.8	13.5	23.1	32.8	16.1	36.0
Information from a website	21.9	21.6	22.4	30.1	19.9	23.7	27.3	21.8	20.2	20.9	27.4	25.5	36.9
I was admitted through an Early Action or Early Decision program	12.9	12.5	13.8	12.8	9.7	16.0	17.6	15.7	14.1	11.1	23.5	10.2	16.7
The athletic department recruited me	6.1	7.7	3.3	6.3	5.4	10.6	8.3	10.0	13.8	2.7	5.3	6.1	6.6
A visit to campus	46.1	46.7	45.0	41.1	40.1	55.2	55.9	52.0	56.1	42.7	53.3	39.5	43.6

WEIGHTED NATIONAL NORMS FOR FRESHMAN WOMEN, FALL 2008

YOUR PROBABLE MAJOR	ALL BACC. INSTS.	ALL 4-YR. COLLEGES	ALL UNIVERSITIES	ALL BLACK COLLEGES	FOUR-YEAR COLLEGES					UNIVERSITIES		BLACK COLLEGES	
					PUBLIC	ALL PRIV.	NONSECT.	CATHOLIC	OTH. REL.	PUBLIC	PRIVATE	PUBLIC	PRIVATE
Arts and Humanities													
Art, fine and applied	3.9	4.6	2.6	0.5	3.4	6.2	10.8	1.8	2.9	2.8	2.2	0.6	0.4
English (language & literature)	2.5	2.5	2.6	1.4	2.0	3.1	3.5	2.3	3.0	2.5	2.9	0.8	2.3
History	1.1	1.1	1.1	0.3	1.0	1.2	1.3	1.0	1.4	1.0	1.4	0.2	0.4
Journalism	2.1	1.9	2.5	1.5	1.8	2.0	2.2	2.1	1.6	2.4	3.1	1.1	2.2
Language and Literature (except English)	0.8	0.7	0.9	0.1	0.6	0.9	0.9	0.5	1.1	0.9	1.1	0.0	0.2
Music	1.2	1.3	1.1	1.0	1.2	1.5	0.9	0.5	2.7	1.0	1.6	0.8	1.4
Philosophy	0.2	0.2	0.2	0.0	0.1	0.2	0.2	0.1	0.2	0.2	0.3	0.0	0.1
Speech	0.1	0.1	0.1	0.1	0.2	0.1	0.1	0.1	0.1	0.1	0.2	0.1	0.1
Theater or Drama	1.4	1.5	1.1	0.7	1.5	1.6	2.0	0.7	1.5	1.0	1.5	0.6	0.8
Theology or Religion	0.2	0.2	0.1	0.0	0.0	0.5	0.1	0.3	1.0	0.0	0.1	0.0	0.0
Other Arts and Humanities	1.5	1.4	1.6	0.6	1.3	1.7	2.4	0.7	1.2	1.5	1.6	0.7	0.6
Biological Science													
Biology (general)	5.9	5.0	7.4	11.4	4.4	5.9	5.4	7.2	5.9	7.1	8.2	9.2	15.0
Biochemistry or Biophysics	1.4	0.9	2.2	0.4	0.8	1.0	0.9	1.2	1.1	2.3	1.8	0.1	0.9
Botany	0.0	0.0	0.1	0.0	0.0	0.0	0.1	0.0	0.0	0.1	0.0	0.0	0.0
Environmental Science	0.7	0.6	1.1	0.2	0.4	0.8	1.0	0.4	0.8	1.2	0.8	0.2	0.2
Marine (Life) Science	0.5	0.5	0.5	0.1	0.5	0.4	0.4	0.1	0.4	0.5	0.3	0.2	0.0
Microbiology or Bacteriology	0.3	0.1	0.6	0.2	0.1	0.2	0.2	0.1	0.1	0.7	0.3	0.1	0.3
Zoology	0.4	0.4	0.6	0.0	0.4	0.4	0.5	0.1	0.4	0.7	0.2	0.0	0.1
Other Biological Science	0.9	0.6	1.4	0.3	0.5	0.6	0.9	0.4	0.4	1.5	1.2	0.3	0.2
Business													
Accounting	2.0	2.1	1.7	3.1	2.2	2.0	2.0	2.1	2.0	1.9	1.4	3.7	2.2
Business Admin. (general)	2.6	2.6	2.5	2.8	2.7	2.5	2.4	2.3	2.6	2.7	2.0	3.1	2.3
Finance	0.8	0.6	1.2	0.4	0.5	0.7	0.8	0.8	0.4	1.0	2.1	0.5	0.4
International Business	1.4	1.2	1.9	0.9	1.0	1.4	1.6	1.6	1.2	1.7	2.4	0.6	1.4
Marketing	2.5	2.4	2.7	1.7	2.4	2.4	2.7	3.0	1.8	2.7	2.8	1.9	1.3
Management	2.4	2.4	2.3	2.9	2.5	2.3	2.6	2.1	2.0	2.6	1.5	3.1	2.5
Secretarial Studies	0.0	0.0	0.0	0.1	0.0	0.0	0.0	0.0	0.0	0.0	0.0	0.1	0.1
Other Business	0.7	0.7	0.7	0.3	0.6	0.9	1.1	0.6	0.7	0.7	0.8	0.4	0.3
Education													
Business Education	0.1	0.1	0.1	0.2	0.1	0.1	0.1	0.0	0.1	0.1	0.1	0.2	0.1
Elementary Education	6.1	7.8	3.0	7.0	8.8	6.5	5.0	6.7	8.2	3.4	1.7	9.1	3.7
Music or Art Education	0.9	1.1	0.4	0.4	1.3	0.9	0.7	0.4	1.4	0.5	0.3	0.4	0.3
Physical Education or Recreation	0.5	0.6	0.2	0.5	0.7	0.4	0.3	0.3	0.7	0.3	0.1	0.7	0.2
Secondary Education	2.3	2.8	1.4	2.1	3.0	2.5	1.8	2.9	3.2	1.5	1.0	2.6	1.3
Special Education	0.8	1.0	0.4	0.5	1.1	0.9	0.6	1.3	1.0	0.4	0.2	0.7	0.3
Other Education	0.5	0.7	0.3	1.0	0.9	0.4	0.2	0.4	0.6	0.3	0.2	1.4	0.3
Engineering													
Aeronautical or Astronautical Engineering	0.3	0.2	0.4	0.0	0.3	0.0	0.1	0.1	0.0	0.5	0.3	0.0	0.0
Civil Engineering	0.4	0.2	0.7	0.3	0.3	0.2	0.1	0.4	0.1	0.7	1.0	0.4	0.2
Chemical Engineering	0.5	0.1	1.0	0.2	0.2	0.1	0.1	0.2	0.1	0.9	1.5	0.1	0.3
Computer Engineering	0.2	0.2	0.3	0.9	0.2	0.2	0.2	0.2	0.1	0.4	0.3	0.9	0.9
Electrical or Electronic Engineering	0.2	0.1	0.4	0.2	0.1	0.1	0.1	0.1	0.0	0.3	0.4	0.2	0.1
Industrial Engineering	0.1	0.0	0.2	0.2	0.0	0.0	0.1	0.0	0.0	0.2	0.2	0.2	0.2
Mechanical Engineering	0.5	0.3	0.8	0.2	0.4	0.2	0.2	0.2	0.2	0.8	0.8	0.3	0.1
Other Engineering	0.9	0.3	1.9	0.5	0.3	0.3	0.4	0.3	0.2	1.7	2.9	0.2	0.9

WEIGHTED NATIONAL NORMS FOR FRESHMAN WOMEN, FALL 2008

YOUR PROBABLE MAJOR	ALL BACC. INSTS.	ALL 4-YR. COLLEGES	ALL UNI-VERSITIES	ALL BLACK COLLEGES	FOUR-YEAR COLLEGES PUBLIC	ALL PRIV.	NONSECT.	CATHOLIC	OTH. REL.	UNIVERSITIES PUBLIC	PRIVATE	BLACK COLLEGES PUBLIC	PRIVATE
Physical Science													
Astronomy	0.1	0.0	0.1	0.0	0.0	0.0	0.0	0.0	0.1	0.1	0.1	0.0	0.0
Atmospheric Science (incl. Meteorology)	0.1	0.1	0.1	0.0	0.1	0.0	0.0	0.0	0.1	0.1	0.1	0.1	0.0
Chemistry	1.2	1.0	1.4	1.7	1.0	1.1	0.9	1.3	1.3	1.3	1.6	0.9	3.1
Earth Science	0.1	0.1	0.1	0.0	0.1	0.1	0.1	0.0	0.0	0.1	0.1	0.0	0.0
Marine Science (incl. Oceanography)	0.2	0.2	0.1	0.1	0.2	0.1	0.2	0.1	0.2	0.1	0.1	0.1	0.1
Mathematics	0.7	0.6	0.9	0.4	0.5	0.6	0.5	0.6	0.8	0.9	1.0	0.3	0.4
Physics	0.2	0.1	0.3	0.1	0.1	0.2	0.2	0.0	0.3	0.2	0.5	0.0	0.1
Other Physical Science	0.2	0.2	0.2	0.2	0.2	0.2	0.2	0.2	0.1	0.2	0.2	0.3	0.1
Professional													
Architecture or Urban Planning	0.5	0.2	1.0	0.2	0.2	0.2	0.3	0.1	0.1	0.9	1.5	0.3	0.1
Family & Consumer Sciences	0.4	0.3	0.6	0.2	0.4	0.2	0.1	0.2	0.2	0.7	0.3	0.3	0.0
Health Technology (medical, dental, laboratory)	0.7	0.7	0.6	0.5	0.8	0.6	0.4	1.0	0.5	0.7	0.4	0.4	0.6
Library or Archival Science	0.1	0.1	0.1	0.2	0.1	0.1	0.1	0.1	0.1	0.1	0.1	0.1	0.5
Medicine, Dentistry, Veterinary Medicine	4.5	3.8	5.8	4.5	3.1	4.8	4.8	4.7	4.8	5.6	6.6	2.2	8.1
Nursing	7.5	9.6	3.9	12.6	11.4	7.3	4.4	13.7	7.5	4.1	3.0	16.9	5.9
Pharmacy	1.6	1.3	2.1	2.8	1.4	1.3	1.0	2.1	1.3	2.1	2.1	1.4	5.0
Therapy (occupational, physical, speech)	2.4	2.5	2.2	1.6	2.5	2.4	1.5	3.3	3.1	2.3	1.6	2.0	1.0
Other Professional	0.8	0.8	0.8	0.5	0.7	1.0	0.9	1.7	0.8	0.8	0.9	0.5	0.4
Social Science													
Anthropology	0.6	0.5	0.8	0.2	0.5	0.6	0.7	0.2	0.6	0.8	0.8	0.1	0.2
Economics	0.4	0.2	0.7	0.6	0.1	0.4	0.8	0.1	0.2	0.5	1.3	0.1	1.5
Ethnic Studies	0.1	0.1	0.1	0.0	0.1	0.1	0.1	0.0	0.1	0.1	0.1	0.0	0.1
Geography	0.1	0.1	0.1	0.1	0.0	0.1	0.1	0.0	0.0	0.0	0.1	0.0	0.2
Political Science (gov't., international relations)	2.9	2.4	4.0	2.6	1.9	2.9	3.3	2.5	2.6	3.4	6.1	1.6	4.0
Psychology	7.2	7.4	6.7	10.0	7.8	7.0	6.9	7.5	6.9	7.0	5.3	9.6	10.5
Public Policy	0.1	0.1	0.2	0.0	0.0	0.1	0.1	0.1	0.1	0.1	0.4	0.1	0.0
Social Work	1.1	1.4	0.5	3.4	1.6	1.1	0.9	1.0	1.5	0.6	0.4	4.5	1.5
Sociology	1.0	0.9	1.0	0.8	1.1	0.7	0.7	0.8	0.8	1.1	0.6	0.5	1.2
Women's Studies	0.0	0.0	0.0	0.0	0.0	0.0	0.0	0.0	0.1	0.0	0.0	0.0	0.1
Other Social Science	0.4	0.4	0.5	1.0	0.4	0.4	0.3	0.4	0.6	0.5	0.5	1.1	0.8
Technical													
Building Trades	0.0	0.0	0.0	0.0	0.0	0.0	0.0	0.0	0.0	0.0	0.0	0.0	0.0
Data Processing or Computer Programming	0.1	0.1	0.1	0.3	0.1	0.1	0.1	0.1	0.1	0.1	0.1	0.5	0.1
Drafting or Design	0.3	0.3	0.2	0.3	0.2	0.4	0.7	0.1	0.2	0.2	0.2	0.4	0.1
Electronics	0.0	0.0	0.1	0.0	0.0	0.0	0.0	0.0	0.0	0.1	0.0	0.0	0.0
Mechanics	0.0	0.0	0.0	0.0	0.0	0.0	0.0	0.0	0.0	0.0	0.0	0.0	0.0
Other Technical	0.0	0.0	0.0	0.0	0.0	0.1	0.1	0.0	0.0	0.0	0.0	0.1	0.0
Other Fields													
Agriculture	0.3	0.2	0.6	0.3	0.2	0.2	0.2	0.0	0.1	0.8	0.1	0.4	0.1
Communications	2.3	2.3	2.3	2.3	2.3	2.3	2.3	2.3	2.3	2.1	3.0	2.6	1.9
Computer Science	0.3	0.3	0.3	1.2	0.3	0.2	0.2	0.2	0.3	0.3	0.4	1.2	1.1
Forestry	0.0	0.0	0.1	0.0	0.0	0.0	0.0	0.0	0.0	0.1	0.0	0.0	0.0
Kinesiology	0.7	0.7	0.6	0.0	1.0	0.4	0.1	0.2	0.8	0.8	0.2	0.0	0.1
Law Enforcement	0.8	1.1	0.3	2.3	1.1	0.9	1.0	1.0	0.8	0.3	0.4	2.3	2.3
Military Science	0.0	0.0	0.0	0.0	0.0	0.0	0.0	0.0	0.0	0.0	0.0	0.0	0.1
Other Field	1.6	1.8	1.3	1.5	1.5	2.1	2.3	1.8	1.8	1.4	1.0	1.3	1.7
Undecided	6.8	6.8	6.8	2.4	7.0	6.4	6.4	6.7	6.3	6.9	6.2	2.4	2.6

WEIGHTED NATIONAL NORMS FOR FRESHMAN WOMEN, FALL 2008

Objectives considered to be "essential" or "very important":	ALL BACC. INSTS.	ALL 4-YR. COLLEGES	ALL UNI-VERSITIES	ALL BLACK COLLEGES	FOUR-YEAR COLLEGES					UNIVERSITIES		BLACK COLLEGES	
					PUBLIC	ALL PRIV.	NONSECT.	CATHOLIC	OTH. REL.	PUBLIC	PRIVATE	PUBLIC	PRIVATE
Becoming accomplished in one of the performing arts (acting, dancing, etc.)	17.2	17.9	15.9	22.6	17.0	19.0	20.3	14.7	19.7	15.2	18.5	21.5	24.5
Becoming an authority in my field	58.5	57.6	60.3	75.7	57.2	58.0	59.7	59.1	55.2	59.0	64.9	74.7	77.2
Obtaining recognition from my colleagues for contributions to my special field	57.2	56.2	59.0	69.2	55.9	56.5	59.9	59.0	51.0	58.2	61.6	68.6	70.2
Influencing the political structure	20.1	19.8	20.7	36.6	19.3	20.5	22.0	21.0	18.2	20.0	23.0	35.2	38.7
Influencing social values	47.3	47.8	46.5	60.1	46.9	48.9	47.8	50.6	49.4	45.9	48.8	59.4	61.2
Raising a family	75.4	75.8	74.6	76.2	76.7	74.7	70.1	80.3	77.3	74.9	73.5	77.3	74.5
Being very well off financially	76.1	76.5	75.3	90.7	79.7	72.5	73.7	79.3	67.1	76.2	72.1	91.2	90.0
Helping others who are in difficulty	75.9	75.5	76.6	83.0	74.9	76.3	73.5	79.5	78.1	76.2	77.9	82.3	84.1
Making a theoretical contribution to science	19.1	17.4	22.0	28.4	17.3	17.5	17.7	20.1	15.9	21.7	23.2	24.8	33.9
Writing original works (poems, novels, short stories, etc.)	16.8	17.3	15.9	25.6	16.0	18.9	21.6	15.5	17.3	15.3	18.1	24.8	26.9
Creating artistic works (painting, sculpture, decorating, etc.)	18.2	19.1	16.8	17.5	17.5	21.1	26.8	15.2	17.2	16.7	17.1	17.2	17.8
Becoming successful in a business of my own	39.9	39.8	40.0	64.0	39.5	40.1	44.5	39.1	35.4	40.5	38.3	62.2	66.7
Becoming involved in programs to clean up the environment	31.8	30.0	35.0	38.1	28.8	31.6	34.9	31.1	27.7	34.7	35.9	37.1	39.6
Developing a meaningful philosophy of life	51.1	49.4	54.1	58.1	47.8	51.4	52.4	49.8	50.9	53.0	57.7	56.2	60.9
Participating in a community action program	34.7	33.1	37.6	51.4	30.8	36.0	35.3	38.2	35.6	36.0	43.5	47.3	57.6
Helping to promote racial understanding	40.0	39.2	41.5	63.3	38.1	40.6	42.9	40.6	37.7	40.8	43.7	61.3	66.4
Keeping up to date with political affairs	37.4	34.2	43.2	51.0	31.9	37.1	40.2	36.2	33.7	41.6	49.0	48.6	54.8
Becoming a community leader	36.4	35.0	38.9	54.0	33.8	36.5	36.2	38.6	35.8	37.7	43.3	51.0	58.6
Improving my understanding of other countries and cultures	56.8	53.4	62.8	59.4	49.6	58.3	61.6	54.7	56.3	61.0	69.3	55.6	65.2
Adopting "green" practices to protect the environment	49.6	46.4	55.3	42.7	43.9	49.5	55.1	48.8	42.8	54.5	58.2	41.3	44.9

WEIGHTED NATIONAL NORMS FOR FRESHMAN WOMEN, FALL 2008

	ALL BACC. INSTS.	ALL 4-YR. COLLEGES	ALL UNI-VERSITIES	ALL BLACK COLLEGES	FOUR-YEAR COLLEGES					UNIVERSITIES		BLACK COLLEGES	
					PUBLIC	ALL PRIV.	NONSECT.	CATHOLIC	OTH. REL.	PUBLIC	PRIVATE	PUBLIC	PRIVATE
Student estimates chances are "very good" that he/she will:													
Change major field	14.4	13.3	16.4	9.5	13.6	12.9	13.7	12.1	12.2	16.6	15.7	9.8	9.0
Change career choice	14.4	13.0	16.8	8.2	12.5	13.7	14.6	12.2	13.2	16.6	17.3	8.1	8.3
Participate in student government	8.2	8.0	8.7	16.9	7.7	8.3	8.4	8.7	7.9	8.3	10.1	14.7	20.3
Get a job to help pay for college expenses	55.7	56.2	54.9	47.4	56.3	56.2	55.5	57.9	56.1	56.2	50.1	48.6	45.6
Work full-time while attending college	8.8	10.2	6.2	12.3	12.4	7.5	8.1	7.8	6.6	6.7	4.4	13.5	10.6
Join a social fraternity or sorority	12.6	11.9	14.0	41.5	14.0	9.3	8.7	7.7	10.8	14.0	14.0	39.7	44.2
Play varsity/intercollegiate athletics	13.2	15.3	9.4	16.6	12.3	19.2	17.1	18.1	22.3	8.8	11.5	16.5	16.7
Make at least a "B" average	63.4	61.9	66.0	68.0	58.7	65.9	66.4	66.6	65.1	64.4	71.7	65.6	71.6
Need extra time to complete your degree requirements	6.8	7.4	5.7	12.5	8.1	6.5	5.9	6.5	7.1	6.2	4.0	13.9	10.5
Participate in student protests or demonstrations	6.9	6.7	7.4	11.7	5.9	7.6	9.1	6.6	6.3	7.0	9.0	10.4	13.7
Transfer to another college before graduating	7.8	9.4	4.9	15.1	11.7	6.4	6.3	6.1	6.8	5.4	2.8	19.3	8.8
Be satisfied with your college	58.9	56.3	63.6	48.9	52.4	61.2	60.5	60.9	62.3	62.1	69.1	41.6	59.9
Participate in volunteer or community service work	36.5	33.5	42.0	49.8	28.3	40.1	37.4	41.7	42.6	38.7	53.7	49.2	50.8
Seek personal counseling	10.7	10.5	11.1	15.1	10.6	10.4	10.7	10.8	9.8	11.5	9.9	13.8	17.2
Communicate regularly with your professors	40.0	39.3	41.2	45.9	34.8	45.1	46.3	43.6	44.6	38.7	50.0	38.3	57.3
Socialize with someone of another racial/ethnic group	69.6	66.9	74.4	61.4	64.7	69.7	71.8	66.8	68.7	73.0	79.6	59.5	64.4
Participate in student clubs/groups	52.6	48.2	60.3	52.4	44.7	52.7	53.8	53.4	51.0	57.8	69.5	47.7	59.5
Participate in a study abroad program	36.9	32.9	44.1	29.8	26.5	41.0	44.4	38.1	38.2	41.0	54.7	26.9	34.1
Have a roommate of different race/ethnicity	32.0	28.8	37.7	21.4	27.2	30.9	34.4	26.9	28.5	35.9	44.1	22.8	19.2
Discuss course content with students outside of class	52.0	47.4	60.3	44.3	43.1	52.7	54.0	50.6	52.3	58.1	68.0	41.1	49.0
Work on a professor's research project	32.0	33.3	29.8	49.4	33.4	33.1	35.5	31.7	31.0	28.8	33.6	47.2	52.6
Get tutoring help in specific courses	37.2	36.8	37.8	57.0	38.5	34.6	34.3	37.1	33.7	39.1	33.2	54.7	60.6
Do you give the Higher Education Research Institute (HERI) permission to include your ID number should your college request the data for additional research analyses?													
Yes	68.0	70.7	63.1	68.4	73.9	66.6	63.8	67.1	69.8	64.3	58.9	67.9	69.1
No	32.0	29.3	36.9	31.6	26.1	33.4	36.2	32.9	30.2	35.7	41.1	32.1	30.9

2008 National Norms

Universities,
by Selectivity Level, by Sex

NOTES

These notes refer to report items that are followed by numbers in [brackets].

[1] Based on the recommendations of the National Commission on Excellence In Education.

[2] Percentage responding "frequently" only.

[3] Recategorization of this item from a longer list is shown in Appendix C.

[4] Percentages will add to more than 100.0 if any student marked more than one category.

WEIGHTED NATIONAL NORMS FOR UNIVERSITIES, FALL 2008

	ALL FRESHMEN					FRESHMAN MEN					FRESHMAN WOMEN				
	PUBLIC			PRIVATE		PUBLIC			PRIVATE		PUBLIC			PRIVATE	
	LOW	MEDIUM	HIGH	HIGH	V. HIGH	LOW	MEDIUM	HIGH	HIGH	V. HIGH	LOW	MEDIUM	HIGH	HIGH	V. HIGH
How old will you be on December 31 of this year?															
16 or younger	0.1	0.0	0.0	0.1	0.1	0.0	0.0	0.0	0.0	0.1	0.1	0.0	0.0	0.1	0.1
17	2.1	1.0	1.8	1.6	2.3	1.8	0.8	1.4	1.3	2.0	2.3	1.2	2.1	1.7	2.5
18	72.3	62.8	73.1	71.0	69.9	69.7	58.3	69.6	67.2	65.2	74.4	66.9	76.2	74.3	74.3
19	24.3	34.8	24.8	26.6	26.8	26.8	38.7	28.4	30.4	31.3	22.2	31.2	21.5	23.4	22.5
20	0.9	0.6	0.3	0.6	0.8	1.2	0.7	0.4	0.8	1.0	0.6	0.4	0.2	0.5	0.7
21 to 24	0.3	0.7	0.1	0.1	0.2	0.3	1.2	0.1	0.2	0.3	0.3	0.1	0.0	0.0	0.0
25 to 29	0.1	0.1	0.0	0.1	0.0	0.1	0.1	0.1	0.0	0.0	0.0	0.0	0.0	0.0	0.0
30 to 39	0.0	0.0	0.0	0.0	0.0	0.0	0.0	0.0	0.0	0.0	0.0	0.0	0.0	0.0	0.0
40 to 54	0.0	0.0	0.0	0.0	0.0	0.0	0.0	0.0	0.0	0.0	0.0	0.0	0.0	0.0	0.0
55 or older	0.0	0.0	0.0	0.0	0.0	0.0	0.0	0.0	0.0	0.0	0.0	0.0	0.0	0.0	0.0
Is English your native language?															
Yes	82.3	92.6	88.3	90.4	85.8	83.3	92.9	88.9	91.0	85.9	81.4	92.4	87.7	89.9	85.8
No	17.7	7.4	11.7	9.6	14.2	16.7	7.1	11.1	9.0	14.1	18.6	7.6	12.3	10.1	14.2
In what year did you graduate from high school?															
2008	98.4	98.4	99.6	98.9	98.4	98.0	97.7	99.5	98.7	98.2	98.7	99.1	99.6	99.1	98.6
2007	0.9	0.8	0.3	0.9	1.3	1.1	0.9	0.4	1.0	1.3	0.8	0.7	0.3	0.8	1.2
2006	0.2	0.2	0.0	0.1	0.1	0.3	0.3	0.0	0.2	0.1	0.2	0.1	0.0	0.1	0.1
2005 or earlier	0.3	0.5	0.0	0.1	0.1	0.4	1.0	0.1	0.1	0.3	0.2	0.1	0.0	0.0	0.0
Did not graduate but passed G.E.D. test	0.1	0.0	0.0	0.0	0.0	0.2	0.1	0.0	0.0	0.0	0.1	0.0	0.0	0.0	0.0
Never completed high school	0.0	0.0	0.0	0.0	0.1	0.0	0.0	0.0	0.0	0.1	0.0	0.0	0.0	0.0	0.1
How many miles is this college from your permanent home?															
5 or less	4.0	3.0	1.8	2.9	1.7	3.8	3.2	2.0	2.7	1.7	4.2	2.8	1.7	3.0	1.6
6 to 10	4.1	2.2	2.3	3.8	1.8	4.1	2.1	2.2	3.5	1.7	4.0	2.4	2.4	4.1	1.9
11 to 50	27.6	16.1	15.1	15.8	11.1	30.3	16.4	15.2	14.8	11.3	25.3	15.8	14.9	13.0	10.9
51 to 100	22.0	25.3	14.9	10.0	5.6	21.9	24.8	14.3	9.7	5.2	22.1	25.7	15.3	10.2	5.9
101 to 500	31.9	45.2	53.2	37.3	33.3	30.0	45.3	54.1	38.2	34.3	33.6	45.2	52.3	36.5	32.4
Over 500	10.5	8.2	12.7	32.2	46.5	10.0	8.3	12.0	31.1	45.7	10.9	8.0	13.4	33.2	47.3
What was your average grade in high school?															
A or A+	13.8	22.5	38.5	34.1	56.0	10.9	19.0	36.1	29.3	54.9	16.3	25.8	40.7	38.2	57.0
A-	20.2	29.1	36.5	35.4	33.0	17.9	27.5	35.7	34.3	32.1	22.1	30.5	37.2	36.3	33.9
B+	24.1	24.8	16.2	19.5	8.7	25.3	26.4	17.5	22.2	9.9	24.8	23.4	15.0	17.2	7.6
B	27.9	18.8	7.5	9.1	1.9	30.6	20.9	9.0	11.5	2.5	25.6	16.9	6.2	7.0	1.4
B-	8.8	3.5	1.0	1.6	0.3	10.5	4.5	1.3	2.2	0.4	7.3	2.6	0.7	1.0	0.1
C+	3.7	0.9	0.2	0.2	0.0	4.8	1.2	0.2	0.2	0.1	2.8	0.6	0.1	0.2	0.0
C	1.5	0.4	0.1	0.1	0.0	2.0	0.5	0.1	0.1	0.0	1.0	0.2	0.1	0.1	0.0
D	0.0	0.0	0.0	0.0	0.0	0.0	0.0	0.1	0.1	0.0	0.0	0.0	0.0	0.0	0.0
From what kind of high school did you graduate?															
Public school (not charter or magnet)	84.3	86.7	77.6	64.6	58.3	84.1	85.8	76.7	63.5	56.5	84.5	87.6	78.5	65.6	60.1
Public charter school	2.5	1.2	1.4	1.0	1.1	2.5	1.2	1.4	0.9	1.0	2.5	1.3	1.3	1.0	1.2
Public magnet school	3.0	1.7	5.4	3.7	5.2	2.5	1.5	5.1	3.2	5.3	3.4	1.8	5.7	4.1	5.1
Private religious/parochial school	7.2	7.2	9.6	17.2	14.7	7.7	7.6	10.2	17.5	16.0	6.8	6.8	9.0	17.0	13.5
Private independent college-prep school	2.7	2.8	5.8	13.0	20.3	3.0	3.5	6.4	14.5	20.8	2.5	2.2	5.3	11.8	19.7
Home school	0.3	0.4	0.3	0.4	0.3	0.3	0.4	0.3	0.5	0.3	0.3	0.3	0.2	0.4	0.3
Prior to this term, have you ever taken courses for credit at this institution?															
No	96.8	94.4	96.2	96.5	95.8	96.4	94.3	95.7	96.2	95.3	97.2	94.5	96.6	96.8	96.3
Yes	3.2	5.6	3.8	3.5	4.2	3.6	5.7	4.3	3.8	4.7	2.8	5.5	3.4	3.2	3.7

WEIGHTED NATIONAL NORMS FOR UNIVERSITIES, FALL 2008

	ALL FRESHMEN						FRESHMAN MEN						FRESHMAN WOMEN					
	PUBLIC			PRIVATE			PUBLIC			PRIVATE			PUBLIC			PRIVATE		
	LOW	MEDIUM	HIGH	MEDIUM	HIGH	V. HIGH	LOW	MEDIUM	HIGH	MEDIUM	HIGH	V. HIGH	LOW	MEDIUM	HIGH	MEDIUM	HIGH	V. HIGH
Since leaving high school, have you ever taken courses, whether for credit or not for credit, at any other institution (university, 4- or 2-year college, technical, vocational, or business school)?																		
No	86.7	86.9	88.5	89.0	87.7	89.1	88.5	88.3	89.2	90.3	88.5	89.1	85.3	85.5	87.8	88.0	87.1	89.0
Yes	13.3	13.1	11.5	11.0	12.3	10.9	11.5	11.7	10.8	9.7	11.5	10.9	14.7	14.5	12.2	12.0	12.9	11.0
Where do you plan to live during the fall term?																		
With my family or other relatives	12.8	4.7	2.3	21.3	5.9	0.7	13.3	4.9	2.4	20.9	5.9	0.6	12.4	4.5	2.2	21.7	5.9	0.7
Other private home, apartment, or room	4.9	4.1	3.8	0.8	0.5	0.2	5.1	4.1	3.7	1.1	0.7	0.2	4.7	4.2	3.9	0.6	0.4	0.2
College residence hall	76.2	86.2	91.0	77.0	92.5	97.0	75.4	85.7	91.2	77.0	92.1	97.3	77.0	86.6	90.9	77.0	92.8	96.8
Fraternity or sorority house	3.7	0.7	0.1	0.1	0.0	0.1	4.3	1.2	0.1	0.1	0.0	0.1	3.2	0.2	0.1	0.1	0.0	0.0
Other campus student housing	2.1	4.0	2.5	0.7	0.9	2.0	1.7	3.8	2.3	0.7	1.1	1.8	2.5	4.3	2.7	0.7	0.8	2.2
Other	0.2	0.3	0.2	0.1	0.1	0.0	0.4	0.3	0.2	0.1	0.2	0.0	0.2	0.2	0.2	0.0	0.0	0.0
To how many colleges other than this one did you apply for admission this year?																		
None	16.9	21.9	7.8	6.1	8.2	9.5	17.9	23.2	9.1	6.9	8.7	9.7	16.1	20.8	6.6	5.5	7.8	9.3
One	11.0	13.5	8.6	6.8	5.6	4.5	10.8	13.3	9.2	7.4	5.3	4.7	11.1	13.7	8.0	6.3	5.9	4.3
Two	13.3	14.1	11.7	11.1	8.0	4.2	13.8	14.4	11.9	11.9	8.0	4.7	12.8	13.8	11.6	10.5	7.9	3.8
Three	15.1	13.8	14.2	16.1	11.0	6.1	16.2	14.2	14.4	16.4	11.3	6.4	14.2	13.5	13.9	15.8	10.8	5.8
Four	12.7	10.7	13.0	15.9	11.7	7.7	12.5	10.5	12.9	17.1	12.5	7.9	12.8	10.8	13.1	14.9	11.0	7.5
Five	9.3	7.7	11.5	13.3	11.9	7.7	9.1	7.8	11.5	12.3	11.9	9.7	9.4	7.7	11.5	14.1	11.8	9.2
Six	7.2	5.9	9.8	10.5	11.4	9.5	7.0	5.4	9.6	9.7	11.6	9.7	7.4	6.4	10.0	11.2	11.3	10.8
Seven to ten	12.3	10.5	19.0	16.2	24.7	34.0	10.9	9.7	17.5	14.6	24.0	32.9	13.5	11.2	20.4	17.5	25.4	35.1
Eleven or more	2.3	1.8	4.4	3.9	7.5	13.6	1.9	1.6	3.9	3.6	6.7	13.0	2.5	2.0	4.8	4.2	8.1	14.1
Were you accepted by your first choice college?																		
Yes	69.6	79.8	72.1	77.2	68.9	65.6	67.4	78.4	69.9	75.2	66.1	62.5	71.4	81.2	74.1	78.8	71.3	68.6
No	30.4	20.2	27.9	22.8	31.1	34.4	32.6	21.6	30.1	24.8	33.9	37.5	28.6	18.8	25.9	21.2	28.7	31.4
Is this college your:																		
First choice?	52.6	66.0	61.4	57.4	58.0	60.9	53.1	66.4	61.6	58.1	57.6	59.3	52.2	65.6	61.1	56.9	58.4	62.5
Second choice?	26.9	22.2	25.2	29.2	25.5	22.5	25.8	22.0	24.6	29.1	25.4	22.9	27.8	22.3	25.7	29.3	25.6	22.2
Third choice?	11.2	7.0	8.9	8.9	10.5	10.0	11.5	7.0	9.2	8.5	10.7	10.5	11.0	7.1	8.7	9.2	10.4	9.6
Less than third choice?	9.3	4.8	4.5	4.4	6.0	6.5	9.5	4.6	4.6	4.2	6.3	7.3	9.0	5.0	4.5	4.6	5.7	5.7
Citizenship status																		
U.S. citizen	95.5	96.7	95.5	95.9	94.4	90.3	95.0	96.3	95.1	96.0	94.4	89.7	96.0	97.1	95.9	95.9	94.5	90.8
Permanent resident (green card)	3.5	1.7	3.2	2.7	2.3	3.4	3.8	1.7	3.4	2.5	2.2	3.7	3.2	1.7	3.0	2.9	2.5	3.1
Neither	1.0	1.5	1.3	1.3	3.2	6.3	1.2	2.0	1.5	1.6	3.4	6.6	0.8	1.2	1.2	1.1	3.0	6.1
Are your parents:																		
Both alive and living with each other?	67.8	76.0	76.9	73.2	78.7	83.6	70.9	77.6	79.4	75.5	81.1	85.0	65.1	74.5	74.6	71.4	76.6	82.3
Both alive, divorced or living apart?	28.2	21.2	20.1	23.1	18.3	14.2	25.1	19.6	17.8	21.1	16.0	12.7	30.8	22.6	22.1	24.7	20.3	15.5
One or both deceased?	4.0	2.8	3.0	3.7	3.0	2.2	4.0	2.8	2.8	3.4	2.9	2.2	4.1	2.8	3.2	3.9	3.1	2.2

WEIGHTED NATIONAL NORMS FOR UNIVERSITIES, FALL 2008

	ALL FRESHMEN					FRESHMEN MEN						FRESHMAN WOMEN					
	PUBLIC			PRIVATE		PUBLIC			PRIVATE			PUBLIC			PRIVATE		
	LOW	MEDIUM	HIGH	HIGH	V. HIGH	LOW	MEDIUM	HIGH	MEDIUM	HIGH	V. HIGH	LOW	MEDIUM	HIGH	MEDIUM	HIGH	V. HIGH
During high school (grades 9-12) how many years did you study each of the following subjects? [1]																	
English (4 years)	98.3	97.7	99.1	98.8	98.8	98.2	97.5	99.0	98.7	98.6	98.5	98.5	98.0	99.2	98.9	99.1	99.0
Mathematics (3 years)	98.6	98.6	99.5	99.4	99.7	98.5	98.9	99.5	99.3	99.3	99.7	98.6	98.4	99.5	99.4	99.6	99.7
Foreign Language (2 years)	92.7	93.4	97.7	97.6	98.2	91.2	93.0	97.4	96.0	97.3	98.2	94.0	93.8	98.0	97.5	97.8	98.2
Physical Science (2 years)	58.1	66.8	71.1	71.2	77.2	62.7	71.4	75.5	65.7	74.3	80.2	54.1	62.4	67.2	59.1	68.4	74.3
Biological Science (2 years)	48.0	49.8	56.9	53.6	56.6	46.7	45.9	53.9	44.7	50.7	52.6	49.1	53.4	59.6	51.7	56.1	60.4
History/Am. Govt. (1 year)	98.8	99.1	99.3	99.1	99.3	99.0	99.2	99.4	99.4	98.9	99.2	98.6	99.1	99.2	99.4	99.2	99.4
Computer Science (1/2 year)	54.7	64.4	52.2	56.7	46.6	60.1	68.8	58.1	65.2	61.1	51.9	50.1	60.3	46.9	53.6	52.8	41.5
Arts and/or Music (1 year)	84.0	86.6	81.4	86.3	87.2	80.1	82.3	76.9	77.3	82.7	83.9	87.2	90.6	85.5	85.6	89.3	90.3
WHAT IS THE HIGHEST ACADEMIC DEGREE THAT YOU INTEND TO OBTAIN?																	
Highest planned																	
None	0.9	0.6	0.4	0.4	0.3	0.9	0.6	0.5	0.9	0.5	0.4	0.9	0.6	0.3	0.6	0.3	0.3
Vocational certificate	0.1	0.1	0.1	0.0	0.0	0.1	0.0	0.0	0.1	0.0	0.0	0.1	0.1	0.1	0.1	0.0	0.0
Associate (A.A. or equivalent)	0.4	0.4	0.1	0.1	0.1	0.4	0.4	0.2	0.2	0.2	0.2	0.4	0.4	0.1	0.2	0.1	0.1
Bachelor's degree (B.A., B.S., etc.)	22.1	27.6	12.6	13.5	8.5	24.2	28.7	13.5	18.5	14.3	8.9	20.3	26.4	11.7	15.1	12.8	8.2
Master's degree (M.A., M.S., etc.)	41.4	42.1	41.5	39.9	38.1	42.8	42.4	42.3	43.2	40.3	38.5	40.2	41.7	40.7	41.5	39.5	37.8
Ph.D. or Ed.D.	19.9	17.2	21.7	20.5	24.1	18.0	18.1	21.6	18.4	20.9	25.9	21.6	16.3	21.8	20.3	20.1	22.3
M.D., D.O., D.D.S., D.V.M.	10.0	8.0	16.5	15.5	18.9	8.9	6.0	14.3	8.7	13.4	16.3	10.9	10.0	18.5	13.3	17.3	21.4
J.D. (Law)	3.5	2.8	5.9	8.3	8.6	3.2	2.7	6.4	7.1	8.5	8.5	3.8	2.9	5.5	6.2	8.1	8.6
B.D. or M.DIV. (Divinity)	0.3	0.1	0.2	0.3	0.2	0.3	0.1	0.2	0.3	0.4	0.3	0.3	0.1	0.1	0.2	0.2	0.2
Other	1.4	1.2	1.0	1.5	1.1	1.3	1.0	0.9	2.7	1.5	1.1	1.5	1.4	1.1	2.5	1.6	1.1
Highest planned at this college																	
None	1.4	1.1	0.4	0.5	0.4	1.3	1.3	0.5	1.1	0.7	0.4	1.4	1.0	0.3	0.8	0.4	0.3
Vocational certificate	0.2	0.1	0.1	0.0	0.1	0.2	0.1	0.1	0.1	0.0	0.1	0.1	0.1	0.1	0.1	0.1	0.1
Associate (A.A. or equivalent)	2.0	1.3	0.5	0.5	0.7	2.0	0.9	0.5	0.6	0.5	0.7	2.0	1.6	0.5	0.9	0.6	0.7
Bachelor's degree (B.A., B.S., etc.)	67.9	70.2	63.8	65.6	72.6	68.1	68.0	61.7	58.0	62.5	69.5	67.7	72.3	65.8	58.5	68.3	75.5
Master's degree (M.A., M.S., etc.)	21.4	20.3	22.5	21.2	17.2	21.8	22.8	24.7	28.3	23.6	19.6	21.1	18.0	20.5	25.3	19.1	14.9
Ph.D. or Ed.D.	4.0	4.0	5.5	4.9	3.6	3.6	4.7	5.7	5.2	5.3	4.2	4.3	3.4	5.2	6.7	4.6	3.0
M.D., D.O., D.D.S., D.V.M.	1.6	1.6	5.4	4.0	3.5	1.4	1.0	5.0	2.2	3.9	3.4	1.8	2.3	5.7	3.3	4.1	3.6
J.D. (Law)	0.5	0.1	1.1	1.7	1.1	0.6	0.1	1.2	1.9	2.0	1.2	0.5	0.1	1.1	1.9	1.5	1.0
B.D. or M.DIV. (Divinity)	0.2	0.0	0.1	0.2	0.1	0.2	0.0	0.1	0.3	0.3	0.2	0.2	0.1	0.1	0.2	0.2	0.0
Other	0.9	1.1	0.6	1.2	0.7	0.9	1.0	0.6	2.4	1.3	0.6	0.9	1.2	0.7	2.5	1.2	0.8
HOW WOULD YOU DESCRIBE THE RACIAL COMPOSITION OF THE:																	
High school I last attended																	
Completely non-White	4.6	2.0	2.8	1.8	2.9	3.7	2.0	2.5	2.4	1.7	2.8	5.4	2.0	3.1	2.5	1.9	2.9
Mostly non-White	22.8	8.5	14.7	10.4	10.1	22.3	7.8	14.1	10.4	9.7	9.5	23.2	9.1	15.3	12.5	11.0	10.7
Roughly half non-White	28.1	21.1	26.4	21.1	22.0	27.0	19.5	25.3	23.0	19.7	21.1	29.0	22.6	27.3	26.3	22.3	22.9
Mostly White	39.6	58.6	49.8	57.7	58.1	41.6	60.0	51.7	55.8	60.2	59.5	37.9	57.3	48.2	50.8	55.5	56.8
Completely White	4.9	9.9	6.2	9.0	6.8	5.3	10.8	6.4	8.4	8.7	7.0	4.5	9.1	6.1	7.8	9.2	6.6
Neighborhood where I grew up																	
Completely non-White	8.2	3.2	4.3	3.5	5.0	6.9	3.1	4.0	4.6	3.4	5.0	9.2	3.4	4.6	5.3	3.7	4.9
Mostly non-White	19.4	7.1	11.2	9.1	9.0	19.1	6.9	10.8	11.5	8.9	8.6	19.7	7.4	11.5	12.5	9.2	9.3
Roughly half non-White	19.0	10.5	13.8	12.7	12.9	19.0	10.2	13.9	15.6	12.5	12.4	19.1	10.8	13.7	16.9	12.8	13.3
Mostly White	41.6	53.7	53.3	54.1	56.2	41.8	53.7	53.9	49.6	54.3	56.5	41.4	53.8	52.8	47.7	54.0	56.0
Completely White	11.8	25.4	17.4	20.6	17.0	13.2	26.1	17.5	18.7	20.9	17.6	10.6	24.7	17.4	17.6	20.3	16.5

WEIGHTED NATIONAL NORMS FOR UNIVERSITIES, FALL 2008

	ALL FRESHMEN					FRESHMAN MEN					FRESHMAN WOMEN				
	PUBLIC			PRIVATE		PUBLIC			PRIVATE		PUBLIC			PRIVATE	
	LOW	MEDIUM	HIGH	HIGH	V. HIGH	LOW	MEDIUM	HIGH	HIGH	V. HIGH	LOW	MEDIUM	HIGH	HIGH	V. HIGH
Do you have a disability?															
Hearing	0.5	0.5	0.4	0.4	0.3	0.6	0.6	0.4	0.3	0.4	0.4	0.5	0.5	0.5	0.2
Speech	0.2	0.2	0.2	0.2	0.2	0.3	0.2	0.3	0.3	0.3	0.1	0.1	0.1	0.1	0.1
Orthopedic	0.4	0.4	0.4	0.5	0.3	0.3	0.4	0.3	0.4	0.3	0.4	0.4	0.4	0.5	0.3
Learning disability	1.9	2.4	1.6	3.7	1.8	2.0	2.7	1.8	4.0	2.2	1.8	2.1	1.4	3.4	1.5
Partially sighted or blind	1.5	1.2	1.5	1.2	1.3	1.6	1.4	1.6	1.5	1.3	1.5	1.0	1.3	0.9	1.3
Health-related	1.5	1.2	1.1	1.4	1.1	1.4	1.1	1.0	1.3	1.2	1.6	1.3	1.2	1.5	0.9
Other	1.0	1.2	0.9	1.2	0.8	1.1	1.4	1.1	1.3	1.0	1.0	1.0	0.8	1.0	0.5
HOW MUCH OF YOUR FIRST YEAR'S EDUCATIONAL EXPENSES (ROOM, BOARD TUITION, AND FEES) DO YOU EXPECT TO COVER FROM:															
Family resources (parents, relatives, spouse, etc.)															
None	20.4	16.6	14.3	12.2	7.8	19.5	16.4	14.0	12.5	7.8	21.2	16.8	14.6	11.9	7.8
Less than $1,000	12.6	10.5	7.4	5.2	3.8	11.5	10.0	6.4	4.4	3.5	13.5	11.0	8.3	5.9	4.0
$1,000 to 2,999	15.0	12.9	10.9	6.7	5.5	13.5	12.4	10.3	6.4	5.2	16.2	13.3	11.3	7.0	5.8
$3,000 to 5,999	15.1	13.4	11.2	7.4	6.4	14.8	13.0	10.8	6.8	6.2	15.4	13.8	11.5	7.8	6.5
$6,000 to 9,999	11.6	13.0	10.8	8.8	7.1	12.2	13.1	10.9	8.4	6.9	11.1	13.0	10.7	9.2	7.3
$10,000 +	25.3	33.6	45.4	59.8	69.5	28.4	35.1	47.5	61.6	70.4	22.6	32.3	43.5	58.2	68.6
My own resources (savings from work, work-study, other income)															
None	31.4	27.7	36.4	39.2	38.5	32.4	28.4	37.0	39.1	39.4	30.5	27.2	36.0	39.3	37.7
Less than $1,000	27.3	26.3	26.4	21.8	22.7	25.0	23.8	24.6	20.3	21.0	29.2	28.5	28.0	23.1	24.4
$1,000 to 2,999	26.5	28.4	24.2	23.0	25.0	26.4	28.9	24.6	23.2	24.4	26.6	28.0	23.9	22.8	25.5
$3,000 to 5,999	10.1	11.6	8.5	8.9	8.2	10.9	12.1	9.0	9.7	8.9	9.5	11.1	8.1	8.2	7.6
$6,000 to 9,999	2.5	3.5	2.4	3.3	2.5	3.0	4.0	2.7	3.6	2.7	2.2	3.0	2.2	3.0	2.2
$10,000 +	2.2	2.6	2.0	3.8	3.1	2.4	2.9	2.2	4.1	3.6	2.0	2.3	1.8	3.6	2.6
Aid which _not_ be repaid (grants, scholarships, military funding, etc.)															
None	34.4	34.8	33.6	21.3	39.4	38.8	36.6	36.2	22.9	40.0	30.6	33.2	31.2	20.0	38.9
Less than $1,000	8.6	11.1	6.4	2.5	4.9	8.7	10.7	6.0	2.3	4.7	8.5	11.3	6.8	2.7	5.1
$1,000 to 2,999	13.3	16.6	14.0	6.3	8.7	12.6	16.2	13.7	5.5	8.1	13.9	17.0	14.3	7.0	9.3
$3,000 to 5,999	13.4	13.6	13.6	7.9	5.8	11.8	13.0	12.9	7.9	5.6	14.7	14.1	14.2	7.9	5.9
$6,000 to 9,999	11.6	10.2	10.8	10.8	4.0	11.0	9.9	10.2	10.4	3.7	12.0	10.4	11.3	11.2	4.3
$10,000 +	18.7	13.8	21.6	51.1	37.2	16.9	13.5	20.9	51.1	37.9	20.3	14.1	22.3	51.2	36.6
Aid which _must_ be repaid (loans, etc.)															
None	48.6	50.6	60.2	50.1	61.4	51.3	51.7	61.0	51.1	61.6	46.2	49.7	59.5	49.2	61.2
Less than $1,000	4.5	3.2	3.2	1.8	2.2	3.8	3.1	3.0	1.7	2.3	5.0	3.4	3.4	2.0	2.1
$1,000 to 2,999	9.9	8.5	7.0	7.7	7.3	9.6	7.9	7.0	7.6	7.5	10.1	9.0	7.0	7.9	7.2
$3,000 to 5,999	17.1	15.3	12.2	14.5	12.0	16.3	14.7	11.8	13.9	11.3	17.7	15.8	12.5	15.1	12.7
$6,000 to 9,999	8.5	9.6	7.2	8.5	5.5	8.2	9.9	7.1	8.5	5.6	8.7	9.3	7.3	8.5	5.5
$10,000 +	11.6	12.8	10.1	17.3	11.5	10.8	12.7	10.0	17.2	11.8	12.3	12.8	10.2	17.3	11.3
Other than above															
None	92.9	94.1	94.8	93.5	94.1	92.8	93.8	94.5	93.1	93.8	93.0	94.5	95.1	93.9	94.4
Less than $1,000	3.1	2.4	2.0	1.8	2.0	3.2	2.6	2.2	1.9	2.2	3.0	2.1	1.7	1.8	1.7
$1,000 to 2,999	1.8	1.5	1.3	1.3	1.2	1.7	1.6	1.3	1.5	1.2	1.8	1.5	1.3	1.1	1.2
$3,000 to 5,999	0.9	0.8	0.7	0.8	0.7	0.9	0.9	0.8	0.9	0.8	0.6	0.7	0.7	0.7	0.7
$6,000 to 9,999	0.5	0.4	0.5	0.7	0.4	0.4	0.4	0.5	0.7	0.3	0.6	0.4	0.4	0.6	0.4
$10,000 +	0.8	0.7	0.8	1.9	1.6	0.9	0.7	0.7	2.0	1.6	0.7	0.8	0.8	1.9	1.6

WEIGHTED NATIONAL NORMS FOR UNIVERSITIES, FALL 2008

	ALL FRESHMEN						FRESHMAN MEN						FRESHMAN WOMEN					
	PUBLIC			PRIVATE			PUBLIC			PRIVATE			PUBLIC			PRIVATE		
	LOW	MEDIUM	HIGH	MEDIUM	HIGH	V. HIGH	LOW	MEDIUM	HIGH	MEDIUM	HIGH	V. HIGH	LOW	MEDIUM	HIGH	MEDIUM	HIGH	V. HIGH
What is your best estimate of your parents' total income last year? Consider income from all sources before taxes																		
Less than $10,000	4.9	2.0	2.1	2.7	1.7	1.7	3.8	1.7	1.7	2.2	1.5	1.5	5.8	2.3	2.4	3.2	1.8	1.9
$10,000 to 14,999	3.5	1.7	1.9	2.2	1.4	1.0	2.8	1.3	1.5	1.9	1.1	0.9	4.1	2.1	2.3	2.5	1.7	1.0
$15,000 to 19,999	3.5	1.6	1.8	2.3	1.3	1.1	3.1	1.4	1.5	2.0	1.0	1.1	3.8	1.7	2.0	2.5	1.6	1.1
$20,000 to 24,999	4.4	2.6	2.6	2.9	1.6	1.4	3.8	2.4	2.1	2.5	1.6	1.1	4.8	2.8	3.0	3.2	1.6	1.6
$25,000 to 29,999	3.8	2.6	2.4	2.7	1.5	1.3	3.5	2.1	2.0	2.3	1.3	1.1	4.1	3.1	2.8	3.1	1.7	1.6
$30,000 to 39,999	7.8	5.3	4.6	6.2	3.5	3.3	6.9	4.6	3.9	5.1	2.7	3.1	8.6	5.9	5.3	7.0	4.2	3.5
$40,000 to 49,999	8.5	6.3	5.0	6.4	4.2	3.4	7.2	5.9	4.3	5.2	3.5	3.2	9.7	6.7	5.6	7.4	4.8	3.5
$50,000 to 59,999	9.1	8.6	5.9	7.4	5.5	4.3	8.2	8.1	5.6	6.9	5.3	4.2	9.9	9.1	6.1	7.9	5.6	4.4
$60,000 to 74,999	11.3	11.5	8.6	11.0	7.5	6.8	10.8	10.6	8.1	10.7	6.8	6.4	11.7	12.3	9.2	11.3	8.1	7.3
$75,000 to 99,999	14.1	16.9	13.9	15.3	13.6	11.0	15.7	17.2	14.1	15.9	14.5	11.3	12.7	16.6	13.6	14.8	12.7	10.7
$100,000 to 149,999	16.2	21.3	22.1	19.8	21.6	20.0	19.0	23.8	24.2	22.5	22.6	20.8	13.8	18.8	20.0	17.6	20.8	19.1
$150,000 to 199,999	6.2	8.9	11.3	8.7	11.8	11.7	6.6	9.5	12.1	9.4	11.8	11.9	5.8	8.2	10.6	8.1	11.9	11.6
$200,000 to 249,999	2.8	4.4	6.6	4.6	7.8	9.3	3.4	4.6	7.1	5.0	7.7	9.6	2.3	4.1	6.0	4.4	7.9	9.1
$250,000 or more	3.9	6.5	11.3	7.7	16.9	23.8	5.1	6.7	11.8	8.5	18.4	23.9	2.9	6.2	10.8	7.1	15.6	23.7
Do you have any concern about your ability to finance your college education?																		
None (I am confident that I will have sufficient funds)	27.1	34.3	40.7	30.9	39.1	43.6	33.5	40.2	46.1	37.5	44.6	47.8	21.7	28.8	35.8	25.7	34.4	39.7
Some (but I probably will have enough funds)	57.6	55.8	50.9	56.8	50.6	49.0	54.9	52.1	47.2	52.8	47.2	45.5	59.9	59.1	54.2	60.0	53.4	52.4
Major (not sure I will have enough funds to complete college)	15.3	10.0	8.4	12.3	10.4	7.4	11.6	7.7	6.7	9.7	8.2	6.7	18.4	12.1	10.0	14.3	12.2	8.0
Your current religious preference																		
Baptist	5.7	5.6	6.6	3.9	8.7	3.4	4.9	5.5	6.3	3.4	7.8	3.5	6.4	5.7	7.0	4.3	9.4	3.4
Buddhist	3.0	1.4	2.1	1.4	1.4	1.7	3.5	1.4	2.1	1.4	1.5	1.5	2.7	1.3	2.1	1.3	1.3	1.8
Church of Christ	5.9	3.4	2.6	2.6	1.6	1.7	6.5	3.8	2.9	3.0	1.8	1.9	5.2	3.0	2.3	2.3	1.4	1.5
Eastern Orthodox	0.8	0.6	0.8	1.5	1.1	1.0	1.0	0.6	0.7	1.4	1.2	1.0	0.6	0.5	0.9	1.7	1.1	1.0
Episcopalian	0.5	0.8	2.0	1.1	2.1	2.1	0.3	0.6	1.9	1.1	1.9	1.9	0.6	1.0	2.0	1.0	2.2	2.3
Hindu	1.8	1.0	1.5	1.9	1.2	2.5	1.7	1.3	1.7	1.5	1.4	2.7	1.9	0.7	1.3	2.3	1.1	2.2
Jewish	1.1	2.2	5.7	2.6	6.7	8.8	1.1	2.0	6.0	2.7	7.2	9.6	1.1	2.3	5.3	2.4	6.4	8.1
LDS (Mormon)	1.4	8.2	0.2	0.1	0.1	0.1	1.1	6.7	0.2	0.1	0.2	0.2	1.7	9.6	0.2	0.2	0.1	0.1
Lutheran	3.5	7.8	2.8	3.0	2.3	1.7	3.4	7.6	2.6	2.5	2.5	1.6	3.6	7.9	2.9	3.3	2.5	1.8
Methodist	1.9	5.2	5.1	2.8	3.4	2.9	1.9	4.8	4.9	2.8	2.6	2.7	1.9	5.6	5.4	2.8	4.1	3.1
Muslim	1.6	0.6	1.0	2.5	1.3	1.3	1.9	0.7	1.2	2.5	1.4	1.3	1.4	0.5	0.9	2.5	1.2	1.2
Presbyterian	2.7	2.2	5.3	2.4	2.6	4.4	3.0	2.3	4.8	2.7	2.2	4.3	2.5	2.1	5.7	2.1	2.9	4.6
Quaker	0.1	0.2	0.2	0.2	0.2	0.2	0.1	0.2	0.2	0.2	0.3	0.2	0.1	0.2	0.1	0.3	0.1	0.2
Roman Catholic	25.3	23.3	24.9	41.8	30.5	28.9	24.4	22.8	24.0	41.3	30.2	28.5	26.1	23.8	25.7	42.1	30.7	29.2
Seventh Day Adventist	0.6	0.2	0.3	0.4	0.4	0.3	0.5	0.1	0.2	0.4	0.2	0.3	0.6	0.2	0.4	0.3	0.3	0.1
United Church of Christ/Congregational	0.5	0.7	0.5	0.4	0.8	0.6	0.5	0.7	0.5	0.4	0.7	0.5	0.5	0.8	0.6	0.4	0.8	0.6
Other Christian	14.9	11.0	10.4	9.1	8.7	8.0	13.1	10.5	9.9	7.6	8.1	6.8	16.4	11.4	10.9	10.2	9.3	9.1
Other Religion	3.7	2.9	2.5	2.7	2.7	2.6	3.8	2.8	2.5	2.6	2.5	2.6	3.6	2.9	2.6	2.8	2.9	2.5
None	25.0	23.0	25.5	19.6	24.3	27.9	27.1	25.6	27.6	22.3	26.7	28.8	23.1	20.5	23.7	17.5	22.2	27.1

WEIGHTED NATIONAL NORMS FOR UNIVERSITIES, FALL 2008

	ALL FRESHMEN					FRESHMAN MEN					FRESHMAN WOMEN				
	PUBLIC			PRIVATE		PUBLIC			PRIVATE		PUBLIC			PRIVATE	
	LOW	MEDIUM	HIGH	HIGH	V. HIGH	LOW	MEDIUM	HIGH	HIGH	V. HIGH	LOW	MEDIUM	HIGH	HIGH	V. HIGH
Father's current religious preference															
Baptist	5.3	6.0	7.1	8.6	3.8	4.6	5.9	6.8	8.1	4.1	6.0	6.1	7.3	9.0	3.6
Buddhist	4.3	1.9	3.3	1.7	2.7	4.7	1.9	3.2	1.8	2.4	4.0	1.9	3.3	1.7	2.9
Church of Christ	5.7	3.8	2.8	2.1	2.0	6.8	4.5	3.4	2.4	2.2	4.7	3.2	2.3	1.8	1.7
Eastern Orthodox	1.0	0.6	0.9	1.2	1.2	1.2	0.6	0.8	1.3	1.1	0.8	0.6	1.0	1.2	1.3
Episcopalian	0.8	1.0	2.3	2.8	2.9	0.6	0.9	2.3	2.7	2.8	0.8	1.1	2.3	2.8	3.0
Hindu	2.1	1.2	1.8	1.6	3.0	2.2	1.6	2.2	1.8	3.5	2.1	0.8	1.6	1.4	2.5
Jewish	1.7	2.8	6.6	8.1	10.1	1.8	2.6	7.2	9.1	11.2	1.7	3.0	6.1	7.2	9.0
LDS (Mormon)	1.7	8.4	0.3	0.2	0.2	1.4	7.0	0.3	0.3	0.2	1.9	9.6	0.2	0.1	0.1
Lutheran	4.4	9.0	3.4	3.2	2.4	4.3	9.1	3.3	2.9	2.4	4.4	8.9	3.5	3.4	2.5
Methodist	2.3	6.0	5.6	4.1	3.5	2.4	6.1	5.6	3.3	3.6	2.1	5.8	5.5	4.7	3.4
Muslim	2.0	0.9	1.4	1.6	1.7	2.3	0.9	1.5	1.8	1.8	1.8	0.9	1.3	1.5	1.7
Presbyterian	3.0	2.6	5.9	3.4	5.2	3.3	2.5	5.7	3.0	5.2	2.7	2.7	6.0	3.8	5.3
Quaker	0.2	0.2	0.2	0.2	0.1	0.2	0.2	0.2	0.2	0.1	0.2	0.1	0.2	0.2	0.2
Roman Catholic	28.6	26.5	27.7	34.4	31.1	27.4	26.5	27.0	34.3	30.8	29.6	26.6	28.3	34.5	31.4
Seventh Day Adventist	0.6	0.3	0.4	0.3	0.2	0.6	0.2	0.2	0.3	0.2	0.7	0.3	0.5	0.3	0.2
United Church of Christ/Congregational	0.5	0.9	0.6	0.8	0.6	0.5	0.9	0.6	0.8	0.7	0.6	0.9	0.6	0.8	0.6
Other Christian	13.8	10.4	9.8	8.3	7.6	13.2	10.6	9.6	8.3	6.9	14.3	10.2	9.9	8.2	8.2
Other Religion	3.0	1.8	1.9	1.8	1.8	3.0	1.6	1.8	1.9	1.7	2.9	2.0	2.0	1.7	1.8
None	19.1	15.7	18.1	15.6	20.0	19.4	16.1	18.2	15.7	19.2	19.0	15.3	18.1	15.6	20.7
Mother's current religious preference															
Baptist	5.9	6.4	7.3	9.0	4.1	5.3	6.6	7.0	8.3	4.3	6.5	6.3	7.6	9.5	4.0
Buddhist	4.6	2.0	3.6	1.8	3.1	5.2	2.0	3.5	1.7	2.7	4.2	2.0	3.6	1.9	3.4
Church of Christ	6.4	4.0	3.1	2.2	2.3	7.7	4.7	3.7	2.5	2.7	5.4	3.4	2.7	2.0	2.0
Eastern Orthodox	0.9	0.7	1.0	1.3	1.3	1.1	0.8	1.0	1.4	1.3	0.8	0.7	1.1	1.2	1.3
Episcopalian	0.8	1.3	2.7	3.1	2.9	0.7	1.1	2.7	3.0	2.7	0.9	1.5	2.6	3.1	3.0
Hindu	2.0	1.1	1.8	1.5	3.0	2.1	1.5	2.1	1.8	3.3	2.0	0.7	1.5	1.4	2.6
Jewish	1.5	2.7	6.4	7.8	9.6	1.6	2.8	6.8	8.5	10.7	1.4	2.7	6.0	7.2	8.6
LDS (Mormon)	1.7	8.5	0.3	0.3	0.3	1.4	7.1	0.3	0.3	0.3	1.9	9.8	0.3	0.2	0.2
Lutheran	4.5	9.1	3.6	3.1	2.6	4.5	9.2	3.6	2.7	2.5	4.4	9.0	3.5	3.3	2.6
Methodist	2.8	6.5	6.2	4.4	3.9	2.8	6.4	6.0	3.8	3.8	2.8	6.7	6.3	4.8	3.9
Muslim	1.7	0.7	1.2	1.4	1.5	1.8	0.8	1.3	1.4	1.5	1.5	0.7	1.1	1.3	1.4
Presbyterian	3.3	2.8	6.4	3.3	5.8	3.8	2.9	6.1	3.1	5.8	2.9	2.7	6.7	3.6	5.8
Quaker	0.2	0.2	0.2	0.2	0.2	0.2	0.2	0.3	0.2	0.2	0.2	0.3	0.1	0.2	0.2
Roman Catholic	30.8	28.1	29.9	36.8	33.6	29.7	28.0	29.2	36.8	33.2	31.7	28.3	30.5	36.8	33.9
Seventh Day Adventist	0.7	0.3	0.4	0.3	0.2	0.5	0.3	0.2	0.3	0.2	0.9	0.3	0.5	0.3	0.2
United Church of Christ/Congregational	0.7	0.9	0.7	1.0	0.7	0.7	0.9	0.7	1.0	0.7	0.6	1.0	0.8	0.9	0.7
Other Christian	15.7	11.4	10.7	9.5	8.2	14.7	11.3	10.6	9.7	7.6	16.5	11.6	10.9	9.4	8.8
Other Religion	2.9	2.1	2.0	2.0	1.8	2.7	2.0	1.9	1.8	1.7	3.1	2.2	2.1	2.1	1.9
None	12.8	10.9	12.5	11.1	15.1	13.5	11.5	13.0	11.5	14.8	12.2	10.4	12.1	10.8	15.4

WEIGHTED NATIONAL NORMS FOR UNIVERSITIES, FALL 2008

	ALL FRESHMEN						FRESHMAN MEN						FRESHMAN WOMEN					
	PUBLIC			PRIVATE			PUBLIC			PRIVATE			PUBLIC			PRIVATE		
	LOW	MEDIUM	HIGH	MEDIUM	HIGH	V. HIGH	LOW	MEDIUM	HIGH	MEDIUM	HIGH	V. HIGH	LOW	MEDIUM	HIGH	MEDIUM	HIGH	V. HIGH
During the past year, student "frequently" or "occasionally":																		
Attended a religious service	71.2	76.1	73.9	78.0	75.3	72.6	68.5	73.5	72.0	75.2	72.9	71.2	73.4	78.5	75.6	80.1	77.3	74.0
Was bored in class [2]	35.0	42.1	42.6	41.1	36.8	37.3	36.1	44.2	44.8	42.2	37.6	39.4	34.1	40.3	40.6	40.3	36.1	35.4
Participated in political demonstrations	27.3	26.7	24.7	25.9	26.3	25.5	26.4	26.7	23.7	25.5	27.1	25.3	28.0	27.3	25.6	26.2	28.5	25.7
Tutored another student	58.4	56.2	69.9	61.8	66.3	77.9	55.4	54.9	68.4	57.5	63.8	77.1	61.0	57.4	71.2	65.0	68.3	78.7
Studied with other students	88.0	89.2	91.8	87.0	90.8	92.8	85.2	86.2	89.5	82.9	88.0	91.0	90.4	91.9	93.8	90.2	93.1	94.5
Was a guest in a teacher's home	18.3	21.8	20.4	18.1	24.0	26.1	18.0	22.3	20.0	19.3	24.1	25.9	18.5	21.5	20.7	17.1	24.0	26.4
Smoked cigarettes [2]	4.4	4.0	2.4	5.1	3.2	1.5	5.5	4.2	2.8	5.4	3.7	1.9	3.5	3.8	2.0	4.8	2.9	1.2
Drank beer	33.1	37.9	40.9	42.9	42.4	41.0	38.7	42.6	46.4	49.6	47.7	46.7	28.4	33.6	36.0	37.7	37.8	35.7
Drank wine or liquor	39.4	42.2	45.9	49.1	47.6	46.5	40.3	41.7	46.4	50.3	48.6	47.4	38.6	42.7	45.4	48.2	45.4	45.6
Felt overwhelmed by all I had to do [2]	25.0	28.0	27.1	29.4	27.2	27.9	16.7	15.9	15.6	18.3	15.5	17.3	32.0	39.0	37.4	38.0	37.1	37.9
Felt depressed [2]	6.8	6.5	4.5	6.9	5.7	5.4	5.6	5.2	3.6	5.7	4.5	4.8	7.7	7.7	5.3	7.7	6.7	6.0
Performed volunteer work	82.0	85.2	91.7	86.9	91.3	93.7	77.1	80.7	88.8	83.0	87.8	91.7	86.1	89.2	94.3	89.9	94.3	95.6
Played a musical instrument	45.0	49.3	47.3	44.9	49.8	55.7	48.2	52.6	51.4	48.2	54.5	58.2	42.2	46.3	43.8	42.3	45.8	53.3
Asked a teacher for advice after class [2]	28.6	28.6	27.9	28.1	31.4	32.1	25.8	25.1	24.6	25.5	28.7	28.3	31.1	31.9	30.9	30.1	33.7	35.7
Voted in a student election [2]	23.0	20.9	24.0	23.9	26.8	26.4	21.3	19.4	21.3	21.9	24.2	24.3	24.5	22.4	26.3	25.4	29.1	28.4
Socialized with someone of another racial/ethnic group [2]	74.3	64.1	74.7	73.2	72.9	75.4	72.3	62.5	74.4	71.4	72.3	74.3	75.6	65.6	75.0	74.6	73.3	76.3
Came late to class	61.1	59.7	62.1	59.3	58.4	60.4	62.0	60.5	64.1	62.1	60.5	61.5	60.3	59.0	60.4	57.1	56.6	59.4
Used the Internet: [2]																		
For research or homework	77.3	77.0	82.3	79.1	84.2	88.2	73.0	70.9	77.3	72.4	80.0	84.9	81.0	82.5	86.7	84.3	87.7	91.2
To read news sites	43.7	42.2	47.6	48.3	53.9	57.9	46.2	46.2	52.2	50.9	57.6	62.5	41.5	38.6	43.5	46.3	50.9	53.5
To read blogs	26.4	24.7	26.1	28.4	26.6	27.8	24.2	21.8	24.8	26.0	25.3	27.9	28.2	27.3	27.2	30.3	27.7	27.7
To blog	15.7	14.5	13.6	16.1	13.4	11.9	13.0	11.3	11.2	13.5	11.6	10.5	17.9	17.5	15.6	18.0	14.9	13.2
Performed community service as part of a class	57.1	58.2	60.0	63.1	64.3	61.1	52.3	53.0	57.1	59.6	61.1	59.9	61.1	62.9	62.6	65.8	67.0	62.3
Discussed religion [2]	29.1	32.6	31.3	33.6	38.9	37.3	26.8	30.7	30.4	31.4	37.8	37.1	31.1	34.3	32.2	35.2	39.8	37.4
Discussed politics [2]	35.3	36.1	42.0	37.9	45.3	48.2	36.6	37.3	43.8	39.6	46.7	49.5	34.2	35.0	40.3	36.7	44.1	47.0
Worked on a local, state or national political campaign	11.5	12.0	13.4	11.9	15.7	15.0	11.0	12.3	13.1	11.9	15.6	15.4	11.9	11.7	13.6	12.0	15.7	14.7
Student rated self "above average" or "highest 10%" as compared with the average person of his/her age in:																		
Academic ability	67.3	75.3	88.4	76.2	87.4	94.6	72.1	80.3	90.7	79.7	89.3	95.2	63.2	70.7	86.3	73.5	85.7	94.1
Artistic ability	29.6	31.1	30.3	31.4	34.3	38.1	27.6	29.3	28.0	29.5	33.1	34.4	31.2	32.9	32.3	32.9	35.4	41.6
Computer skills	41.1	39.0	41.5	40.6	41.4	42.8	51.4	51.5	54.0	52.4	54.1	56.6	32.4	27.5	30.3	31.6	30.5	29.8
Cooperativeness	74.8	74.3	77.5	75.2	76.4	77.8	74.1	73.4	75.7	73.6	75.9	76.8	75.5	75.1	79.0	76.4	76.9	78.8
Creativity	57.7	56.5	56.2	58.8	63.6	62.8	57.6	56.2	55.8	59.7	62.2	62.5	57.7	56.2	56.5	58.2	59.4	63.0
Drive to achieve	74.8	74.6	82.9	78.0	81.9	89.1	71.3	71.3	79.0	74.5	78.6	86.1	77.8	77.7	86.4	80.8	84.6	91.9
Emotional health	55.8	55.9	62.1	54.4	59.9	63.4	62.4	61.8	68.2	61.9	65.7	68.8	50.2	50.4	56.7	48.6	55.0	58.3
Leadership ability	61.8	61.8	66.7	62.3	67.4	72.4	62.6	63.7	68.4	64.9	69.6	74.8	61.1	60.2	65.2	60.3	65.6	70.1
Mathematical ability	43.8	50.0	61.3	48.9	57.9	73.0	54.5	63.2	72.8	60.0	67.9	81.3	34.7	37.8	51.0	40.4	49.4	65.3
Physical health	54.5	56.6	62.3	54.0	58.9	63.2	66.1	66.9	71.0	64.5	67.0	69.6	44.7	47.2	54.6	45.9	52.1	57.2
Popularity	37.7	37.2	43.0	39.8	42.0	46.6	44.2	43.6	49.0	47.4	48.6	53.4	35.1	31.3	37.6	33.8	36.5	40.2
Public speaking ability	37.1	37.1	42.3	38.8	45.6	53.0	39.6	40.0	45.1	41.8	49.3	56.7	32.1	34.4	39.8	36.9	42.6	49.5
Self-confidence (intellectual)	58.9	60.7	69.0	61.9	68.3	76.9	63.1	69.4	77.4	69.8	76.2	83.3	55.1	52.7	61.3	55.8	61.5	71.0
Self-confidence (social)	54.8	50.9	55.0	52.1	53.4	54.9	58.5	54.1	58.5	56.4	57.1	58.2	51.8	47.9	51.9	48.8	50.2	51.9
Self-understanding	60.7	58.2	63.1	59.1	63.3	67.7	64.9	62.3	66.8	63.0	67.8	70.6	57.1	54.4	59.8	56.0	59.6	65.0
Spirituality	40.5	40.2	37.5	37.3	40.2	40.5	38.9	38.4	36.5	36.7	39.8	40.4	41.9	41.8	38.5	37.8	40.6	40.5
Understanding of others	69.1	67.3	69.4	69.5	71.0	72.4	67.3	64.9	66.3	67.6	69.6	70.0	70.7	69.6	72.2	71.0	72.2	74.5
Writing ability	45.4	46.9	54.7	51.2	57.6	64.8	43.0	43.6	51.9	48.9	55.7	62.8	47.4	50.0	57.1	52.9	59.2	66.7

WEIGHTED NATIONAL NORMS FOR UNIVERSITIES, FALL 2008

| | ALL FRESHMEN | | | | | | FRESHMAN MEN | | | | | | FRESHMAN WOMEN | | | | | |
| | PUBLIC | | | PRIVATE | | | PUBLIC | | | PRIVATE | | | PUBLIC | | | PRIVATE | | |
	LOW	MEDIUM	HIGH	MEDIUM	HIGH	V. HIGH	LOW	MEDIUM	HIGH	MEDIUM	HIGH	V. HIGH	LOW	MEDIUM	HIGH	MEDIUM	HIGH	V. HIGH
Student rated self "above average" or "highest 10%" as compared with the average person of his/her age in:																		
Ability to see the world from someone else's perspective	67.4	67.0	71.7	68.6	74.1	77.4	67.2	67.3	71.5	67.6	74.0	76.7	67.5	66.7	71.8	69.4	74.2	78.1
Tolerance of others with different beliefs	76.2	75.8	79.9	77.5	80.7	84.5	75.6	74.8	78.6	75.6	80.3	82.5	76.8	76.8	81.0	79.0	81.1	86.3
Openness to having my own views challenged	62.2	58.0	61.6	60.5	63.8	67.5	63.4	60.6	63.8	61.8	65.7	68.6	61.2	55.6	59.6	59.5	62.2	66.4
Ability to discuss and negotiate controversial issues	65.5	63.5	69.6	67.1	71.5	74.9	69.3	69.7	75.1	71.9	76.9	79.8	62.3	57.8	64.7	63.4	66.9	70.4
Ability to work cooperatively with diverse people	81.6	78.9	83.4	81.6	83.9	86.0	81.0	78.3	83.0	80.4	83.4	85.6	82.1	79.4	83.8	82.6	84.4	86.3
WHAT IS THE HIGHEST LEVEL OF FORMAL EDUCATION OBTAINED BY YOUR PARENTS?																		
Father																		
Grammar school or less	6.8	2.8	3.0	3.8	2.2	1.1	5.3	2.2	2.5	3.5	2.1	1.2	8.0	3.3	3.4	4.0	2.2	1.1
Some high school	6.9	2.9	3.2	5.0	2.4	1.6	5.8	2.7	2.8	4.0	2.2	1.5	7.9	3.0	3.5	5.7	2.6	1.6
High school graduate	19.8	15.9	12.0	18.4	9.6	5.6	18.0	15.1	10.8	18.0	9.5	5.3	21.4	16.7	13.1	18.8	9.6	5.9
Postsecondary school other than college	3.3	3.8	2.3	3.6	2.2	1.4	3.1	3.5	2.0	3.4	1.8	1.4	3.5	4.2	2.6	3.7	2.4	1.4
Some college	17.5	14.8	11.6	15.2	10.5	7.2	16.8	14.0	10.8	14.8	9.8	6.9	18.0	15.6	12.3	15.5	11.1	7.5
College degree	25.4	33.2	30.5	28.7	31.6	27.1	27.8	34.9	31.5	29.7	32.2	27.5	23.2	31.7	29.5	27.9	31.0	26.7
Some graduate school	1.9	2.3	2.9	2.4	3.2	3.6	2.1	2.3	3.0	2.5	3.1	3.4	1.7	2.3	2.8	2.3	3.4	3.8
Graduate degree	18.4	24.3	34.5	23.0	38.3	52.4	21.0	25.4	36.5	24.1	39.2	52.9	16.3	23.2	32.8	22.1	37.6	51.9
Mother																		
Grammar school or less	6.3	2.5	3.0	3.5	1.8	1.1	5.0	2.0	2.4	3.5	1.7	1.0	7.5	2.9	3.4	3.6	1.9	1.1
Some high school	6.1	2.4	2.5	3.7	1.7	1.3	5.1	2.0	2.2	2.9	1.6	1.2	6.9	2.8	2.8	4.3	1.8	1.4
High school graduate	19.7	15.3	12.2	18.1	9.4	6.3	19.0	15.3	11.8	17.9	9.1	6.7	20.2	15.3	12.6	18.2	9.7	5.8
Postsecondary school other than college	3.5	3.6	2.7	3.5	2.6	2.2	3.0	3.5	2.5	3.7	2.3	1.7	3.9	3.6	2.8	3.5	2.9	2.2
Some college	20.2	18.0	13.7	16.4	12.5	8.6	19.1	15.9	12.8	15.5	11.4	8.5	21.1	19.9	14.6	17.1	13.3	8.6
College degree	27.5	37.3	38.1	32.9	38.9	38.7	30.2	39.3	39.4	34.0	39.5	39.0	25.2	35.5	36.9	32.1	38.3	38.4
Some graduate school	2.6	2.7	3.6	2.8	4.5	4.5	2.7	2.7	3.7	2.7	4.6	4.1	2.5	2.7	3.5	2.9	4.4	4.9
Graduate degree	14.2	18.3	24.2	19.1	28.7	37.6	15.8	19.3	25.2	19.9	29.8	37.7	12.8	17.3	23.4	18.4	27.7	37.6
During the past year, did you "frequently":																		
Ask questions in class	49.9	53.1	57.5	55.3	60.6	65.9	45.4	49.1	53.6	50.6	57.3	63.6	53.7	56.7	61.0	58.9	63.4	68.1
Support your opinions with a logical argument	54.9	58.9	66.9	61.7	70.2	79.2	57.4	62.7	70.2	63.9	73.1	81.7	52.7	55.5	63.9	60.0	67.8	76.8
Seek solutions to problems and explain them to others	49.8	52.1	59.8	55.4	63.3	73.3	49.2	52.7	59.8	53.5	63.0	73.0	50.3	51.6	59.8	56.9	63.5	73.5
Revise your papers to improve your writing	43.8	47.1	49.3	46.7	53.4	59.8	35.0	36.9	39.8	35.4	44.1	51.2	51.2	56.5	57.6	55.4	61.2	67.8
Evaluate the quality or reliability of information you received	37.2	37.0	42.1	39.0	47.4	53.5	36.9	37.5	42.6	38.7	47.3	53.6	37.5	36.7	41.6	39.3	47.5	53.4
Take a risk because you feel you have more to gain	40.4	38.4	39.6	40.2	41.7	43.6	43.7	41.8	43.2	43.8	44.9	47.5	37.5	35.4	36.4	37.3	39.1	40.0
Seek alternative solutions to a problem	44.4	44.0	46.7	47.1	50.6	53.8	45.9	46.9	48.2	48.2	52.2	55.6	43.1	41.4	45.4	46.3	49.2	52.0
Look up scientific research articles and resources	22.2	22.9	25.6	23.7	29.0	33.4	25.0	25.7	28.2	25.0	31.3	35.4	19.7	20.4	23.3	22.8	27.1	31.6
Explore topics on your own, even though it was not required for a class	31.8	31.8	33.6	34.2	39.4	43.3	34.9	36.1	37.9	37.8	43.6	48.3	29.1	27.8	29.7	31.5	35.8	38.5
Accept mistakes as part of the learning process	54.5	51.2	52.6	51.7	53.5	55.6	53.2	50.4	51.7	50.1	53.6	55.8	55.6	51.9	53.5	52.9	53.5	55.5
Seek feedback on your academic work	46.9	46.0	50.9	48.1	53.4	58.4	40.5	39.1	44.0	40.3	46.7	52.7	52.3	52.3	57.1	54.2	59.0	63.8
Take notes during class	64.1	63.8	67.0	69.6	70.1	73.0	49.7	49.7	51.7	54.5	56.4	59.8	76.3	76.7	80.5	81.1	81.6	85.3

WEIGHTED NATIONAL NORMS FOR UNIVERSITIES, FALL 2008

| | ALL FRESHMEN | | | | | | FRESHMAN MEN | | | | | | FRESHMAN WOMEN | | | | | |
| | PUBLIC | | | PRIVATE | | | PUBLIC | | | PRIVATE | | | PUBLIC | | | PRIVATE | | |
Your probable career occupation	LOW	MEDIUM	HIGH	MEDIUM	HIGH	V. HIGH	LOW	MEDIUM	HIGH	MEDIUM	HIGH	V. HIGH	LOW	MEDIUM	HIGH	MEDIUM	HIGH	V. HIGH
Accountant or actuary	3.4	2.2	1.8	3.2	1.9	1.0	4.4	2.4	2.1	3.9	2.2	1.1	2.5	2.0	1.6	2.7	1.7	1.0
Actor or entertainer	0.8	0.9	0.7	1.3	1.2	1.7	0.8	0.8	0.6	0.9	0.9	1.6	0.9	1.0	0.8	1.5	1.4	1.9
Architect or urban planner	1.2	0.9	1.6	0.5	1.8	1.9	1.6	1.1	1.7	0.8	1.7	1.7	0.8	0.8	1.5	0.3	1.9	2.0
Artist	1.5	2.2	1.0	1.9	1.1	1.4	1.2	1.5	0.6	1.3	0.7	1.0	1.6	2.8	1.4	2.3	1.4	1.9
Business (clerical)	1.1	0.6	0.6	0.8	0.5	0.4	1.2	0.6	0.6	0.9	0.5	0.5	0.9	0.7	0.5	0.7	0.5	0.4
Business executive (management, administrator)	8.1	7.0	8.6	8.8	9.1	12.4	10.3	8.4	10.4	12.1	11.7	15.6	6.2	5.8	6.9	6.2	6.9	9.4
Business owner or proprietor	3.8	2.6	2.6	3.1	3.2	3.2	4.9	3.6	3.5	4.6	4.8	4.5	2.9	1.8	1.7	1.9	1.8	2.0
Business salesperson or buyer	0.9	1.1	0.8	0.9	0.8	0.4	1.0	1.1	0.7	0.9	0.8	0.5	0.8	1.1	0.8	0.9	0.8	0.3
Clergy (minister, priest)	0.1	0.0	0.1	0.1	0.2	0.1	0.1	0.1	0.1	0.2	0.4	0.2	0.0	0.0	0.1	0.0	0.1	0.0
Clergy (other religious)	0.0	0.0	0.0	0.0	0.1	0.0	0.0	0.1	0.0	0.0	0.1	0.0	0.0	0.0	0.1	0.0	0.1	0.0
Clinical psychologist	1.4	1.2	1.2	1.5	1.0	0.9	0.7	0.5	0.5	0.6	0.4	0.4	2.0	1.8	1.8	2.1	1.6	1.5
College administrator/staff	0.0	0.1	0.0	0.0	0.0	0.1	0.0	0.1	0.0	0.0	0.0	0.1	0.1	0.0	0.1	0.0	0.0	0.1
College teacher	0.5	0.4	0.5	0.4	0.6	1.2	0.4	0.5	0.4	0.3	0.7	1.4	0.5	0.3	0.5	0.4	0.5	1.0
Computer programmer or analyst	1.8	2.5	1.7	1.6	1.9	1.8	3.6	4.7	3.1	3.4	3.7	3.1	0.3	0.5	0.4	0.1	0.5	0.5
Conservationist or forester	0.6	0.5	0.3	0.1	0.1	0.2	0.8	0.5	0.3	0.1	0.1	0.1	0.4	0.4	0.4	0.1	0.2	0.3
Dentist (including orthodontist)	1.5	1.0	1.7	1.7	1.2	0.8	1.3	0.9	1.6	1.6	1.1	0.8	1.6	1.2	1.7	1.8	1.3	0.9
Dietitian or nutritionist	0.5	1.1	0.5	0.3	0.3	0.2	0.3	0.2	0.1	0.2	0.1	0.1	0.7	2.0	0.9	0.4	0.4	0.3
Engineer	7.7	16.1	12.8	9.9	9.9	11.9	14.0	27.2	21.8	18.4	16.5	15.9	2.4	5.8	4.9	3.3	4.3	8.1
Farmer or rancher	0.2	0.7	0.2	0.1	0.2	0.1	0.4	1.0	0.2	0.1	0.2	0.1	0.1	0.3	0.2	0.1	0.1	0.1
Foreign service worker (including diplomat)	0.7	0.6	1.0	1.3	2.7	1.7	0.5	0.3	0.5	0.7	1.7	1.0	0.8	0.9	1.5	1.7	3.5	2.4
Homemaker (full-time)	0.1	0.1	0.1	0.0	0.0	0.1	0.0	0.0	0.1	0.0	0.0	0.0	0.1	0.3	0.1	0.0	0.1	0.1
Interior decorator (including designer)	0.4	0.8	0.2	0.4	0.3	0.2	0.1	0.1	0.0	0.0	0.0	0.0	0.6	1.5	0.4	0.6	0.5	0.3
Lab technician or hygienist	0.2	0.2	0.1	0.2	0.1	0.1	0.2	0.1	0.1	0.2	0.1	0.1	0.2	0.2	0.1	0.2	0.1	0.0
Law enforcement officer	1.2	0.4	0.2	0.8	0.5	0.1	1.8	0.7	0.3	1.3	0.7	0.1	0.7	0.2	0.1	0.4	0.2	0.1
Lawyer (attorney) or judge	3.3	2.4	4.8	5.3	6.0	5.7	2.8	2.1	4.6	5.2	5.9	5.4	3.7	2.6	5.0	5.5	6.1	5.9
Military service (career)	0.6	0.4	0.6	0.4	0.4	0.2	1.0	0.8	1.2	0.8	0.7	0.3	0.2	0.1	0.1	0.2	0.2	0.2
Musician (performer, composer)	1.5	1.5	0.9	1.7	2.1	1.6	1.9	1.9	1.2	2.7	3.0	1.8	1.1	1.2	0.7	1.0	1.4	1.4
Nurse	3.9	2.0	1.9	3.7	1.7	1.6	0.8	0.3	0.3	0.7	0.2	0.1	6.5	3.6	3.3	6.0	3.0	1.0
Optometrist	0.6	0.2	0.4	0.4	0.3	0.2	0.5	0.2	0.3	0.1	0.2	0.1	0.7	0.3	0.6	0.6	0.3	0.3
Pharmacist	2.2	2.5	2.9	4.8	1.8	0.5	2.1	2.1	2.2	3.8	1.5	0.2	2.2	2.8	3.5	5.6	2.2	0.8
Physician	7.0	4.7	11.9	8.8	12.0	14.9	6.2	4.1	10.8	6.4	10.0	13.2	7.7	5.3	13.0	10.6	13.7	16.4
Policymaker/Government	0.7	0.7	1.3	0.9	2.3	1.9	0.8	0.9	1.5	1.1	2.5	1.9	0.5	0.5	1.2	0.7	2.1	1.8
School counselor	0.4	0.2	0.1	0.3	0.1	0.1	0.1	0.1	0.0	0.0	0.1	0.0	0.7	0.4	0.2	0.4	0.1	0.1
School principal or superintendent	0.0	0.0	0.0	0.1	0.0	0.0	0.0	0.0	0.0	0.1	0.0	0.0	0.0	0.0	0.0	0.1	0.0	0.1
Scientific researcher	1.7	2.8	2.8	1.6	3.1	4.4	2.1	3.0	3.2	1.9	3.1	4.6	1.5	2.7	2.6	1.4	3.2	4.2
Social, welfare, or recreation worker	1.2	0.8	0.6	0.8	0.7	0.3	0.4	0.3	0.2	0.2	0.2	0.1	1.9	1.3	0.9	1.2	1.0	0.5
Therapist (physical, occupational, speech)	3.1	2.6	1.9	2.9	2.1	0.6	1.9	1.3	0.8	1.4	0.9	0.2	4.2	3.8	3.0	4.0	3.0	0.9
Teacher or administrator (elementary)	3.1	3.0	1.2	2.3	0.9	0.6	0.6	0.4	0.2	0.5	0.1	0.1	5.1	5.5	2.0	3.7	1.7	1.0
Teacher or administrator (secondary)	4.0	2.9	1.9	3.0	1.1	0.9	3.5	2.3	1.5	2.3	1.0	0.6	4.5	3.5	2.2	3.6	1.2	1.1
Veterinarian	1.1	2.3	1.4	0.3	0.4	0.7	0.5	0.7	0.5	0.0	0.2	0.3	1.5	3.7	2.2	0.6	0.6	1.1
Writer or journalist	2.4	2.5	2.8	3.2	3.6	4.0	1.5	1.7	1.5	2.0	1.9	2.3	3.1	3.3	4.0	4.1	4.9	5.7
Skilled trades	0.2	0.3	0.1	0.2	0.1	0.1	0.4	0.5	0.2	0.3	0.2	0.1	0.1	0.1	0.1	0.1	0.1	0.0
Laborer (unskilled)	0.4	0.3	0.3	0.2	0.2	0.1	0.7	0.5	0.4	0.4	0.3	0.1	0.2	0.2	0.2	0.1	0.1	0.0
Semi-skilled worker	0.2	0.2	0.2	0.2	0.2	0.1	0.3	0.3	0.3	0.3	0.3	0.1	0.1	0.1	0.2	0.1	0.1	0.1
Unemployed	1.8	0.8	1.2	1.1	1.2	0.6	1.7	0.8	1.2	1.0	1.3	0.8	1.9	0.9	1.3	1.2	1.0	0.5
Other	9.3	9.1	6.2	8.6	6.7	3.7	7.2	6.9	4.7	6.6	4.9	2.9	11.1	11.1	7.5	10.1	8.2	4.4
Undecided	13.7	14.2	16.1	10.7	14.3	16.5	13.0	12.7	13.8	9.7	12.3	14.8	14.2	15.5	18.0	11.4	15.9	18.2

WEIGHTED NATIONAL NORMS FOR UNIVERSITIES, FALL 2008

| | ALL FRESHMEN | | | | | | FRESHMAN MEN | | | | | | FRESHMAN WOMEN | | | | | |
| | PUBLIC | | | PRIVATE | | | PUBLIC | | | PRIVATE | | | PUBLIC | | | PRIVATE | | |
	LOW	MEDIUM	HIGH	MEDIUM	HIGH	V. HIGH	LOW	MEDIUM	HIGH	MEDIUM	HIGH	V. HIGH	LOW	MEDIUM	HIGH	MEDIUM	HIGH	V. HIGH
Your father's occupation [3]																		
Artist	0.9	1.2	1.2	0.8	1.4	1.5	1.0	1.2	1.3	0.8	1.5	1.6	0.9	1.2	1.2	0.9	1.3	1.4
Business	24.6	28.6	30.5	29.3	34.6	35.8	26.8	28.7	31.6	30.8	35.6	36.7	22.8	28.5	29.6	28.2	33.7	34.8
Business (clerical)	1.5	1.3	1.3	1.6	1.3	1.1	1.6	1.3	1.4	2.0	1.5	1.1	1.3	1.3	1.2	1.3	1.1	1.1
Clergy	0.6	0.5	0.6	0.6	0.7	0.7	0.6	0.6	0.6	0.5	0.7	0.7	0.6	0.3	0.6	0.6	0.7	0.7
College teacher	0.4	0.7	0.9	0.6	1.0	2.3	0.5	0.7	1.1	0.7	0.9	2.4	0.3	0.6	0.8	0.6	1.1	2.2
Doctor (MD or DDS)	1.7	2.2	5.3	3.6	6.1	9.2	2.2	2.6	5.6	3.6	6.4	9.3	1.2	1.9	5.0	3.6	5.9	9.2
Education (secondary)	2.0	2.4	1.8	1.7	1.8	1.9	2.1	2.6	1.9	1.8	1.8	2.1	1.8	2.2	1.7	1.7	1.8	1.7
Education (elementary)	0.8	0.6	0.7	0.6	0.6	0.4	0.9	0.6	0.8	0.7	0.6	0.5	0.7	0.7	0.6	0.5	0.5	0.3
Engineer	9.6	11.7	11.5	8.4	9.7	9.9	10.1	12.4	11.9	9.0	9.5	9.5	9.1	11.1	11.1	7.8	9.9	10.3
Farmer or forester	1.5	3.5	0.6	0.7	0.7	0.6	1.4	3.5	0.6	0.6	0.7	0.6	1.6	3.4	0.7	0.8	0.8	0.6
Health professional	1.4	1.6	1.7	1.7	1.6	1.5	1.6	1.7	1.7	1.5	1.6	1.5	1.2	1.6	1.7	1.8	1.7	1.4
Homemaker (full-time)	0.3	0.2	0.3	0.3	0.2	0.2	0.3	0.3	0.4	0.3	0.3	0.2	0.2	0.2	0.2	0.2	0.2	0.2
Lawyer	1.2	2.0	4.0	2.2	5.3	7.0	1.3	2.0	4.2	2.3	5.4	6.9	1.1	2.0	3.9	2.2	5.3	7.1
Military (career)	1.5	1.0	1.4	0.7	1.0	0.6	1.4	0.9	1.4	0.7	0.9	0.7	1.6	1.0	1.4	0.7	1.1	0.6
Nurse	0.6	0.4	0.4	0.6	0.4	0.2	0.6	0.5	0.5	0.6	0.3	0.2	0.6	0.4	0.4	0.6	0.4	0.2
Research scientist	0.7	1.0	1.3	0.6	1.3	2.5	0.7	1.1	1.3	0.6	1.5	2.5	0.6	1.0	1.2	0.6	1.1	2.5
Social/welfare/rec worker	0.6	0.5	0.4	0.5	0.4	0.4	0.7	0.6	0.5	0.6	0.4	0.5	0.6	0.4	0.3	0.5	0.5	0.3
Skilled worker	6.7	7.0	4.9	7.4	4.5	2.8	7.3	7.8	4.9	8.0	4.2	2.8	6.1	6.4	5.0	7.0	4.7	2.8
Semi-skilled worker	3.7	2.8	2.3	2.4	1.6	1.3	3.6	2.9	2.2	2.5	1.7	1.4	3.7	2.6	2.3	2.3	1.4	1.2
Unskilled worker	4.5	2.5	2.3	2.4	1.3	1.0	4.3	2.3	2.1	2.1	1.3	0.9	4.6	2.7	2.5	2.6	1.3	1.0
Unemployed	4.0	2.5	2.7	3.0	2.0	1.8	2.7	2.2	2.1	2.6	1.6	1.5	5.1	2.8	3.2	3.3	2.2	2.1
Other	31.5	25.7	23.8	30.4	22.5	17.3	28.4	23.6	22.0	27.8	21.6	16.4	34.2	27.8	25.4	32.4	23.3	18.3
Your mother's occupation [3]																		
Artist	1.4	2.1	2.3	1.7	2.7	3.3	1.7	2.2	2.3	1.7	3.0	3.5	1.1	2.0	2.2	1.8	2.4	3.1
Business	17.0	16.4	16.9	16.1	18.4	16.9	17.5	16.2	16.7	16.2	18.0	16.6	16.6	16.5	17.2	16.0	18.7	17.2
Business (clerical)	4.0	4.5	3.9	4.2	3.9	2.8	4.2	4.6	3.9	4.4	4.0	3.1	3.9	4.5	3.9	4.0	3.8	2.6
Clergy	0.2	0.2	0.2	0.1	0.3	0.3	0.3	0.3	0.2	0.1	0.4	0.3	0.1	0.1	0.2	0.1	0.2	0.4
College teacher	0.2	0.5	0.6	0.4	0.7	1.4	0.3	0.6	0.6	0.5	0.6	1.4	0.1	0.5	0.6	0.3	0.9	1.5
Doctor (MD or DDS)	1.0	1.2	2.0	1.3	2.4	4.4	1.1	1.5	2.2	1.6	2.5	4.3	0.9	0.9	1.8	1.1	2.3	4.6
Education (secondary)	3.7	5.1	4.5	3.7	4.9	4.6	4.2	5.1	4.7	3.9	4.9	5.0	3.2	5.0	4.3	3.5	5.0	4.3
Education (elementary)	7.0	9.2	8.0	7.7	7.9	5.8	7.7	9.4	8.5	8.2	7.9	6.0	6.3	8.9	7.6	7.4	7.9	5.7
Engineer	0.8	1.1	1.6	0.8	1.3	2.0	0.9	1.1	1.7	0.9	1.3	2.0	0.7	1.1	1.6	0.7	1.4	2.0
Farmer or forester	0.3	0.4	0.2	0.1	0.1	0.2	0.3	0.3	0.2	0.1	0.2	0.2	0.3	0.4	0.2	0.1	0.1	0.2
Health professional	3.2	4.0	4.1	4.0	3.9	3.6	3.4	4.2	4.0	4.3	4.0	4.0	3.1	3.8	4.2	3.8	3.7	3.2
Homemaker (full-time)	8.1	9.8	11.1	9.0	11.9	17.2	6.9	8.8	10.3	8.0	10.9	16.5	9.0	10.7	11.8	9.8	12.8	18.0
Lawyer	0.6	0.8	1.7	1.0	2.4	3.3	0.6	0.9	1.9	1.2	2.6	3.2	0.5	0.7	0.9	0.8	2.2	3.4
Military (career)	0.2	0.1	0.1	0.1	0.2	0.1	0.2	0.1	0.1	0.2	0.2	0.1	0.2	0.1	0.2	0.1	0.2	0.1
Nurse	7.8	7.9	7.2	9.6	7.2	5.2	7.7	8.1	7.4	9.6	7.4	5.1	7.8	7.7	7.0	9.5	7.0	5.3
Research scientist	0.4	0.6	0.8	0.4	0.7	1.5	0.4	0.6	0.8	0.5	0.9	1.7	0.3	0.6	0.8	0.3	0.5	1.3
Social/welfare/rec worker	1.5	1.6	1.6	1.7	1.6	1.5	1.4	1.7	1.7	2.0	1.5	1.5	1.7	1.5	1.5	1.4	1.6	1.6
Skilled worker	1.6	1.5	1.4	1.3	0.9	0.9	1.7	1.8	1.4	1.7	1.0	1.0	1.6	1.2	1.3	1.1	0.9	0.8
Semi-skilled worker	2.5	1.9	1.6	1.8	1.1	1.2	2.9	2.1	1.8	2.3	1.5	1.3	2.2	1.7	1.5	1.5	0.8	1.1
Unskilled worker	2.7	1.6	1.6	1.4	0.8	0.7	2.7	1.7	1.5	1.3	0.8	0.7	2.7	1.5	1.6	1.5	0.8	0.6
Unemployed	8.5	5.6	6.6	6.8	6.1	6.2	8.4	6.1	6.9	6.5	6.6	7.0	8.6	5.2	6.3	7.0	5.7	5.4
Other	27.3	24.0	22.2	26.7	20.5	16.7	25.4	22.6	21.2	24.8	19.9	15.6	28.9	25.2	23.0	28.2	21.1	17.7
How would you characterize your political views?																		
Far left	2.8	3.3	3.2	3.5	4.1	4.4	3.3	3.7	3.7	3.9	4.4	4.4	2.3	2.9	2.8	3.2	3.8	4.4
Liberal	32.8	31.1	37.1	35.1	37.0	41.4	28.7	27.2	32.3	28.9	32.1	37.0	36.4	34.7	41.4	40.0	41.2	45.5
Middle-of-the-road	45.7	42.0	38.1	43.2	36.5	35.2	47.2	43.5	39.5	45.4	37.9	36.1	44.4	40.5	36.9	41.6	35.4	34.4
Conservative	17.4	22.0	20.1	16.7	20.9	17.7	19.0	23.2	22.5	19.4	23.4	20.5	15.9	20.9	18.0	14.6	18.7	15.1
Far right	1.4	1.6	1.4	1.5	1.5	1.3	1.8	2.3	2.1	2.5	2.2	1.9	1.0	1.0	0.8	0.6	0.9	0.6

WEIGHTED NATIONAL NORMS FOR UNIVERSITIES, FALL 2008

	ALL FRESHMEN					FRESHMAN MEN					FRESHMAN WOMEN				
	PUBLIC			PRIVATE		PUBLIC			PRIVATE		PUBLIC			PRIVATE	
Student agrees "strongly" or "somewhat":	LOW	MEDIUM	HIGH	HIGH	V. HIGH	LOW	MEDIUM	HIGH	HIGH	V. HIGH	LOW	MEDIUM	HIGH	HIGH	V. HIGH
There is too much concern in the courts for the rights of criminals	57.7	57.6	53.7	52.7	49.2	60.5	60.6	55.9	54.9	51.7	55.3	54.8	51.7	50.9	46.8
Abortion should be legal	60.5	57.6	67.0	65.5	71.5	62.1	58.6	66.7	65.7	70.9	59.1	56.8	67.3	65.4	72.0
The death penalty should be abolished	32.9	34.2	37.0	42.9	49.8	30.3	30.7	32.7	39.1	45.5	35.1	37.5	40.9	46.1	53.9
Marijuana should be legalized	39.0	40.3	44.8	44.3	45.2	44.9	45.9	50.2	48.4	49.7	34.0	35.2	40.0	40.9	40.9
It is important to have laws prohibiting homosexual relationships	21.3	23.8	18.1	19.3	15.0	26.9	29.9	23.0	23.0	18.7	16.5	18.2	13.8	16.1	11.5
Racial discrimination is no longer a major problem in America	18.1	20.8	18.7	20.1	17.6	22.3	25.8	23.1	24.8	21.8	14.6	16.2	14.7	16.2	13.6
Realistically, an individual can do little to bring about changes in our society	28.8	26.4	22.5	22.8	22.0	32.4	30.9	26.8	27.6	26.1	25.7	22.1	18.7	18.7	18.1
Wealthy people should pay a larger share of taxes than they do now	60.8	60.3	58.5	57.3	57.1	61.1	59.1	58.0	57.3	56.7	60.5	61.3	58.9	57.4	57.4
Same-sex couples should have the right to legal marital status	70.1	65.4	71.6	71.6	76.4	63.7	59.0	65.7	66.9	72.1	75.5	71.2	76.8	75.6	80.4
Affirmative action in college admissions should be abolished	45.3	50.7	57.1	55.7	60.3	51.6	56.3	61.4	60.1	63.7	39.8	45.3	53.2	51.9	57.0
Federal military spending should be increased	23.3	26.0	22.7	25.7	19.6	26.3	29.5	26.7	30.1	23.7	20.7	22.7	19.0	21.9	15.8
The federal government should do more to control the sale of handguns	72.9	69.5	73.8	74.5	79.5	65.6	60.5	66.0	67.7	73.4	79.1	77.8	80.9	80.4	85.4
Only volunteers should serve in the armed forces	65.7	67.8	69.2	70.9	75.6	64.6	66.2	68.4	70.3	75.4	66.6	69.2	69.9	71.5	75.8
The federal government is not doing enough to control environmental pollution	81.1	77.3	82.4	80.7	85.7	77.9	73.5	79.3	77.6	82.6	83.9	80.8	85.2	83.4	88.6
A national health care plan is needed to cover everybody's medical costs	71.3	67.3	65.9	66.6	67.5	67.5	62.3	61.1	61.7	62.6	74.5	72.0	70.3	70.8	72.1
Undocumented immigrants should be denied access to public education	43.5	49.8	44.7	43.6	37.5	48.8	55.5	49.2	48.6	42.2	39.0	44.6	40.7	39.4	33.0
Through hard work, everybody can succeed in American society	81.4	78.8	77.7	74.8	70.6	81.3	79.6	78.5	75.9	72.6	81.6	78.0	77.0	73.7	68.8
Dissent is a critical component of the political process	59.1	62.1	70.8	71.9	82.1	62.6	66.5	74.1	74.7	83.7	56.0	57.8	67.7	69.4	80.5
Colleges have the right to ban extreme speakers from campus	36.0	41.5	37.0	41.6	41.8	38.0	43.7	40.8	45.2	46.4	34.2	39.4	33.5	38.5	37.5
Students from disadvantaged social backgrounds should be given preferential treatment in college admissions	41.6	36.9	35.1	35.3	37.6	43.1	37.6	36.7	38.1	39.8	40.3	36.2	33.7	32.9	35.4
The federal government should raise taxes to reduce the deficit	28.0	30.6	34.7	34.1	39.5	32.7	35.6	39.2	38.8	43.8	23.9	25.9	30.6	30.0	35.4
Addressing global warming should be a federal priority	75.6	71.7	78.4	77.2	81.4	71.6	67.5	74.7	73.6	78.0	79.0	75.5	81.7	80.3	84.7

101

WEIGHTED NATIONAL NORMS FOR UNIVERSITIES, FALL 2008

DURING YOUR LAST YEAR IN HIGH SCHOOL, HOW MUCH TIME DID YOU SPEND DURING A TYPICAL WEEK DOING THE FOLLOWING?

| | ALL FRESHMEN | | | | | FRESHMAN MEN | | | | | FRESHMAN WOMEN | | | | |
| | PUBLIC | | | PRIVATE | | PUBLIC | | | PRIVATE | | PUBLIC | | | PRIVATE | |
	LOW	MEDIUM	HIGH	HIGH	V. HIGH	LOW	MEDIUM	HIGH	HIGH	V. HIGH	LOW	MEDIUM	HIGH	HIGH	V. HIGH
Studying/homework															
None	1.5	1.8	1.1	1.5	0.7	2.3	3.1	2.1	2.5	1.2	0.8	0.7	0.3	0.6	0.2
Less than one hour	9.9	10.0	6.9	5.8	3.0	13.0	13.1	9.9	8.9	4.7	7.4	7.1	4.2	3.3	1.4
1 to 2 hours	22.7	20.6	15.6	14.3	8.0	25.7	23.4	19.1	17.2	10.7	20.2	18.0	12.4	11.8	5.4
3 to 5 hours	31.1	29.6	28.3	25.2	18.4	30.1	28.7	28.7	26.5	21.8	31.9	30.4	27.9	24.1	15.3
6 to 10 hours	20.1	21.4	24.0	24.1	24.5	17.4	18.7	21.6	23.0	24.6	22.3	24.0	26.2	26.2	24.4
11 to 15 hours	8.3	9.6	12.6	14.1	19.8	6.5	7.7	10.0	11.7	17.6	9.9	11.4	14.9	16.2	21.8
16 to 20 hours	3.5	4.1	6.7	8.0	13.4	2.8	3.1	4.8	5.8	10.1	4.1	5.1	8.4	9.9	16.5
Over 20 hours	2.8	2.8	4.8	6.3	12.2	2.3	2.3	3.8	4.5	9.4	3.3	3.3	5.8	7.8	14.9
Socializing with friends															
None	0.4	0.3	0.2	0.4	0.2	0.6	0.4	0.3	0.6	0.3	0.3	0.2	0.1	0.2	0.1
Less than one hour	1.9	1.0	1.0	1.1	0.8	1.6	1.2	1.0	1.2	1.0	2.1	0.9	1.0	0.9	0.6
1 to 2 hours	8.9	5.4	5.8	5.7	5.1	8.0	5.3	5.3	5.9	5.0	9.6	5.5	6.1	5.5	5.1
3 to 5 hours	21.4	18.7	20.0	18.1	20.1	19.9	18.1	18.9	16.6	18.8	22.8	19.3	20.9	19.4	21.2
6 to 10 hours	25.5	27.7	29.9	28.5	31.3	25.8	27.1	29.0	28.3	30.1	25.3	28.3	30.7	28.6	32.5
11 to 15 hours	17.0	20.0	19.8	19.9	20.5	17.6	19.7	19.7	19.9	20.6	16.5	20.3	19.8	20.0	20.4
16 to 20 hours	9.9	11.9	11.0	11.9	11.1	10.3	11.3	11.2	11.6	11.3	9.5	12.5	10.8	12.1	11.0
Over 20 hours	15.0	14.9	12.3	14.5	10.9	16.2	17.0	14.5	15.9	12.9	13.9	13.1	10.5	13.2	9.1
Talking with teachers outside of class															
None	10.0	8.9	8.5	6.3	5.7	12.2	11.2	10.8	7.9	7.4	8.2	6.9	6.5	5.0	4.1
Less than one hour	43.3	43.6	44.3	36.6	36.9	44.9	44.9	46.3	38.1	39.0	42.0	42.4	42.5	35.4	35.0
1 to 2 hours	30.6	32.0	32.8	37.0	37.5	29.9	30.2	30.5	35.3	36.2	31.2	33.7	34.7	38.5	38.7
3 to 5 hours	10.9	11.4	10.8	14.4	15.1	8.8	10.0	9.2	13.3	12.9	12.6	12.6	12.1	15.3	17.1
6 to 10 hours	3.2	2.7	2.5	3.7	3.4	2.7	2.4	2.1	3.6	3.1	3.6	3.0	2.8	3.8	3.6
11 to 15 hours	1.1	0.9	0.6	1.0	0.8	0.8	0.8	0.5	0.8	0.8	1.4	1.0	0.7	1.2	0.9
16 to 20 hours	0.4	0.2	0.3	0.4	0.3	0.2	0.2	0.2	0.4	0.2	0.5	0.3	0.4	0.5	0.3
Over 20 hours	0.5	0.3	0.3	0.5	0.3	0.5	0.4	0.3	0.6	0.4	0.4	0.3	0.2	0.3	0.2
Exercise or sports															
None	5.6	3.5	3.2	3.4	2.6	3.6	2.8	2.2	2.9	1.9	7.2	4.1	4.0	5.0	3.3
Less than one hour	10.3	8.5	7.9	7.5	7.1	7.3	6.6	5.7	5.8	5.7	12.8	10.2	9.8	9.0	8.4
1 to 2 hours	17.5	15.5	14.2	14.4	13.5	15.3	13.3	12.2	13.3	12.0	19.4	17.4	15.9	15.4	14.9
3 to 5 hours	20.4	20.2	20.7	21.9	21.2	19.8	19.4	19.8	20.9	20.3	20.8	20.8	21.5	22.7	22.1
6 to 10 hours	17.9	20.6	22.0	20.5	22.2	19.8	21.5	22.9	20.5	23.0	16.3	19.8	21.2	20.5	21.4
11 to 15 hours	12.3	14.5	15.3	14.7	16.1	13.7	15.8	16.7	16.2	16.7	11.2	13.4	14.1	13.3	15.6
16 to 20 hours	6.9	8.3	8.4	8.5	8.4	8.1	9.3	9.6	9.2	9.1	5.9	7.4	7.5	7.9	7.8
Over 20 hours	9.1	9.0	8.3	9.1	8.8	12.4	11.2	10.9	11.3	11.2	6.4	6.9	6.1	7.3	6.5
Partying															
None	31.6	30.8	27.3	28.3	28.1	28.1	27.0	23.8	24.8	24.9	34.5	34.3	30.3	31.2	31.2
Less than one hour	15.5	15.7	16.6	15.7	17.0	15.8	16.0	16.8	15.9	16.7	15.2	15.5	16.5	15.5	17.3
1 to 2 hours	18.6	18.4	20.0	18.4	19.0	19.2	19.1	20.4	18.9	19.4	18.1	17.8	19.7	18.0	18.7
3 to 5 hours	18.3	18.2	19.9	19.6	21.0	18.5	18.9	20.3	19.9	21.5	18.1	17.6	19.5	19.4	20.5
6 to 10 hours	9.2	10.2	10.2	11.2	10.2	9.6	11.0	10.9	12.0	11.3	8.8	9.5	9.5	10.6	9.0
11 to 15 hours	3.5	3.8	3.6	3.6	2.6	4.5	4.2	4.3	4.2	3.2	2.6	3.4	2.9	3.1	2.1
16 to 20 hours	1.5	1.4	1.3	1.7	1.1	1.9	1.8	1.5	1.9	1.5	1.2	1.1	1.1	1.5	0.7
Over 20 hours	1.8	1.4	1.2	1.5	0.9	2.4	2.0	2.0	2.3	1.5	1.4	0.8	0.5	0.8	0.4

WEIGHTED NATIONAL NORMS FOR UNIVERSITIES, FALL 2008

	ALL FRESHMEN						FRESHMAN MEN						FRESHMAN WOMEN					
	PUBLIC			PRIVATE			PUBLIC			PRIVATE			PUBLIC			PRIVATE		
	LOW	MEDIUM	HIGH	MEDIUM	HIGH	V. HIGH	LOW	MEDIUM	HIGH	MEDIUM	HIGH	V. HIGH	LOW	MEDIUM	HIGH	MEDIUM	HIGH	V. HIGH
DURING YOUR LAST YEAR IN HIGH SCHOOL, HOW MUCH TIME DID YOU SPEND DURING A TYPICAL WEEK DOING THE FOLLOWING?																		
Working (for pay)																		
None	38.4	28.8	40.6	33.3	40.3	53.4	40.3	31.3	43.0	35.3	43.1	56.5	36.7	26.5	38.4	31.8	37.9	50.5
Less than one hour	2.2	3.0	3.6	2.5	3.8	4.6	2.6	3.7	4.2	3.2	4.5	4.9	1.8	2.5	3.0	2.0	3.2	4.3
1 to 2 hours	3.5	4.0	5.4	3.8	5.5	7.0	3.8	4.3	5.9	4.3	5.8	6.6	3.2	3.7	4.9	3.4	5.2	7.5
3 to 5 hours	6.2	7.3	9.2	7.7	8.9	10.0	6.6	7.0	8.8	7.3	8.7	9.4	6.0	7.6	9.6	8.0	9.1	10.6
6 to 10 hours	10.2	13.8	12.8	12.8	11.8	10.3	9.1	12.1	11.4	11.5	9.9	8.7	11.2	15.4	14.0	13.7	13.4	11.8
11 to 15 hours	11.2	15.2	11.9	13.1	11.9	6.8	10.1	13.0	10.3	11.4	10.1	6.0	12.2	17.3	13.3	14.3	13.4	7.5
16 to 20 hours	13.0	14.3	9.6	13.3	9.4	4.6	11.8	13.5	8.8	12.2	8.6	4.2	14.1	15.0	10.4	14.2	10.1	4.9
Over 20 hours	15.2	13.5	7.0	13.6	8.3	3.2	15.7	15.2	7.6	14.8	9.1	3.7	14.8	12.1	6.4	12.6	7.6	2.9
Volunteer work																		
None	31.5	26.6	19.0	25.5	18.7	16.3	38.5	32.7	24.3	32.5	24.4	19.9	25.6	20.9	14.3	20.1	13.9	12.9
Less than one hour	20.4	26.1	22.4	20.9	20.5	20.5	20.9	27.8	24.6	23.1	22.1	22.5	20.0	24.6	20.4	19.1	19.1	18.6
1 to 2 hours	23.1	25.9	30.1	25.5	29.4	31.7	20.4	23.3	28.1	22.6	27.6	30.4	25.3	28.3	31.9	27.8	30.9	32.9
3 to 5 hours	13.6	12.9	17.4	15.3	18.3	20.3	11.0	9.5	13.8	11.2	15.2	17.6	15.7	16.0	20.6	18.5	21.0	22.9
6 to 10 hours	6.0	4.9	6.6	6.6	7.6	7.0	4.9	4.0	5.4	5.6	6.1	5.8	7.0	5.7	7.6	7.3	8.8	8.2
11 to 15 hours	2.1	1.7	2.2	2.6	2.6	2.2	1.6	1.2	1.8	1.9	2.1	1.9	2.5	2.2	2.6	3.1	3.1	2.4
16 to 20 hours	1.3	0.9	0.9	1.2	1.1	0.9	0.9	0.5	0.8	0.8	0.7	0.6	1.6	1.2	1.0	1.5	1.4	1.1
Over 20 hours	2.1	1.1	1.4	2.4	1.8	1.1	1.8	0.9	1.3	2.3	1.8	1.3	2.3	1.2	1.5	2.5	1.9	1.0
Student clubs/groups																		
None	32.1	27.3	16.9	22.0	15.0	9.4	39.5	34.9	22.7	28.8	20.2	12.3	25.9	20.3	11.7	16.8	10.7	6.7
Less than one hour	13.7	15.0	15.3	12.8	12.2	10.9	14.1	15.6	17.2	13.8	13.6	12.2	13.3	14.4	13.6	12.1	11.0	9.8
1 to 2 hours	23.8	25.0	31.1	27.9	28.8	29.2	21.5	22.9	30.0	25.8	28.7	29.2	25.8	26.9	32.2	29.6	28.8	29.2
3 to 5 hours	15.5	17.3	21.2	19.7	23.1	26.8	13.0	14.4	17.7	17.5	20.5	25.1	17.5	20.0	24.2	21.4	25.4	28.5
6 to 10 hours	7.5	8.0	8.9	9.0	11.3	13.0	5.7	6.4	7.1	7.0	9.1	11.1	9.0	9.6	10.4	10.5	13.2	14.8
11 to 15 hours	3.2	3.6	3.3	3.8	4.7	5.2	2.6	2.6	2.5	3.2	3.7	4.9	3.7	4.5	4.1	4.2	5.4	5.6
16 to 20 hours	1.7	1.7	1.5	2.0	2.2	2.5	1.3	1.3	1.2	1.4	1.7	2.2	2.1	2.0	1.8	2.5	2.7	2.7
Over 20 hours	2.4	2.1	1.8	2.8	2.7	2.9	2.2	2.0	1.6	2.6	2.5	2.9	2.6	2.3	1.9	2.9	2.8	2.8
Watching TV																		
None	7.3	6.7	7.1	6.4	6.7	9.1	7.4	6.8	7.2	6.3	7.1	9.7	7.1	6.6	7.0	6.5	6.5	8.6
Less than one hour	16.3	14.8	14.3	14.0	13.3	13.8	14.4	13.3	12.7	12.0	12.5	12.8	17.8	16.2	15.8	15.6	14.0	14.7
1 to 2 hours	25.1	25.2	25.8	23.8	24.8	23.9	24.5	23.3	23.5	22.8	22.8	22.3	25.7	26.9	27.9	24.6	26.6	25.3
3 to 5 hours	25.9	28.1	29.0	28.0	28.9	28.8	25.3	27.8	28.4	26.3	27.9	27.3	26.5	28.4	29.5	29.2	29.7	30.3
6 to 10 hours	14.6	15.2	15.2	15.7	16.4	16.0	15.2	16.4	17.3	17.7	17.8	17.4	14.0	14.1	13.3	14.1	15.2	14.8
11 to 15 hours	5.7	5.5	4.8	6.1	5.6	4.9	6.9	6.5	5.9	7.3	6.8	6.1	4.7	4.5	3.9	5.1	4.6	3.9
16 to 20 hours	2.2	2.0	1.9	2.6	2.3	1.7	2.9	2.4	2.4	3.0	2.6	2.2	1.6	1.6	1.4	2.3	2.0	1.3
Over 20 hours	2.9	2.5	1.9	3.4	1.9	1.7	3.2	3.5	2.7	4.6	2.5	2.3	2.7	1.7	1.2	2.4	1.5	1.2
Household/childcare duties																		
None	17.1	17.8	16.7	17.5	18.6	19.8	22.9	23.9	21.4	23.3	23.8	23.4	12.2	12.2	12.5	13.2	14.2	16.4
Less than one hour	18.0	21.2	23.0	19.1	20.4	23.0	19.4	22.1	22.8	19.8	20.0	22.3	16.8	20.4	23.2	18.6	20.8	23.7
1 to 2 hours	30.9	32.1	34.1	31.3	32.8	33.0	30.3	30.3	32.7	30.3	31.1	31.6	31.4	33.8	35.4	32.0	34.3	34.3
3 to 5 hours	20.7	19.3	18.3	20.0	18.9	17.4	18.0	16.5	16.3	17.3	17.4	16.3	22.9	21.9	20.1	22.0	20.3	18.5
6 to 10 hours	7.5	6.0	5.2	7.1	6.1	4.6	5.7	4.7	4.7	5.8	5.3	4.4	9.0	7.2	5.6	8.1	6.7	4.7
11 to 15 hours	2.5	1.8	1.4	2.4	1.8	1.2	1.7	1.2	1.2	1.8	1.4	1.1	3.2	2.2	1.7	2.9	2.1	1.3
16 to 20 hours	1.3	0.8	0.5	1.0	0.6	0.5	0.9	0.4	0.3	0.7	0.4	0.4	1.6	1.1	0.7	1.3	0.8	0.6
Over 20 hours	2.1	1.0	0.7	1.5	0.8	0.5	1.3	0.8	0.6	1.1	0.8	0.6	2.9	1.2	0.8	1.9	0.8	0.4

WEIGHTED NATIONAL NORMS FOR UNIVERSITIES, FALL 2008

| | ALL FRESHMEN | | | | | | FRESHMAN MEN | | | | | | FRESHMAN WOMEN | | | | | |
| | PUBLIC | | | PRIVATE | | | PUBLIC | | | PRIVATE | | | PUBLIC | | | PRIVATE | | |
	LOW	MEDIUM	HIGH	MEDIUM	HIGH	V. HIGH	LOW	MEDIUM	HIGH	MEDIUM	HIGH	V. HIGH	LOW	MEDIUM	HIGH	MEDIUM	HIGH	V. HIGH
DURING YOUR LAST YEAR IN HIGH SCHOOL, HOW MUCH TIME DID YOU SPEND DURING A TYPICAL WEEK DOING THE FOLLOWING?																		
Reading for pleasure																		
None	24.2	23.1	20.5	23.1	17.0	15.2	30.6	30.0	25.9	30.1	21.7	17.7	18.8	16.8	15.7	17.7	13.1	12.8
Less than one hour	24.3	24.2	26.4	24.1	23.1	24.7	25.7	24.9	27.9	25.2	24.4	26.3	23.1	23.5	25.1	23.3	22.0	23.2
1 to 2 hours	24.2	24.2	27.2	24.4	27.1	29.4	22.7	22.3	24.6	22.8	25.7	28.4	25.4	26.0	29.5	25.6	28.3	30.3
3 to 5 hours	15.3	16.7	16.3	15.7	19.2	19.0	12.1	13.9	13.8	12.5	16.8	17.0	18.1	19.3	18.5	18.2	21.3	20.9
6 to 10 hours	7.0	7.1	6.2	7.2	8.1	7.9	5.2	5.6	5.0	5.3	6.7	7.1	8.5	8.6	7.3	8.7	9.4	8.6
11 to 15 hours	2.7	2.7	2.0	2.8	3.2	2.2	2.2	1.8	1.6	2.2	2.7	1.9	3.1	3.5	2.4	3.3	3.6	2.6
16 to 20 hours	0.9	0.9	0.7	1.2	1.1	0.7	0.4	0.7	0.5	0.9	0.8	0.5	1.4	1.0	0.8	1.5	1.3	0.9
Over 20 hours	1.4	1.0	0.6	1.5	1.1	0.8	1.0	0.7	0.6	1.2	1.2	1.0	1.7	1.3	0.7	1.7	1.0	0.7
Playing video/computer games																		
None	38.5	37.1	41.6	39.1	41.5	43.6	16.0	14.1	16.9	16.0	16.5	19.6	57.5	58.3	63.6	56.7	62.5	66.1
Less than one hour	18.8	20.2	19.9	19.3	18.7	18.5	17.2	17.7	19.1	16.8	17.5	18.7	20.0	22.4	20.6	21.1	19.7	18.3
1 to 2 hours	16.1	15.8	15.5	16.2	15.2	15.3	21.0	21.4	22.4	22.1	21.6	21.9	12.0	10.6	9.4	11.8	9.8	9.2
3 to 5 hours	12.8	13.0	11.9	12.1	12.3	12.1	20.6	21.4	20.7	20.0	20.9	20.8	6.3	5.3	4.1	6.1	5.1	3.9
6 to 10 hours	6.8	7.1	6.2	6.9	6.6	6.0	11.9	12.5	11.6	12.7	12.4	10.9	2.4	2.0	1.5	2.5	1.8	1.5
11 to 15 hours	3.1	3.5	2.4	3.1	2.7	2.5	6.0	6.3	4.7	5.7	5.3	4.5	0.7	0.9	0.5	1.1	0.6	0.6
16 to 20 hours	1.5	1.5	1.0	1.2	1.2	0.9	2.8	2.7	1.9	2.5	2.3	1.7	0.4	0.3	0.3	0.3	0.3	0.2
Over 20 hours	2.4	2.0	1.5	2.1	1.7	1.1	4.5	3.8	2.8	4.3	3.5	2.0	0.6	0.3	0.2	0.5	0.3	0.2
Online social networks (MySpace, Facebook, etc.)																		
None	13.2	11.8	9.7	8.8	8.0	7.1	16.5	14.6	12.2	12.1	10.5	8.7	10.5	9.2	7.5	6.3	6.0	5.7
Less than one hour	21.2	19.0	18.6	17.3	16.5	15.2	23.0	21.7	20.6	19.4	19.1	18.1	19.7	16.5	16.9	15.7	14.3	12.4
1 to 2 hours	26.3	27.8	29.9	27.4	28.7	29.3	25.7	27.8	29.7	27.2	29.2	30.4	26.8	27.7	30.1	27.6	28.2	28.3
3 to 5 hours	21.2	23.7	25.5	24.7	26.8	28.9	18.5	20.8	22.5	21.4	23.1	25.5	23.5	26.4	28.2	27.2	29.9	32.1
6 to 10 hours	9.5	10.3	9.9	11.7	11.8	12.2	8.5	8.7	8.7	10.7	10.6	10.4	10.4	11.7	11.0	12.5	12.9	13.9
11 to 15 hours	4.2	3.8	3.2	4.6	4.2	3.9	3.8	3.1	3.1	4.2	4.0	3.4	4.5	4.4	3.3	4.8	4.5	4.3
16 to 20 hours	1.5	1.7	1.4	2.2	1.8	1.6	1.3	1.3	1.2	1.8	1.3	1.5	1.7	2.0	1.6	2.4	2.2	1.7
Over 20 hours	2.9	2.0	1.7	3.3	2.2	1.8	2.7	2.0	1.9	3.3	2.3	2.0	3.0	2.1	1.5	3.4	2.1	1.6
Are you: [4]																		
White/Caucasian	55.8	82.7	70.2	68.7	75.9	67.1	57.9	83.1	71.2	72.2	76.7	68.2	54.0	82.3	69.3	66.1	75.1	66.0
African American/Black	10.2	3.9	5.4	9.8	5.2	5.8	8.0	3.4	4.4	8.1	4.2	4.5	12.0	4.4	6.3	11.2	6.1	7.1
American Indian/Alaska Native	3.2	1.7	1.4	1.9	1.9	1.4	2.8	1.6	1.2	1.7	1.8	1.2	3.5	1.9	1.6	2.1	1.9	1.5
Asian American/Asian	17.6	8.9	17.9	13.5	11.7	24.2	20.1	9.7	18.5	13.0	12.4	24.1	15.5	8.2	17.3	13.9	11.2	24.4
Native Hawaiian/Pacific Islander	2.7	0.9	1.3	1.3	1.0	0.7	2.7	0.9	1.4	1.2	1.0	0.7	2.8	0.9	1.3	1.4	1.1	0.8
Mexican American/Chicano	13.9	4.7	4.8	2.8	3.8	3.5	12.1	3.7	4.1	2.4	3.8	3.5	15.5	5.6	5.5	3.1	3.8	3.5
Puerto Rican	1.3	0.6	0.8	2.9	1.5	1.2	1.2	0.6	0.7	2.8	1.6	1.0	1.4	0.7	0.9	2.9	1.4	1.3
Other Latino	5.3	2.2	4.4	5.6	6.1	4.8	4.5	1.9	3.8	5.1	5.5	4.7	6.0	2.5	4.9	6.1	6.6	4.9
Other	5.1	3.0	3.5	5.0	4.6	3.6	5.0	2.9	3.6	4.3	4.8	3.2	5.2	3.0	3.5	5.6	4.5	4.0

WEIGHTED NATIONAL NORMS FOR UNIVERSITIES, FALL 2008

| | ALL FRESHMEN | | | | | | FRESHMAN MEN | | | | | | FRESHMAN WOMEN | | | | | |
| | PUBLIC | | | PRIVATE | | | PUBLIC | | | PRIVATE | | | PUBLIC | | | PRIVATE | | |
Reasons noted as "very important" in influencing student's decision to attend this particular college	LOW	MEDIUM	HIGH	MEDIUM	HIGH	V. HIGH	LOW	MEDIUM	HIGH	MEDIUM	HIGH	V. HIGH	LOW	MEDIUM	HIGH	MEDIUM	HIGH	V. HIGH
My parents wanted me to come here	16.3	11.3	12.5	14.8	13.1	14.7	13.9	9.9	10.7	13.6	12.5	13.3	18.3	12.6	14.1	15.8	13.7	16.1
My relatives wanted me to come here	6.1	4.4	4.5	5.3	4.7	5.1	5.7	4.2	4.4	5.6	4.8	5.6	6.5	4.7	4.5	5.1	4.6	4.6
My teacher advised me	7.5	4.9	5.2	6.1	6.5	6.9	6.5	5.0	4.9	6.4	6.6	6.9	8.3	4.9	5.4	6.0	6.3	6.9
This college has a very good academic reputation	52.1	64.2	78.0	71.5	77.3	88.6	45.3	62.1	75.1	67.2	74.5	88.0	57.9	66.1	80.5	74.8	79.6	89.2
This college has a good reputation for its social activities	34.1	40.2	47.9	37.2	39.5	41.2	31.3	37.6	47.8	34.6	37.6	42.1	36.6	42.6	47.9	39.3	41.1	40.5
I was offered financial assistance	41.0	32.3	30.6	63.0	53.1	34.0	34.4	27.4	26.8	58.5	50.1	32.5	46.6	36.9	33.9	66.5	55.7	35.4
The cost of attending this college	46.3	36.3	32.2	35.9	26.6	22.2	41.1	32.5	28.9	30.8	23.1	20.5	50.7	39.9	35.0	39.9	29.5	23.8
High school counselor advised me	10.7	6.7	7.5	11.5	10.0	9.9	9.5	6.3	7.1	11.2	10.3	10.0	11.7	7.0	7.9	11.7	9.8	9.9
Private college counselor advised me	3.1	1.9	2.2	4.4	4.9	4.3	2.7	2.0	2.2	4.7	5.2	4.8	3.4	1.7	2.1	4.1	4.6	3.9
I wanted to live near home	22.7	14.8	10.7	22.5	11.7	6.3	19.0	11.7	8.7	18.5	10.2	5.8	25.8	17.6	12.5	25.5	12.9	6.8
Not offered aid by first choice	9.4	7.6	7.5	11.3	9.3	5.9	8.1	6.8	6.5	10.3	8.4	5.3	10.5	8.3	8.4	12.0	10.2	6.5
Could not afford first choice	13.3	11.2	9.3	11.9	8.5	5.0	11.1	9.6	7.8	10.1	7.3	4.3	15.2	12.8	10.7	13.2	9.5	5.7
This college's graduates gain admission to top graduate/professional schools	30.9	30.2	46.6	45.4	48.2	58.2	25.3	26.9	41.6	39.2	43.6	55.8	35.6	33.3	51.0	50.1	52.0	60.4
This college's graduates get good jobs	46.6	53.2	60.2	67.6	67.3	71.8	41.6	51.4	56.7	64.2	64.1	70.5	50.8	54.9	63.2	70.2	70.0	73.1
I was attracted by the religious affiliation/orientation of the college	3.3	4.3	2.3	9.2	14.3	7.7	2.5	3.1	2.2	7.1	11.2	7.4	3.9	5.4	2.4	10.7	16.9	7.9
I wanted to go to a school about the size of this college	32.7	31.6	29.2	42.5	43.5	39.6	27.2	26.3	26.1	35.4	36.8	34.2	37.3	36.4	32.0	47.9	49.1	44.6
Rankings in national magazines	13.7	17.6	32.6	20.7	28.2	41.8	13.3	18.3	31.6	18.9	27.0	40.4	14.0	16.9	33.5	22.0	29.1	43.2
Information from a website	17.9	15.5	20.5	21.0	23.1	27.2	14.1	12.7	17.6	16.5	19.4	23.5	21.2	18.0	23.1	24.4	26.2	30.6
I was admitted through an Early Action or Early Decision program	10.4	7.0	12.5	14.9	26.2	22.9	8.8	6.0	11.7	12.6	24.2	21.7	11.9	7.9	13.1	16.6	27.9	24.1
The athletic department recruited me	4.2	2.9	2.8	5.8	5.1	7.0	5.0	3.3	3.3	7.3	5.9	7.5	3.5	2.5	2.3	4.6	4.5	6.5
A visit to campus	32.2	37.0	40.8	42.4	49.8	51.3	26.9	30.0	35.1	36.7	43.7	46.0	36.7	43.4	45.8	46.7	54.9	56.3

WEIGHTED NATIONAL NORMS FOR UNIVERSITIES, FALL 2008

YOUR PROBABLE MAJOR	ALL FRESHMEN — PUBLIC LOW	ALL FRESHMEN — PUBLIC MEDIUM	ALL FRESHMEN — PUBLIC HIGH	ALL FRESHMEN — PRIVATE MEDIUM	ALL FRESHMEN — PRIVATE HIGH	ALL FRESHMEN — PRIVATE V. HIGH	FRESHMAN MEN — PUBLIC LOW	FRESHMAN MEN — PUBLIC MEDIUM	FRESHMAN MEN — PUBLIC HIGH	FRESHMAN MEN — PRIVATE MEDIUM	FRESHMAN MEN — PRIVATE HIGH	FRESHMAN MEN — PRIVATE V. HIGH	FRESHMAN WOMEN — PUBLIC LOW	FRESHMAN WOMEN — PUBLIC MEDIUM	FRESHMAN WOMEN — PUBLIC HIGH	FRESHMAN WOMEN — PRIVATE MEDIUM	FRESHMAN WOMEN — PRIVATE HIGH	FRESHMAN WOMEN — PRIVATE V. HIGH
Arts and Humanities																		
Art, fine and applied	1.8	3.0	1.4	2.2	1.3	1.4	1.3	1.7	0.7	1.2	0.7	0.8	2.2	4.2	2.0	3.0	1.9	2.0
English (language & literature)	1.7	1.6	2.1	1.8	1.9	2.6	0.9	1.1	1.3	1.2	1.0	1.8	2.4	2.1	2.8	2.2	2.7	3.5
History	1.3	1.0	1.2	1.2	1.4	1.7	1.7	1.2	1.3	1.5	1.4	1.6	0.9	0.9	1.1	1.0	1.3	1.7
Journalism	1.6	1.6	1.8	2.2	2.3	2.1	1.1	0.9	0.8	1.1	1.2	1.1	2.0	2.2	2.7	3.1	3.2	3.0
Language and Literature (except English)	0.5	0.7	0.8	0.6	0.7	1.0	0.3	0.5	0.4	0.4	0.3	0.6	0.7	0.9	1.1	0.8	1.0	1.4
Music	1.2	1.5	0.8	1.7	2.2	1.8	1.3	1.6	1.0	2.4	2.8	2.0	1.1	0.2	0.7	1.2	1.7	1.6
Philosophy	0.4	0.3	0.4	0.3	0.4	0.5	0.4	0.4	0.5	0.5	0.1	0.7	0.3	0.1	0.2	0.2	0.2	0.3
Speech	0.1	0.1	0.1	0.4	0.1	0.0	0.0	0.1	0.0	0.1	0.1	0.1	0.1	0.1	0.1	0.6	0.1	0.0
Theater or Drama	1.0	0.8	0.7	0.9	0.9	1.7	0.7	0.5	0.5	0.5	0.5	1.4	1.2	1.1	0.9	1.2	1.2	2.0
Theology or Religion	0.1	0.0	0.1	0.1	0.2	0.1	0.1	0.0	0.1	0.1	0.2	0.1	0.1	0.0	0.1	0.1	0.1	0.1
Other Arts and Humanities	1.2	1.4	0.9	1.7	1.2	1.5	0.8	0.9	0.5	1.2	1.0	1.3	1.6	1.9	1.2	2.0	1.4	1.6
Biological Science																		
Biology (general)	6.7	4.0	7.7	7.0	6.9	7.2	6.1	2.9	6.6	5.7	5.6	5.8	7.2	5.0	8.8	8.0	8.0	8.6
Biochemistry or Biophysics	2.6	1.5	2.7	1.1	1.8	2.2	2.4	1.4	2.8	0.9	1.8	2.2	2.9	1.5	2.7	1.3	1.8	2.2
Botany	0.1	0.1	0.1	0.1	0.0	0.1	0.2	0.1	0.1	0.0	0.0	0.1	0.0	0.1	0.1	0.1	0.0	0.1
Environmental Science	0.7	1.0	1.2	0.4	0.6	0.8	0.7	0.9	1.0	0.3	0.3	0.5	0.7	1.1	1.5	0.4	0.8	1.1
Marine (Life) Science	0.2	0.6	0.4	0.1	0.4	0.1	0.1	0.3	0.3	0.1	0.4	0.1	0.2	0.8	0.5	0.1	0.5	0.2
Microbiology or Bacteriology	0.6	0.3	1.0	0.1	0.3	0.4	0.5	0.2	1.0	0.1	0.3	0.3	0.6	0.3	1.1	0.2	0.3	0.4
Zoology	0.5	0.4	0.6	0.1	0.1	0.2	0.4	0.2	0.4	0.1	0.0	0.1	0.6	0.6	0.7	0.1	0.1	0.3
Other Biological Science	1.2	1.0	1.6	0.3	0.9	1.5	1.2	0.7	1.4	0.3	0.7	1.1	1.1	1.2	1.9	0.3	1.0	2.0
Business																		
Accounting	3.6	2.0	1.8	2.9	1.8	0.8	4.7	2.2	2.1	3.7	2.2	0.9	2.6	1.7	1.5	2.4	1.5	0.6
Business Admin. (general)	5.2	2.2	3.4	2.8	2.6	3.5	6.5	2.8	4.4	4.6	3.5	4.7	4.1	1.7	2.5	1.5	1.9	2.3
Finance	1.8	1.7	2.5	2.9	4.0	4.4	2.9	2.7	3.8	4.6	6.3	6.5	0.9	0.7	1.2	1.6	2.1	2.4
International Business	1.2	1.0	2.3	2.0	2.8	2.3	1.0	1.0	2.1	2.2	2.7	2.3	1.4	1.0	2.4	1.9	2.8	2.4
Marketing	3.1	2.4	2.2	3.2	3.0	1.5	3.7	2.0	1.9	3.0	2.4	1.0	2.7	2.9	2.5	3.3	3.5	2.0
Management	3.8	4.2	2.0	3.4	2.2	2.0	4.8	4.9	2.5	5.4	3.4	2.5	3.0	3.5	1.6	1.9	1.2	1.6
Secretarial Studies	0.0	0.0	0.0	0.0	0.0	0.0	0.0	0.0	0.0	0.0	0.0	0.0	0.0	0.0	0.0	0.0	0.0	0.0
Other Business	1.0	1.0	0.8	1.6	1.3	0.7	1.3	1.1	1.1	2.6	1.7	0.7	0.7	0.8	0.6	0.9	0.9	0.7
Education																		
Business Education	0.2	0.0	0.1	0.1	0.0	0.1	0.1	0.1	0.1	0.1	0.0	0.1	0.2	0.0	0.1	0.1	0.0	0.1
Elementary Education	2.6	2.7	0.8	2.1	0.8	0.5	0.4	0.2	0.1	0.3	0.1	0.0	4.4	5.0	1.5	3.4	1.4	1.0
Music or Art Education	0.7	0.5	0.2	0.5	0.3	0.1	0.6	0.4	0.2	0.4	0.2	0.1	0.8	0.5	0.2	0.5	0.3	0.1
Physical Education or Recreation	0.7	0.4	0.1	0.3	0.1	0.0	0.9	0.3	0.1	0.4	0.1	0.0	0.4	0.4	0.1	0.2	0.1	0.0
Secondary Education	1.9	1.3	0.6	1.9	0.3	0.4	1.3	0.9	0.4	1.3	0.3	0.2	2.4	1.6	0.8	2.4	0.4	0.6
Special Education	0.3	0.4	0.1	0.3	0.2	0.1	0.0	0.0	0.0	0.1	0.0	0.0	0.5	0.7	0.2	0.5	0.1	0.1
Other Education	0.4	0.2	0.1	0.1	0.1	0.1	0.3	0.1	0.0	0.0	0.1	0.0	0.5	0.3	0.1	0.2	0.2	0.1
Engineering																		
Aeronautical or Astronautical Engineering	0.2	2.4	1.7	0.5	0.9	0.9	0.3	4.3	3.2	1.0	1.6	1.4	0.1	0.7	0.5	0.1	0.2	0.4
Civil Engineering	1.1	2.2	1.8	1.9	1.3	1.6	2.0	3.9	3.0	3.5	2.1	1.8	0.3	0.7	0.8	0.8	0.6	1.4
Chemical Engineering	0.6	2.1	2.0	0.9	1.2	3.3	0.9	2.9	3.1	1.6	1.6	3.9	0.3	1.3	1.0	0.4	0.8	2.7
Computer Engineering	1.4	2.0	2.0	1.1	1.2	1.3	2.6	3.8	3.8	2.3	2.4	2.3	0.4	0.3	0.4	0.1	0.3	0.4
Electrical or Electronic Engineering	1.3	1.8	1.6	0.9	1.2	1.6	2.7	3.5	2.9	2.0	2.3	2.6	0.2	0.3	0.4	0.1	0.3	0.7
Industrial Engineering	0.1	0.5	0.4	0.2	0.2	0.4	0.2	0.7	0.5	0.3	0.3	0.5	0.0	0.4	0.2	0.1	0.1	0.3
Mechanical Engineering	3.3	4.4	3.7	3.4	3.0	3.2	6.3	8.3	7.0	7.0	5.6	5.4	0.7	0.8	0.7	0.6	0.7	1.0
Other Engineering	1.6	3.2	3.1	2.4	3.2	4.5	2.3	4.7	4.4	3.4	4.2	4.9	1.0	1.9	2.0	1.6	2.4	4.0

WEIGHTED NATIONAL NORMS FOR UNIVERSITIES, FALL 2008

YOUR PROBABLE MAJOR	ALL FRESHMEN					FRESHMAN MEN						FRESHMAN WOMEN					
	PUBLIC			PRIVATE		PUBLIC			PRIVATE			PUBLIC			PRIVATE		
	LOW	MEDIUM	HIGH	HIGH	V. HIGH	LOW	MEDIUM	HIGH	MEDIUM	HIGH	V. HIGH	LOW	MEDIUM	HIGH	MEDIUM	HIGH	V. HIGH
Physical Science																	
Astronomy	0.3	0.2	0.1	0.0	0.2	0.4	0.3	0.2	0.0	0.0	0.2	0.2	0.1	0.0	0.0	0.1	0.1
Atmospheric Science (incl. Meteorology)	0.1	0.3	0.0	0.1	0.1	0.1	0.3	0.0	0.0	0.1	0.1	0.1	0.2	0.0	0.0	0.1	0.1
Chemistry	1.2	1.3	1.6	1.4	2.0	1.3	1.3	1.7	1.3	1.5	2.1	1.2	1.2	1.6	1.4	1.4	1.8
Earth Science	0.2	0.2	0.1	0.1	0.2	0.3	0.2	0.2	0.0	0.1	0.1	0.1	0.2	0.1	0.1	0.1	0.2
Marine Science (incl. Oceanography)	0.1	0.1	0.1	0.2	0.1	0.0	0.1	0.1	0.0	0.1	0.0	0.1	0.1	0.2	0.0	0.3	0.1
Mathematics	0.8	0.8	1.2	0.9	1.8	0.8	0.8	1.5	0.8	1.1	2.0	0.8	0.7	1.0	0.6	0.8	1.5
Physics	0.4	0.7	0.8	1.0	1.6	0.9	1.3	1.3	1.2	1.7	2.5	0.1	0.2	0.3	0.3	0.5	0.7
Other Physical Science	0.2	0.1	0.2	0.2	0.2	0.2	0.1	0.2	0.1	0.2	0.2	0.3	0.1	0.2	0.2	0.2	0.2
Professional																	
Architecture or Urban Planning	0.8	0.7	1.5	1.8	1.8	1.2	0.9	1.5	0.6	1.7	1.6	0.5	0.5	1.4	0.2	1.9	2.0
Family & Consumer Sciences	0.3	0.8	0.0	0.3	0.0	0.0	0.1	0.0	0.1	0.0	0.0	0.6	1.5	0.1	0.2	0.6	0.0
Health Technology (medical, dental, laboratory)	0.8	0.5	0.4	0.3	0.2	0.4	0.4	0.4	0.5	0.2	0.2	1.1	0.7	0.5	0.5	0.3	0.3
Library or Archival Science	0.1	0.1	0.1	0.0	0.0	0.1	0.0	0.1	0.0	0.0	0.0	0.1	0.1	0.1	0.1	0.1	0.0
Medicine, Dentistry, Veterinary Medicine	3.5	4.0	5.5	5.7	6.5	2.6	2.5	4.3	2.9	4.7	5.2	4.2	5.4	6.6	4.8	6.6	7.8
Nursing	3.8	1.8	1.8	1.8	0.5	0.8	0.2	0.2	0.8	0.2	0.0	6.4	3.4	3.3	6.2	3.1	0.9
Pharmacy	1.0	2.0	2.1	1.7	0.2	0.9	1.7	1.5	3.9	1.3	0.1	1.0	2.3	2.5	5.0	2.0	0.4
Therapy (occupational, physical, speech)	2.1	1.6	1.3	1.4	0.2	1.4	0.9	0.5	1.0	0.6	0.1	2.8	2.3	2.0	2.9	2.2	0.3
Other Professional	0.6	0.7	0.5	0.6	0.2	0.4	0.6	0.3	1.6	0.4	0.1	0.8	0.9	0.6	2.2	0.7	0.2
Social Science																	
Anthropology	0.4	0.6	0.7	0.7	0.6	0.2	0.4	0.4	0.2	0.3	0.2	0.5	0.8	1.0	0.4	1.0	1.0
Economics	0.4	0.5	1.4	1.3	3.8	0.7	0.7	2.0	0.6	1.9	5.1	0.1	0.4	0.9	0.2	0.8	2.5
Ethnic Studies	0.1	0.1	0.1	0.1	0.1	0.0	0.1	0.1	0.0	0.0	0.1	0.1	0.1	0.1	0.1	0.2	0.1
Geography	0.1	0.0	0.1	0.1	0.0	0.1	0.0	0.1	0.0	0.0	0.0	0.0	0.0	0.1	0.0	0.1	0.0
Political Science (gov't., international relations)	3.0	1.9	4.2	7.9	4.9	2.9	1.8	3.8	3.1	7.3	4.4	3.2	2.0	4.6	4.0	8.4	5.3
Psychology	5.9	4.5	4.6	3.8	2.9	3.0	2.3	2.2	2.4	1.8	1.5	8.3	6.5	6.7	6.8	5.4	4.3
Public Policy	0.1	0.1	0.1	0.2	0.6	0.1	0.0	0.1	0.1	0.2	0.4	0.1	0.1	0.2	0.1	0.2	0.7
Social Work	0.5	0.4	0.2	0.3	0.1	0.1	0.1	0.0	0.1	0.1	0.1	0.8	0.6	0.4	0.7	0.4	0.2
Sociology	1.3	0.7	0.7	0.5	0.5	1.0	0.4	0.4	0.2	0.3	0.4	1.6	1.0	1.0	0.5	0.6	0.6
Women's Studies	0.0	0.0	0.0	0.1	0.0	0.0	0.0	0.0	0.0	0.0	0.0	0.0	0.1	0.0	0.0	0.0	0.0
Other Social Science	0.5	0.3	0.4	0.4	0.3	0.4	0.1	0.2	0.1	0.3	0.1	0.5	0.4	0.5	0.3	0.6	0.5
Technical																	
Building Trades	0.0	0.2	0.0	0.0	0.0	0.0	0.3	0.1	0.0	0.0	0.0	0.0	0.0	0.0	0.0	0.0	0.0
Data Processing or Computer Programming	0.5	0.7	0.3	0.6	0.5	1.0	1.4	0.6	1.0	1.0	0.9	0.0	0.1	0.1	0.1	0.1	0.1
Drafting or Design	0.1	0.3	0.1	0.1	0.1	0.1	0.3	0.1	0.2	0.0	0.0	0.1	0.3	0.1	0.2	0.1	0.2
Electronics	0.0	0.1	0.0	0.0	0.0	0.1	0.2	0.1	0.1	0.0	0.0	0.0	0.0	0.0	0.0	0.0	0.0
Mechanics	0.0	0.1	0.0	0.0	0.0	0.1	0.3	0.0	0.0	0.0	0.0	0.0	0.0	0.0	0.0	0.0	0.0
Other Technical	0.1	0.2	0.0	0.0	0.1	0.2	0.4	0.0	0.1	0.1	0.1	0.0	0.1	0.0	0.1	0.0	0.0
Other Fields																	
Agriculture	0.4	1.7	0.4	0.0	0.2	0.4	1.3	0.3	0.0	0.0	0.2	0.4	1.5	0.4	0.0	0.0	0.3
Communications	1.1	1.3	1.8	2.5	1.7	0.7	0.3	0.7	1.6	1.3	0.9	1.4	1.8	2.7	3.1	3.5	2.5
Computer Science	1.1	1.4	0.8	1.4	1.4	2.1	2.5	1.4	2.0	2.7	2.2	0.2	0.3	0.3	0.3	0.4	0.6
Forestry	0.5	0.1	0.1	0.0	0.0	0.8	0.2	0.1	0.0	0.1	0.0	0.2	0.0	0.0	0.0	0.0	0.0
Kinesiology	0.4	1.0	0.5	0.2	0.2	0.5	0.8	0.4	0.1	0.1	0.1	0.3	1.2	0.7	0.9	0.3	0.2
Law Enforcement	1.0	0.4	0.1	0.6	0.1	1.3	0.6	0.1	1.4	0.8	0.1	0.7	0.3	0.1	0.9	0.4	0.1
Military Science	0.1	0.0	0.0	0.0	0.0	0.1	0.1	0.0	0.1	0.1	0.0	0.0	0.0	0.0	0.1	0.0	0.0
Other Field	1.0	1.7	0.8	0.7	0.7	1.1	1.1	0.6	1.2	0.7	0.5	1.0	2.2	1.0	1.6	0.8	0.8
Undecided	5.7	6.2	6.2	5.8	5.4	5.2	5.1	4.9	3.6	4.6	4.4	6.1	7.1	7.2	5.4	6.7	6.4

107

WEIGHTED NATIONAL NORMS FOR UNIVERSITIES, FALL 2008

| | ALL FRESHMEN | | | | | | FRESHMAN MEN | | | | | | FRESHMAN WOMEN | | | | | |
| | PUBLIC | | | PRIVATE | | | PUBLIC | | | PRIVATE | | | PUBLIC | | | PRIVATE | | |
Objectives considered to be "essential" or "very important":	LOW	MEDIUM	HIGH	MEDIUM	HIGH	V. HIGH	LOW	MEDIUM	HIGH	MEDIUM	HIGH	V. HIGH	LOW	MEDIUM	HIGH	MEDIUM	HIGH	V. HIGH
Becoming accomplished in one of the performing arts (acting, dancing, etc.)	16.3	14.4	13.0	16.7	16.8	19.1	14.7	13.5	12.4	16.3	16.3	17.5	17.6	15.3	13.6	17.0	17.2	20.6
Becoming an authority in my field	60.5	56.9	62.0	63.0	64.6	68.5	61.2	58.7	62.6	64.5	66.1	68.8	60.0	55.3	61.4	61.8	63.4	68.2
Obtaining recognition from my colleagues for contributions to my special field	60.1	56.3	58.9	63.0	61.3	62.0	60.3	56.4	59.0	63.9	62.1	61.8	60.0	56.2	58.7	62.4	60.5	62.2
Influencing the political structure	24.2	19.3	21.6	24.8	25.7	23.9	25.6	21.1	23.3	27.1	27.2	26.4	22.9	17.7	20.1	23.1	24.5	21.6
Influencing social values	46.7	40.3	40.8	47.0	46.9	43.3	42.9	35.7	36.6	43.0	42.5	40.1	50.0	44.5	44.4	50.1	50.6	46.3
Raising a family	74.3	76.8	74.6	75.3	73.7	74.4	75.4	76.4	75.3	75.1	75.1	75.9	73.4	77.2	73.9	75.4	72.6	73.1
Being very well off financially	80.4	76.0	77.2	80.2	72.7	71.6	81.8	77.6	78.9	81.1	75.9	74.3	79.1	74.6	75.6	79.4	70.0	69.1
Helping others who are in difficulty	71.5	66.5	69.5	70.8	72.1	72.6	63.2	57.9	61.8	61.5	64.6	67.2	78.4	74.3	76.3	77.8	78.3	77.6
Making a theoretical contribution to science	23.8	23.6	27.0	24.5	25.2	27.8	26.7	28.0	30.9	26.9	28.8	31.4	21.4	19.6	23.5	22.6	22.3	24.4
Writing original works (poems, novels, short stories, etc.)	16.0	14.4	13.8	17.4	16.9	19.3	14.7	13.9	13.2	17.8	17.2	18.6	17.1	14.9	14.4	17.2	16.6	20.0
Creating artistic works (painting, sculpture, decorating, etc.)	16.1	16.3	12.7	16.2	15.8	16.4	14.3	13.1	11.3	14.9	14.8	15.0	17.7	19.2	14.0	17.2	16.6	17.6
Becoming successful in a business of my own	47.8	40.2	42.9	45.6	41.9	41.1	51.2	42.7	46.4	50.9	46.8	46.1	44.9	37.9	39.9	41.5	37.9	36.4
Becoming involved in programs to clean up the environment	32.8	28.6	33.0	31.7	33.0	33.9	29.5	25.4	28.9	28.7	28.9	30.9	35.6	31.5	36.7	34.0	36.5	36.7
Developing a meaningful philosophy of life	52.1	50.9	54.2	53.5	57.3	62.1	51.7	50.0	53.8	53.5	58.0	62.9	52.4	51.7	54.5	53.5	56.7	61.3
Participating in a community action program	31.2	26.8	32.2	33.6	37.7	38.5	25.0	21.1	24.7	27.1	29.7	30.5	36.5	32.0	38.8	38.5	44.4	46.0
Helping to promote racial understanding	42.6	32.5	36.8	40.1	40.1	40.0	37.8	28.3	32.2	36.2	35.6	35.7	46.6	36.3	40.8	43.1	43.7	44.1
Keeping up to date with political affairs	39.2	38.6	46.9	41.0	51.1	53.6	40.2	39.4	47.1	43.2	51.6	53.4	38.4	37.8	46.7	39.3	50.6	53.9
Becoming a community leader	35.6	31.8	38.6	37.1	43.3	43.7	33.5	30.0	35.6	35.7	40.8	42.6	37.3	33.5	41.3	38.2	45.4	44.8
Improving my understanding of other countries and cultures	54.6	50.0	59.4	56.3	63.8	67.4	48.4	43.4	52.0	50.1	56.4	60.0	59.7	56.0	65.8	60.9	70.0	74.2
Adopting "green" practices to protect the environment	48.5	45.6	52.4	49.8	51.9	55.2	43.5	40.0	45.2	43.5	45.2	48.9	52.6	50.8	58.8	54.5	57.5	61.2

WEIGHTED NATIONAL NORMS FOR UNIVERSITIES, FALL 2008

| | ALL FRESHMEN | | | | | | FRESHMAN MEN | | | | | | FRESHMAN WOMEN | | | | | |
| | PUBLIC | | | PRIVATE | | | PUBLIC | | | PRIVATE | | | PUBLIC | | | PRIVATE | | |
	LOW	MEDIUM	HIGH	MEDIUM	HIGH	V. HIGH	LOW	MEDIUM	HIGH	MEDIUM	HIGH	V. HIGH	LOW	MEDIUM	HIGH	MEDIUM	HIGH	V. HIGH
Student estimates chances are "very good" that he/she will:																		
Change major field	12.2	13.7	18.1	11.0	13.2	17.0	11.6	12.4	15.2	9.5	11.4	14.8	12.8	14.8	20.6	12.1	14.6	19.1
Change career choice	11.8	13.4	17.7	10.2	14.2	19.6	10.7	11.3	14.9	8.5	11.5	17.0	12.8	15.3	20.2	11.4	16.4	22.0
Participate in student government	6.1	5.4	8.4	7.7	9.6	9.5	4.6	4.4	6.0	6.5	7.9	8.6	7.4	6.3	10.6	8.6	11.0	10.2
Get a job to help pay for college expenses	55.5	52.6	44.4	49.9	44.1	42.4	48.2	45.4	37.8	42.5	37.6	37.2	61.6	59.3	50.2	55.4	49.5	47.2
Work full-time while attending college	8.5	5.7	3.8	7.1	4.0	2.3	6.4	4.6	3.0	6.3	3.8	2.2	10.2	6.8	4.4	7.7	4.2	2.4
Join a social fraternity or sorority	13.3	9.2	11.4	10.9	11.7	11.7	10.6	6.5	7.6	7.6	7.8	9.6	15.7	11.7	14.7	13.3	14.9	13.7
Play varsity/intercollegiate athletics	11.3	9.0	10.8	12.4	12.9	15.2	13.1	10.4	12.6	15.6	15.7	17.3	9.7	7.7	9.2	10.0	10.6	13.3
Make at least a "B" average	60.0	63.8	67.8	68.2	72.1	74.9	58.1	63.6	69.4	68.2	71.7	76.3	61.7	64.1	66.5	68.1	72.3	73.5
Need extra time to complete your degree requirements	8.1	6.1	4.6	5.6	4.0	3.0	7.8	5.5	4.6	5.3	3.9	3.3	8.3	6.6	4.6	5.8	4.2	2.6
Participate in student protests or demonstrations	6.0	5.4	7.0	6.6	8.2	8.3	5.4	4.6	5.9	5.7	6.6	7.0	6.6	6.0	8.0	7.3	9.5	9.5
Transfer to another college before graduating	8.9	5.4	2.6	4.7	3.2	1.6	8.4	4.8	2.8	4.9	3.2	2.0	9.4	5.9	2.5	4.5	3.3	1.3
Be satisfied with your college	50.1	56.2	66.3	54.4	64.6	75.6	45.1	52.1	63.4	50.2	61.0	73.1	54.3	59.9	68.9	57.6	67.6	77.9
Participate in volunteer or community service work	25.4	24.3	35.0	33.2	43.2	48.1	15.5	14.2	22.0	20.6	29.1	35.6	33.7	33.4	46.4	42.7	55.0	59.8
Seek personal counseling	11.9	7.7	10.0	8.1	9.1	8.8	9.5	6.3	7.9	6.7	7.8	7.5	13.9	9.1	11.9	9.1	10.2	10.0
Communicate regularly with your professors	35.0	31.1	37.9	35.8	45.5	54.2	30.3	27.6	33.1	31.3	40.9	50.5	39.0	34.3	42.1	39.3	49.3	57.7
Socialize with someone of another racial/ethnic group	68.7	62.4	73.6	66.9	74.3	81.9	63.4	57.3	68.9	60.3	69.2	77.8	73.2	67.0	77.8	71.8	78.5	85.7
Participate in student clubs/groups	42.3	45.8	57.8	51.8	60.3	70.4	33.8	37.3	47.7	42.0	51.3	62.5	49.5	53.5	66.7	59.1	67.8	77.7
Participate in a study abroad program	24.4	27.9	39.3	34.7	43.7	49.9	15.3	18.2	26.7	22.3	31.0	36.9	32.1	36.8	50.4	44.1	54.2	62.1
Have a roommate of different race/ethnicity	32.7	26.3	36.3	31.9	38.1	47.2	27.6	22.6	31.7	26.8	33.1	43.1	37.1	29.7	40.4	35.8	42.3	51.0
Discuss course content with students outside of class	47.1	49.9	58.1	48.1	61.7	72.1	4C.7	43.4	51.8	40.2	54.4	66.5	52.4	55.9	63.6	54.1	67.7	77.3
Work on a professor's research project	31.0	23.8	27.4	30.4	29.3	35.3	28.1	22.0	26.2	27.6	27.2	33.9	33.5	25.4	28.5	32.5	31.0	36.7
Get tutoring help in specific courses	37.5	30.3	30.5	29.2	29.2	25.9	29.8	22.8	22.6	22.9	22.3	20.3	44.0	37.2	37.5	34.0	34.9	31.2
Do you give the Higher Education Research Institute (HERI) permission to include your ID number should your college request the data for additional research analyses?																		
Yes	70.6	64.5	60.4	57.9	58.0	61.0	71.0	64.5	60.5	56.4	58.1	62.4	70.3	64.6	60.2	59.0	57.9	59.7
No	29.4	35.5	39.6	42.1	42.0	39.0	29.0	35.5	39.5	43.6	41.9	37.6	29.7	35.4	39.8	41.0	42.1	40.3

2008 National Norms

Four-Year Colleges, by Selectivity Level

NOTES

These notes refer to report items that are followed by numbers in [brackets].

[1] Based on the recommendations of the National Commission on Excellence In Education.

[2] Percentage responding "frequently" <u>only</u>.

[3] Recategorization of this item from a longer list is shown in Appendix C.

[4] Percentages will add to more than 100.0 if any student marked more than one category.

WEIGHTED NATIONAL NORMS FOR FOUR-YEAR COLLEGES, FALL 2008

	PUBLIC			NONSECTARIAN				CATHOLIC			OTHER RELIGIOUS		
	LOW	MEDIUM	HIGH	LOW	MEDIUM	HIGH	V. HIGH	LOW	MEDIUM	HIGH	LOW	MEDIUM	HIGH
How old will you be on December 31 of this year?													
16 or younger	0.0	0.1	0.0	0.0	0.0	0.0	0.1	0.0	0.1	0.0	0.0	0.4	0.0
17	1.6	1.3	1.4	2.1	1.3	1.6	1.7	2.4	1.6	1.6	1.3	1.4	1.1
18	74.7	71.6	65.7	71.2	72.0	68.9	66.7	71.4	67.1	69.6	63.4	63.5	62.8
19	21.5	25.2	30.8	23.3	25.1	27.7	29.7	23.9	30.3	27.9	32.5	33.2	34.7
20	1.2	0.8	1.2	2.0	1.3	1.2	1.5	1.3	0.6	0.6	1.9	1.2	1.1
21 to 24	0.8	0.9	0.6	1.2	0.2	0.4	0.3	0.6	0.3	0.2	0.7	0.3	0.3
25 to 29	0.1	0.1	0.1	0.1	0.1	0.0	0.0	0.2	0.1	0.0	0.0	0.0	0.0
30 to 39	0.1	0.1	0.1	0.0	0.0	0.0	0.0	0.1	0.0	0.0	0.0	0.0	0.0
40 to 54	0.0	0.0	0.0	0.0	0.0	0.0	0.0	0.1	0.0	0.0	0.0	0.0	0.0
55 or older	0.0	0.0	0.0	0.0	0.0	0.0	0.0	0.0	0.0	0.0	0.0	0.0	0.0
Is English your native language?													
Yes	85.4	96.1	96.1	91.3	94.4	91.9	90.1	90.1	91.9	95.2	96.5	95.7	95.7
No	14.6	3.9	3.9	8.7	5.6	8.1	9.9	9.9	8.1	4.8	3.5	4.3	4.3
In what year did you graduate from high school?													
2008	97.3	97.4	97.2	95.8	98.3	97.6	97.0	96.9	98.9	98.8	96.9	97.8	98.1
2007	1.5	1.3	1.8	2.2	1.1	1.7	2.5	1.7	0.7	0.8	1.9	1.1	1.4
2006	0.4	0.3	0.4	0.8	0.3	0.4	0.3	0.4	0.1	0.2	0.5	0.3	0.2
2005 or earlier	0.5	0.8	0.5	0.9	0.2	0.2	0.1	0.7	0.2	0.2	0.4	0.3	0.1
Did not graduate but passed G.E.D. test	0.3	0.2	0.2	0.2	0.1	0.1	0.0	0.3	0.1	0.1	0.3	0.2	0.1
Never completed high school	0.0	0.0	0.0	0.0	0.0	0.0	0.0	0.0	0.0	0.0	0.0	0.3	0.0
How many miles is this college from your permanent home?													
5 or less	13.2	6.8	4.9	8.3	6.2	3.4	1.5	10.6	9.3	4.3	4.4	5.9	2.7
6 to 10	11.3	7.8	6.9	11.0	7.5	3.6	1.1	11.1	11.8	5.6	4.7	5.8	2.9
11 to 50	35.5	31.4	27.3	30.5	31.6	20.4	6.5	38.2	37.4	27.8	23.1	22.3	15.5
51 to 100	14.7	20.4	17.9	13.8	18.1	18.1	9.2	12.7	14.7	17.2	21.2	18.0	17.1
101 to 500	20.2	28.5	25.9	19.7	19.0	36.4	39.0	14.3	21.6	31.5	35.1	29.9	39.3
Over 500	5.0	5.1	17.0	16.7	17.7	18.0	42.6	13.1	5.3	13.6	11.5	18.2	22.4
What was your average grade in high school?													
A or A+	9.2	12.9	22.5	9.4	15.3	23.2	36.1	13.8	19.4	21.7	14.4	26.2	29.8
A-	14.1	20.2	24.3	13.1	22.3	26.9	36.8	17.0	21.4	29.4	17.4	25.7	29.7
B+	22.7	23.0	21.5	21.5	24.4	23.0	17.9	21.6	21.3	24.3	19.5	19.2	19.5
B	30.1	28.0	20.5	28.1	24.4	18.4	7.8	25.3	23.9	18.4	23.4	18.3	15.0
B-	12.9	9.8	7.0	13.9	9.3	5.7	1.2	11.9	7.9	4.4	12.1	6.3	4.1
C+	8.2	4.3	3.1	9.4	3.2	2.2	0.2	7.2	4.3	1.3	8.9	3.0	1.4
C	2.8	1.7	1.0	4.2	1.1	0.6	0.0	3.1	1.8	0.5	4.1	1.2	0.4
D	0.2	0.1	0.0	0.4	0.1	0.0	0.0	0.1	0.0	0.0	0.1	0.0	0.0
From what kind of high school did you graduate?													
Public school (not charter or magnet)	79.2	87.8	81.8	69.9	76.3	73.8	57.8	63.3	73.9	63.5	81.6	71.8	70.2
Public charter school	4.4	1.5	1.6	2.2	1.4	1.4	1.4	4.9	0.8	0.9	1.8	1.7	1.3
Public magnet school	6.4	1.8	2.1	3.8	3.2	2.4	2.9	5.6	1.5	0.7	3.0	1.5	2.8
Private religious/parochial school	7.2	5.9	9.4	16.8	12.5	11.4	9.3	20.1	17.7	26.2	9.0	17.6	13.5
Private independent college-prep school	2.6	2.4	4.4	6.9	6.1	9.9	28.2	5.8	5.7	7.6	3.0	3.9	10.2
Home school	0.3	0.6	0.7	0.4	0.5	1.1	0.3	0.3	0.3	1.2	1.6	3.4	2.0
Prior to this term, have you ever taken courses for credit at this institution?													
No	93.3	95.1	95.9	94.7	95.0	96.1	97.3	93.6	95.1	96.4	95.6	94.8	96.4
Yes	6.7	4.9	4.1	5.3	5.0	3.9	2.7	6.4	4.9	3.6	4.4	5.2	3.6

113

WEIGHTED NATIONAL NORMS FOR FOUR-YEAR COLLEGES, FALL 2008

	PUBLIC			NONSECTARIAN				CATHOLIC			OTHER RELIGIOUS		
	LOW	MEDIUM	HIGH	LOW	MEDIUM	HIGH	V. HIGH	LOW	MEDIUM	HIGH	LOW	MEDIUM	HIGH
Since leaving high school, have you ever taken courses, whether for credit or not for credit, at any other institution (university, 4- or 2-year college, technical, vocational, or business school)?													
No	85.9	90.6	90.4	89.9	89.8	88.9	89.0	89.3	87.5	89.9	88.6	86.1	88.7
Yes	14.1	9.4	9.6	10.1	10.2	11.1	11.0	10.7	12.5	10.1	11.4	13.9	11.3
Where do you plan to live during the fall term?													
With my family or other relatives	38.2	21.7	17.3	26.6	18.4	8.2	0.8	27.0	24.4	7.3	10.1	8.1	3.2
Other private home, apartment, or room	10.1	8.9	3.2	3.4	2.0	1.1	0.1	2.2	0.9	0.9	1.6	0.7	0.3
College residence hall	46.1	65.7	76.5	68.0	78.1	87.4	97.9	68.9	73.6	90.9	84.9	89.6	95.6
Fraternity or sorority house	0.1	0.1	0.2	0.1	0.0	1.7	0.0	0.1	0.0	0.0	0.1	0.0	0.1
Other campus student housing	4.6	3.1	2.3	1.6	1.2	1.2	1.1	1.4	0.8	0.8	2.8	1.3	0.7
Other	0.9	0.4	0.4	0.3	0.2	0.3	0.1	0.4	0.2	0.1	0.4	0.2	0.2
To how many colleges other than this one did you apply for admission this year?													
None	17.1	21.0	19.9	10.7	11.4	12.5	14.6	10.8	13.8	8.4	16.1	19.9	13.6
One	10.8	14.0	14.0	8.3	9.8	8.7	5.0	9.7	11.4	7.5	12.0	13.1	10.5
Two	14.7	17.4	16.8	12.0	14.3	11.1	4.5	14.5	16.4	11.7	16.3	17.1	13.5
Three	17.3	17.9	17.2	17.7	18.1	13.5	6.6	18.5	19.3	15.1	20.4	17.9	15.6
Four	14.4	12.3	12.4	17.3	15.9	13.7	8.0	15.2	16.0	15.2	14.8	13.1	14.1
Five	10.2	7.5	7.5	13.1	11.4	11.3	9.0	11.2	9.5	12.5	9.0	8.0	9.9
Six	7.5	4.5	4.8	8.6	7.8	9.2	10.1	7.5	5.2	9.6	4.5	4.5	7.2
Seven to ten	6.5	4.6	6.1	10.1	9.4	15.7	29.8	10.3	6.8	16.5	5.1	5.4	12.3
Eleven or more	1.5	0.8	1.2	2.2	2.0	4.2	12.3	2.4	1.5	3.4	1.7	1.1	3.4
Were you accepted by your first choice college?													
Yes	75.7	81.5	86.3	74.2	79.7	78.8	67.8	80.5	87.9	79.0	83.8	91.3	84.5
No	24.3	18.5	13.7	25.8	20.3	21.2	32.2	19.5	12.1	21.0	16.2	8.7	15.5
Is this college your:													
First choice?	50.9	60.6	69.0	51.7	63.3	62.7	60.9	55.4	63.2	62.3	55.9	73.7	70.0
Second choice?	32.1	28.6	23.3	29.7	27.8	25.0	23.7	31.5	27.3	26.9	27.1	19.4	21.4
Third choice?	11.4	7.6	5.4	11.8	6.5	8.6	9.8	9.4	7.0	7.6	10.8	4.8	5.9
Less than third choice?	5.6	3.1	2.3	6.7	2.3	3.8	5.6	3.6	2.5	3.2	6.1	2.0	2.6
Citizenship status													
U.S. citizen	96.2	98.5	98.0	94.0	95.8	95.5	92.5	96.0	97.2	98.0	97.4	97.3	96.9
Permanent resident (green card)	2.5	1.2	1.2	2.4	1.4	1.8	1.8	2.1	2.1	1.0	0.9	1.0	0.9
Neither	1.3	0.3	0.8	3.6	2.8	2.7	5.7	1.9	0.7	1.0	1.7	1.6	2.1
Are your parents:													
Both alive and living with each other?	58.9	65.9	71.6	57.8	69.1	71.3	78.4	58.0	70.7	78.0	62.0	75.3	77.6
Both alive, divorced or living apart?	36.0	29.6	25.1	37.0	26.6	25.3	18.7	36.1	25.4	18.9	33.1	21.2	19.2
One or both deceased?	5.0	4.5	3.3	5.2	4.3	3.4	2.8	5.9	3.9	3.1	4.9	3.5	3.1

WEIGHTED NATIONAL NORMS FOR FOUR-YEAR COLLEGES, FALL 2008

	PUBLIC			NONSECTARIAN				CATHOLIC			OTHER RELIGIOUS		
	LOW	MEDIUM	HIGH	LOW	MEDIUM	HIGH	V. HIGH	LOW	MEDIUM	HIGH	LOW	MEDIUM	HIGH
During high school (grades 9-12) how many years did you study each of the following subjects? [1]													
English (4 years)	97.8	97.0	98.0	96.7	98.4	97.8	98.4	97.8	98.6	98.4	96.3	97.0	97.7
Mathematics (3 years)	97.0	97.5	99.1	98.1	98.9	98.9	99.4	98.7	99.2	99.2	97.2	97.7	98.6
Foreign Language (2 years)	89.9	86.9	93.2	89.1	94.2	93.7	97.6	91.8	93.4	96.5	87.5	90.3	95.1
Physical Science (2 years)	55.1	54.5	58.6	59.5	61.4	52.2	73.4	49.6	61.2	64.1	53.6	58.1	64.1
Biological Science (2 years)	44.6	46.0	46.2	47.0	47.9	49.6	56.3	47.6	54.3	50.0	48.4	48.9	51.9
History/Am. Govt. (1 year)	98.4	99.0	98.9	98.7	99.1	98.9	99.0	98.5	99.0	99.4	97.8	98.7	99.0
Computer Science (1/2 year)	69.1	68.5	62.8	62.3	62.7	58.9	41.9	65.8	64.5	59.2	64.5	63.4	58.0
Arts and/or Music (1 year)	85.1	80.2	76.1	81.5	84.7	84.2	88.4	78.0	76.6	83.4	75.9	82.7	87.2
WHAT IS THE HIGHEST ACADEMIC DEGREE THAT YOU INTEND TO OBTAIN?													
Highest planned													
None	1.5	0.7	0.8	1.9	1.1	0.9	0.5	1.5	1.1	0.7	1.7	0.9	0.6
Vocational certificate	0.1	0.2	0.2	0.6	0.2	0.1	0.0	0.1	0.1	0.1	0.3	0.2	0.1
Associate (A.A. or equivalent)	0.8	0.9	0.6	0.9	0.6	0.4	0.1	1.4	0.7	0.4	1.5	0.9	0.4
Bachelor's degree (B.A., B.S., etc.)	26.5	32.4	24.4	26.8	27.4	19.5	10.2	20.3	21.9	19.7	27.7	28.1	22.0
Master's degree (M.A., M.S., etc.)	42.7	42.1	45.5	42.5	46.0	44.2	42.5	35.6	48.0	47.2	40.2	41.0	39.7
Ph.D. or Ed.D.	18.0	13.9	16.2	14.0	14.0	19.4	24.1	21.2	15.5	16.1	16.7	15.9	19.4
M.D., D.O., D.D.S., D.V.M.	5.3	5.8	7.0	5.9	5.5	8.5	11.8	14.3	7.1	8.7	5.8	7.9	10.6
J.D. (Law)	2.8	2.5	3.3	3.9	2.7	4.2	8.8	3.4	2.9	5.4	3.0	2.6	4.8
B.D. or M.DIV. (Divinity)	0.4	0.2	0.3	0.8	0.2	0.4	0.2	0.4	0.5	0.2	0.6	0.7	0.6
Other	1.9	1.2	1.7	2.8	2.3	2.2	1.6	2.0	2.2	1.4	2.5	1.8	1.7
Highest planned at this college													
None	2.4	2.2	2.1	2.0	1.0	0.8	0.6	1.5	1.0	0.9	2.6	1.3	0.8
Vocational certificate	0.2	0.2	0.3	0.3	0.2	0.3	0.2	0.0	0.1	0.2	0.4	0.3	0.2
Associate (A.A. or equivalent)	3.8	4.6	2.7	3.4	1.4	1.1	0.7	4.0	2.3	1.6	4.4	3.3	1.0
Bachelor's degree (B.A., B.S., etc.)	65.0	70.5	71.7	71.1	70.8	73.3	89.2	62.3	59.4	72.2	71.2	76.1	83.2
Master's degree (M.A., M.S., etc.)	21.9	18.8	18.2	18.0	20.8	18.2	6.9	19.6	29.6	20.0	15.6	15.1	10.6
Ph.D. or Ed.D.	3.5	1.9	2.4	2.1	2.8	3.0	1.0	7.4	4.2	2.2	2.2	1.9	1.7
M.D., D.O., D.D.S., D.V.M.	0.7	0.5	0.8	0.7	0.6	0.9	0.5	2.8	0.8	0.7	0.6	0.5	0.6
J.D. (Law)	0.5	0.1	0.4	0.6	0.5	0.4	0.2	0.4	0.6	0.8	0.5	0.1	0.6
B.D. or M.DIV. (Divinity)	0.4	0.1	0.2	0.4	0.1	0.2	0.1	0.3	0.2	0.1	0.5	0.3	0.1
Other	1.7	1.0	1.4	1.4	1.9	1.9	0.8	1.6	1.8	1.2	2.1	1.2	1.2
HOW WOULD YOU DESCRIBE THE RACIAL COMPOSITION OF THE:													
High school I last attended													
Completely non-White	9.9	1.3	1.5	5.6	1.5	2.7	3.0	10.3	3.2	1.4	3.9	1.4	1.2
Mostly non-White	25.9	8.8	7.3	16.6	8.3	8.6	8.1	23.5	9.5	5.9	13.6	7.3	6.9
Roughly half non-White	27.7	27.0	23.9	26.9	24.8	21.0	19.2	22.1	21.0	16.7	29.7	22.3	21.2
Mostly White	32.2	55.7	57.1	44.4	57.5	57.3	61.2	38.6	57.1	65.0	45.6	57.9	60.6
Completely White	4.2	7.2	10.1	6.5	7.9	10.4	8.5	5.4	9.1	11.1	7.2	11.0	10.0
Neighborhood where I grew up													
Completely non-White	16.6	3.4	2.7	11.5	3.4	4.5	5.0	16.9	5.7	2.4	8.5	3.0	2.6
Mostly non-White	23.6	8.2	6.3	17.3	8.9	8.3	6.8	21.7	9.2	5.9	13.3	6.9	6.1
Roughly half non-White	18.3	12.7	11.8	14.3	12.8	11.6	11.0	16.0	13.2	10.1	14.7	11.8	10.5
Mostly White	31.3	52.4	54.8	41.1	54.3	51.1	53.9	32.1	47.8	54.5	43.2	53.5	54.9
Completely White	10.2	23.4	24.5	15.8	20.7	24.5	23.3	13.1	24.1	27.2	20.3	24.9	25.8

WEIGHTED NATIONAL NORMS FOR FOUR-YEAR COLLEGES, FALL 2008

	PUBLIC			NONSECTARIAN				CATHOLIC			OTHER RELIGIOUS		
	LOW	MEDIUM	HIGH	LOW	MEDIUM	HIGH	V. HIGH	LOW	MEDIUM	HIGH	LOW	MEDIUM	HIGH
Do you have a disability?													
Hearing	0.6	0.7	0.6	0.7	0.6	0.6	0.6	0.7	0.5	0.6	0.8	0.6	0.6
Speech	0.3	0.4	0.2	0.4	0.3	0.3	0.2	0.3	0.3	0.3	0.4	0.2	0.3
Orthopedic	0.5	0.5	0.4	0.6	0.6	0.5	0.5	0.4	0.5	0.5	0.5	0.6	0.6
Learning disability	2.4	4.8	2.8	6.7	4.9	5.6	4.5	3.9	3.4	4.0	5.2	3.5	4.7
Partially sighted or blind	1.4	1.8	1.4	1.2	0.9	1.4	1.2	1.3	1.0	1.1	1.4	1.2	1.3
Health-related	1.4	1.8	1.1	1.8	1.6	1.8	1.2	1.7	1.9	1.4	1.9	1.7	1.5
Other	1.3	1.5	1.2	1.6	1.6	1.7	1.2	1.6	1.1	1.2	1.9	1.4	1.5
HOW MUCH OF YOUR FIRST YEAR'S EDUCATIONAL EXPENSES (ROOM, BOARD TUITION, AND FEES) DO YOU EXPECT TO COVER FROM:													
Family resources (parents, relatives, spouse, etc.)													
None	29.4	20.3	29.8	26.0	17.3	19.4	7.9	26.1	19.8	14.1	24.9	18.9	13.5
Less than $1,000	21.0	15.0	11.3	12.2	9.6	9.6	4.6	14.7	11.6	8.1	16.1	11.7	8.7
$1,000 to 2,999	20.1	18.2	13.8	13.7	11.8	11.2	6.3	17.9	16.8	9.9	17.2	14.1	10.8
$3,000 to 5,999	12.6	14.9	13.1	13.5	12.0	10.3	6.5	14.3	16.9	11.1	14.5	14.9	11.5
$6,000 to 9,999	6.3	11.4	10.8	10.5	11.8	11.2	7.0	10.1	11.8	11.9	9.8	12.4	11.9
$10,000 +	10.6	20.1	21.2	24.1	37.5	38.3	67.6	16.9	23.3	44.9	17.4	28.0	43.5
My own resources (savings from work, work-study, other income)													
None	39.1	31.1	42.3	38.1	35.6	32.0	37.2	37.0	28.3	27.8	39.9	30.1	31.7
Less than $1,000	32.8	32.0	25.4	24.8	25.4	25.1	23.5	28.7	27.3	24.1	27.1	26.9	24.9
$1,000 to 2,999	19.7	24.9	19.9	22.1	23.4	25.6	26.2	22.7	26.2	27.3	21.1	25.9	25.8
$3,000 to 5,999	5.9	8.4	7.9	9.2	8.3	10.1	8.3	7.1	11.1	12.6	7.6	10.1	10.4
$6,000 to 9,999	1.4	2.3	2.2	2.5	3.5	3.6	1.9	2.2	3.9	4.1	2.2	3.8	3.6
$10,000 +	1.1	1.4	2.2	3.4	3.8	3.6	2.9	2.2	3.3	4.1	2.1	3.3	3.5
Aid which need not be repaid (grants, scholarships, military funding, etc.)													
None	37.0	35.5	35.6	23.6	21.6	19.1	41.6	18.9	13.5	17.0	16.2	13.6	18.0
Less than $1,000	8.7	11.2	8.6	5.4	4.5	3.1	3.6	4.5	3.2	3.3	3.8	3.1	3.0
$1,000 to 2,999	19.3	19.6	15.2	11.3	10.4	6.6	6.2	10.2	7.9	8.1	9.2	9.3	7.3
$3,000 to 5,999	17.9	16.3	14.2	15.7	13.9	9.1	5.0	15.3	11.6	10.8	14.1	12.7	9.8
$6,000 to 9,999	9.6	8.6	7.9	16.7	15.7	13.0	4.8	17.2	17.4	14.2	16.1	17.5	12.5
$10,000 +	7.5	8.8	18.6	27.4	33.9	49.1	38.9	33.9	46.3	46.6	40.7	43.9	49.5
Aid which must be repaid (loans, etc.)													
None	56.6	51.6	57.6	36.7	36.6	41.2	62.0	33.3	29.9	37.9	34.1	36.1	42.6
Less than $1,000	5.9	5.0	4.2	3.4	3.2	2.6	2.4	4.7	4.0	3.0	4.7	3.5	2.5
$1,000 to 2,999	11.9	12.1	8.9	9.2	8.7	9.0	7.7	11.4	12.5	9.9	12.3	10.1	8.9
$3,000 to 5,999	15.2	15.6	12.2	16.7	17.3	16.4	12.4	19.0	22.7	19.6	21.1	19.9	18.0
$6,000 to 9,999	6.0	8.3	7.4	12.7	12.6	11.9	5.4	13.9	14.6	11.8	13.4	14.1	12.8
$10,000 +	4.4	7.3	9.7	21.2	21.6	18.8	10.1	17.7	16.3	17.9	14.3	16.3	15.1
Other than above													
None	93.0	94.2	94.5	92.6	92.9	92.9	95.0	91.6	90.4	92.1	91.2	92.6	93.3
Less than $1,000	2.9	2.9	2.1	2.4	2.2	2.3	1.5	3.1	3.6	2.7	3.3	2.4	2.3
$1,000 to 2,999	2.1	1.5	1.1	1.4	1.5	1.6	1.1	1.8	2.0	1.7	2.1	1.7	1.3
$3,000 to 5,999	0.9	0.6	0.8	1.3	1.2	1.1	0.7	1.2	1.4	1.1	1.4	1.2	1.0
$6,000 to 9,999	0.4	0.2	0.3	0.8	0.7	0.7	0.3	0.8	0.8	0.7	0.9	0.7	0.5
$10,000 +	0.6	0.5	1.2	1.5	1.6	1.5	1.4	1.6	1.8	1.7	1.3	1.4	1.5

WEIGHTED NATIONAL NORMS FOR FOUR-YEAR COLLEGES, FALL 2008

	PUBLIC			NONSECTARIAN				CATHOLIC			OTHER RELIGIOUS		
	LOW	MEDIUM	HIGH	LOW	MEDIUM	HIGH	V. HIGH	LOW	MEDIUM	HIGH	LOW	MEDIUM	HIGH
What is your best estimate of your parents' total income last year? Consider income from all sources before taxes													
Less than $10,000	7.9	3.8	2.5	6.1	2.5	3.6	2.5	8.1	3.8	2.2	6.1	2.8	2.5
$10,000 to 14,999	6.2	3.1	1.9	4.1	2.5	2.6	1.5	5.8	3.2	1.4	4.0	2.3	1.9
$15,000 to 19,999	4.8	2.7	1.7	3.7	2.0	2.3	1.3	4.6	2.6	1.5	3.2	2.4	1.5
$20,000 to 24,999	6.3	3.7	2.5	3.9	3.0	3.5	1.8	6.6	4.1	2.0	5.1	3.2	2.3
$25,000 to 29,999	5.4	3.7	2.7	4.3	3.0	3.4	1.6	5.1	3.0	2.0	5.1	3.5	2.6
$30,000 to 39,999	9.2	7.1	5.5	8.1	6.6	5.7	3.5	9.6	7.8	4.8	8.7	7.0	5.0
$40,000 to 49,999	9.9	8.5	7.0	9.0	7.2	7.4	4.1	9.2	10.0	5.9	10.2	9.1	6.7
$50,000 to 59,999	9.0	10.2	8.7	10.5	8.6	8.3	5.3	9.0	10.1	7.9	10.5	9.5	8.5
$60,000 to 74,999	10.6	13.4	12.1	12.0	11.7	10.8	7.7	10.9	12.7	11.7	12.5	13.7	11.3
$75,000 to 99,999	11.1	14.6	16.3	13.1	15.9	13.9	11.6	12.6	15.7	15.4	12.5	16.7	14.9
$100,000 to 149,999	10.5	15.3	20.9	12.3	17.8	17.9	17.8	10.3	15.1	20.4	12.0	16.1	18.2
$150,000 to 199,999	4.3	6.7	8.7	6.3	8.5	8.4	10.7	4.2	6.0	10.5	4.5	5.6	8.9
$200,000 to 249,999	1.7	2.9	3.6	2.3	4.0	4.4	8.4	1.8	2.5	5.2	2.3	2.9	5.1
$250,000 or more	3.1	4.3	5.8	4.3	6.7	7.7	22.2	2.0	3.4	9.2	3.4	5.2	10.5
Do you have any concern about your ability to finance your college education?													
None (I am confident that I will have sufficient funds)	30.3	31.6	47.2	30.6	33.7	34.1	46.6	26.2	31.4	35.3	33.4	32.7	37.1
Some (but I probably will have enough funds)	55.7	57.1	45.1	53.3	54.9	55.1	46.7	57.2	56.5	55.3	53.8	56.2	53.9
Major (not sure I will have enough funds to complete college)	14.0	11.3	7.7	16.1	11.4	10.9	6.7	16.5	12.1	9.5	12.8	11.1	9.1
Your current religious preference													
Baptist	17.9	14.8	11.5	14.5	6.1	7.4	1.9	18.0	4.9	2.7	31.8	13.0	9.6
Buddhist	1.2	0.6	0.6	1.1	1.0	1.2	1.8	1.2	0.6	0.7	0.4	0.2	0.9
Church of Christ	7.6	4.5	4.1	7.1	3.8	3.9	1.5	4.7	4.0	2.6	5.6	8.0	2.6
Eastern Orthodox	0.5	0.4	0.5	0.7	0.7	0.6	0.9	0.7	1.0	0.7	0.4	0.5	0.4
Episcopalian	0.4	1.1	1.8	0.9	1.2	2.3	3.9	0.8	0.5	1.2	1.0	0.8	2.6
Hindu	0.2	0.1	0.5	0.7	0.4	1.3	1.1	0.4	0.3	0.2	0.1	0.1	0.5
Jewish	1.6	1.3	1.7	1.1	3.2	2.6	9.2	0.2	0.4	0.4	0.3	0.4	2.1
LDS (Mormon)	0.2	10.9	0.6	0.1	0.1	0.2	0.2	0.1	0.1	0.1	0.3	0.1	0.1
Lutheran	2.0	1.9	3.9	1.7	3.0	2.8	2.4	1.7	4.3	4.1	2.8	7.8	9.2
Methodist	3.1	4.9	6.0	2.9	4.3	4.8	2.3	3.5	3.8	1.9	8.4	6.4	7.3
Muslim	0.8	0.4	1.1	1.3	0.6	1.1	1.0	1.2	0.9	0.3	0.4	0.3	0.5
Presbyterian	1.4	2.3	3.8	1.4	2.8	3.0	4.4	1.1	1.6	2.0	2.9	4.9	5.6
Quaker	0.1	0.2	0.1	0.2	0.1	0.2	0.7	0.2	0.1	0.1	0.2	0.2	0.7
Roman Catholic	24.9	18.0	27.5	28.4	33.5	24.8	17.2	40.5	52.9	58.5	12.0	14.7	14.6
Seventh Day Adventist	0.7	0.2	0.3	0.8	0.3	0.2	0.2	0.5	0.3	0.2	0.3	4.6	0.2
United Church of Christ/Congregational	0.6	0.7	0.9	0.8	0.9	1.1	1.4	0.6	0.6	0.9	0.6	1.1	1.0
Other Christian	15.4	12.5	13.4	12.0	10.7	13.3	6.9	12.7	9.2	7.7	20.3	25.5	21.2
Other Religion	3.5	3.5	2.7	2.9	3.1	3.8	4.0	2.5	2.1	2.0	2.4	1.9	3.3
None	17.9	21.5	19.0	21.5	24.0	25.2	39.0	9.5	12.3	13.7	9.8	9.3	17.6

117

WEIGHTED NATIONAL NORMS FOR FOUR-YEAR COLLEGES, FALL 2008

	PUBLIC			NONSECTARIAN				CATHOLIC			OTHER RELIGIOUS		
	LOW	MEDIUM	HIGH	LOW	MEDIUM	HIGH	V. HIGH	LOW	MEDIUM	HIGH	LOW	MEDIUM	HIGH
Father's current religious preference													
Baptist	16.8	15.5	12.3	13.5	6.9	8.3	2.3	16.1	5.1	3.1	29.9	13.0	10.1
Buddhist	1.6	0.6	0.6	1.3	0.7	1.3	2.0	1.5	0.4	0.6	0.4	0.2	0.8
Church of Christ	7.1	4.6	4.2	7.4	4.3	4.1	1.7	4.8	4.0	2.8	5.2	7.0	2.7
Eastern Orthodox	0.6	0.5	0.6	1.0	0.9	0.9	1.0	0.9	1.1	0.9	0.3	0.5	0.5
Episcopalian	0.5	1.4	2.1	1.2	1.6	2.5	4.9	0.8	0.8	1.5	0.9	0.9	3.2
Hindu	0.3	0.2	0.6	0.8	0.5	1.5	1.4	0.6	0.4	0.2	0.2	0.1	0.6
Jewish	2.4	1.5	2.2	2.0	4.9	3.9	11.7	0.5	0.7	1.0	0.5	0.7	3.0
LDS (Mormon)	0.2	11.3	0.6	0.3	0.1	0.2	0.8	0.1	0.1	0.1	0.3	0.2	0.2
Lutheran	2.3	2.2	4.9	1.9	3.6	3.5	3.3	1.4	4.8	5.4	3.3	8.8	10.1
Methodist	3.0	4.9	6.7	3.2	5.3	5.4	3.0	3.2	4.1	2.4	7.9	6.1	7.9
Muslim	1.5	0.6	1.4	2.3	0.7	1.5	1.4	1.7	1.2	0.6	0.6	0.6	0.7
Presbyterian	1.8	2.9	4.5	1.6	3.5	3.9	5.6	1.6	2.2	2.4	3.2	5.0	6.3
Quaker	0.1	0.2	0.1	0.1	0.2	0.2	0.6	0.1	0.1	0.1	0.2	0.2	0.5
Roman Catholic	28.9	21.5	30.6	32.2	38.2	28.5	21.8	42.2	54.7	58.1	13.8	16.9	17.9
Seventh Day Adventist	0.7	0.3	0.3	0.8	0.5	0.3	0.4	0.6	0.4	0.3	0.4	4.3	0.3
United Church of Christ/Congregational	0.6	0.9	0.8	0.8	0.9	1.2	1.7	0.5	0.6	0.8	0.7	0.9	1.1
Other Christian	14.2	11.8	12.0	11.2	10.1	12.4	7.7	11.1	7.9	7.3	18.4	22.4	18.4
Other Religion	2.8	2.3	1.8	2.3	1.9	2.2	2.5	2.1	1.7	1.5	2.0	1.6	2.1
None	14.7	16.6	13.7	16.1	15.2	18.1	26.7	10.3	9.7	10.9	11.5	10.5	13.7
Mother's current religious preference													
Baptist	17.9	16.2	12.9	15.6	7.1	8.7	2.6	18.9	5.3	3.1	31.8	14.0	10.7
Buddhist	1.6	0.6	0.6	1.5	0.7	1.4	2.1	1.4	0.4	0.7	0.3	0.3	0.8
Church of Christ	8.0	5.3	4.6	8.3	4.6	4.7	2.2	5.2	4.5	2.9	5.7	7.5	2.9
Eastern Orthodox	0.6	0.6	0.5	0.9	1.0	0.7	1.1	0.7	0.8	0.8	0.4	0.4	0.5
Episcopalian	0.6	1.5	2.2	1.3	1.8	2.9	5.7	0.7	0.8	1.5	1.2	1.0	3.5
Hindu	0.3	0.2	0.6	0.6	0.5	1.4	1.4	0.5	0.3	0.2	0.1	0.1	0.6
Jewish	2.3	1.5	2.0	1.4	4.4	3.5	10.6	0.3	0.5	0.6	0.4	0.5	2.6
LDS (Mormon)	0.3	11.7	0.7	0.1	0.2	0.2	0.2	0.2	0.1	0.2	0.4	0.2	0.2
Lutheran	2.4	2.4	4.9	2.6	3.7	3.8	3.6	1.7	4.8	5.1	3.6	9.0	10.5
Methodist	3.5	6.0	7.4	3.3	5.6	6.1	3.7	3.6	4.5	2.7	8.7	6.9	8.9
Muslim	1.0	0.5	1.2	1.6	0.6	1.2	1.2	1.1	1.0	0.4	0.4	0.4	0.5
Presbyterian	1.8	3.2	4.7	2.1	3.6	4.2	6.3	1.6	2.1	2.5	3.4	5.2	6.9
Quaker	0.2	0.3	0.2	0.1	0.3	0.3	0.6	0.2	0.3	0.2	0.3	0.2	0.6
Roman Catholic	30.6	22.6	32.3	33.1	40.2	30.2	23.9	42.5	56.9	62.1	14.0	17.6	18.6
Seventh Day Adventist	0.8	0.3	0.4	0.9	0.6	0.3	0.4	0.5	0.5	0.3	0.4	4.6	0.3
United Church of Christ/Congregational	0.7	1.0	0.9	1.0	1.1	1.4	2.2	0.6	0.7	1.0	0.8	1.1	1.4
Other Christian	15.7	12.9	13.1	12.9	11.9	13.7	8.8	12.9	9.2	7.7	19.6	23.4	19.5
Other Religion	3.1	2.4	1.9	2.4	2.1	2.6	3.1	2.4	1.5	1.5	2.0	1.6	2.4
None	8.6	10.8	8.9	10.2	10.0	12.6	20.2	5.1	5.9	6.5	6.5	6.0	8.5

118

WEIGHTED NATIONAL NORMS FOR FOUR-YEAR COLLEGES, FALL 2008

	PUBLIC			NONSECTARIAN				CATHOLIC			OTHER RELIGIOUS		
	LOW	MEDIUM	HIGH	LOW	MEDIUM	HIGH	V. HIGH	LOW	MEDIUM	HIGH	LOW	MEDIUM	HIGH
During the past year, student "frequently" or "occasionally":													
Attended a religious service	75.2	75.1	77.4	71.8	69.6	71.4	65.1	83.9	80.7	84.1	86.1	89.1	83.0
Was bored in class [2]	35.8	43.0	43.9	36.1	37.1	37.5	36.4	29.5	36.6	36.3	37.9	36.2	37.2
Participated in political demonstrations	28.0	25.8	21.2	26.9	22.6	26.5	31.6	28.6	24.2	26.7	26.4	23.1	27.0
Tutored another student	52.0	48.4	53.5	45.5	44.5	54.5	63.2	54.2	49.2	55.3	49.7	51.8	54.8
Studied with other students	86.3	84.6	85.6	84.0	84.1	86.7	91.6	87.5	87.6	90.1	84.8	87.6	89.0
Was a guest in a teacher's home	18.8	20.9	21.2	18.0	18.5	25.3	32.0	18.3	17.5	19.8	25.9	29.4	29.0
Smoked cigarettes [2]	4.4	5.7	6.1	7.0	6.5	5.1	3.7	4.2	4.9	3.4	4.1	2.5	3.5
Drank beer	31.5	35.2	41.8	39.9	45.5	45.2	57.3	27.6	37.5	44.7	29.2	25.1	35.7
Drank wine or liquor	40.6	40.7	46.8	49.3	50.6	49.9	62.4	37.0	43.8	49.3	35.6	29.1	41.6
Felt overwhelmed by all I had to do [2]	27.3	31.1	27.1	27.9	29.3	30.2	31.3	26.2	31.2	29.8	28.1	30.0	30.6
Felt depressed [2]	8.6	8.3	6.2	9.0	7.2	8.3	6.8	7.2	7.8	6.0	7.9	6.7	6.6
Performed volunteer work	77.4	81.1	81.0	79.1	81.6	85.8	90.8	83.8	82.2	90.8	82.9	88.3	89.5
Played a musical instrument	40.7	41.8	42.2	37.2	40.0	45.2	51.4	36.7	38.1	40.0	40.2	48.8	53.3
Asked a teacher for advice after class [2]	26.5	27.2	24.3	28.1	25.6	31.0	36.5	29.9	26.9	30.5	27.4	29.0	31.5
Voted in a student election [2]	23.0	22.3	19.5	21.1	20.2	23.2	27.1	25.7	20.2	25.4	22.8	22.7	23.2
Socialized with someone of another racial/ethnic group [2]	70.3	69.6	66.9	71.4	68.2	67.1	71.5	70.1	64.9	64.6	69.6	65.9	65.8
Came late to class	62.2	62.6	59.7	61.4	56.3	58.3	65.0	55.3	53.2	57.3	58.0	57.3	57.8
Used the Internet: [2]													
For research or homework	71.5	67.6	73.8	73.9	75.7	76.3	85.2	76.0	78.6	81.3	68.9	74.8	77.7
To read news sites	39.0	36.1	41.0	42.7	43.5	44.0	53.1	44.2	44.5	44.2	36.4	38.3	42.6
To read blogs	24.5	22.5	24.2	26.8	27.9	25.3	23.8	26.6	26.6	23.0	24.5	25.2	24.7
To blog	15.8	12.9	14.4	15.9	16.5	13.9	10.2	17.4	17.4	13.0	16.3	16.7	14.7
Performed community service as part of a class	57.6	55.0	53.5	58.4	58.2	60.5	59.9	64.7	64.3	67.7	57.6	62.7	61.2
Discussed religion [2]	25.9	32.3	31.2	26.8	26.5	32.0	35.8	30.8	28.8	35.7	33.8	43.6	41.5
Discussed politics [2]	27.7	32.3	35.0	30.0	30.3	36.7	51.3	27.6	29.9	38.6	28.5	31.8	39.5
Worked on a local, state or national political campaign	12.5	9.1	10.0	10.3	8.6	11.9	16.8	13.8	10.1	12.0	10.7	10.6	13.3
Student rated self "above average" or "highest 10%" as compared with the average person of his/her age in:													
Academic ability	52.8	60.2	68.9	49.4	60.0	70.3	88.3	55.5	62.1	71.7	54.2	66.9	75.8
Artistic ability	28.7	29.6	28.3	33.8	38.5	33.9	39.9	24.4	25.6	24.9	25.9	28.9	34.6
Computer skills	39.3	36.5	38.3	38.5	39.0	34.9	31.4	39.8	36.8	35.0	35.8	31.7	32.1
Cooperativeness	68.6	73.2	72.8	69.9	73.1	74.5	74.6	71.7	74.0	77.2	70.9	74.8	74.1
Creativity	55.3	55.9	54.2	61.0	61.4	58.7	64.0	54.0	54.1	53.5	54.1	54.5	58.5
Drive to achieve	69.9	68.8	73.7	72.9	73.4	75.3	80.9	76.9	75.0	76.5	72.9	74.2	74.3
Emotional health	49.4	49.1	54.6	48.9	50.4	52.2	56.3	52.0	50.4	55.5	52.7	54.7	53.5
Leadership ability	57.1	56.7	63.7	57.6	57.7	60.7	65.5	59.5	59.5	63.5	60.8	62.0	62.2
Mathematical ability	32.8	36.1	45.9	30.4	35.0	42.0	50.9	34.8	37.4	42.5	35.2	38.6	42.5
Physical health	48.8	50.6	58.7	51.8	52.6	54.2	59.6	53.7	54.5	59.3	57.5	55.5	55.4
Popularity	37.8	36.3	40.8	41.1	37.6	37.3	39.6	40.0	36.3	40.0	41.0	37.1	35.9
Public speaking ability	33.7	34.3	37.5	33.6	33.7	36.4	46.2	32.3	32.9	37.8	32.6	36.5	40.2
Self-confidence (intellectual)	57.3	53.9	59.5	56.1	53.6	58.7	66.9	57.6	56.1	58.3	58.4	57.7	60.5
Self-confidence (social)	54.5	49.7	52.3	54.5	50.3	48.3	48.8	54.3	50.9	51.3	54.6	50.7	48.4
Self-understanding	56.5	54.1	56.2	57.8	56.1	57.3	64.0	57.5	54.3	57.1	56.9	55.9	58.4
Spirituality	42.0	39.5	38.8	37.7	34.1	37.3	32.4	44.4	38.6	38.6	46.9	50.6	45.4
Understanding of others	64.6	67.2	64.4	65.8	66.8	67.3	70.4	64.6	66.7	68.8	63.6	66.7	68.3
Writing ability	40.3	41.2	48.0	42.8	44.4	47.7	63.5	43.2	42.5	50.1	39.4	45.0	51.6

119

WEIGHTED NATIONAL NORMS FOR FOUR-YEAR COLLEGES, FALL 2008

	PUBLIC			NONSECTARIAN				CATHOLIC			OTHER RELIGIOUS		
	LOW	MEDIUM	HIGH	LOW	MEDIUM	HIGH	V. HIGH	LOW	MEDIUM	HIGH	LOW	MEDIUM	HIGH
Student rated self "above average" or "highest 10%" as compared with the average person of his/her age in:													
Ability to see the world from someone else's perspective	59.3	62.5	63.2	59.9	63.3	66.5	75.6	58.3	61.7	64.7	55.7	61.2	67.3
Tolerance of others with different beliefs	66.0	71.7	70.4	67.3	71.3	75.7	84.4	66.6	69.7	73.8	61.9	66.4	73.7
Openness to having my own views challenged	57.1	56.5	55.5	58.1	57.4	59.2	66.7	55.9	55.5	56.5	52.5	51.6	56.9
Ability to discuss and negotiate controversial issues	58.5	60.3	63.0	59.7	60.6	63.4	72.6	56.6	59.7	62.0	55.3	56.7	62.7
Ability to work cooperatively with diverse people	74.7	77.6	77.0	74.7	77.3	79.4	84.6	75.6	75.9	79.1	71.6	74.7	78.6
WHAT IS THE HIGHEST LEVEL OF FORMAL EDUCATION OBTAINED BY YOUR PARENTS?													
Father													
Grammar school or less	10.6	2.8	2.5	5.8	3.0	3.0	1.3	7.2	5.2	2.1	4.8	2.5	1.7
Some high school	10.6	5.4	3.9	8.1	4.4	4.3	1.7	8.9	6.1	2.8	8.1	4.2	2.3
High school graduate	27.5	25.8	20.9	27.5	23.7	18.6	6.3	30.9	26.8	16.6	30.7	21.1	13.9
Postsecondary school other than college	3.2	3.7	4.1	3.5	4.4	3.3	1.8	4.5	5.7	4.2	4.1	3.9	3.5
Some college	17.9	18.3	15.1	16.8	16.3	13.3	7.7	17.2	15.6	14.5	17.3	16.0	12.6
College degree	18.8	27.1	29.2	22.6	28.2	30.2	26.7	18.3	24.4	32.1	22.8	29.4	31.3
Some graduate school	1.1	1.3	2.3	1.3	1.9	2.5	3.6	1.6	1.6	2.5	1.5	2.4	3.0
Graduate degree	10.3	15.6	21.9	14.4	18.2	24.7	50.7	11.3	14.6	25.0	10.6	20.4	31.7
Mother													
Grammar school or less	10.0	2.4	2.2	5.2	2.5	2.6	1.1	6.8	3.7	2.1	4.5	2.0	1.5
Some high school	8.3	3.4	2.7	5.9	2.5	3.1	1.4	5.7	4.5	2.0	4.8	2.4	1.4
High school graduate	22.6	22.1	19.5	23.5	20.8	16.1	6.3	26.5	24.9	15.5	25.6	19.4	12.1
Postsecondary school other than college	3.6	4.0	4.3	3.8	4.9	3.5	2.1	4.6	5.7	4.1	4.2	4.2	3.4
Some college	21.1	22.1	17.2	18.3	17.7	15.5	8.6	18.7	17.6	16.0	21.0	19.4	15.3
College degree	22.4	31.2	33.4	27.6	32.5	35.1	34.9	23.9	28.3	37.4	27.4	34.5	37.6
Some graduate school	1.4	1.9	2.7	2.2	2.4	3.0	5.4	1.8	1.7	3.2	1.8	2.7	4.0
Graduate degree	10.6	13.0	17.9	13.5	16.7	21.1	40.2	12.1	13.6	19.8	10.8	15.4	24.7
During the past year, did you "frequently":													
Ask questions in class	48.7	50.9	53.6	50.5	51.9	56.0	68.5	53.2	51.4	57.7	50.2	53.0	57.6
Support your opinions with a logical argument	47.0	52.9	59.2	51.1	54.5	59.9	76.0	48.8	50.5	59.5	46.2	53.1	60.3
Seek solutions to problems and explain them to others	44.6	45.9	50.9	45.4	48.0	52.9	65.8	46.6	45.9	52.6	41.6	48.4	53.1
Revise your papers to improve your writing	42.2	41.8	44.3	44.4	45.0	48.5	58.9	47.6	50.1	51.6	43.4	49.4	53.0
Evaluate the quality or reliability of information you received	32.4	32.4	35.4	32.8	33.6	38.0	49.1	36.0	34.0	37.1	30.2	33.5	39.1
Take a risk because you feel you have more to gain	39.8	39.0	40.8	43.1	40.8	39.3	42.1	39.2	40.5	39.3	39.1	37.7	37.8
Seek alternative solutions to a problem	41.4	42.2	43.2	43.4	44.2	45.4	50.2	44.2	43.0	43.5	39.7	42.1	43.5
Look up scientific research articles and resources	18.7	18.7	21.6	19.3	18.9	23.0	28.1	23.8	20.5	21.9	17.9	18.0	22.1
Explore topics on your own, even though it was not required for a class	27.8	28.2	31.2	30.0	30.1	34.4	42.7	27.8	27.9	28.9	24.0	26.4	32.9
Accept mistakes as part of the learning process	51.4	51.5	50.0	52.4	50.9	51.1	54.7	53.5	49.1	50.0	48.4	48.5	49.3
Seek feedback on your academic work	43.9	45.8	45.3	47.9	46.2	49.6	59.7	49.8	48.5	49.9	43.1	46.4	50.0
Take notes during class	63.3	61.8	63.0	69.7	67.9	68.1	71.7	70.9	74.6	72.4	66.0	66.3	68.3

WEIGHTED NATIONAL NORMS FOR FOUR-YEAR COLLEGES, FALL 2008

	PUBLIC			NONSECTARIAN				CATHOLIC			OTHER RELIGIOUS		
	LOW	MEDIUM	HIGH	LOW	MEDIUM	HIGH	V. HIGH	LOW	MEDIUM	HIGH	LOW	MEDIUM	HIGH
Your probable career occupation													
Accountant or actuary	2.4	2.5	2.3	3.0	3.7	3.4	0.8	2.1	3.9	3.5	3.0	2.3	1.9
Actor or entertainer	1.8	2.0	1.0	1.4	4.7	2.3	1.8	0.8	0.8	0.8	1.0	1.6	1.7
Architect or urban planner	0.5	0.5	0.4	0.6	0.3	0.4	1.0	0.1	0.3	0.3	0.5	0.3	0.4
Artist	2.5	2.5	2.6	11.4	9.9	5.5	3.1	1.0	2.0	0.7	1.6	2.3	2.2
Business (clerical)	0.6	0.6	0.8	0.8	0.9	1.1	0.6	0.8	0.7	0.9	0.7	0.8	0.6
Business executive (management, administrator)	6.6	5.6	6.3	8.6	7.5	9.0	8.6	5.2	6.2	10.6	7.0	6.6	6.4
Business owner or proprietor	3.4	3.7	3.1	4.8	3.7	3.9	2.7	2.6	2.5	3.8	4.5	2.8	2.5
Business salesperson or buyer	1.0	1.0	1.0	1.5	1.0	1.1	0.5	0.5	1.1	1.2	0.9	0.6	0.6
Clergy (minister, priest)	0.1	0.0	0.1	0.0	0.1	0.2	0.1	0.0	0.1	0.3	1.0	1.4	0.8
Clergy (other religious)	0.0	0.0	0.0	0.0	0.0	0.1	0.1	0.1	0.1	0.1	0.3	0.7	0.4
Clinical psychologist	1.6	1.7	1.3	1.7	1.2	1.2	1.2	1.2	1.8	1.9	1.5	1.5	1.4
College administrator/staff	0.1	0.1	0.0	0.1	0.0	0.0	0.0	0.1	0.1	0.1	0.1	0.0	0.0
College teacher	0.4	0.5	0.3	0.5	0.3	0.6	1.5	0.2	0.2	0.5	0.5	0.6	1.0
Computer programmer or analyst	2.4	1.9	1.6	1.6	1.3	1.4	0.5	1.2	1.4	1.0	1.5	1.3	1.1
Conservationist or forester	0.2	0.2	0.2	0.0	0.5	0.5	0.3	0.1	0.1	0.2	0.3	0.2	0.5
Dentist (including orthodontist)	1.1	1.1	1.3	1.0	0.5	0.7	0.6	1.8	0.7	1.3	1.0	1.0	0.9
Dietitian or nutritionist	0.5	0.6	0.4	0.1	0.3	0.2	0.2	0.4	1.1	0.3	0.3	0.3	0.4
Engineer	4.8	3.8	7.5	1.1	2.9	6.3	3.0	1.0	1.1	5.6	1.6	2.2	3.7
Farmer or rancher	0.2	0.2	0.1	0.2	0.4	0.2	0.2	0.1	0.0	0.1	0.4	0.3	0.3
Foreign service worker (including diplomat)	0.2	0.5	0.7	0.1	0.3	1.2	3.3	0.4	0.5	0.9	0.4	0.7	1.5
Homemaker (full-time)	0.0	0.2	0.1	0.1	0.0	0.1	0.1	0.0	0.1	0.1	0.1	0.2	0.2
Interior decorator (including designer)	0.3	0.5	0.2	1.3	0.5	0.2	0.2	0.1	0.3	0.1	0.4	0.1	0.3
Lab technician or hygienist	0.2	0.4	0.2	0.3	0.2	0.1	0.1	0.6	0.3	0.1	0.1	0.2	0.1
Law enforcement officer	2.1	2.1	1.4	2.0	1.6	0.5	0.1	2.0	2.2	0.9	2.5	1.1	0.5
Lawyer (attorney) or judge	2.7	2.3	2.7	3.6	2.3	3.4	5.7	3.2	2.9	4.5	2.8	2.2	3.9
Military service (career)	0.5	0.4	0.4	0.4	0.5	0.3	0.2	0.4	0.4	0.7	0.4	0.5	0.4
Musician (performer, composer)	2.4	2.1	1.4	1.1	1.5	1.3	1.6	1.0	0.8	0.7	2.1	2.8	3.9
Nurse	7.1	7.4	6.2	3.1	4.7	1.7	0.2	15.3	11.9	5.0	5.3	6.4	3.2
Optometrist	0.7	0.2	0.3	0.2	0.2	0.2	0.1	0.6	0.4	0.4	0.3	0.3	0.3
Pharmacist	1.6	1.7	2.0	0.5	1.9	3.3	0.4	7.0	2.3	1.2	1.7	2.2	1.2
Physician	3.0	3.5	4.2	3.5	3.2	5.0	8.6	10.4	6.1	6.3	4.0	5.3	7.7
Policymaker/Government	0.4	0.6	0.9	0.4	0.6	1.1	2.6	0.6	0.5	1.3	0.5	0.6	1.4
School counselor	0.5	0.4	0.4	0.3	0.1	0.3	0.1	0.4	0.5	0.5	0.6	0.5	0.3
School principal or superintendent	0.1	0.0	0.0	0.1	0.0	0.1	0.0	0.0	0.0	0.0	0.0	0.0	0.0
Scientific researcher	0.8	1.4	1.7	0.6	1.9	2.4	4.0	0.8	0.9	1.6	1.0	1.1	2.7
Social, welfare, or recreation worker	2.1	1.3	0.8	1.0	0.8	0.7	0.6	1.4	1.3	0.9	1.7	1.6	1.2
Therapist (physical, occupational, speech)	4.1	4.1	2.7	1.9	2.7	2.5	1.1	2.8	6.0	3.5	4.3	4.7	3.2
Teacher or administrator (elementary)	5.9	7.0	5.0	4.2	4.8	3.0	0.8	4.3	7.0	4.6	7.7	6.7	3.7
Teacher or administrator (secondary)	6.1	5.8	5.2	3.2	3.7	3.9	2.3	2.7	6.3	4.7	7.4	6.7	4.9
Veterinarian	1.0	0.8	0.6	2.5	2.2	1.5	0.8	0.9	0.6	0.7	1.4	1.3	1.2
Writer or journalist	2.3	2.5	2.1	2.6	3.5	3.0	6.2	1.6	3.3	3.4	2.5	2.6	4.1
Skilled trades	0.3	0.5	0.3	0.4	0.3	0.2	0.2	0.2	0.2	0.2	0.3	0.3	0.3
Laborer (unskilled)	0.3	0.4	0.3	0.5	0.2	0.3	0.1	0.3	0.3	0.2	0.3	0.3	0.2
Semi-skilled worker	0.2	0.3	0.3	0.3	0.2	0.2	0.1	0.2	0.1	0.2	0.2	0.2	0.2
Unemployed	2.4	1.1	0.9	1.5	1.1	1.1	0.9	2.4	0.1	0.8	1.7	1.2	1.1
Other	9.7	10.5	7.3	13.7	10.8	9.0	5.7	11.9	10.2	7.3	10.8	10.3	8.5
Undecided	12.9	13.6	12.4	12.6	11.0	15.1	27.2	9.1	9.2	16.0	11.6	13.0	16.9

WEIGHTED NATIONAL NORMS FOR FOUR-YEAR COLLEGES, FALL 2008

	PUBLIC			NONSECTARIAN				CATHOLIC			OTHER RELIGIOUS		
	LOW	MEDIUM	HIGH	LOW	MEDIUM	HIGH	V. HIGH	LOW	MEDIUM	HIGH	LOW	MEDIUM	HIGH
Your father's occupation [3]													
Artist	1.2	1.0	0.9	1.9	1.6	1.6	3.0	1.0	0.9	0.9	1.0	1.0	1.7
Business	20.0	25.1	27.2	24.2	30.1	28.7	32.0	18.5	23.9	33.9	22.4	25.8	28.8
Business (clerical)	1.3	1.1	1.5	1.4	1.5	1.3	1.1	1.1	1.3	1.4	1.2	1.3	1.4
Clergy	0.6	0.7	0.7	0.5	0.3	0.8	0.6	0.8	0.4	0.3	2.1	3.9	2.7
College teacher	0.3	0.4	0.5	0.6	0.6	1.0	2.7	0.6	0.3	0.6	0.4	0.9	1.5
Doctor (MD or DDS)	0.5	1.3	2.2	1.3	1.7	2.6	8.1	1.2	1.5	3.2	1.0	2.2	4.7
Education (secondary)	1.7	2.2	2.5	1.5	1.7	2.7	3.0	1.6	2.1	2.2	2.4	3.2	3.4
Education (elementary)	0.6	0.6	0.6	0.7	0.4	0.8	0.8	0.6	0.7	0.8	0.7	1.0	1.0
Engineer	6.5	7.5	8.9	6.3	7.3	7.8	5.9	5.4	7.6	7.9	5.9	6.8	7.6
Farmer or forester	1.2	1.2	1.3	0.4	0.8	1.1	0.9	0.8	0.9	1.1	2.2	2.3	2.1
Health professional	1.1	1.2	1.5	1.2	1.5	1.9	1.2	1.3	1.2	1.3	1.1	1.5	1.5
Homemaker (full-time)	0.3	0.3	0.2	0.4	0.3	0.4	0.3	0.2	0.2	0.2	0.3	0.2	0.2
Lawyer	0.7	1.4	1.9	1.5	1.7	2.4	8.2	0.7	1.0	3.3	0.7	1.3	3.8
Military (career)	2.3	1.6	3.6	1.4	1.1	1.2	0.5	1.9	0.7	1.0	2.2	1.4	1.0
Nurse	0.6	0.5	0.6	0.6	0.4	0.5	0.3	0.8	0.5	0.6	0.5	0.7	0.5
Research scientist	0.3	0.6	0.5	0.3	0.4	0.8	1.8	0.2	0.4	0.5	0.2	0.3	0.9
Social/welfare/rec worker	0.8	0.7	0.5	0.5	0.4	0.6	0.5	1.0	0.5	0.6	0.6	0.5	0.6
Skilled worker	7.1	9.7	8.1	7.5	8.8	7.1	3.3	7.8	9.7	7.1	8.6	7.4	5.6
Semi-skilled worker	4.1	3.2	2.7	2.6	2.6	2.7	1.3	3.4	3.9	2.3	3.5	2.7	2.0
Unskilled worker	5.3	3.9	2.9	3.4	2.6	2.6	1.2	4.3	5.8	2.3	3.7	3.2	1.8
Unemployed	5.1	3.5	2.4	5.3	2.8	3.0	2.3	5.9	4.3	2.2	4.4	2.7	1.9
Other	38.3	32.4	28.9	36.4	31.5	28.4	21.1	40.8	32.2	26.4	35.0	29.8	25.4
Your mother's occupation [3]													
Artist	1.2	1.7	1.7	2.0	2.8	2.7	5.1	0.9	1.1	1.7	1.4	1.5	2.8
Business	15.3	16.1	17.2	15.6	18.1	16.1	14.7	15.6	15.9	16.6	16.6	14.5	14.7
Business (clerical)	3.6	4.3	4.6	5.0	4.6	4.0	2.6	4.0	4.6	4.4	4.6	4.4	3.6
Clergy	0.1	0.2	0.2	0.1	0.2	0.4	0.4	0.1	0.3	0.2	0.5	0.8	0.8
College teacher	0.2	0.3	0.4	0.3	0.4	0.7	1.8	0.1	0.4	0.6	0.3	0.5	1.2
Doctor (MD or DDS)	0.7	0.8	1.1	1.2	0.9	1.5	3.9	1.4	0.8	1.2	0.9	0.8	2.0
Education (secondary)	3.4	4.3	5.2	3.9	3.9	5.0	5.4	3.0	3.3	4.9	4.8	5.2	5.7
Education (elementary)	6.8	7.7	8.5	6.7	7.5	8.1	6.9	6.1	7.5	9.0	7.9	9.9	9.6
Engineer	0.6	0.6	0.8	0.4	0.6	0.8	1.0	0.5	0.3	0.6	0.4	0.4	0.7
Farmer or forester	0.2	0.2	0.3	0.1	0.2	0.3	0.4	0.1	0.1	0.2	0.3	0.3	0.3
Health professional	2.4	3.0	3.6	2.9	3.6	3.6	3.8	2.9	3.1	3.7	2.5	3.3	3.8
Homemaker (full-time)	5.4	6.6	7.9	5.5	7.3	9.0	13.5	5.6	6.5	10.3	6.4	10.2	11.0
Lawyer	0.4	0.4	0.9	0.6	0.8	1.1	4.2	0.3	0.1	1.0	0.4	0.4	1.4
Military (career)	0.3	0.2	0.4	0.4	0.2	0.1	0.1	0.4	0.1	0.1	0.4	0.2	0.1
Nurse	8.5	9.1	9.2	8.8	8.4	7.8	5.1	9.7	9.9	9.3	8.9	9.5	8.0
Research scientist	0.2	0.3	0.3	0.2	0.2	0.4	1.0	0.2	0.2	0.2	0.2	0.1	0.5
Social/welfare/rec worker	2.3	1.6	1.6	1.6	1.8	2.1	2.4	2.7	1.6	1.9	1.7	1.6	2.2
Skilled worker	1.9	1.9	1.6	1.5	1.4	1.4	0.9	1.3	1.9	1.4	1.8	1.3	1.1
Semi-skilled worker	2.2	2.0	2.0	1.6	2.0	1.3	1.0	1.7	2.6	1.5	1.7	1.8	1.3
Unskilled worker	3.0	2.1	1.4	1.6	1.1	1.2	0.7	1.8	2.3	1.1	1.8	1.4	1.0
Unemployed	9.1	7.4	5.9	7.3	6.1	6.5	5.7	7.8	7.3	5.7	7.0	5.9	5.3
Other	32.1	29.1	25.3	32.4	27.8	25.9	19.4	33.8	30.2	24.2	29.5	25.9	22.6
How would you characterize your political views?													
Far left	3.3	2.6	2.5	4.3	3.5	4.2	7.8	2.7	2.5	2.5	2.2	1.7	4.0
Liberal	30.9	27.0	23.8	33.0	32.2	34.3	51.4	30.3	27.5	29.7	18.6	17.8	29.5
Middle-of-the-road	47.7	48.0	45.1	46.6	47.3	41.4	28.7	49.6	48.9	42.5	47.8	40.9	37.4
Conservative	16.4	20.6	25.9	14.5	15.7	18.5	11.4	16.1	19.6	23.5	28.4	36.2	27.1
Far right	1.7	1.9	2.6	1.6	1.3	1.6	0.8	1.3	1.6	1.9	3.0	3.3	2.1

WEIGHTED NATIONAL NORMS FOR FOUR-YEAR COLLEGES, FALL 2008

Student agrees "strongly" or "somewhat":	PUBLIC			NONSECTARIAN				CATHOLIC			OTHER RELIGIOUS		
	LOW	MEDIUM	HIGH	LOW	MEDIUM	HIGH	V. HIGH	LOW	MEDIUM	HIGH	LOW	MEDIUM	HIGH
There is too much concern in the courts for the rights of criminals	60.1	59.7	62.9	54.3	59.6	55.6	39.4	54.2	62.6	57.7	63.2	61.7	53.6
Abortion should be legal	54.9	55.4	55.0	60.4	63.8	53.1	82.7	48.7	49.7	54.0	41.3	34.8	52.0
The death penalty should be abolished	34.0	29.0	28.1	38.2	34.5	37.8	56.1	37.5	36.1	40.9	29.1	29.8	40.6
Marijuana should be legalized	41.4	39.9	39.8	46.3	44.4	45.8	57.4	34.6	36.1	40.9	34.1	26.4	38.4
It is important to have laws prohibiting homosexual relationships	26.0	23.7	26.1	22.8	18.6	20.5	8.3	25.8	22.6	21.5	40.1	43.0	27.2
Racial discrimination is no longer a major problem in America	20.7	19.8	23.6	19.7	18.9	19.1	13.3	18.6	20.3	19.0	24.2	22.3	19.8
Realistically, an individual can do little to bring about changes in our society	34.2	27.0	28.6	31.6	28.0	25.4	21.0	31.8	29.2	24.1	33.6	23.8	22.9
Wealthy people should pay a larger share of taxes than they do now	63.4	61.1	57.0	65.9	63.9	62.5	66.4	63.8	64.3	59.7	59.5	56.5	58.9
Same-sex couples should have the right to legal marital status	65.2	64.6	62.4	68.8	73.5	70.4	85.2	63.2	68.2	67.3	47.4	41.3	59.0
Affirmative action in college admissions should be abolished	39.8	42.4	48.9	39.9	44.6	48.8	50.6	35.6	44.5	50.0	40.4	41.9	48.5
Federal military spending should be increased	27.5	29.2	40.0	27.3	27.4	25.3	14.4	30.3	29.8	27.3	36.7	33.7	25.6
The federal government should do more to control the sale of handguns	73.7	70.5	65.9	79.7	76.7	71.7	80.9	78.9	76.3	74.1	68.7	66.0	69.9
Only volunteers should serve in the armed forces	65.2	64.5	63.4	68.3	68.3	68.6	77.6	65.0	66.8	66.4	59.8	60.4	67.3
The federal government is not doing enough to control environmental pollution	79.3	77.6	74.7	81.5	82.7	81.0	89.2	79.2	79.5	78.9	73.0	70.0	77.2
A national health care plan is needed to cover everybody's medical costs	77.6	71.6	64.3	80.9	77.5	71.0	77.4	80.4	75.9	70.9	70.1	63.0	65.0
Undocumented immigrants should be denied access to public education	42.0	53.2	55.6	43.0	49.6	45.8	31.2	41.7	49.1	49.0	51.3	52.0	45.2
Through hard work, everybody can succeed in American society	81.2	80.5	81.4	76.6	78.7	76.0	61.9	79.7	80.4	78.8	80.9	81.0	73.8
Dissent is a critical component of the political process	55.9	58.2	60.6	54.4	57.2	61.5	79.4	52.4	56.8	62.7	54.9	57.8	65.3
Colleges have the right to ban extreme speakers from campus	37.4	41.8	43.9	38.1	39.8	38.9	33.1	40.4	42.1	44.4	46.8	50.9	44.2
Students from disadvantaged social backgrounds should be given preferential treatment in college admissions	49.4	38.3	34.8	45.6	38.2	37.8	42.7	48.4	38.6	35.4	46.1	40.3	38.1
The federal government should raise taxes to reduce the deficit	25.7	23.3	26.0	24.6	22.1	28.3	44.1	24.8	22.4	26.8	21.8	22.4	31.6
Addressing global warming should be a federal priority	75.8	71.3	69.3	79.4	78.9	76.6	87.0	77.1	76.1	75.1	67.1	60.0	70.4

WEIGHTED NATIONAL NORMS FOR FOUR-YEAR COLLEGES, FALL 2008

DURING YOUR LAST YEAR IN HIGH SCHOOL, HOW MUCH TIME DID YOU SPEND DURING A TYPICAL WEEK DOING THE FOLLOWING?

	PUBLIC			NONSECTARIAN				CATHOLIC			OTHER RELIGIOUS		
	LOW	MEDIUM	HIGH	LOW	MEDIUM	HIGH	V. HIGH	LOW	MEDIUM	HIGH	LOW	MEDIUM	HIGH
Studying/homework													
None	2.7	2.6	2.6	2.5	2.3	1.6	0.5	2.0	1.7	1.2	2.6	2.0	1.3
Less than one hour	14.2	14.3	14.0	13.5	12.5	9.6	2.9	11.0	11.0	7.3	13.5	10.6	7.6
1 to 2 hours	30.3	27.5	23.5	26.8	23.4	19.6	9.0	27.2	22.8	17.5	27.4	21.8	17.1
3 to 5 hours	29.2	31.0	28.3	30.4	30.0	27.9	20.4	27.4	32.0	28.9	30.0	30.3	28.5
6 to 10 hours	14.3	15.6	18.3	15.1	19.3	21.8	26.6	18.4	18.5	24.3	16.2	19.3	23.1
11 to 15 hours	5.2	5.2	7.8	6.2	7.2	10.3	19.0	7.4	7.8	11.7	5.7	9.1	12.0
16 to 20 hours	2.3	2.4	3.3	2.8	3.2	5.3	12.7	3.4	3.3	5.7	2.5	4.3	6.2
Over 20 hours	1.8	1.4	2.3	2.8	2.1	4.0	8.8	3.2	2.7	3.5	2.0	2.6	4.3
Socializing with friends													
None	0.5	0.3	0.3	0.5	0.2	0.3	0.2	0.7	0.3	0.2	0.4	0.3	0.2
Less than one hour	2.4	1.7	1.3	1.8	1.4	1.8	0.8	2.2	1.1	0.9	1.9	1.5	1.4
1 to 2 hours	9.1	6.9	5.7	6.0	5.9	6.8	4.6	8.8	6.3	4.8	6.7	6.6	6.1
3 to 5 hours	22.4	19.0	17.6	18.9	18.2	18.9	17.2	20.4	18.0	17.2	20.4	19.5	19.7
6 to 10 hours	24.5	25.6	25.8	23.3	24.6	26.3	29.5	23.6	27.8	27.5	25.5	26.7	28.1
11 to 15 hours	15.3	18.1	19.3	17.5	18.7	18.3	21.6	15.6	18.7	21.1	17.7	18.9	19.5
16 to 20 hours	9.1	11.5	12.4	12.5	12.7	12.1	12.6	10.3	12.1	13.5	10.4	11.7	11.8
Over 20 hours	16.8	16.9	17.6	19.5	18.3	15.5	13.5	18.4	15.7	14.9	17.1	14.7	13.2
Talking with teachers outside of class													
None	11.5	9.4	11.5	10.7	10.4	7.2	3.8	9.4	10.0	6.9	10.1	8.5	7.2
Less than one hour	40.4	44.5	43.3	39.3	41.1	37.3	33.0	39.1	42.1	41.2	39.9	42.1	39.2
1 to 2 hours	29.9	31.5	30.0	29.9	29.7	34.9	40.0	28.7	31.1	34.9	30.9	32.0	35.8
3 to 5 hours	11.8	10.4	10.6	12.7	12.8	13.9	17.3	14.3	11.8	12.5	12.4	11.9	12.8
6 to 10 hours	3.8	2.8	2.8	4.3	3.5	4.1	4.0	4.6	3.2	3.0	4.0	3.4	3.2
11 to 15 hours	1.4	0.9	1.0	1.7	1.3	1.6	1.1	1.5	1.0	0.8	1.5	1.0	1.0
16 to 20 hours	0.6	0.3	0.3	0.6	0.7	0.5	0.4	0.9	0.4	0.4	0.4	0.4	0.4
Over 20 hours	0.7	0.4	0.4	0.9	0.5	0.5	0.4	1.3	0.5	0.3	0.8	0.7	0.4
Exercise or sports													
None	6.8	5.8	3.9	7.4	5.5	4.4	3.1	7.6	4.2	2.5	5.5	3.7	4.0
Less than one hour	11.1	10.7	7.9	9.9	8.7	8.9	7.1	9.9	8.3	6.2	7.6	8.6	8.4
1 to 2 hours	18.2	16.4	13.4	15.7	14.9	14.9	13.0	17.1	15.1	12.8	12.4	14.5	14.9
3 to 5 hours	20.2	19.1	17.6	17.3	19.6	17.6	19.0	18.1	18.8	18.5	14.7	18.1	18.6
6 to 10 hours	15.8	17.0	20.1	16.0	16.7	18.6	20.8	15.6	17.4	19.6	16.4	17.8	18.3
11 to 15 hours	10.0	13.6	15.9	11.7	13.8	15.0	17.5	11.7	14.2	17.7	14.3	14.7	15.0
16 to 20 hours	6.7	7.8	9.5	9.0	8.5	9.1	10.3	6.8	9.1	10.6	10.9	9.8	9.9
Over 20 hours	11.2	9.8	11.6	13.0	12.3	11.4	9.2	13.1	12.9	12.0	18.2	12.8	10.9
Partying													
None	26.1	31.7	27.1	23.6	24.8	29.8	26.0	24.9	25.8	25.9	32.9	43.5	37.7
Less than one hour	13.7	15.5	14.4	12.4	14.0	15.5	16.2	13.9	13.5	14.9	13.7	15.4	16.6
1 to 2 hours	19.1	16.9	17.9	17.6	17.2	16.9	18.6	18.8	20.2	18.0	16.4	15.1	17.0
3 to 5 hours	20.1	17.6	18.8	20.6	20.6	18.0	21.3	21.4	20.0	20.6	17.6	13.1	15.2
6 to 10 hours	10.7	10.3	11.7	13.0	13.0	10.6	12.1	11.2	11.3	12.7	9.4	7.1	8.2
11 to 15 hours	4.9	4.3	5.2	6.3	5.4	4.9	3.4	4.5	5.2	4.7	5.2	2.9	2.8
16 to 20 hours	2.1	1.7	2.4	3.0	2.6	2.1	1.4	2.2	1.9	1.6	1.8	1.5	1.4
Over 20 hours	3.2	2.0	2.5	3.5	2.4	2.2	1.0	3.1	2.1	1.6	2.9	1.4	1.3

WEIGHTED NATIONAL NORMS FOR FOUR-YEAR COLLEGES, FALL 2008

DURING YOUR LAST YEAR IN HIGH SCHOOL, HOW MUCH TIME DID YOU SPEND DURING A TYPICAL WEEK DOING THE FOLLOWING?

	PUBLIC			NONSECTARIAN				CATHOLIC			OTHER RELIGIOUS		
	LOW	MEDIUM	HIGH	LOW	MEDIUM	HIGH	V. HIGH	LOW	MEDIUM	HIGH	LOW	MEDIUM	HIGH
Working (for pay)													
None	34.8	25.4	28.9	29.2	26.5	34.2	51.6	31.2	27.3	28.9	30.6	30.2	36.9
Less than one hour	2.5	2.2	2.8	2.7	2.6	3.0	4.2	2.6	2.2	2.9	3.1	3.0	3.5
1 to 2 hours	3.2	3.6	4.0	3.2	3.6	4.6	6.4	3.3	3.6	4.1	4.1	4.6	5.2
3 to 5 hours	7.0	7.3	7.5	6.8	7.6	8.2	9.1	7.6	7.3	9.0	8.1	8.5	8.8
6 to 10 hours	11.1	11.8	12.6	13.2	13.1	12.6	10.8	13.1	13.8	15.1	12.3	14.0	13.2
11 to 15 hours	10.0	14.5	14.2	12.6	14.8	12.3	7.6	12.0	14.4	14.8	11.5	13.5	12.0
16 to 20 hours	13.1	17.1	14.6	14.7	15.7	11.6	5.6	12.2	15.0	13.1	12.0	13.3	10.3
Over 20 hours	18.3	18.2	15.5	17.6	16.2	13.4	4.8	18.1	16.4	12.1	18.3	12.9	10.1
Volunteer work													
None	35.8	32.1	30.8	32.4	30.9	25.8	21.6	26.0	30.9	19.7	29.8	23.6	21.5
Less than one hour	17.8	23.5	24.1	17.0	21.4	22.7	22.3	17.3	21.7	22.3	20.6	23.4	24.2
1 to 2 hours	21.1	22.2	24.3	22.2	23.3	25.5	28.9	25.6	22.5	28.7	23.2	26.1	27.7
3 to 5 hours	12.7	12.6	12.0	14.2	13.5	14.1	17.1	15.3	13.4	17.7	13.5	15.4	15.4
6 to 10 hours	5.9	5.1	4.5	6.3	5.2	6.3	5.9	7.4	5.9	6.5	6.4	5.9	6.1
11 to 15 hours	2.3	1.8	1.8	3.0	2.4	2.4	2.0	3.2	2.2	2.1	2.6	2.4	2.3
16 to 20 hours	1.3	1.0	1.0	1.7	1.3	1.2	1.0	1.7	1.3	1.1	1.4	1.3	1.0
Over 20 hours	2.9	1.5	1.5	3.2	2.0	2.0	1.2	3.6	2.1	1.8	2.4	1.8	1.7
Student clubs/groups													
None	37.9	36.8	30.3	37.1	30.9	25.1	16.9	27.4	29.6	24.3	33.5	29.6	23.8
Less than one hour	12.6	14.7	15.7	11.9	14.0	14.0	12.0	13.7	13.3	14.9	14.7	15.0	13.9
1 to 2 hours	20.7	22.3	24.5	21.6	23.6	26.4	28.0	24.4	24.6	26.7	22.5	24.4	26.1
3 to 5 hours	13.9	13.7	15.5	15.0	16.6	18.4	23.0	17.5	17.4	19.0	15.2	16.8	19.5
6 to 10 hours	6.9	6.2	7.2	7.0	7.3	8.6	11.2	8.3	8.0	8.3	7.3	7.7	8.7
11 to 15 hours	3.2	2.9	3.1	3.4	3.4	3.3	4.7	3.7	3.0	3.6	3.1	3.3	4.1
16 to 20 hours	1.7	1.3	1.5	1.9	1.7	2.0	2.0	1.7	1.8	1.5	1.3	1.5	1.7
Over 20 hours	3.2	2.1	2.1	2.2	2.5	2.2	2.3	3.3	2.3	1.6	2.3	1.9	2.1
Watching TV													
None	5.6	6.2	6.1	6.4	5.7	7.1	11.3	5.4	4.0	5.5	5.1	7.0	7.8
Less than one hour	15.0	15.5	15.5	13.0	13.6	14.8	15.1	15.9	14.7	13.8	13.0	15.2	14.3
1 to 2 hours	24.8	24.9	25.2	24.5	24.1	23.9	23.7	23.7	24.0	24.6	23.5	24.7	24.1
3 to 5 hours	26.7	26.4	27.7	26.5	27.8	27.6	27.9	25.5	28.6	29.4	26.6	27.1	28.6
6 to 10 hours	14.4	15.6	15.2	15.4	15.7	15.9	14.3	15.2	16.1	17.0	16.8	15.6	15.8
11 to 15 hours	6.3	5.8	5.4	6.8	6.8	5.9	4.7	6.7	6.5	5.5	7.2	5.7	5.1
16 to 20 hours	2.9	2.5	2.2	2.4	3.1	2.0	1.5	2.7	2.3	2.1	3.1	2.0	2.1
Over 20 hours	4.2	3.0	2.6	5.0	3.1	2.7	1.4	4.9	3.8	2.0	4.9	2.7	2.0
Household/childcare duties													
None	20.5	17.2	17.3	19.8	20.1	20.1	24.4	16.3	14.5	15.7	20.1	16.3	19.1
Less than one hour	17.4	18.2	19.9	17.4	18.4	18.5	22.8	14.8	18.5	19.7	16.8	19.7	20.9
1 to 2 hours	27.1	31.4	31.2	27.8	29.5	30.4	31.1	28.3	31.5	33.0	28.2	31.4	32.6
3 to 5 hours	19.4	20.3	19.9	18.9	20.1	19.2	15.7	21.7	21.4	20.8	20.0	20.3	18.2
6 to 10 hours	8.1	7.4	6.9	8.4	7.2	7.0	4.1	9.6	8.1	6.7	7.6	7.0	5.6
11 to 15 hours	3.1	2.6	2.3	3.4	2.3	2.3	1.2	3.9	3.0	2.3	3.1	2.6	1.9
16 to 20 hours	1.5	1.1	1.0	1.4	1.0	1.2	0.3	1.9	1.0	0.8	1.5	1.2	0.7
Over 20 hours	2.9	1.7	1.5	2.9	1.4	1.2	0.4	3.6	2.0	1.1	2.7	1.5	1.0

WEIGHTED NATIONAL NORMS FOR FOUR-YEAR COLLEGES, FALL 2008

	PUBLIC			NONSECTARIAN				CATHOLIC			OTHER RELIGIOUS		
	LOW	MEDIUM	HIGH	LOW	MEDIUM	HIGH	V. HIGH	LOW	MEDIUM	HIGH	LOW	MEDIUM	HIGH
DURING YOUR LAST YEAR IN HIGH SCHOOL, HOW MUCH TIME DID YOU SPEND DURING A TYPICAL WEEK DOING THE FOLLOWING?													
Reading for pleasure													
None	30.0	28.6	25.8	28.6	25.6	21.9	13.3	25.8	28.2	23.9	33.0	25.2	19.4
Less than one hour	24.4	22.8	23.7	22.5	22.5	22.5	21.5	23.4	23.7	25.3	22.2	23.4	22.3
1 to 2 hours	22.0	21.6	22.8	20.9	23.4	24.0	29.1	24.1	23.3	24.7	19.1	22.6	25.5
3 to 5 hours	12.8	14.3	15.2	14.7	15.0	16.9	22.1	13.5	13.8	15.4	13.2	15.9	18.1
6 to 10 hours	5.8	7.2	7.2	6.8	7.2	8.4	9.0	6.8	6.1	6.4	6.6	7.5	9.0
11 to 15 hours	2.3	2.9	2.8	3.1	3.3	3.3	3.0	2.9	2.8	2.5	2.6	3.0	3.5
16 to 20 hours	1.3	1.3	1.1	1.3	1.4	1.5	1.1	1.7	0.9	0.9	1.2	1.2	1.1
Over 20 hours	1.5	1.3	1.4	2.0	1.5	1.4	1.0	1.8	1.3	1.0	2.0	1.3	1.0
Playing video/computer games													
None	39.4	40.0	38.0	37.7	40.2	39.2	49.3	42.7	39.8	43.6	35.8	41.4	43.2
Less than one hour	19.5	20.5	20.8	19.7	19.4	20.3	18.5	21.2	19.9	20.1	20.8	20.8	19.6
1 to 2 hours	16.4	15.9	16.0	16.5	15.3	16.3	13.2	15.0	16.9	14.8	17.2	15.2	15.0
3 to 5 hours	11.7	11.0	12.1	13.2	12.3	12.1	10.8	10.2	12.0	11.4	12.1	11.4	11.0
6 to 10 hours	6.3	6.4	6.8	6.1	6.5	6.4	4.8	6.0	6.1	5.5	6.8	6.2	6.1
11 to 15 hours	2.7	3.0	3.0	3.1	3.0	2.8	1.8	2.3	2.8	2.5	3.3	2.6	2.7
16 to 20 hours	1.5	1.6	1.2	1.3	1.4	1.2	0.7	1.1	1.1	1.0	1.5	1.0	1.0
Over 20 hours	2.5	1.8	2.0	2.5	2.0	1.7	0.9	1.6	1.5	1.0	2.5	1.4	1.5
Online social networks (MySpace, Facebook, etc.)													
None	12.0	14.4	11.7	9.7	9.7	9.8	7.0	12.2	9.8	9.2	10.8	11.4	8.8
Less than one hour	19.2	20.6	19.1	17.7	16.5	16.7	15.5	18.9	17.3	16.9	16.3	15.9	15.5
1 to 2 hours	27.7	25.1	27.2	24.9	25.7	27.2	30.2	23.9	26.6	29.1	25.4	26.1	28.3
3 to 5 hours	20.7	21.4	22.6	23.0	25.3	24.6	29.3	21.5	25.0	25.7	23.0	24.4	27.2
6 to 10 hours	10.5	9.8	10.7	11.6	11.5	12.0	11.4	11.2	10.3	11.3	11.9	12.6	12.2
11 to 15 hours	4.1	4.2	4.3	5.6	5.1	5.0	3.5	5.3	5.6	4.1	5.6	4.8	4.2
16 to 20 hours	2.2	1.8	1.8	3.0	2.6	2.1	1.5	2.6	2.4	1.9	2.6	2.2	1.9
Over 20 hours	3.7	2.7	2.6	4.4	3.5	2.6	1.6	4.5	2.9	1.8	4.4	2.6	2.0
Are you: [4]													
White/Caucasian	42.6	82.9	85.9	56.9	82.3	80.9	80.0	44.1	77.5	86.8	68.0	85.4	88.0
African American/Black	24.9	11.2	7.0	28.5	8.5	7.3	5.7	37.5	9.9	4.1	26.8	7.6	4.9
American Indian/Alaska Native	5.5	2.9	2.2	2.7	2.2	2.6	1.9	2.0	1.7	1.5	2.9	2.6	2.3
Asian American/Asian	6.4	2.7	4.2	6.2	4.6	7.1	11.9	8.0	2.6	4.7	1.8	3.5	4.7
Native Hawaiian/Pacific Islander	2.7	1.1	0.8	1.1	0.6	0.9	0.8	3.4	0.7	1.2	0.6	0.8	0.7
Mexican American/Chicano	17.5	2.9	2.3	1.7	1.0	2.1	2.4	4.9	7.7	2.8	3.1	3.0	2.5
Puerto Rican	1.5	0.8	1.2	5.1	2.6	1.8	1.2	2.8	3.1	1.2	1.3	1.4	0.8
Other Latino	8.7	2.4	2.5	5.9	4.3	3.6	4.2	6.2	2.2	3.7	2.6	2.8	2.2
Other	6.4	3.1	2.9	5.9	3.9	4.4	4.1	4.7	3.2	3.0	3.5	3.3	3.4

WEIGHTED NATIONAL NORMS FOR FOUR-YEAR COLLEGES, FALL 2008

	PUBLIC			NONSECTARIAN				CATHOLIC			OTHER RELIGIOUS		
	LOW	MEDIUM	HIGH	LOW	MEDIUM	HIGH	V. HIGH	LOW	MEDIUM	HIGH	LOW	MEDIUM	HIGH
Reasons noted as "very important" in influencing student's decision to attend this particular college													
My parents wanted me to come here	20.2	12.8	14.2	16.3	12.4	13.6	10.1	20.3	17.6	14.9	19.2	17.2	12.8
My relatives wanted me to come here	9.5	4.8	5.6	7.4	4.5	4.8	2.8	9.3	7.2	5.2	8.5	6.3	4.4
My teacher advised me	10.2	6.2	6.0	9.9	7.2	8.8	7.4	10.5	8.0	5.7	7.1	5.6	5.6
This college has a very good academic reputation	50.8	59.1	63.1	58.8	63.7	70.8	80.9	70.9	70.3	71.5	55.3	63.5	71.8
This college has a good reputation for its social activities	33.5	38.5	34.3	37.0	35.8	37.2	39.4	35.0	37.8	42.7	36.8	40.7	38.8
I was offered financial assistance	40.6	36.0	35.6	56.6	55.3	63.6	39.0	64.3	71.6	61.3	66.4	63.2	59.2
The cost of attending this college	51.8	47.7	49.1	40.5	32.2	35.3	22.2	41.4	42.1	32.7	36.6	30.7	28.1
High school counselor advised me	15.7	9.1	9.3	14.1	10.4	12.2	12.7	16.6	12.7	9.8	9.0	6.8	8.3
Private college counselor advised me	4.5	2.2	2.4	6.2	4.0	6.5	6.4	7.1	5.6	4.0	6.3	5.4	5.1
I wanted to live near home	30.3	25.7	20.9	25.6	24.9	16.0	6.7	31.9	34.8	20.2	23.7	20.7	14.1
Not offered aid by first choice	10.3	7.3	6.8	11.6	8.0	10.1	5.7	12.3	12.0	9.6	11.7	6.9	7.8
Could not afford first choice	15.9	11.8	11.3	13.1	8.5	10.5	5.6	13.8	12.5	10.5	11.6	7.3	7.7
This college's graduates gain admission to top graduate/professional schools	25.7	27.7	31.0	35.9	34.3	41.8	47.2	45.2	37.3	37.5	28.9	30.4	38.1
This college's graduates get good jobs	42.8	46.9	54.4	56.4	61.5	63.9	58.4	63.2	62.2	61.3	49.8	51.0	55.6
I was attracted by the religious affiliation/orientation of the college	4.6	4.9	3.2	7.0	2.9	7.6	1.8	14.0	14.6	18.7	24.6	40.5	23.7
I wanted to go to a school about the size of this college	30.3	40.2	33.2	43.0	48.9	49.7	58.0	44.4	52.0	56.1	50.1	54.6	57.4
Rankings in national magazines	8.3	11.2	13.8	16.2	11.7	18.4	27.1	18.8	15.1	15.7	9.6	11.5	17.3
Information from a website	16.5	17.1	17.7	24.2	22.9	21.1	24.3	23.9	18.5	17.0	16.9	15.6	18.9
I was admitted through an Early Action or Early Decision program	7.2	9.8	9.6	10.5	13.0	16.1	30.7	12.5	9.5	16.3	8.7	12.1	16.1
The athletic department recruited me	7.1	6.0	8.2	14.5	10.3	14.9	14.4	14.7	17.1	11.3	28.5	18.9	15.2
A visit to campus	30.4	38.8	38.8	45.5	51.7	53.6	61.6	40.0	49.0	51.3	46.1	51.1	55.4

WEIGHTED NATIONAL NORMS FOR FOUR-YEAR COLLEGES, FALL 2008

YOUR PROBABLE MAJOR	PUBLIC			NONSECTARIAN				CATHOLIC			OTHER RELIGIOUS		
	LOW	MEDIUM	HIGH	LOW	MEDIUM	HIGH	V. HIGH	LOW	MEDIUM	HIGH	LOW	MEDIUM	HIGH
Arts and Humanities													
Art, fine and applied	2.9	3.1	3.0	12.6	11.1	6.9	4.3	1.1	2.8	1.1	1.8	2.7	2.9
English (language & literature)	1.3	1.9	1.5	1.3	1.7	2.5	6.3	1.2	1.2	2.7	1.5	1.9	3.4
History	0.9	1.8	2.0	0.7	0.9	1.8	3.4	0.5	1.1	2.0	1.3	1.7	2.2
Journalism	1.9	1.2	1.3	1.6	2.3	1.5	1.9	0.8	3.1	2.0	1.4	1.5	1.4
Language and Literature (except English)	0.3	0.4	0.7	0.1	0.2	0.9	2.2	0.2	0.2	0.5	0.3	0.6	1.3
Music	2.4	1.8	1.4	0.7	1.1	1.4	1.7	0.8	1.0	0.5	2.2	2.9	4.1
Philosophy	0.2	0.3	0.2	0.1	0.1	0.4	1.0	0.2	0.2	0.6	0.2	0.2	0.6
Speech	0.1	0.1	0.1	0.0	0.1	0.1	0.1	0.1	0.1	0.0	0.1	0.1	0.0
Theater or Drama	1.1	2.2	1.1	0.9	3.9	2.3	2.0	0.5	0.6	0.7	0.9	1.6	1.6
Theology or Religion	0.0	0.1	0.0	0.0	0.0	0.3	0.2	0.1	0.2	0.5	1.2	2.3	1.1
Other Arts and Humanities	1.6	1.2	0.7	2.1	3.6	1.1	2.1	0.4	0.5	0.8	0.9	0.8	1.5
Biological Science													
Biology (general)	4.1	3.5	3.9	4.2	3.0	4.8	6.5	9.7	5.3	6.3	4.3	4.7	6.1
Biochemistry or Biophysics	0.9	0.7	1.0	0.4	0.4	1.3	2.0	0.9	0.8	1.4	0.7	1.3	1.6
Botany	0.0	0.0	0.0	0.0	0.1	0.1	0.1	0.0	0.0	0.0	0.0	0.0	0.0
Environmental Science	0.3	0.6	0.6	0.2	0.5	1.7	2.3	0.2	0.5	0.7	0.9	0.4	1.5
Marine (Life) Science	0.3	0.5	0.7	0.1	0.9	0.5	0.3	0.1	0.3	0.2	0.3	0.3	0.6
Microbiology or Bacteriology	0.2	0.1	0.2	0.1	0.1	0.1	0.3	0.0	0.0	0.1	0.1	0.1	0.2
Zoology	0.3	0.5	0.3	0.2	0.9	0.3	0.4	0.1	0.1	0.1	0.3	0.3	0.4
Other Biological Science	0.4	0.4	0.5	0.6	1.1	0.5	0.9	0.6	0.2	0.3	0.3	0.4	0.5
Business													
Accounting	2.9	2.6	2.4	3.5	3.7	3.0	0.5	2.3	3.7	3.4	3.3	2.3	1.6
Business Admin. (general)	4.4	3.8	3.9	5.5	3.6	3.7	2.2	2.8	2.8	4.4	5.2	4.1	3.7
Finance	0.9	1.0	1.5	1.2	1.7	3.2	2.2	0.6	1.5	3.1	0.6	1.2	1.1
International Business	0.7	1.2	1.4	1.6	1.7	2.7	2.4	1.4	1.1	2.5	1.0	1.3	1.6
Marketing	2.9	2.5	2.7	3.1	2.5	3.7	1.5	1.8	2.7	4.6	2.6	2.2	1.9
Management	4.6	3.3	3.6	6.7	4.7	3.4	1.7	3.8	3.2	4.4	5.4	3.5	2.7
Secretarial Studies	0.0	0.0	0.0	0.0	0.0	0.0	0.0	0.0	0.0	0.0	0.0	0.0	0.0
Other Business	0.9	0.8	0.6	1.9	1.7	1.0	0.6	0.6	0.7	1.2	0.7	0.7	1.4
Education													
Business Education	0.2	0.1	0.1	0.2	0.0	0.2	0.1	0.1	0.1	0.1	0.2	0.1	0.1
Elementary Education	5.4	6.2	4.2	4.1	4.2	2.4	0.4	4.2	5.5	4.2	6.6	6.0	3.2
Music or Art Education	1.2	1.1	1.1	0.6	1.0	0.7	0.2	0.5	0.4	0.2	1.1	1.3	1.2
Physical Education or Recreation	1.5	1.4	0.8	1.9	0.3	0.4	0.0	0.5	1.1	0.7	3.0	1.3	0.6
Secondary Education	3.1	2.2	2.8	2.0	2.6	2.0	0.6	1.4	4.2	2.9	4.2	4.1	2.2
Special Education	0.8	0.8	0.5	0.5	0.5	0.4	0.0	0.6	1.6	0.7	1.0	0.7	0.4
Other Education	0.6	0.9	0.3	0.2	0.2	0.3	0.1	0.2	0.4	0.2	0.6	0.4	0.3
Engineering													
Aeronautical or Astronautical Engineering	0.2	0.4	2.6	0.3	0.0	0.1	0.1	0.0	0.4	0.1	0.1	0.2	0.1
Civil Engineering	1.1	0.7	2.0	0.1	0.2	0.2	0.5	0.3	0.2	1.4	0.3	0.5	0.7
Chemical Engineering	0.3	0.1	0.5	0.1	0.1	0.3	0.4	0.1	0.1	0.5	0.0	0.1	0.3
Computer Engineering	1.3	0.5	1.1	0.7	0.3	0.6	0.2	0.3	0.4	0.7	0.6	0.2	0.4
Electrical or Electronic Engineering	0.7	0.5	1.3	0.2	0.6	0.9	0.2	0.3	0.2	0.8	0.2	0.3	0.4
Industrial Engineering	0.1	0.1	0.1	0.1	0.1	0.2	0.0	0.0	0.0	0.0	0.0	0.0	0.0
Mechanical Engineering	1.6	1.2	3.4	0.2	1.3	3.0	0.7	0.3	0.3	2.3	0.4	0.8	1.2
Other Engineering	0.6	1.0	1.6	0.1	0.6	1.3	0.7	0.2	0.2	0.6	0.1	0.4	0.9

WEIGHTED NATIONAL NORMS FOR FOUR-YEAR COLLEGES, FALL 2008

YOUR PROBABLE MAJOR	PUBLIC			NONSECTARIAN				CATHOLIC			OTHER RELIGIOUS		
	LOW	MEDIUM	HIGH	LOW	MEDIUM	HIGH	V. HIGH	LOW	MEDIUM	HIGH	LOW	MEDIUM	HIGH
Physical Science													
Astronomy	0.1	0.1	0.1	0.0	0.0	0.1	0.1	0.0	0.0	0.0	0.0	0.1	0.1
Atmospheric Science (incl. Meteorology)	0.0	0.0	0.2	0.0	0.0	0.0	0.1	0.0	0.1	0.0	0.0	0.0	0.3
Chemistry	0.7	1.1	1.4	0.4	1.1	1.4	1.7	2.4	1.1	1.1	0.9	1.2	1.5
Earth Science	0.1	0.2	0.1	0.1	0.1	0.3	0.4	0.0	0.1	0.1	0.1	0.0	0.2
Marine Science (incl. Oceanography)	0.1	0.1	0.5	0.0	0.3	0.1	0.2	0.1	0.1	0.0	0.1	0.1	0.3
Mathematics	0.5	0.6	0.8	0.2	0.2	1.0	1.6	0.3	0.6	1.1	0.8	0.8	1.2
Physics	0.2	0.3	0.7	0.1	0.1	0.6	1.5	0.2	0.0	0.2	0.2	0.5	0.9
Other Physical Science	0.2	0.2	0.2	0.2	0.2	0.1	0.3	0.3	0.3	0.1	0.3	0.2	0.2
Professional													
Architecture or Urban Planning	0.2	0.4	0.2	0.4	0.1	0.3	0.6	0.0	0.2	0.1	0.4	0.2	0.2
Family & Consumer Sciences	0.4	0.2	0.1	0.1	0.1	0.1	0.0	0.2	0.3	0.0	0.1	0.0	0.2
Health Technology (medical, dental, laboratory)	0.8	0.6	0.6	0.5	0.3	0.3	0.2	2.0	0.5	0.4	0.5	0.5	0.4
Library or Archival Science	0.0	0.0	0.1	0.1	0.1	0.1	0.0	0.2	0.1	0.0	0.1	0.0	0.1
Medicine, Dentistry, Veterinary Medicine	2.1	2.5	3.2	3.7	3.4	3.5	3.9	6.0	4.1	3.6	3.7	3.8	4.7
Nursing	7.0	7.6	6.3	3.9	4.7	1.5	0.1	15.2	11.7	5.0	5.1	6.8	3.1
Pharmacy	0.8	1.2	1.5	0.2	1.7	2.9	0.1	5.4	1.8	0.6	1.3	1.4	0.8
Therapy (occupational, physical, speech)	1.9	2.7	1.9	1.5	2.0	1.8	0.4	1.4	5.3	2.5	3.4	3.7	2.0
Other Professional	0.7	0.8	0.6	1.2	0.8	0.6	0.2	1.5	2.4	0.9	1.0	0.7	0.5
Social Science													
Anthropology	0.2	0.4	0.5	0.1	0.0	0.5	1.7	0.1	0.0	0.3	0.2	0.2	0.8
Economics	0.1	0.1	0.5	0.5	0.2	1.2	5.0	0.1	0.1	0.6	0.0	0.2	1.0
Ethnic Studies	0.0	0.0	0.1	0.0	0.0	0.1	0.2	0.0	0.0	0.0	0.0	0.1	0.2
Geography	0.0	0.1	0.1	0.1	0.0	0.1	0.2	0.1	0.0	0.0	0.0	0.0	0.1
Political Science (gov't., international relations)	1.5	1.9	3.7	1.4	1.7	3.1	8.9	2.2	1.8	3.6	1.8	2.0	4.5
Psychology	6.7	5.3	4.6	6.0	4.1	4.7	4.3	6.8	4.6	5.5	5.1	5.0	4.7
Public Policy	0.1	0.0	0.0	0.1	0.0	0.2	0.3	0.1	0.1	0.1	0.0	0.1	0.1
Social Work	1.5	0.9	0.6	0.8	0.6	0.3	0.2	0.7	0.9	0.5	1.1	1.1	0.7
Sociology	1.4	0.7	0.3	0.4	0.3	0.5	0.9	1.1	0.4	0.6	0.8	0.6	0.8
Women's Studies	0.0	0.0	0.0	0.0	0.0	0.0	0.1	0.0	0.0	0.0	0.0	0.0	0.1
Other Social Science	0.4	0.4	0.4	0.2	0.2	0.2	0.5	0.3	0.5	0.2	0.4	0.4	0.5
Technical													
Building Trades	0.0	0.0	0.0	0.0	0.0	0.0	0.0	0.0	0.0	0.0	0.1	0.0	0.0
Data Processing or Computer Programming	0.7	0.6	0.5	0.6	0.6	0.5	0.2	0.3	0.6	0.3	0.4	0.5	0.4
Drafting or Design	0.3	0.3	0.2	1.0	0.4	0.3	0.1	0.1	0.2	0.1	0.4	0.3	0.2
Electronics	0.1	0.0	0.0	0.0	0.0	0.1	0.0	0.0	0.0	0.0	0.1	0.1	0.0
Mechanics	0.0	0.0	0.0	0.0	0.0	0.0	0.0	0.2	0.2	0.0	0.0	0.0	0.0
Other Technical	0.1	0.2	0.0	0.2	0.2	0.1	0.0	0.1	0.2	0.2	0.2	0.1	0.1
Other Fields													
Agriculture	0.5	0.2	0.1	0.2	0.7	0.2	0.0	0.1	0.0	0.0	0.3	0.1	0.1
Communications	2.0	2.3	1.3	2.0	3.2	2.3	0.7	1.9	1.6	2.2	1.9	2.6	1.9
Computer Science	1.4	1.1	1.0	0.8	0.5	0.7	0.4	1.1	0.6	0.6	1.1	0.8	0.7
Forestry	0.1	0.1	0.0	0.0	0.1	0.0	0.0	0.0	0.1	0.0	0.1	0.0	0.1
Kinesiology	2.0	1.1	0.3	0.1	0.1	0.1	0.1	0.2	0.2	0.3	1.4	0.8	0.6
Law Enforcement	2.3	2.4	1.7	3.0	2.0	0.5	0.1	2.6	2.8	1.1	3.2	1.1	0.5
Military Science	0.1	0.1	0.5	0.1	0.1	0.1	0.0	0.0	0.0	0.1	0.1	0.1	0.0
Other Field	1.6	2.0	0.9	3.8	1.5	1.1	0.5	2.4	2.5	1.0	2.4	1.7	1.5
Undecided	5.3	8.1	6.4	4.7	4.2	6.4	10.6	4.6	4.9	7.5	5.2	6.8	7.0

WEIGHTED NATIONAL NORMS FOR FOUR-YEAR COLLEGES, FALL 2008

Objectives considered to be "essential" or "very important":	PUBLIC			NONSECTARIAN				CATHOLIC			OTHER RELIGIOUS		
	LOW	MEDIUM	HIGH	LOW	MEDIUM	HIGH	V. HIGH	LOW	MEDIUM	HIGH	LOW	MEDIUM	HIGH
Becoming accomplished in one of the performing arts (acting, dancing, etc.)	20.9	16.9	13.6	18.9	21.7	18.0	21.3	16.6	13.8	12.7	18.4	17.7	20.7
Becoming an authority in my field	61.7	56.6	60.0	64.5	59.3	58.4	59.8	64.1	62.4	57.9	61.1	55.3	55.7
Obtaining recognition from my colleagues for contributions to my special field	59.5	54.4	55.5	63.9	60.8	57.1	55.0	61.0	61.8	56.1	55.6	49.1	51.6
Influencing the political structure	25.5	18.8	21.4	25.3	19.6	23.3	26.6	28.2	20.5	22.4	23.3	17.8	21.2
Influencing social values	48.1	43.4	42.7	49.3	43.4	45.2	44.6	50.4	46.9	48.4	48.3	48.9	46.6
Raising a family	75.0	77.4	76.2	72.8	72.7	71.8	68.2	77.1	81.0	80.3	79.2	80.5	74.3
Being very well off financially	84.9	77.6	75.6	82.2	78.9	71.9	61.1	85.3	82.5	75.4	77.6	66.2	62.3
Helping others who are in difficulty	70.4	69.3	66.7	69.3	66.0	68.5	70.8	75.7	73.2	73.4	71.7	74.9	72.1
Making a theoretical contribution to science	21.2	17.1	19.0	19.1	17.6	19.5	18.8	28.9	20.8	17.5	18.8	15.8	17.9
Writing original works (poems, novels, short stories, etc.)	19.8	15.1	13.9	21.7	18.6	19.2	24.5	19.6	14.9	13.9	17.3	15.9	19.2
Creating artistic works (painting, sculpture, decorating, etc.)	19.5	16.0	14.5	27.7	23.7	21.4	20.8	16.9	15.3	12.6	17.2	14.6	17.8
Becoming successful in a business of my own	52.5	39.8	36.9	56.9	45.9	44.4	35.1	52.0	42.3	41.0	48.2	36.1	35.1
Becoming involved in programs to clean up the environment	31.1	25.2	24.3	30.6	28.7	32.6	38.8	33.6	26.5	28.7	27.7	22.2	28.6
Developing a meaningful philosophy of life	48.5	49.4	47.1	49.7	49.1	53.0	64.1	51.0	47.0	51.7	48.2	50.3	55.6
Participating in a community action program	31.5	27.1	23.9	32.0	25.8	30.9	35.7	37.4	29.2	34.5	32.7	31.0	32.6
Helping to promote racial understanding	41.6	37.4	29.9	42.7	35.3	38.3	42.4	48.3	35.7	36.0	38.7	33.5	35.5
Keeping up to date with political affairs	34.6	33.7	37.7	36.5	34.3	41.2	58.1	37.7	31.7	41.7	33.7	32.4	40.7
Becoming a community leader	35.9	32.6	35.5	36.8	31.1	37.6	41.0	41.1	33.9	39.3	37.8	36.2	37.1
Improving my understanding of other countries and cultures	47.7	48.0	47.4	51.8	49.6	57.7	73.2	52.5	45.8	54.7	44.6	50.5	58.7
Adopting "green" practices to protect the environment	41.9	40.4	39.1	44.5	46.1	50.4	63.8	44.3	42.7	47.0	35.9	34.4	46.5

130

WEIGHTED NATIONAL NORMS FOR FOUR-YEAR COLLEGES, FALL 2008

	PUBLIC			NONSECTARIAN				CATHOLIC			OTHER RELIGIOUS		
	LOW	MEDIUM	HIGH	LOW	MEDIUM	HIGH	V. HIGH	LOW	MEDIUM	HIGH	LOW	MEDIUM	HIGH
Student estimates chances are "very good" that he/she will:													
Change major field	12.2	13.7	12.5	10.0	9.3	12.1	22.9	7.7	8.8	14.4	9.3	11.5	14.3
Change career choice	10.3	12.5	11.4	8.5	8.8	13.2	28.0	6.9	7.5	15.5	8.4	11.4	16.8
Participate in student government	7.6	6.3	6.3	7.6	6.1	8.2	8.4	9.2	5.6	8.0	7.8	6.2	7.0
Get a job to help pay for college expenses	51.0	55.0	43.4	51.0	50.0	51.2	44.7	49.8	53.9	52.7	46.1	53.5	49.2
Work full-time while attending college	13.8	9.2	9.8	10.6	6.5	5.7	2.3	9.9	9.0	4.5	7.9	4.7	4.0
Join a social fraternity or sorority	14.8	9.8	8.6	11.0	4.8	6.9	8.0	14.8	5.9	3.8	10.9	7.2	9.6
Play varsity/intercollegiate athletics	15.3	14.3	18.5	24.1	17.8	24.8	27.1	23.3	24.0	21.3	36.9	28.0	24.7
Make at least a "B" average	56.0	56.5	57.8	62.6	64.5	64.7	70.4	63.5	64.8	67.2	59.0	64.4	64.8
Need extra time to complete your degree requirements	9.7	7.2	6.0	7.8	5.7	5.1	2.9	8.3	7.7	4.5	8.6	6.5	4.9
Participate in student protests or demonstrations	6.6	5.5	4.4	7.3	5.9	7.2	12.3	7.5	4.8	6.2	5.7	4.3	7.4
Transfer to another college before graduating	13.2	11.7	9.3	9.6	5.2	5.5	2.5	8.1	6.4	4.8	10.9	7.0	4.4
Be satisfied with your college	42.4	51.9	51.7	49.4	56.1	58.6	69.5	52.3	55.5	61.0	47.9	60.0	62.6
Participate in volunteer or community service work	21.7	24.4	20.2	24.0	24.5	31.2	41.9	30.5	27.5	38.3	26.5	36.6	38.2
Seek personal counseling	11.2	8.7	7.4	9.7	6.9	9.8	9.9	11.8	8.6	8.7	8.4	7.8	9.2
Communicate regularly with your professors	29.8	34.7	31.7	35.4	35.2	44.9	58.0	39.0	34.3	42.3	33.6	38.5	45.4
Socialize with someone of another racial/ethnic group	57.7	64.1	60.4	62.3	62.7	67.8	80.4	61.9	61.3	65.1	61.0	64.5	66.6
Participate in student clubs/groups	35.3	42.1	39.2	36.7	42.0	48.7	66.1	41.0	40.4	51.9	35.7	42.4	49.2
Participate in a study abroad program	20.0	22.0	21.9	25.8	29.3	41.5	61.5	24.0	22.1	40.9	19.9	27.5	44.5
Have a roommate of different race/ethnicity	27.2	24.9	24.5	28.2	28.1	30.0	41.3	27.4	22.0	23.4	27.1	25.2	26.4
Discuss course content with students outside of class	35.6	39.9	41.4	37.4	41.8	50.7	70.5	41.1	39.9	49.5	37.2	45.6	53.4
Work on a professor's research project	34.4	32.4	25.9	39.3	28.9	28.3	27.7	38.3	28.9	25.5	34.2	26.6	25.3
Get tutoring help in specific courses	37.6	33.4	28.3	33.5	28.4	29.8	24.6	41.4	29.4	29.0	35.1	26.7	26.9
Do you give the Higher Education Research Institute (HERI) permission to include your ID number should your college request the data for additional research analyses?													
Yes	77.2	72.1	71.8	63.5	62.6	65.9	63.2	63.7	70.6	65.1	68.9	71.2	67.2
No	22.8	27.9	28.2	36.5	37.4	34.1	36.8	36.3	29.4	34.9	31.1	28.8	32.8

Appendix A

Research Methodology

Appendix A
Research Methodology

The data reported here have been weighted to provide a normative picture of the American college freshman population for persons engaged in policy analysis, human resource planning, campus administration, educational research, and guidance and counseling, as well as for the general community of students and parents. This Appendix provides a brief overview of the CIRP methodology and describes the procedures used to weight the annual freshman survey results to produce the national normative estimates.

HISTORICAL OVERVIEW

From 1966 to 1970, approximately 15 percent of the nation's institutions of higher education were selected by sampling procedures and invited to participate in the program. As the academic community became aware of the value of program participation, additional institutions asked to participate. Beginning in 1971, all institutions that have entering freshman classes and that respond to the U.S. Department of Education's Higher Education General Information Survey were invited to participate (see 'The National Population' below). A minimal charge plus a unit rate based on the number of forms processed helps to defray the direct costs of the survey. In Fall 1974 and 1975, samples of proprietary institutions also participated in the survey.

THE NATIONAL POPULATION FOR 2008

For the purposes of the 2008 CIRP Freshmen Survey, the population has been defined as all institutions of higher education admitting first time freshmen and granting a baccalaureate-level degree or higher listed in the Opening Fall Enrollment (OFE) files of the U.S. Department of Education's Higher Education General Information Survey (HEGIS, since 1986 known as IPEDS— Integrated Postsecondary Education Data System). An institution is considered eligible if it was operating at the time of the HEGIS/IPEDS survey and had a first-time full-time (FTFT) freshman class of at least 25 students. In addition, a small number of institutions or their branches are included even though their separate enrollments were not available from the OFE files, because they were part of prior HEGIS/IPEDS populations and are known to be functioning with FTFT students. The 2008 population figures were obtained from the on-line OFE Survey for Fall 2007. In 2008, the national population included 1,693 institutions.

Figure A1: 2008 Data Bank Population
(N = 1,694)

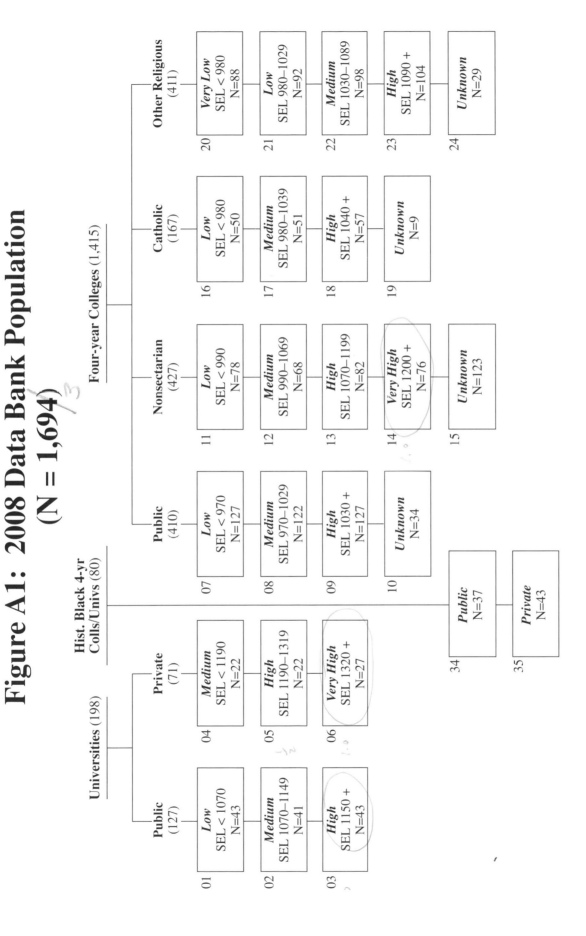

The broad categories of institutional type are defined by data submitted to Integrated Postsecondary Educational Data System (IPEDS). Selectivity (SEL) is based on median SAT Verbal + Math scores and/or ACT composite scores of the entering class as reported to IPEDS. Institutions with unknown selectivity are grouped with the low-selectivity institutions when computing National Norms.

The stratification design presented here is used to group schools to develop population weights and should not be used as a measure of institutional or program quality.

It should be noted that the population reflects institutions of "higher education," rather than "postsecondary education." Most proprietary, special vocational or semiprofessional institutions are not currently included in the population. Beginning with the Fall 1993 survey, only institutions with regional accreditation (including provisional accreditation) were included.

INSTITUTIONAL STRATIFICATION DESIGN

The institutions identified as part of the national population are divided into 26 stratification groups based on institutional race (predominantly non-black vs. predominantly black), type (four-year college, university[1]), control (public, private nonsectarian, Roman Catholic and other religious[2]) and the "selectivity level" of the institution. Selectivity, defined as the median SAT Verbal & Math scores of the entering class (or ACT composite score), was made an integral part of the stratification design in 1968. The selectivity figures were revised and updated in 1975, 2001, and 2008. Figure A1 shows the distribution of institutions across the 26 stratification cells.

It should be noted that the dividing lines between low, medium and high selectivity levels are different for different types of institutions, as shown in the table below.

| | Universities | | | | Four-year institutions | | | | | | | |
| | Public | | Private | | Public | | Nonsectarian | | Catholic | | Oth. Relig. | |
Dividing Line Between	SAT V+M	ACT	SAT V+M	ACT	SAT V+M	ACT	SAT V+M	ACT	SAT V+M	ACT	SAT V+M	ACT
Low–medium	1070	23.0	—	—	970	20.5	990	21.0	980	20.8	980	20.8
Medium–high	1150	25.0	1190	26.0	1030	22.0	1070	23.0	1040	22.3	1090	23.5
High–Very high	—	—	1320	29.5	—	—	1200	26.3	—	—	—	—

In 2008 a comprehensive restratification of the national population was undertaken, reviewing not only institutions' selectivity scores, but also their type, control, and religious affiliation (if any). All decisions on stratification cell assignment were based on data reported to IPEDS by the institutions themselves. One result of this review was the increase of the national population by 124 institutions that were formerly classified as two-year colleges, but whose programs had been expanded to include the offering of baccalaureate degrees.

---

[1] For stratification purposes, we define a "university" as an institution that awards a certain minimal number of earned doctoral degrees. Institutions that offer postbaccalaureate programs but do not award a sufficient number of doctoral degrees are considered four-year colleges. The stratification design presented here is used to group schools to develop population weights and should not be used as a measure of institutional or program quality.

[2] This type of institution was labeled "Protestant" in publications prior to 2000. "Other Religious" more correctly characterizes the institutions that have always been in this group, which include all institutions affiliated with a religion other than Roman Catholic.

Table A1. Uses of 2008 CIRP Freshman Survey Items in Previous CIRP Surveys

Item No.	Item	08	07	06	05	04	03	02	01	00	99	98	97	96	95	94	93	92	91	90	89	88	87	86	85	84	83	82	81	80	79	78	77	76	75	74	73	72	71	70	69	68	67	66
1	Sex	X	X	X	X	X	X	X	X	X	X	X	X	X	X	X	X	X	X	X	X	X	X	X	X	X	X	X	X	X	X	X	X	X	X	X	X	X	X	X	X	X	X	X
2	Age	X	X	X	X	X	X	X	X	X	X	X	X	X	X	X	X	X	X	X	X	X	X	X	X	X	X	X	X	X	X	X	X	X	X	X	X	X	X	X	X	X	X	X
3	English native language	X	X	X	X	X	X	X	X	X	X	X	X	X	X	X	X	X	X	X	X	X	X	-	-	-	-	-	-	-	-	-	-	-	-	-	-	-	-	-	-	-	-	-
4	Year graduated from high school	X	X	X	X	X	X	X	X	X	X	X	X	X	X	X	X	X	X	X	X	X	X	X	X	X	X	X	X	X	X	X	X	X	X	X	X	-	-	-	-	-	-	-
5	Enrollment status	X	X	X	X	X	X	X	X	X	X	X	X	X	X	X	X	X	X	X	X	X	X	X	X	X	X	X	X	X	X	X	X	X	X	X	-	-	-	-	-	-	-	-
6	Miles from home to college	X	X	X	X	X	X	X	X	X	X	X	X	X	X	X	X	X	X	X	X	X	X	X	X	X	X	X	X	X	X	X	X	X	X	X	X	X	X	X	X	X	X	-
7	High school grade average	X	X	X	X	X	X	X	X	X	X	X	X	X	X	X	X	X	X	X	X	X	X	X	X	X	X	X	X	X	X	X	X	X	X	X	X	X	X	X	X	X	-	-
8	Scores on the SAT and/or ACT	X	X	X	X	X	X	X	X	X	X	X	X	X	X	X	X	X	X	X	X	X	X	X	X	X	X	X	X	X	X	X	X	X	X	-	-	X	X	X	X	X	X	X
9	Type of High School	-	-	X	-	X	-	-	-	-	-	-	-	-	-	X	X	-	-	-	-	-	-	-	-	X	-	-	-	X	X	-	X	-	-	-	-	X	-	X	-	-	-	-
10	Prior enrollment at this college	X	X	X	X	X	X	X	X	X	X	X	X	X	X	X	X	X	X	X	X	X	X	X	X	X	X	X	X	X	X	X	X	X	X	X	X	X	X	X	X	-	-	-
11	Transfer status	X	X	X	X	X	X	X	X	X	X	X	X	X	X	X	X	X	X	X	X	X	X	X	X	X	X	X	X	X	X	X	X	X	X	X	X	X	X	X	X	X	X	-
12	Residence during fall term	X	X	X	X	X	X	X	X	X	X	X	X	X	X	X	X	X	X	X	X	X	X	X	X	X	X	X	X	X	X	X	X	X	X	X	-	X	X	-	X	X	X	-
13	Number of other applications	X	X	X	X	X	X	X	X	X	X	X	X	X	X	X	X	X	X	X	X	X	X	X	X	X	X	-	X	-	X	X	X	X	X	-	X	X	-	-	-	X	X	-
14	Accepted to first-choice college	X	X	-	-	-	-	-	-	X	X	X	X	X	X	X	-	X	-	-	-	-	-	-	-	-	-	-	-	-	-	-	-	-	-	-	-	-	-	-	-	-	-	-
15	Rank of college choice	X	X	X	X	X	X	X	X	X	X	X	X	X	X	X	X	X	X	X	X	X	X	X	X	X	X	X	X	X	X	X	X	X	X	X	X	X	X	X	X	X	X	X
16	Citizenship Status	X	X	X	X	X	X	X	X	X	X	X	X	X	X	X	X	X	X	X	X	X	X	X	X	X	X	X	-	-	-	-	-	-	-	-	-	-	-	-	-	-	-	-
17	Parents' marital status	-	X	X	X	-	X	-	-	X	X	X	-	X	X	X	X	X	X	X	X	X	-	-	-	-	-	-	-	-	X	-	-	-	-	-	-	X	-	X	-	-	-	-
18	Years of high school study	X	-	X	-	X	-	X	X	-	X	X	-	X	-	X	X	X	-	X	X	X	X	X	X	X	X	-	X	-	X	X	X	-	-	-	X	X	-	X	-	X	X	X
19	Degree aspirations	X	X	X	X	X	X	X	X	X	X	X	X	X	X	X	X	X	X	X	X	X	X	X	X	X	X	X	X	X	X	X	X	X	X	X	X	X	X	X	X	X	X	X
20	Racial Composition of HS/neighborhood	X	X	X	-	-	-	-	-	-	-	-	-	-	-	X	-	-	-	X	-	X	-	-	-	-	X	X	-	X	-	-	-	-	-	-	-	-	-	-	-	-	-	-
21	Disabilities	X	X	-	-	-	-	-	-	-	-	-	-	-	-	-	-	-	-	-	-	-	-	-	-	-	-	-	-	-	-	-	-	-	-	-	-	-	-	-	-	-	-	-
22	Sources of financial support for college	X	X	X	X	X	X	X	X	X	X	X	X	X	X	X	X	X	X	X	X	X	X	X	X	X	X	X	X	X	X	X	X	X	X	X	X	X	X	X	X	X	X	X
23	Parental/family income	X	X	X	X	X	X	X	X	X	X	X	X	X	X	X	X	X	X	X	X	X	X	X	X	X	X	X	X	X	X	X	X	X	X	X	X	X	X	X	X	X	X	X
24	Concern about financing college	X	X	X	X	X	X	X	X	X	X	X	X	X	X	-	X	X	-	-	X	X	-	X	-	X	X	X	X	X	X	X	X	X	X	X	X	X	X	X	X	X	X	X
25	Religious preference of student and parents	X	X	X	X	X	X	X	X	X	X	X	X	X	X	X	X	X	X	X	X	X	X	X	X	X	X	X	X	X	X	X	X	X	X	X	X	X	s	s	s	s	s	s
26	Activities in past year	X	X	X	X	X	X	X	X	X	X	X	X	X	X	X	X	X	X	X	X	X	X	X	X	X	X	X	X	X	X	X	X	X	X	X	X	X	X	X	X	X	X	X
27	Self-rating of abilities (traditional)	X	X	X	X	X	X	X	X	X	X	X	X	X	X	X	X	X	X	X	X	X	X	X	-	-	X	-	-	X	-	X	X	X	-	X	-	X	-	-	-	X	X	-
28	Self-rating of abilities (new)	X	-	-	-	-	-	-	-	-	-	-	-	-	-	-	-	-	-	-	-	-	-	-	-	-	-	-	-	-	-	-	-	-	-	-	-	-	-	-	-	-	-	-
29	Parental education	X	X	X	X	X	X	X	X	X	X	X	X	X	X	X	X	X	X	X	X	X	X	X	X	X	X	X	X	X	X	X	X	X	X	X	X	X	X	X	X	X	X	X
30	Habits of Mind	X	X	-	-	-	-	-	-	-	-	-	-	-	-	-	-	-	-	-	-	-	-	-	-	-	-	-	-	-	-	-	-	-	-	-	-	-	-	-	-	-	-	-
31	Student's career choice and parental occupation	X	X	X	X	X	X	X	X	X	X	X	X	X	X	X	X	X	X	X	X	X	X	X	X	X	X	X	X	X	X	X	X	X	X	X	X	X	X	X	X	X	X	X
32	Political orientation	X	X	X	X	X	X	X	X	X	X	X	X	X	X	X	X	X	X	X	X	X	X	X	X	X	X	X	X	X	X	X	X	X	X	X	X	X	X	X	X	X	-	-
33	Political and social attitudes	X	X	X	X	X	X	X	X	X	X	X	X	X	X	X	X	X	X	X	X	X	X	X	X	X	X	X	X	X	X	X	X	X	X	X	X	X	X	X	-	X	X	X
34	Time diary last year	X	X	X	X	X	X	X	X	X	X	X	X	X	X	X	X	X	X	X	X	X	X	X	-	-	-	-	-	-	-	-	-	-	-	-	-	-	-	-	-	-	-	-
35	Racial background	X	X	X	X	X	X	X	X	X	X	X	X	X	X	X	X	X	X	X	X	X	X	X	X	X	X	X	X	X	X	X	X	X	X	X	X	X	X	X	X	X	X	X
36	Reasons for choosing this college	X	X	X	X	X	X	X	X	X	X	X	X	X	X	X	X	X	X	X	X	X	X	X	X	X	X	X	X	X	X	X	X	X	X	X	X	X	X	X	X	X	X	X
37	Undergraduate major	X	X	X	X	X	X	X	X	X	X	X	X	X	X	X	X	X	X	X	X	X	X	X	X	X	X	X	X	X	X	X	X	X	X	X	X	X	X	-	-	X	X	-
38	Values and life goals	X	X	X	X	X	X	X	X	X	X	X	X	X	X	X	X	X	X	X	X	X	X	X	X	X	X	X	X	X	X	X	X	X	X	X	X	X	X	X	X	X	X	X
39	Expectations during college	X	X	X	X	X	X	X	X	X	X	X	X	X	X	X	X	X	X	X	X	X	X	X	X	X	X	X	X	X	X	X	X	X	X	X	X	X	X	X	X	X	X	X
40	Permission to use Student I.D.	X	X	X	X	X	X	X	X	X	X	X	X	X	X	X	X	X	X	X	X	X	X	X	X	X	X	-	-	-	-	-	X	X	X	X	X	X	X	X	-	-	-	-

Notes: The language of some survey questions may have varied since the inception of the CIRP survey project. Please refer to the survey form for that particular year (www.heri.ucla.edu) for the exact language.

137

Changes in stratification assignment do occur based on changing circumstances at individual institutions. Institutional requests for review are honored each year. Appendix D lists the current stratification cell assignment of institutions that participated in the CIRP Freshman Survey in 2008.

Having defined the population in terms of the stratification cell scheme, the OFE file is used to compute the male and female FTFT population in each cell. These population counts form the target counts of the weighting procedure.

IDENTIFYING THE NORMS SAMPLE

Generally speaking, an institution is included in the National Norms sample if it provided a representative sample of its FTFT population. The minimum percentage required of a sample is based on the type of institution from which it was collected. For four-year colleges the minimum is 75 percent, while for universities, the minimum is 65 percent. Institutions whose sample proportions were less than but close to these cutoffs are included if the method used to administer the survey showed no systematic biases in freshman class coverage.

Information about the FTFT population and the method of survey administration is obtained from participating institutions at the time they return their completed surveys. In the event an institution did not return FTFT information, counts from the most recent OFE survey are used. This procedure, although not optimal, is adequate unless the institution experienced a substantial change in its FTFT population since the last HEGIS/IPEDS survey.

THE 2008 DATA

Although 328,182 respondents at 522 colleges and universities[3] returned their forms in time for their data to be included in the 2008 norms, the normative data presented here are based on responses from 240,580 FTFT freshmen entering 340 baccalaureate institutions.

The normative data presented here were collected by administering the 2008 CIRP Freshman Survey during registration, freshman orientation, or the first few weeks of classes (i.e., before the students have had any substantial experience with college life).[4] The survey is designed to elicit a wide range of biographic and demographic data, as well as data on the student's high school background, career plans, educational aspirations, financial arrangements, high school activities, and current attitudes. In addition to standard biographic and demographic items that have been administered annually to each entering class, the survey also contains other research-oriented items that may have been modified from previous years (e.g., see the list of attitudinal questions listed under item #33, Appendix B). The inclusion of modified items permits a more thorough coverage of

---

[3] Including 1,418 respondents attending 8 two-year colleges. As of 2000, two-year colleges are no longer included in the normative data. See "The American Freshman: National Norms for Fall 2000."

[4] A total of 76 institutions administered in this manner to all or some of their entering class.

student characteristics but also represents a compromise between two mutually exclusive objectives: (1) comparability of information from year to year which is required for assessing trends; and (2) flexibility in item content to meet changing information and research needs. Table A1 lists the 2008 survey items and indicates previous survey years in which comparable items have been used.

The survey, reproduced as Appendix B, has been developed in collaboration with students, professional associations, participating institutions, government agencies, educational researchers, administrators, policy makers, and members of the CIRP Advisory Committee. It is designed for self-administration under proctored conditions and for processing onto magnetic tape with a mark reflex reader. The survey content is reviewed annually by the CIRP project staff, with the assistance of the CIRP Advisory Committee as well as others interested in the annual freshman survey program.

Four data files are developed from the survey each year: (1) an institutional summary file containing institutional identification numbers and an institutional summary of the responses for men and women; (2) a file containing individual responses and a student identification number, but no names and addresses; (3) a name-and-address file containing a second, independent student identification number; and (4) a "link" file containing *only* the two independent identification numbers. This last file is maintained under an elaborate system developed to ensure strict confidentiality of individual student data and to protect against misuse of the name-and-address file (Astin & Boruch, 1970).

Those data from institutions meeting minimal quality requirements for inclusion in the 2008 norms (above) were differentially weighted to represent the population of entering freshmen at all higher educational institutions in the United States (see 'Weighting the Sample' below). Part-time students and those who are not first-time college students (i.e., transfers and former enrollees) were excluded from the normative sample. Since the 1972 survey, special care has been taken to define these enrollment statuses; in surveys before 1972, the participating institutions were asked to exclude part-time students, while non-first-time students were excluded during the data processing stage by screening out those who indicated that they had previously attended college. Since that time, all students who did not identify themselves as part-time were included in the national norms if they either graduated from high school in the year of the survey or had never attended any post-secondary institution.

WEIGHTING THE SAMPLE

Those institutions identified as being part of the Norms sample are weighted by a two-step procedure. The first weight is designed to adjust for nonparticipation within institutions. Counts of the male and female FTFT population for each institution are divided by that institution's male and female FTFT respondent count. The resulting weights, when applied to each respondent, bring the male and female respondent counts up to the corresponding counts for the population at that institution.

Table A2. Institutional Sample and Population Weights Used to Compute the 2008 Freshman Norms

| Stratification Cell for Sampling | Number of Institutions | | | Cell Weights [1] Applied to Data Collected from | |
	Population	Participants [2] Total	Used in Norms	Men	Women
Public universities					
01 Less than 1,070 [3]	43	8	5	7.76	7.90
02 1,070–1,149	41	12	7	4.80	5.28
03 1,150 or more	43	16	10	4.57	4.30
Private universities					
04 Less than 1,190	22	16	10	1.89	2.03
05 1,190–1,319	22	12	10	2.25	2.38
06 1,320 or more	27	18	12	2.17	2.27
Public four-year colleges					
07,10 Less than 970 or unknown	161	18	8	14.43	12.98
08 970–1,029	122	24	10	18.47	14.02
09 1,030 or more	127	29	20	7.24	8.66
Private nonsectarian four-year colleges					
11,15 Less than 990 or unknown	201	25	14	18.92	14.49
12 990–1,069	68	22	15	4.38	3.56
13 1,070–1,199	82	36	26	3.62	3.28
14 1,200 or more	76	47	30	2.26	2.20
Catholic four-year colleges					
16,19 Less than 980 or unknown	59	22	15	3.38	3.20
17 980–1,039	51	15	9	4.74	4.40
18 1,040 or more	57	27	23	2.51	2.36
Other religious four-year colleges					
20,24 Less than 980 or unknown	117	19	11	9.27	7.57
21 980–1,029	92	27	21	3.85	3.58
22 1,030–1,089	98	40	32	2.92	2.85
23 1,090 or more	104	58	40	2.87	2.89
Predominantly Black colleges					
34 Public	37	10	5	8.04	7.86
35 Private	43	12	7	3.92	5.74
ALL INSTITUTIONS	1693	513	340		

[1] Ratio between the number of 2008 first-time, full-time students enrolled in all colleges and the number of first-time, full-time students enrolled at colleges in the 2008 CIRP sample.

[2] The 8 two-year colleges participating in 2008 are not included in this table. Two-year colleges are not included in the Norms.

[3] Categories within types are based on selectivity—the average SAT Verbal + Math scores of the entering class.

The second weight is designed to compensate for nonparticipating institutions within each stratification cell. The weighted male and female counts for all participating institutions in each stratification cell are first summed, and then are divided into the national male and female FTFT counts for all institutions in that stratification cell, producing a second set of ("cell") weights. (The last two columns of Table A2 show the final weights that were applied to the 2008 data.) The final weight is simply the product of the first and second weights.

Weighting each respondent using this final weight brings the male and female counts for each stratification cell up to the corresponding national counts for all institutions in that stratification cell.

COMPARISON GROUPS

Weighted data are combined separately to form various comparison (or Norms) groups. Most norms groups are hierarchically organized, allowing participating institutions to compare their results at different levels of specificity. A college assigned to stratification cell #14, for example, can compare its results with the following five Norms groups (in declining order of specificity):

> Private nonsectarian four-year colleges, very high selectivity
> All private nonsectarian four-year colleges
> All private four-year colleges
> All four-year colleges
> All baccalaureate institutions

Table A3 shows the 2008 distribution of schools and respondents across the 32 Norms groups printed in the annual *American Freshman* report, as well as a summary of distribution by national region. The weighted results reported here represent the "all baccalaureate institutions" group—the overall weighted summary based on all 240,580 respondents whose institutions were included in the national norms.

Table A3. Number of Institutions and Students Used in Computing the Weighted National Norms, Fall 2008

Norm Group	Number of Institutions in the 2008 Norms	Number of Entering First-time, Full-time Freshmen			
		Unweighted Participants	Weighted Number	% Men	% Women
All institutions	340	240,580	1,447,920	45.4	54.6
All universities	54	111,087	552,758	47.1	52.9
All four-year colleges	286	129,493	895,162	44.3	55.7
Black colleges (1)	12	5,304	50,474	40.8	59.2
Public universities	22	67,765	438,662	47.3	52.7
Low selectivity	5	11,600	103,467	46.0	54.0
Medium selectivity	7	19,442	141,135	48.1	51.9
High selectivity	10	36,723	194,060	47.4	52.6
Private universities	32	43,322	114,096	46.6	53.4
Medium selectivity	10	11,977	27,854	43.8	56.2
High selectivity	10	14,700	40,874	46.1	53.9
Very high selectivity	12	16,645	45,368	48.6	51.4
Public four-year colleges	43	39,525	511,796	45.1	54.9
Low selectivity (2)	13	10,914	165,649	43.8	56.2
Medium selectivity	10	9,341	160,601	44.7	55.3
High selectivity	20	19,270	185,546	46.5	53.5
Private four-year colleges	243	89,968	383,366	43.3	56.7
Nonsectarian	88	35,227	176,513	44.3	55.7
Low selectivity (2)	17	4,844	73,742	44.5	55.5
Medium selectivity	15	6,743	30,693	42.4	57.6
High selectivity	26	9,561	36,838	45.7	54.3
Very high selectivity	30	14,079	35,241	43.8	56.2
Catholic	48	20,619	69,926	39.6	60.4
Low selectivity (2)	16	4,133	17,752	35.2	64.8
Medium selectivity	9	3,276	16,289	38.9	61.1
High selectivity	23	13,210	35,886	42.0	58.0
Other Religious	107	34,122	136,927	43.9	56.1
Low selectivity (2)	35	8,631	52,099	46.0	54.0
Medium selectivity	32	10,005	33,847	42.6	57.4
High selectivity	40	15,486	50,982	42.6	57.4
Public Black College	5	2,500	31,834	41.6	58.4
Private Black Colleges	7	2,804	18,640	39.4	60.6
Eastern region	127	81,994	432,652	46.8	53.2
Midwestern region	83	53,345	295,774	46.7	53.3
Southern region	73	45,418	291,225	42.8	57.2
Western region	57	59,823	428,269	44.8	55.2

(1) Black colleges are also included in the appropriate four-year college or university norm group according to their type.

(2) Includes those institutions with unknown selectivity.

Note: The weighted counts may not always sum to identical totals due to rounding error.

142

Appendix B

The 2008 CIRP Freshman Survey Instrument

2008 CIRP FRESHMAN SURVEY

PLEASE PRINT NAME AND PERMANENT/HOME ADDRESS (one letter or number per box).

FIRST   MI   LAST   **When were you born?**

NAME:

ADDRESS: Month   Day   Year
                                                             (01-12) (01-31)

CITY: STATE: ZIP: PHONE: —   —

STUDENT ID# *(as instructed):*   EMAIL *(print letters carefully):*

---

1. Your sex: ○ Male   ○ Female

2. How old will you be on December 31 of this year? (Mark one)

16 or younger . ○   21-24 ..... ○
17 .... ○   25-29 ..... ○
18 .... ○   30-39 ..... ○
19 .... ○   40-54 ..... ○
20 .... ○   55 or older . ○

3. Is English your native language?
○ Yes   ○ No

4. In what year did you graduate from high school? (Mark one)

2008 ...... ○   Did not graduate but
2007 ...... ○   passed G.E.D. test. ○
2006 ...... ○   Never completed
2005 or earlier ○   high school ...... ○

5. Are you enrolled (or enrolling) as a:
(Mark one)   Full-time student? .... ○
              Part-time student? ... ○

6. How many miles is this college from your permanent home? (Mark one)

5 or less ○   11-50 ○   101-500 ○
6-10 ○   51-100 ○   Over 500 ○

7. What was your average grade in high school? (Mark one)

A or A+ ○   B ○   C ○
A– ○   B– ○   D ○
B+ ○   C+ ○

8. What were your scores on the SAT I and/or ACT?

SAT VERBAL ....
SAT MATH ....
SAT WRITING ....
ACT Composite ....

9. From what kind of high school did you graduate? (Mark one)

○ Public school (not charter or magnet)
○ Public charter school
○ Public magnet school
○ Private religious/parochial school
○ Private independent college-prep school
○ Home school

10. Prior to this term, have you ever taken courses for credit at this institution?
○ Yes   ○ No

11. Since leaving high school, have you ever taken courses, whether for credit or not for credit, at any other institution (university, 4- or 2-year college, technical, vocational, or business school)?
○ Yes   ○ No

12. Where do you plan to live during the fall term? (Mark one)

With my family or other relatives ...... ○
Other private home, apartment, or room. ○
College residence hall .... ○
Fraternity or sorority house .... ○
Other campus student housing .... ○
Other .... ○

13. To how many colleges other than this one did you apply for admission this year?

None   1 ○   4 ○   7-10 ○
○   2 ○   5 ○   11 or more ○
     3 ○   6 ○

14. Were you accepted by your first choice college?
○ Yes   ○ No

15. Is this college your: (Mark one)

First choice? ..... ○   Less than third
Second choice? .. ○   choice? .... ○
Third choice? .... ○

16. Citizenship status:
○ U.S. citizen
○ Permanent resident (green card)
○ Neither

17. Are your parents: (Mark one)

Both alive and living with each other? .. ○
Both alive, divorced or living apart? ... ○
One or both deceased? .... ○

18. During high school (grades 9-12) how many years did you study each of the following subjects? (Mark one for each item)

	None	1/2	1	2	3	4	5 or more
English	○	○	○	○	○	○	○
Mathematics	○	○	○	○	○	○	○
Foreign Language ...	○	○	○	○	○	○	○
Physical Science	○	○	○	○	○	○	○
Biological Science ...	○	○	○	○	○	○	○
History/Am. Gov't ...	○	○	○	○	○	○	○
Computer Science ...	○	○	○	○	○	○	○
Arts and/or Music....	○	○	○	○	○	○	○

19. What is the highest academic degree that you intend to obtain?
(Mark one in each column)

	Highest Planned	Highest Planned at This College
None	○	○
Vocational certificate	○	○
Associate (A.A. or equivalent)	○	○
Bachelor's degree (B.A., B.S., etc.) ..	○	○
Master's degree (M.A., M.S., etc.)...	○	○
Ph.D. or Ed.D.	○	○
M.D., D.O., D.D.S., or D.V.M.	○	○
J.D. (Law)	○	○
B.D. or M.DIV. (Divinity)	○	○
Other........................	○	○

20. How would you describe the racial composition of the high school you last attended and the neighborhood where you grew up? (Mark one in each row)

	Completely non-White	Mostly non-White	Roughly half non-White	Mostly White	Completely White
High school I last attended ..	○	○	○	○	○
Neighborhood where I grew up.	○	○	○	○	○

21. Do you have a disability? (Mark all that apply)

○ None   ○ Learning disability
○ Hearing   ○ Partially sighted or blind
○ Speech   ○ Health-related
○ Orthopedic   ○ Other

145

22. How much of your first year's educational expenses (room, board, tuition, and fees) do you expect to cover from each of the sources listed below?
(Mark one answer for each possible source)

	None	Less than $1,000	$1,000 to 2,999	$3,000 to 5,999	$6,000 to 9,999	$10,000+
Family resources (parents, relatives, spouse, etc.)....	○	○	○	○	○	○
My own resources (savings from work, work-study, other income)	○	○	○	○	○	○
Aid which need not be repaid (grants, scholarships, military funding, etc.)	○	○	○	○	○	○
Aid which must be repaid (loans, etc.)............	○	○	○	○	○	○
Other than above..........	○	○	○	○	○	○

23. What is your best estimate of your parents' total income last year? Consider income from all sources before taxes. (Mark one)

- ○ Less than $10,000
- ○ $10,000-14,999
- ○ $15,000-19,999
- ○ $20,000-24,999
- ○ $25,000-29,999
- ○ $30,000-39,999
- ○ $40,000-49,999
- ○ $50,000-59,999
- ○ $60,000-74,999
- ○ $75,000-99,999
- ○ $100,000-149,999
- ○ $150,000-199,999
- ○ $200,000-249,999
- ○ $250,000 or more

24. Do you have any concern about your ability to finance your college education? (Mark one)

- None (I am confident that I will have sufficient funds)........................ ○
- Some (but I probably will have enough funds)... ○
- Major (not sure I will have enough funds to complete college).................... ○

25. Current religious preference:
(Mark one in each column)

	Yours	Father's	Mother's
Baptist	Y	F	M
Buddhist	Y	F	M
Church of Christ	Y	F	M
Eastern Orthodox	Y	F	M
Episcopalian	Y	F	M
Hindu............................	Y	F	M
Jewish	Y	F	M
LDS (Mormon)	Y	F	M
Lutheran	Y	F	M
Methodist	Y	F	M
Muslim...........................	Y	F	M
Presbyterian	Y	F	M
Quaker...........................	Y	F	M
Roman Catholic	Y	F	M
Seventh Day Adventist	Y	F	M
United Church of Christ/Congregational.	Y	F	M
Other Christian	Y	F	M
Other Religion....................	Y	F	M
None	Y	F	M

26. For the activities below, indicate which ones you did during the past year. If you engaged in an activity frequently, mark Ⓕ. If you engaged in an activity one or more times, but not frequently, mark Ⓞ (Occasionally). Mark Ⓝ (Not at all) if you have not performed the activity during the past year.
(Mark one for each item)

	Frequently	Occasionally	Not at All
Attended a religious service....	F	O	N
Was bored in class	F	O	N
Participated in political demonstrations	F	O	N
Tutored another student	F	O	N
Studied with other students	F	O	N
Was a guest in a teacher's home .	F	O	N
Smoked cigarettes	F	O	N
Drank beer..................	F	O	N
Drank wine or liquor	F	O	N
Felt overwhelmed by all I had to do .	F	O	N
Felt depressed	F	O	N
Performed volunteer work	F	O	N
Played a musical instrument ...	F	O	N
Asked a teacher for advice after class.................	F	O	N
Voted in a student election.....	F	O	N
Socialized with someone of another racial/ethnic group ...	F	O	N
Came late to class	F	O	N
Used the Internet:			
For research or homework	F	O	N
To read news sites	F	O	N
To read blogs	F	O	N
To blog	F	O	N
Performed community service as a part of a class...........	F	O	N
Discussed religion............	F	O	N
Discussed politics	F	O	N
Worked on a local, state, or national political campaign ...	F	O	N

27. Rate yourself on each of the following traits as compared with the average person your age. We want the most accurate estimate of how you see yourself.
(Mark one in each row)

	Highest 10%	Above Average	Average	Below Average	Lowest 10%
Academic ability.....	○	○	○	○	○
Artistic ability........	○	○	○	○	○
Computer skills......	○	○	○	○	○
Cooperativeness	○	○	○	○	○
Creativity...........	○	○	○	○	○
Drive to achieve	○	○	○	○	○
Emotional health	○	○	○	○	○
Leadership ability....	○	○	○	○	○
Mathematical ability ..	○	○	○	○	○
Physical health	○	○	○	○	○
Popularity	○	○	○	○	○
Public speaking ability .	○	○	○	○	○
Self-confidence (intellectual).......	○	○	○	○	○
Self-confidence (social).	○	○	○	○	○
Self-understanding...	○	○	○	○	○
Spirituality.........	○	○	○	○	○
Understanding of others............	○	○	○	○	○
Writing ability	○	○	○	○	○

28. Rate yourself on each of the following traits as compared with the average person your age. We want the most accurate estimate of how you see yourself.
(Mark one for each item)

	Highest 10%	Above Average	Average	Below Average	Lowest 10%
Ability to see the world from someone else's perspective	○	○	○	○	○
Tolerance of others with different beliefs.	○	○	○	○	○
Openness to having my own views challenged........	○	○	○	○	○
Ability to discuss and negotiate controversial issues	○	○	○	○	○
Ability to work cooperatively with diverse people.....	○	○	○	○	○

29. What is the highest level of formal education obtained by your parents?
(Mark one in each column)

	Father	Mother
Grammar school or less	○	○
Some high school	○	○
High school graduate	○	○
Postsecondary school other than college........	○	○
Some college.............	○	○
College degree	○	○
Some graduate school	○	○
Graduate degree	○	○

30. How often in the past year did you?
(Mark one for each item)

	Frequently	Occasionally	Not at All
Ask questions in class......	F	O	N
Support your opinions with a logical argument	F	O	N
Seek solutions to problems and explain them to others .	F	O	N
Revise your papers to improve your writing......	F	O	N
Evaluate the quality or reliability of information you received	F	O	N
Take a risk because you feel you have more to gain	F	O	N
Seek alternative solutions to a problem	F	O	N
Look up scientific research articles and resources	F	O	N
Explore topics on your own, even though it was not required for a class	F	O	N
Accept mistakes as part of the learning process	F	O	N
Seek feedback on your academic work	F	O	N
Take notes during class	F	O	N

31. Mark only three responses, one in each column.

Ⓜ Your mother's occupation ─┐
Ⓕ Your father's occupation ─┐
Ⓨ Your probable career occupation ─┐

Accountant or actuary............	Ⓨ Ⓕ Ⓜ
Actor or entertainer.............	Ⓨ Ⓕ Ⓜ
Architect or urban planner	Ⓨ Ⓕ Ⓜ
Artist	Ⓨ Ⓕ Ⓜ
Business (clerical)..............	Ⓨ Ⓕ Ⓜ
Business executive (management, administrator)....	Ⓨ Ⓕ Ⓜ
Business owner or proprietor......	Ⓨ Ⓕ Ⓜ
Business salesperson or buyer	Ⓨ Ⓕ Ⓜ
Clergy (minister, priest)	Ⓨ Ⓕ Ⓜ
Clergy (other religious)..........	Ⓨ Ⓕ Ⓜ
Clinical psychologist	Ⓨ Ⓕ Ⓜ
College administrator/staff........	Ⓨ Ⓕ Ⓜ
College teacher................	Ⓨ Ⓕ Ⓜ
Computer programmer or analyst ..	Ⓨ Ⓕ Ⓜ
Conservationist or forester........	Ⓨ Ⓕ Ⓜ
Dentist (including orthodontist)	Ⓨ Ⓕ Ⓜ
Dietitian or nutritionist	Ⓨ Ⓕ Ⓜ
Engineer	Ⓨ Ⓕ Ⓜ
Farmer or rancher..............	Ⓨ Ⓕ Ⓜ
Foreign service worker (including diplomat)...........	Ⓨ Ⓕ Ⓜ
Homemaker (full-time)	Ⓨ Ⓕ Ⓜ
Interior decorator (including designer) .	Ⓨ Ⓕ Ⓜ
Lab technician or hygienist	Ⓨ Ⓕ Ⓜ
Law enforcement officer..........	Ⓨ Ⓕ Ⓜ
Lawyer (attorney) or judge	Ⓨ Ⓕ Ⓜ
Military service (career)	Ⓨ Ⓕ Ⓜ
Musician (performer, composer) ...	Ⓨ Ⓕ Ⓜ
Nurse	Ⓨ Ⓕ Ⓜ
Optometrist	Ⓨ Ⓕ Ⓜ
Pharmacist	Ⓨ Ⓕ Ⓜ
Physician	Ⓨ Ⓕ Ⓜ
Policymaker/Government	Ⓨ Ⓕ Ⓜ
School counselor	Ⓨ Ⓕ Ⓜ
School principal or superintendent .	Ⓨ Ⓕ Ⓜ
Scientific researcher	Ⓨ Ⓕ Ⓜ
Social, welfare, or recreation worker .	Ⓨ Ⓕ Ⓜ
Therapist (physical, occupational, speech)....................	Ⓨ Ⓕ Ⓜ
Teacher or administrator (elementary)	Ⓨ Ⓕ Ⓜ
Teacher or administrator (secondary)	Ⓨ Ⓕ Ⓜ
Veterinarian	Ⓨ Ⓕ Ⓜ
Writer or journalist	Ⓨ Ⓕ Ⓜ
Skilled trades	Ⓨ Ⓕ Ⓜ
Laborer (unskilled)	Ⓨ Ⓕ Ⓜ
Semi-skilled worker	Ⓨ Ⓕ Ⓜ
Unemployed	Ⓨ Ⓕ Ⓜ
Other	Ⓨ Ⓕ Ⓜ
Undecided	Ⓨ

32. How would you characterize your political views? (Mark one)

○ Far left
○ Liberal
○ Middle-of-the-road
○ Conservative
○ Far right

33. Mark one in each row:

① Disagree Strongly ─┐
② Disagree Somewhat ─┐
③ Agree Somewhat ─┐
④ Agree Strongly ─┐

There is too much concern in the courts for the rights of criminals..............	④ ③ ② ①
Abortion should be legal..	④ ③ ② ①
The death penalty should be abolished.............................	④ ③ ② ①
Marijuana should be legalized	④ ③ ② ①
It is important to have laws prohibiting homosexual relationships..............	④ ③ ② ①
Racial discrimination is no longer a major problem in America	④ ③ ② ①
Realistically, an individual can do little to bring about changes in our society	④ ③ ② ①
Wealthy people should pay a larger share of taxes than they do now	④ ③ ② ①
Same-sex couples should have the right to legal marital status	④ ③ ② ①
Affirmative action in college admissions should be abolished.................	④ ③ ② ①
Federal military spending should be increased.........................	④ ③ ② ①
The federal government should do more to control the sale of handguns	④ ③ ② ①
Only volunteers should serve in the armed forces	④ ③ ② ①
The federal government is not doing enough to control environmental pollution ...	④ ③ ② ①
A national health care plan is needed to cover everybody's medical costs	④ ③ ② ①
Undocumented immigrants should be denied access to public education	④ ③ ② ①
Through hard work, everybody can succeed in American society..............	④ ③ ② ①
Dissent is a critical component of the political process	④ ③ ② ①
Colleges have the right to ban extreme speakers from campus	④ ③ ② ①
Students from disadvantaged social backgrounds should be given preferential treatment in college admissions	④ ③ ② ①
The federal government should raise taxes to reduce the deficit	④ ③ ② ①
Addressing global warming should be a federal priority.....................	④ ③ ② ①

34. During your last year in high school, how much time did you spend during a typical week doing the following activities?

Hours per week: None / Less than 1 hour / 1-2 / 3-5 / 6-10 / 11-15 / 16-20 / Over 20

Activity	None	<1	1-2	3-5	6-10	11-15	16-20	Over 20
Studying/homework ..	○	○	○	○	○	○	○	○
Socializing with friends.	○	○	○	○	○	○	○	○
Talking with teachers outside of class	○	○	○	○	○	○	○	○
Exercise or sports ...	○	○	○	○	○	○	○	○
Partying	○	○	○	○	○	○	○	○
Working (for pay)	○	○	○	○	○	○	○	○
Volunteer work	○	○	○	○	○	○	○	○
Student clubs/groups.	○	○	○	○	○	○	○	○
Watching TV	○	○	○	○	○	○	○	○
Household/childcare duties	○	○	○	○	○	○	○	○
Reading for pleasure .	○	○	○	○	○	○	○	○
Playing video/ computer games...	○	○	○	○	○	○	○	○
Online social networks (MySpace, Facebook, etc.).	○	○	○	○	○	○	○	○

35. Are you: (Mark all that apply)

White/Caucasian	○
African American/Black	○
American Indian/Alaska Native.......	○
Asian American/Asian	○
Native Hawaiian/Pacific Islander......	○
Mexican American/Chicano	○
Puerto Rican	○
Other Latino	○
Other.........................	○

36. Below are some reasons that might have influenced your decision to attend this particular college. How important was each reason in your decision to come here? (Mark one answer for each possible reason)

Very Important / Somewhat Important / Not Important

My parents wanted me to come here.	Ⓥ Ⓢ Ⓝ
My relatives wanted me to come here.	Ⓥ Ⓢ Ⓝ
My teacher advised me	Ⓥ Ⓢ Ⓝ
This college has a very good academic reputation	Ⓥ Ⓢ Ⓝ
This college has a good reputation for its social activities	Ⓥ Ⓢ Ⓝ
I was offered financial assistance ..	Ⓥ Ⓢ Ⓝ
The cost of attending this college ..	Ⓥ Ⓢ Ⓝ
High school counselor advised me .	Ⓥ Ⓢ Ⓝ
Private college counselor advised me.	Ⓥ Ⓢ Ⓝ
I wanted to live near home	Ⓥ Ⓢ Ⓝ
Not offered aid by first choice	Ⓥ Ⓢ Ⓝ
Could not afford first choice.......	Ⓥ Ⓢ Ⓝ
This college's graduates gain admission to top graduate/ professional schools	Ⓥ Ⓢ Ⓝ
This college's graduates get good jobs .	Ⓥ Ⓢ Ⓝ
I was attracted by the religious affiliation/orientation of the college .	Ⓥ Ⓢ Ⓝ
I wanted to go to a school about the size of this college..........	Ⓥ Ⓢ Ⓝ
Rankings in national magazines ...	Ⓥ Ⓢ Ⓝ
Information from a website	Ⓥ Ⓢ Ⓝ
I was admitted through an Early Action or Early Decision program .	Ⓥ Ⓢ Ⓝ
The athletic department recruited me .	Ⓥ Ⓢ Ⓝ
A visit to the campus	Ⓥ Ⓢ Ⓝ

37. **Below is a list of different undergraduate major fields grouped into general categories. Mark only one oval to indicate your probable field of study.**

ARTS AND HUMANITIES
- Art, fine and applied ...... ①
- English (language and literature) .... ②
- History.................. ③
- Journalism .... ④
- Language and Literature (except English) .... ⑤
- Music .... ⑥
- Philosophy .... ⑦
- Speech.................. ⑧
- Theater or Drama .... ⑨
- Theology or Religion ...... ⑩
- Other Arts and Humanities . ⑪

BIOLOGICAL SCIENCE
- Biology (general) .... ⑫
- Biochemistry or Biophysics .... ⑬
- Botany .... ⑭
- Environmental Science .... ⑮
- Marine (Life) Science ..... ⑯
- Microbiology or Bacteriology .... ⑰
- Zoology.................. ⑱
- Other Biological Science... ⑲

BUSINESS
- Accounting .... ⑳
- Business Admin. (general) . ㉑
- Finance................. ㉒
- International Business..... ㉓
- Marketing .... ㉔
- Management .... ㉕
- Secretarial Studies .... ㉖
- Other Business .... ㉗

EDUCATION
- Business Education....... ㉘
- Elementary Education..... ㉙
- Music or Art Education .... ㉚
- Physical Education or Recreation .... ㉛
- Secondary Education ..... ㉜
- Special Education .... ㉝
- Other Education .... ㉞

ENGINEERING
- Aeronautical or Astronautical Eng .... ㉟
- Civil Engineering .... ㊱
- Chemical Engineering..... ㊲
- Computer Engineering .... ㊳
- Electrical or Electronic Engineering............ ㊴
- Industrial Engineering ..... ㊵
- Mechanical Engineering ... ㊶
- Other Engineering .... ㊷

PHYSICAL SCIENCE
- Astronomy .... ㊸
- Atmospheric Science (incl. Meteorology) ...... ㊹
- Chemistry............... ㊺
- Earth Science............ ㊻
- Marine Science (incl. Oceanography).......... ㊼
- Mathematics .... ㊽
- Physics................. ㊾
- Other Physical Science.... ㊿

PROFESSIONAL
- Architecture or Urban Planning............... (51)
- Family & Consumer Sciences. (52)
- Health Technology (medical, dental, laboratory) ... (53)
- Library or Archival Science . (54)
- Medicine, Dentistry, Veterinary Medicine ..... (55)
- Nursing................. (56)
- Pharmacy............... (57)
- Therapy (occupational, physical, speech) .... (58)
- Other Professional........ (59)

SOCIAL SCIENCE
- Anthropology .... (60)
- Economics .... (61)
- Ethnic Studies .... (62)
- Geography .... (63)
- Political Science (gov't., international relations) ... (64)
- Psychology.............. (65)
- Public Policy............. (66)
- Social Work .... (67)
- Sociology .... (68)
- Women's Studies......... (69)
- Other Social Science...... (70)

TECHNICAL
- Building Trades .... (71)
- Data Processing or Computer Programming.. (72)
- Drafting or Design .... (73)
- Electronics .... (74)
- Mechanics .... (75)
- Other Technical .... (76)

OTHER FIELDS
- Agriculture .... (77)
- Communications .... (78)
- Computer Science........ (79)
- Forestry .... (80)
- Kinesiology.............. (81)
- Law Enforcement .... (82)
- Military Science .... (83)
- Other Field .... (84)
- Undecided .... (85)

38. **Please indicate the importance to you personally of each of the following:**
(Mark one for each item)

Ⓝ Not Important
Ⓢ Somewhat Important
Ⓥ Very Important
Ⓔ Essential

Becoming accomplished in one of the performing arts (acting, dancing, etc.).	Ⓔ	Ⓥ	Ⓢ	Ⓝ
Becoming an authority in my field	Ⓔ	Ⓥ	Ⓢ	Ⓝ
Obtaining recognition from my colleagues for contributions to my special field	Ⓔ	Ⓥ	Ⓢ	Ⓝ
Influencing the political structure	Ⓔ	Ⓥ	Ⓢ	Ⓝ
Influencing social values	Ⓔ	Ⓥ	Ⓢ	Ⓝ
Raising a family	Ⓔ	Ⓥ	Ⓢ	Ⓝ
Being very well off financially	Ⓔ	Ⓥ	Ⓢ	Ⓝ
Helping others who are in difficulty	Ⓔ	Ⓥ	Ⓢ	Ⓝ
Making a theoretical contribution to science	Ⓔ	Ⓥ	Ⓢ	Ⓝ
Writing original works (poems, novels, short stories, etc.)	Ⓔ	Ⓥ	Ⓢ	Ⓝ
Creating artistic works (painting, sculpture, decorating, etc.)	Ⓔ	Ⓥ	Ⓢ	Ⓝ
Becoming successful in a business of my own	Ⓔ	Ⓥ	Ⓢ	Ⓝ
Becoming involved in programs to clean up the environment	Ⓔ	Ⓥ	Ⓢ	Ⓝ
Developing a meaningful philosophy of life	Ⓔ	Ⓥ	Ⓢ	Ⓝ
Participating in a community action program	Ⓔ	Ⓥ	Ⓢ	Ⓝ
Helping to promote racial understanding	Ⓔ	Ⓥ	Ⓢ	Ⓝ
Keeping up to date with political affairs	Ⓔ	Ⓥ	Ⓢ	Ⓝ
Becoming a community leader	Ⓔ	Ⓥ	Ⓢ	Ⓝ
Improving my understanding of other countries and cultures	Ⓔ	Ⓥ	Ⓢ	Ⓝ
Adopting "green" practices to protect the environment	Ⓔ	Ⓥ	Ⓢ	Ⓝ

39. **What is your best guess as to the chances that you will:**
(Mark one for each item)

Ⓝ No Chance
Ⓛ Very Little Chance
Ⓢ Some Chance
Ⓥ Very Good Chance

Change major field?	Ⓥ	Ⓢ	Ⓛ	Ⓝ
Change career choice?	Ⓥ	Ⓢ	Ⓛ	Ⓝ
Participate in student government?	Ⓥ	Ⓢ	Ⓛ	Ⓝ
Get a job to help pay for college expenses?	Ⓥ	Ⓢ	Ⓛ	Ⓝ
Work full-time while attending college?	Ⓥ	Ⓢ	Ⓛ	Ⓝ
Join a social fraternity or sorority?	Ⓥ	Ⓢ	Ⓛ	Ⓝ
Play varsity/intercollegiate athletics?	Ⓥ	Ⓢ	Ⓛ	Ⓝ
Make at least a "B" average?	Ⓥ	Ⓢ	Ⓛ	Ⓝ
Need extra time to complete your degree requirements?	Ⓥ	Ⓢ	Ⓛ	Ⓝ
Participate in student protests or demonstrations?	Ⓥ	Ⓢ	Ⓛ	Ⓝ
Transfer to another college before graduating?	Ⓥ	Ⓢ	Ⓛ	Ⓝ
Be satisfied with your college?	Ⓥ	Ⓢ	Ⓛ	Ⓝ
Participate in volunteer or community service work?	Ⓥ	Ⓢ	Ⓛ	Ⓝ
Seek personal counseling?	Ⓥ	Ⓢ	Ⓛ	Ⓝ
Communicate regularly with your professors?	Ⓥ	Ⓢ	Ⓛ	Ⓝ
Socialize with someone of another racial/ethnic group?	Ⓥ	Ⓢ	Ⓛ	Ⓝ
Participate in student clubs/groups?	Ⓥ	Ⓢ	Ⓛ	Ⓝ
Participate in a study abroad program?	Ⓥ	Ⓢ	Ⓛ	Ⓝ
Have a roommate of a different race/ethnicity?	Ⓥ	Ⓢ	Ⓛ	Ⓝ
Discuss course content with students outside of class?	Ⓥ	Ⓢ	Ⓛ	Ⓝ
Work on a professor's research project?	Ⓥ	Ⓢ	Ⓛ	Ⓝ
Get tutoring help in specific courses?	Ⓥ	Ⓢ	Ⓛ	Ⓝ

40. **Do you give the Higher Education Research Institute (HERI) permission to include your ID number should your college request the data for additional research analyses? HERI maintains strict standards of confidentiality and would require your college to sign a pledge of confidentiality.**

◯ Yes ◯ No

The remaining ovals are provided for questions specifically designed by your college rather than the Higher Education Research Institute. If your college has chosen to use the ovals, please observe carefully the supplemental directions given to you.

41. Ⓐ Ⓑ Ⓒ Ⓓ Ⓔ	**45.** Ⓐ Ⓑ Ⓒ Ⓓ Ⓔ	**49.** Ⓐ Ⓑ Ⓒ Ⓓ Ⓔ	**53.** Ⓐ Ⓑ Ⓒ Ⓓ Ⓔ	**57.** Ⓐ Ⓑ Ⓒ Ⓓ Ⓔ
42. Ⓐ Ⓑ Ⓒ Ⓓ Ⓔ	**46.** Ⓐ Ⓑ Ⓒ Ⓓ Ⓔ	**50.** Ⓐ Ⓑ Ⓒ Ⓓ Ⓔ	**54.** Ⓐ Ⓑ Ⓒ Ⓓ Ⓔ	**58.** Ⓐ Ⓑ Ⓒ Ⓓ Ⓔ
43. Ⓐ Ⓑ Ⓒ Ⓓ Ⓔ	**47.** Ⓐ Ⓑ Ⓒ Ⓓ Ⓔ	**51.** Ⓐ Ⓑ Ⓒ Ⓓ Ⓔ	**55.** Ⓐ Ⓑ Ⓒ Ⓓ Ⓔ	**59.** Ⓐ Ⓑ Ⓒ Ⓓ Ⓔ
44. Ⓐ Ⓑ Ⓒ Ⓓ Ⓔ	**48.** Ⓐ Ⓑ Ⓒ Ⓓ Ⓔ	**52.** Ⓐ Ⓑ Ⓒ Ⓓ Ⓔ	**56.** Ⓐ Ⓑ Ⓒ Ⓓ Ⓔ	**60.** Ⓐ Ⓑ Ⓒ Ⓓ Ⓔ

THANK YOU!

© Prepared by the Higher Education Research Institute, University of California, Los Angeles, California 90095-1521

Data Recognition Corp.-6G8044-8704-54321

Appendix C

Coding Scheme for Collapsed Items

Father's and Mother's Occupation

Collapsed Category	Item Response Alternatives
Artist	Actor or entertainer; Artist; Interior decorator (or designer); Musician (composer, performer); Writer or journalist.
Business	Accountant or actuary; Business executive; Business owner or proprietor; Salesperson or buyer.
Business (clerical)	Business (clerical).
Clergy	Clergy (minister, priest); Clergy (other religious).
College Teacher	College teacher.
Doctor (MD or DDS)	Dentist (including orthodontist); Physician.
Education (secondary)	School counselor; School principal or superintendent; Teacher or administrator (secondary).
Education (elementary)	Teacher or administrator (elementary).
Engineer	Engineer.
Farmer or Forester	Conservationist or forester; Farmer or rancher.
Health Professional	Dietitian or nutritionist; Lab technician or hygienist; Optometrist; Pharmacist; Therapist (physical, occupational, or speech); Veterinarian.
Homemaker (full-time)	Homemaker (full-time).
Lawyer	Lawyer, attorney or judge.
Military (career)	Military service (career).
Nurse	Nurse.
Research Scientist	Scientific researcher.
Social/welfare/recreation Worker	Social, welfare or recreation worker.
Skilled Trades	Skilled trades.
Semi-skilled Worker	Semi-skilled worker.
Laborer (unskilled)	Laborer (unskilled).
Unemployed	Unemployed.
Other	Architect or urban planner; Clinical psychologist; College administrator/ staff; Computer programmer or analyst; Foreign Service (incl. Diplomat) Law enforcement officer; Policymaker/government; Other occupation.

Appendix D

Institutions Participating in the

2008 Freshman Survey

The complete participation history for the CIRP Freshman Survey can be found on the HERI website at http://www.heri.ucla.edu

PARTICIPANTS IN THE 2008 CIRP FRESHMAN SURVEY

Institution	City	State	Stratification Cell	Included in National Norms
Abilene Christian University	Abilene	TX	22	No
Adelphi University	Garden City	NY	04	**Yes**
Adrian College	Adrian	MI	21	**Yes**
Alabama A & M University	Normal	AL	34	**Yes**
Alaska Pacific University	Anchorage	AK	13	**Yes**
Albertus Magnus College	New Haven	CT	16	**Yes**
Albion College	Albion	MI	23	No
Albright College	Reading	PA	21	**Yes**
Alfred State College	Alfred	NY	07	No
Alfred University	Alfred	NY	13	**Yes**
Allegheny College	Meadville	PA	23	No
Alma College	Alma	MI	23	**Yes**
American University	Washington	DC	05	**Yes**
Amherst College	Amherst	MA	14	No
Anderson University	Anderson	IN	22	No
Arkansas State University	State University	AR	08	No
Armstrong Atlantic State U	Savannah	GA	08	No
Art Center College of Design	Pasadena	CA	12	No
Asbury College	Wilmore	KY	13	**Yes**
Assumption College	Worcester	MA	18	**Yes**
Augsburg College	Minneapolis	MN	22	**Yes**
Austin College	Sherman	TX	23	**Yes**
Ave Maria University	Ave Maria	FL	18	**Yes**
Averett University	Danville	VA	11	**Yes**
Azusa Pacific University	Azusa	CA	22	**Yes**
Babson College	Babson Park	MA	14	**Yes**
Bard College	Annandale-on-Hudson	NY	14	**Yes**
Barnard College	New York	NY	14	**Yes**
Barry University	Miami Shores	FL	16	No
Barton College	Wilson	NC	20	**Yes**
Bates College	Lewiston	ME	14	**Yes**
Baylor University	Waco	TX	05	**Yes**
Belmont University	Nashville	TN	23	**Yes**
Beloit College	Beloit	WI	14	**Yes**
Benedictine College	Atchison	KS	18	**Yes**
Bennett College for Women	Greensboro	NC	35	No
Berea College	Berea	KY	13	**Yes**
Berry College	Mount Berry	GA	13	**Yes**
Bethany College	Bethany	WV	21	**Yes**
Bethany Lutheran College	Mankato	MN	22	**Yes**
Bethel College	North Newton	KS	23	**Yes**
Bethel College	Mishawaka	IN	22	**Yes**
Bethel University	Saint Paul	MN	23	No
Bethune-Cookman University	Daytona Beach	FL	35	**Yes**
Biola University	La Mirada	CA	04	No
Bloomfield College	Bloomfield	NJ	20	No

Stratification Cell definitions can be found in Appendix A, Table A2.

PARTICIPANTS IN THE 2008 CIRP FRESHMAN SURVEY

Institution	City	State	Stratification Cell	Included in National Norms
Bluffton University	Bluffton	OH	21	**Yes**
Boston College	Chestnut Hill	MA	06	**Yes**
Bowdoin College	Brunswick	ME	14	**Yes**
Bradley University	Peoria	IL	04	**Yes**
Brandeis University	Waltham	MA	06	No
Brevard College	Brevard	NC	21	No
Bridgewater State College	Bridgewater	MA	08	**Yes**
Brown University	Providence	RI	06	**Yes**
Brunswick Cmty College	Supply	NC	26	No
Bryant University	Smithfield	RI	13	**Yes**
Bryn Athyn Coll of the New Church	Bryn Athyn	PA	23	No
Bryn Mawr College	Bryn Mawr	PA	14	No
Bucknell University	Lewisburg	PA	14	**Yes**
Buena Vista University	Storm Lake	IA	21	**Yes**
Butler University	Indianapolis	IN	04	**Yes**
Cabrini College	Radnor	PA	16	No
Cal State Univ-Monterey Bay	Seaside	CA	08	No
California Baptist University	Riverside	CA	21	**Yes**
California College of the Arts	San Francisco	CA	12	No
California Institute of Technology	Pasadena	CA	06	**Yes**
California State U-Long Beach	Long Beach	CA	08	No
California State U-Los Angeles	Los Angeles	CA	07	No
California State U-Northridge	Northridge	CA	07	**Yes**
California State U-San Marcos	San Marcos	CA	07	**Yes**
Canisius College	Buffalo	NY	18	No
Cardinal Stritch University	Milwaukee	WI	17	No
Carleton College	Northfield	MN	14	**Yes**
Carnegie-Mellon University	Pittsburgh	PA	06	**Yes**
Carthage College	Kenosha	WI	22	**Yes**
Castleton State College	Castleton	VT	08	**Yes**
Catawba College	Salisbury	NC	21	**Yes**
Catholic University of America	Washington	DC	04	No
Cazenovia College	Cazenovia	NY	11	No
Centenary College of Louisiana	Shreveport	LA	23	**Yes**
Central Connecticut State U	New Britain	CT	08	No
Central Michigan University	Mount Pleasant	MI	09	No
Central State University	Wilberforce	OH	34	**Yes**
Centre College	Danville	KY	23	**Yes**
Chaminade University of Honolulu	Honolulu	HI	16	**Yes**
Chapman University	Orange	CA	23	**Yes**
Charleston Southern University	Charleston	SC	20	No
Chowan University	Murfreesboro	NC	20	**Yes**
Christian Brothers University	Memphis	TN	18	**Yes**
Claremont McKenna College	Claremont	CA	14	**Yes**
Clarkson University	Potsdam	NY	04	**Yes**

Stratification Cell definitions can be found in Appendix A, Table A2.

PARTICIPANTS IN THE 2008 CIRP FRESHMAN SURVEY

Institution	City	State	Stratification Cell	Included in National Norms
Coker College	Hartsville	SC	11	**Yes**
Colby College	Waterville	ME	14	**Yes**
Colgate University	Hamilton	NY	14	**Yes**
College of Charleston	Charleston	SC	09	**Yes**
College of Mount Saint Vincent	Riverdale	NY	16	No
College of New Rochelle	New Rochelle	NY	11	**Yes**
College of Saint Catherine	Saint Paul	MN	18	**Yes**
College of Saint Mary	Omaha	NE	16	**Yes**
College of Santa Fe	Santa Fe	NM	13	No
College of William and Mary	Williamsburg	VA	09	No
College of Wooster	Wooster	OH	14	**Yes**
Colorado Christian University	Lakewood	CO	22	**Yes**
Colorado College	Colorado Springs	CO	14	**Yes**
Colorado State University	Fort Collins	CO	02	No
Columbia College	Columbia	SC	20	**Yes**
Columbia University	New York	NY	06	No
Columbus College of Art and Design	Columbus	OH	11	No
Concordia College	Bronxville	NY	20	**Yes**
Connecticut College	New London	CT	14	**Yes**
Converse College	Spartanburg	SC	13	**Yes**
Corban College	Salem	OR	22	**Yes**
Corcoran College of Art & Design	Washington	DC	12	No
Cornell College	Mount Vernon	IA	23	**Yes**
Cornell University	Ithaca	NY	06	**Yes**
Cornerstone University	Grand Rapids	MI	22	**Yes**
Cornish College of the Arts	Seattle	WA	15	No
Cottey College	Nevada	MO	31	No
Creighton University	Omaha	NE	05	**Yes**
Culver-Stockton College	Canton	MO	21	**Yes**
Daemen College	Amherst	NY	12	**Yes**
Dana College	Blair	NE	21	**Yes**
Dartmouth College	Hanover	NH	14	**Yes**
Davidson College	Davidson	NC	23	No
Delaware Valley College	Doylestown	PA	12	**Yes**
Denison University	Granville	OH	14	No
DePaul University	Chicago	IL	04	No
Dickinson College	Carlisle	PA	14	**Yes**
Dominican College of Blauvelt	Orangeburg	NY	11	**Yes**
Dominican University	River Forest	IL	17	**Yes**
Drexel University	Philadelphia	PA	04	**Yes**
Duke University	Durham	NC	06	No
Earlham College	Richmond	IN	23	**Yes**
East Texas Baptist University	Marshall	TX	20	**Yes**
Eastern Kentucky University	Richmond	KY	07	No

Stratification Cell definitions can be found in Appendix A, Table A2.

PARTICIPANTS IN THE 2008 CIRP FRESHMAN SURVEY

Institution	City	State	Stratification Cell	Included in National Norms
Eastern Mennonite University	Harrisonburg	VA	22	No
Eastern Michigan University	Ypsilanti	MI	08	No
Eckerd College	Saint Petersburg	FL	23	**Yes**
Elizabeth City State University	Elizabeth City	NC	34	**Yes**
Elmhurst College	Elmhurst	IL	22	**Yes**
Elon University	Elon	NC	23	No
Emerson College	Boston	MA	14	**Yes**
Emmanuel College	Boston	MA	18	**Yes**
Emory and Henry College	Emory	VA	21	No
Emory University	Atlanta	GA	06	**Yes**
Erskine College	Due West	SC	22	**Yes**
Fairfield University	Fairfield	CT	18	No
Ferrum College	Ferrum	VA	20	**Yes**
Fisher College	Boston	MA	15	No
Fisk University	Nashville	TN	35	No
Florida College	Temple Terrace	FL	22	**Yes**
Florida Memorial University	Miami	FL	35	No
Florida Southern College	Lakeland	FL	22	**Yes**
Florida State University	Tallahassee	FL	03	No
Fordham University	New York	NY	05	**Yes**
Freed-Hardeman University	Henderson	TN	22	**Yes**
Fresno Pacific University	Fresno	CA	21	**Yes**
Gannon University	Erie	PA	18	**Yes**
Geneva College	Beaver Falls	PA	22	**Yes**
George Washington University	Washington	DC	05	No
Georgetown College	Georgetown	KY	22	**Yes**
Georgia Institute of Technology	Atlanta	GA	03	No
Gettysburg College	Gettysburg	PA	23	**Yes**
Gonzaga University	Spokane	WA	18	**Yes**
Gordon College	Wenham	MA	23	**Yes**
Goshen College	Goshen	IN	23	**Yes**
Grace College	Winona Lake	IN	22	**Yes**
Grand View College	Des Moines	IA	20	No
Grinnell College	Grinnell	IA	14	No
Guilford College	Greensboro	NC	23	**Yes**
Gustavus Adolphus College	Saint Peter	MN	23	**Yes**
Gwynedd-Mercy College	Gwynedd Valley	PA	16	**Yes**
Hamilton College	Clinton	NY	14	**Yes**
Hamline University	Saint Paul	MN	23	**Yes**
Hannibal-LaGrange College	Hannibal	MO	21	**Yes**
Harcum College	Bryn Mawr	PA	32	No
Hartwick College	Oneonta	NY	13	**Yes**
Haverford College	Haverford	PA	14	No

Stratification Cell definitions can be found in Appendix A, Table A2.

PARTICIPANTS IN THE 2008 CIRP FRESHMAN SURVEY

Institution	City	State	Stratification Cell	Included in National Norms
Hendrix College	Conway	AR	23	No
Herbert H Lehman College	Bronx	NY	07	No
Hiram College	Hiram	OH	12	**Yes**
Hobart and William Smith Colleges	Geneva	NY	13	**Yes**
Hollins University	Roanoke	VA	13	No
Holy Family University	Philadelphia	PA	16	No
Holy Names University	Oakland	CA	16	**Yes**
Hood College	Frederick	MD	13	**Yes**
Houghton College	Houghton	NY	23	**Yes**
Howard University	Washington	DC	35	No
Hunter College	New York	NY	09	No
Huntingdon College	Montgomery	AL	22	**Yes**
Huntington University	Huntington	IN	23	**Yes**
Husson University	Bangor	ME	11	No
Illinois College	Jacksonville	IL	22	**Yes**
Illinois Institute of Technology	Chicago	IL	14	No
Indiana Wesleyan University	Marion	IN	23	**Yes**
Iowa State University	Ames	IA	02	**Yes**
Iowa Wesleyan College	Mount Pleasant	IA	20	**Yes**
John Carroll University	University Heights	OH	18	No
Johns Hopkins University	Baltimore	MD	06	**Yes**
Johnson C Smith University	Charlotte	NC	35	**Yes**
Judson University	Elgin	IL	22	No
Juniata College	Huntingdon	PA	13	**Yes**
Kansas City Art Institute	Kansas City	MO	12	**Yes**
Kennesaw State University	Marietta	GA	09	**Yes**
Kenyon College	Gambier	OH	14	No
Kettering University	Flint	MI	13	**Yes**
King College	Bristol	TN	23	No
King's College	Wilkes-Barre	PA	17	No
Knox College	Galesburg	IL	14	No
Lafayette College	Easton	PA	23	**Yes**
Laguna College of Art & Design	Laguna Beach	CA	15	**Yes**
Lake Forest College	Lake Forest	IL	13	**Yes**
Lakeland College	Plymouth	WI	20	No
Lawrence University	Appleton	WI	14	**Yes**
Lawson State Cmty College	Birmingham	AL	36	No
Le Moyne College	Syracuse	NY	18	**Yes**
Lebanon Valley College	Annville	PA	23	**Yes**
Lenoir-Rhyne College	Hickory	NC	21	No
Lewis and Clark College	Portland	OR	14	**Yes**
Lewis University	Romeoville	IL	17	**Yes**

Stratification Cell definitions can be found in Appendix A, Table A2.

PARTICIPANTS IN THE 2008 CIRP FRESHMAN SURVEY

Institution	City	State	Stratification Cell	Included in National Norms
Lincoln Memorial University	Harrogate	TN	11	No
Lincoln University	Jefferson City	MO	07	No
Lincoln University	Lincoln University	PA	34	No
Longwood University	Farmville	VA	09	No
Loyola Marymount University	Los Angeles	CA	04	No
Loyola University of Chicago	Chicago	IL	04	**Yes**
Loyola University-New Orleans	New Orleans	LA	04	**Yes**
Luther College	Decorah	IA	23	**Yes**
Lycoming College	Williamsport	PA	22	**Yes**
Lyon College	Batesville	AR	23	**Yes**
Macalester College	Saint Paul	MN	23	**Yes**
Maine Maritime Academy	Castine	ME	08	**Yes**
Manchester College	North Manchester	IN	21	**Yes**
Manhattan College	Riverdale	NY	18	**Yes**
Manor College	Jenkintown	PA	31	No
Mansfield U of Pennsylvania	Mansfield	PA	07	**Yes**
Marian College of Fond du Lac	Fond du Lac	WI	16	No
Marietta College	Marietta	OH	13	**Yes**
Mary Baldwin College	Staunton	VA	22	**Yes**
Maryland Institute College of Art	Baltimore	MD	13	**Yes**
Marymount Manhattan College	New York	NY	12	**Yes**
Maryville Univ. of Saint Louis	Saint Louis	MO	13	No
Marywood University	Scranton	PA	17	**Yes**
Massachusetts Coll of Liberal Arts	North Adams	MA	08	No
Massachusetts College of Art	Boston	MA	09	**Yes**
Master's College	Newhall	CA	23	**Yes**
McKendree University	Lebanon	IL	21	**Yes**
McPherson College	McPherson	KS	21	**Yes**
Medaille College	Buffalo	NY	11	**Yes**
Medgar Evers College	Brooklyn	NY	34	No
Mercer County Cmty College	West Windsor	NJ	29	No
Mercer University	Macon	GA	23	**Yes**
Meredith College	Raleigh	NC	12	**Yes**
Miami University	Oxford	OH	03	**Yes**
Middlebury College	Middlebury	VT	14	**Yes**
Mills College	Oakland	CA	13	**Yes**
Molloy College	Rockville Centre	NY	12	**Yes**
Monmouth College	Monmouth	IL	13	No
Montclair State University	Upper Montclair	NJ	08	No
Montserrat College of Art	Beverly	MA	12	**Yes**
Moore College of Art and Design	Philadelphia	PA	11	**Yes**
Moravian College	Bethlehem	PA	22	**Yes**
Morehouse College	Atlanta	GA	35	**Yes**
Morgan State University	Baltimore	MD	34	No
Mount Aloysius College	Cresson	PA	16	**Yes**

Stratification Cell definitions can be found in Appendix A, Table A2.

PARTICIPANTS IN THE 2008 CIRP FRESHMAN SURVEY

Institution	City	State	Stratification Cell	Included in National Norms
Mount Holyoke College	South Hadley	MA	14	No
Mount Ida College	Newton Centre	MA	11	**Yes**
Mount Mercy College	Cedar Rapids	IA	17	**Yes**
Mount Saint Mary's College	Los Angeles	CA	16	**Yes**
Mount Saint Mary's University	Emmitsburg	MD	18	**Yes**
Mount Vernon Nazarene University	Mount Vernon	OH	21	**Yes**
Muhlenberg College	Allentown	PA	23	No
Naropa University	Boulder	CO	15	No
Neumann College	Aston	PA	16	**Yes**
Niagara University	Niagara University	NY	18	**Yes**
North Carolina Wesleyan College	Rocky Mount	NC	20	No
North Central College	Naperville	IL	23	No
North Dakota State University	Fargo	ND	02	No
Northeastern State University	Tahlequah	OK	07	**Yes**
Northeastern University	Boston	MA	05	**Yes**
Northern Arizona University	Flagstaff	AZ	01	**Yes**
Northern Illinois University	De Kalb	IL	01	**Yes**
Northland College	Ashland	WI	23	**Yes**
Northwest Nazarene University	Nampa	ID	22	**Yes**
Northwest University	Kirkland	WA	21	**Yes**
Northwestern College	Orange City	IA	23	**Yes**
Northwestern College	Saint Paul	MN	23	No
Northwestern University	Evanston	IL	06	**Yes**
Nyack College	Nyack	NY	20	No
Oberlin College	Oberlin	OH	14	No
Occidental College	Los Angeles	CA	14	**Yes**
Oglethorpe University	Atlanta	GA	13	No
Ohio Dominican University	Columbus	OH	17	No
Ohio Northern University	Ada	OH	23	No
Oklahoma Christian University	Oklahoma City	OK	22	No
Oklahoma City University	Oklahoma City	OK	23	No
Oklahoma State U	Stillwater	OK	02	No
Oklahoma Wesleyan University	Bartlesville	OK	22	No
Oral Roberts University	Tulsa	OK	22	**Yes**
Oregon College of Art & Craft	Portland	OR	15	No
Otis College of Art and Design	Los Angeles	CA	12	No
Otterbein College	Westerville	OH	22	**Yes**
Our Lady of the Lake University	San Antonio	TX	16	No
Pace University	Pleasantville	NY	13	**Yes**
Pacific University	Forest Grove	OR	13	No
Palm Beach Atlantic University	West Palm Beach	FL	22	**Yes**
Patrick Henry College	Purcellville	VA	24	No
Peace College	Raleigh	NC	20	**Yes**

Stratification Cell definitions can be found in Appendix A, Table A2.

PARTICIPANTS IN THE 2008 CIRP FRESHMAN SURVEY

Institution	City	State	Stratification Cell	Included in National Norms
Penn State Erie-The Behrend College	Erie	PA	09	**Yes**
Pepperdine University	Malibu	CA	23	No
Philander Smith College	Little Rock	AR	35	**Yes**
Pine Manor College	Chestnut Hill	MA	11	**Yes**
Point Loma Nazarene University	San Diego	CA	23	**Yes**
Point Park University	Pittsburgh	PA	12	**Yes**
Polytechnic University	Brooklyn	NY	13	No
Pratt Institute	Brooklyn	NY	04	No
Presbyterian College	Clinton	SC	23	**Yes**
Princeton University	Princeton	NJ	06	No
Principia College	Elsah	IL	13	**Yes**
Providence College	Providence	RI	18	**Yes**
Purdue University	West Lafayette	IN	02	**Yes**
Quinnipiac University	Hamden	CT	13	No
Radford University	Radford	VA	08	No
Ramapo College of New Jersey	Mahwah	NJ	09	**Yes**
Randolph College	Lynchburg	VA	23	**Yes**
Reed College	Portland	OR	14	No
Regis College	Weston	MA	16	**Yes**
Reinhardt College	Waleska	GA	20	**Yes**
Rensselaer Polytechnic Institute	Troy	NY	05	**Yes**
Rhode Island College	Providence	RI	07	**Yes**
Rhode Island School of Design	Providence	RI	14	**Yes**
Rhodes College	Memphis	TN	23	**Yes**
Rice University	Houston	TX	06	**Yes**
Richard Bland College	Petersburg	VA	27	No
Richard Stockton College of NJ	Pomona	NJ	09	**Yes**
Rider University	Lawrenceville	NJ	12	**Yes**
Ringling School of Art and Design	Sarasota	FL	15	No
Roanoke Bible College	Elizabeth City	NC	20	No
Rockford College	Rockford	IL	11	**Yes**
Rosemont College	Rosemont	PA	16	**Yes**
Russell Sage College	Troy	NY	13	**Yes**
Rutgers University-Camden	Camden	NJ	09	**Yes**
Rutgers University-Newark	Newark	NJ	01	**Yes**
Sacred Heart University	Fairfield	CT	18	**Yes**
Sage College of Albany	Troy	NY	11	No
Saint Andrews Presbyterian College	Laurinburg	NC	21	**Yes**
Saint Augustine's College	Raleigh	NC	35	No
Saint Bonaventure University	Saint Bonaventure	NY	17	**Yes**
Saint Catharine College	Saint Catharine	KY	19	**Yes**
Saint Francis College	Brooklyn	NY	11	**Yes**
Saint Francis University	Loretto	PA	17	**Yes**

Stratification Cell definitions can be found in Appendix A, Table A2.

PARTICIPANTS IN THE 2008 CIRP FRESHMAN SURVEY

Institution	City	State	Stratification Cell	Included in National Norms
Saint John Fisher College	Rochester	NY	22	**Yes**
Saint John's University-Queens	Jamaica	NY	04	**Yes**
Saint Joseph College	West Hartford	CT	17	**Yes**
Saint Joseph's College of Maine	Standish	ME	16	**Yes**
Saint Lawrence University	Canton	NY	13	**Yes**
Saint Mary's College	Notre Dame	IN	18	**Yes**
Saint Mary's College of California	Moraga	CA	18	**Yes**
Saint Mary's U of Minnesota	Winona	MN	17	No
Saint Mary's University	San Antonio	TX	17	No
Saint Michael's College	Colchester	VT	18	**Yes**
Saint Norbert College	De Pere	WI	18	**Yes**
Saint Peter's College	Jersey City	NJ	16	**Yes**
Saint Vincent College	Latrobe	PA	18	**Yes**
Saint Xavier University	Chicago	IL	17	**Yes**
Salem State College	Salem	MA	07	No
San Jose State University	San Jose	CA	08	No
Santa Clara University	Santa Clara	CA	05	**Yes**
Sarah Lawrence College	Bronxville	NY	14	No
School of the Art Inst of Chicago	Chicago	IL	15	**Yes**
School of Visual Arts	New York	NY	12	**Yes**
Scripps College	Claremont	CA	14	**Yes**
Seattle Pacific University	Seattle	WA	23	**Yes**
Seattle University	Seattle	WA	18	**Yes**
Seton Hall University	South Orange	NJ	04	**Yes**
Seton Hill University	Greensburg	PA	16	**Yes**
Simmons College	Boston	MA	13	No
Simpson College	Indianola	IA	23	**Yes**
Simpson University	Redding	CA	21	No
Smith College	Northampton	MA	14	No
Sonoma State University	Rohnert Park	CA	08	**Yes**
South Dakota State University	Brookings	SD	01	No
Southeast Missouri State U	Cape Girardeau	MO	09	**Yes**
Southern Adventist U	Collegedale	TN	22	**Yes**
Southern Illinois U-Edwardsville	Edwardsville	IL	09	**Yes**
Southern Methodist University	Dallas	TX	05	No
Southern New Hampshire University	Manchester	NH	11	**Yes**
Southern University-New Orleans	New Orleans	LA	34	No
Southern Utah University	Cedar City	UT	08	**Yes**
Southwestern University	Georgetown	TX	23	**Yes**
Spelman College	Atlanta	GA	35	**Yes**
Spring Hill College	Mobile	AL	18	No
Stephens College	Columbia	MO	13	**Yes**
Stonehill College	North Easton	MA	18	**Yes**
Suffolk University	Boston	MA	12	No
SUNY College-Brockport	Brockport	NY	09	**Yes**
SUNY College-Geneseo	Geneseo	NY	09	No

Stratification Cell definitions can be found in Appendix A, Table A2.

PARTICIPANTS IN THE 2008 CIRP FRESHMAN SURVEY

Institution	City	State	Stratification Cell	Included in National Norms
SUNY College-Old Westbury	Old Westbury	NY	07	No
SUNY College-Potsdam	Potsdam	NY	09	**Yes**
SUNY College-Purchase	Purchase	NY	09	No
SUNY Institute of Technology	Utica	NY	09	No
Susquehanna University	Selinsgrove	PA	23	**Yes**
Swarthmore College	Swarthmore	PA	14	No
Sweet Briar College	Sweet Briar	VA	13	**Yes**
Tabor College	Hillsboro	KS	22	**Yes**
Taylor University	Upland	IN	23	No
Taylor University at Fort Wayne	Fort Wayne	IN	22	**Yes**
Texas A&M University-Kingsville	Kingsville	TX	07	**Yes**
Texas Christian University	Fort Worth	TX	04	No
Texas Tech University	Lubbock	TX	02	No
The Citadel	Charleston	SC	09	**Yes**
The University of Tampa	Tampa	FL	12	**Yes**
Touro College	New York	NY	12	No
Trinity (Washington) University	Washington	DC	16	**Yes**
Trinity Christian College	Palos Heights	IL	22	No
Trinity College	Hartford	CT	14	No
Trinity University	San Antonio	TX	23	No
Troy University	Troy	AL	07	No
Tulane University	New Orleans	LA	05	**Yes**
Tusculum College	Greeneville	TN	20	**Yes**
U of Alabama	Tuscaloosa	AL	02	No
U of Arkansas-Little Rock	Little Rock	AR	07	No
U of Arkansas-Pine Bluff	Pine Bluff	AR	34	No
U of Bridgeport	Bridgeport	CT	11	**Yes**
U of California-Los Angeles	Los Angeles	CA	03	**Yes**
U of California-Riverside	Riverside	CA	01	**Yes**
U of California-San Diego	La Jolla	CA	03	**Yes**
U of California-Santa Barbara	Santa Barbara	CA	03	**Yes**
U of California-Santa Cruz	Santa Cruz	CA	02	**Yes**
U of Central Oklahoma	Edmond	OK	08	No
U of Chicago	Chicago	IL	06	No
U of Colorado-Colorado Springs	Colorado Springs	CO	01	No
U of Florida	Gainesville	FL	03	**Yes**
U of Georgia	Athens	GA	03	No
U of Idaho	Moscow	ID	01	**Yes**
U of Illinois-Springfield	Springfield	IL	09	**Yes**
U of Illinois-Urbana-Champaign	Champaign	IL	03	No
U of Maine-Fort Kent	Fort Kent	ME	07	No
U of Maine-Presque Isle	Presque Isle	ME	07	**Yes**
U of Massachusetts-Amherst	Amherst	MA	02	**Yes**
U of Massachusetts-Boston	Boston	MA	01	No

Stratification Cell definitions can be found in Appendix A, Table A2.

PARTICIPANTS IN THE 2008 CIRP FRESHMAN SURVEY

Institution	City	State	Stratification Cell	Included in National Norms
U of Massachusetts-Dartmouth	North Dartmouth	MA	09	**Yes**
U of Miami	Coral Gables	FL	05	**Yes**
U of Michigan	Ann Arbor	MI	03	**Yes**
U of Michigan-Dearborn	Dearborn	MI	09	**Yes**
U of Michigan-Flint	Flint	MI	08	**Yes**
U of Minnesota-Duluth	Duluth	MN	02	**Yes**
U of Montevallo	Montevallo	AL	08	**Yes**
U of Nebraska-Omaha	Omaha	NE	09	No
U of North Carolina-Chapel Hill	Chapel Hill	NC	03	No
U of North Carolina-Greensboro	Greensboro	NC	08	**Yes**
U of North Carolina-Wilmington	Wilmington	NC	09	No
U of North Texas	Denton	TX	02	**Yes**
U of Northern Colorado	Greeley	CO	09	**Yes**
U of Notre Dame	South Bend	IN	06	**Yes**
U of Pennsylvania	Philadelphia	PA	06	No
U of Pittsburgh	Pittsburgh	PA	03	**Yes**
U of Pittsburgh-Bradford	Bradford	PA	08	**Yes**
U of Pittsburgh-Johnstown	Johnstown	PA	08	No
U of Portland	Portland	OR	18	**Yes**
U of Puget Sound	Tacoma	WA	14	**Yes**
U of Redlands	Redlands	CA	13	**Yes**
U of Rochester	Rochester	NY	05	**Yes**
U of Saint Thomas	Saint Paul	MN	18	**Yes**
U of Sioux Falls	Sioux Falls	SD	21	No
U of South Carolina-Aiken	Aiken	SC	08	**Yes**
U of South Carolina-Columbia	Columbia	SC	03	**Yes**
U of South Florida-St Petersburg	Saint Petersburg	FL	08	No
U of Southern California	Los Angeles	CA	06	**Yes**
U of Texas-Austin	Austin	TX	03	No
U of the Arts	Philadelphia	PA	12	No
U of the Pacific	Stockton	CA	04	**Yes**
U of the Sciences in Philadelphia	Philadelphia	PA	13	**Yes**
U of the South	Sewanee	TN	23	**Yes**
U of the Virgin Islands	Saint Thomas	VI	34	**Yes**
U of Vermont	Burlington	VT	03	**Yes**
Union University	Jackson	TN	23	No
US Air Force Academy	Colorado Springs	CO	09	**Yes**
US Coast Guard Academy	New London	CT	09	**Yes**
US Military Academy	West Point	NY	09	**Yes**
US Naval Academy	Annapolis	MD	09	**Yes**
Utah State University	Logan	UT	02	**Yes**
Utica College of Syracuse U	Utica	NY	11	No
Valley City State University	Valley City	ND	07	**Yes**
Valparaiso University	Valparaiso	IN	23	**Yes**
Vanderbilt University	Nashville	TN	06	**Yes**

Stratification Cell definitions can be found in Appendix A, Table A2.

PARTICIPANTS IN THE 2008 CIRP FRESHMAN SURVEY

Institution	City	State	Stratification Cell	Included in National Norms
Vanguard U of Southern California	Costa Mesa	CA	21	**Yes**
Vassar College	Poughkeepsie	NY	14	**Yes**
Villa Julie College	Stevenson	MD	12	**Yes**
Villa Maria College of Buffalo	Buffalo	NY	16	No
Virginia Polytechnic Inst and St U	Blacksburg	VA	03	**Yes**
Voorhees College	Denmark	SC	35	**Yes**
Wabash College	Crawfordsville	IN	13	**Yes**
Wallace State Cmty College	Hanceville	AL	28	No
Walsh University	Canton	OH	17	No
Warner Southern College	Lake Wales	FL	20	**Yes**
Warren Wilson College	Swannanoa	NC	23	**Yes**
Wartburg College	Waverly	IA	22	**Yes**
Washington and Lee University	Lexington	VA	14	**Yes**
Wayne State College	Wayne	NE	08	No
Waynesburg University	Waynesburg	PA	21	**Yes**
Webb Institute	Glen Cove	NY	14	**Yes**
Webster University	Saint Louis	MO	13	**Yes**
Wesleyan College	Macon	GA	22	**Yes**
Wesleyan University	Middletown	CT	14	No
West Virginia Wesleyan College	Buckhannon	WV	22	**Yes**
Western New England College	Springfield	MA	12	**Yes**
Westminster College	New Wilmington	PA	22	No
Westmont College	Santa Barbara	CA	13	No
Wheeling Jesuit University	Wheeling	WV	17	**Yes**
Whitman College	Walla Walla	WA	14	No
Wilkes University	Wilkes-Barre	PA	12	**Yes**
Willamette University	Salem	OR	14	**Yes**
Williams Baptist College	Walnut Ridge	AR	21	No
Williams College	Williamstown	MA	14	**Yes**
Wilmington College	Wilmington	OH	20	No
Wilson College	Chambersburg	PA	21	**Yes**
Wingate University	Wingate	NC	21	**Yes**
Winston-Salem State University	Winston-Salem	NC	34	**Yes**
Wittenberg University	Springfield	OH	23	**Yes**
Wofford College	Spartanburg	SC	23	No
Xavier University of Louisiana	New Orleans	LA	35	**Yes**

Stratification Cell definitions can be found in Appendix A, Table A2.

Appendix E

The Precision of the

Normative Data and Their Comparisons

Appendix E

The Precision of the
Normative Data and Their Comparisons

A common question asked about sample surveys relates to the precision of the data, which is typically reported as the accuracy of a percentage "plus or minus x percentage points." This figure, which is known as a confidence interval, can be estimated for items of interest if one knows the response percentage and its standard error.

Given the CIRP's large normative sample, the calculated standard error associated with any particular response percentage will be small (as will its confidence interval). It is important to note, however, that traditional methods of calculating standard error assume conditions which, (as is the case with most real sample survey data), do not apply here. Moreover, there are other possible sources of error which should be considered in comparing data across normative groups, across related item categories, and over time. In reference to the precision of the CIRP data, these concerns include:

1) Traditional methods of calculating standard error assume that the <u>individuals</u> were selected through simple random sampling. Given the complex stratified design of the CIRP, where whole <u>institutions</u> participate, it is likely that the actual standard errors will be somewhat larger than the standard error estimates produced through traditional computational methods. In addition, while every effort has been made to maximize the comparability of the institutional sample from year to year (repeat participation runs about 90 percent), comparability is reduced by non-repeat participation and year-to-year variation in the quality of data collected by continuing institutional participants. While the CIRP stratification and weighting procedures are designed to minimize this institutional form of "response bias," an unknown amount of non-random variation is introduced into the results.

2) The wording of some questions in the survey instrument, the text and number of response options, and their order of presentation have changed over the years. We have found that even small changes can produce large order and context effects. Given this, the *exact* wording and order of items on the survey instrument (which is produced as Appendix B) should be examined carefully prior to making comparisons across survey years.

3) Substantial changes in the institutional stratification scheme were made in 1968, 1971, 1975 and 2000. These changes resulted in a revision of the weights applied to individual institutions between 1966 and 2007. Stratification cell assignments of a few institutions may also change from time to time, but the scale of these changes and their effect on the national normative results are likely to be small in comparison to other sources of bias.

Since it is impractical to report statistical indicators for every percentage in every CIRP norms group, it is important for those who are interested to be able to estimate the precision of the data. Toward this end, Table E1 provides estimates of standard errors for norms groups of various sizes and for different percentages[1] which can be used to derive confidence interval estimates.

For example, suppose the item we are interested in has a response percentage of 15.7 percent among students at all nonsectarian four-year colleges (a normative group that is 39,525 in size). First, we choose the <u>column</u> that is closest to the observed percentage 15.7—in this case "15%."[2] Next, we select the <u>row</u> closest to the unweighted sample size of 39,525—in this case "40,000." Consulting Table E1, we find the estimated standard error would be .179.

To calculate the confidence interval at the 95% probability level, we multiply the estimated standard error by the critical value of *t* for the unweighted sample size (which, for all CIRP norms groups, will be equal to 1.96 at the .05 level of probability).[3] In this example, we would multiply the estimated standard error of .179 by 1.96, which yields .350. If we round this figure to a single decimal point we would then estimate our confidence interval to be 15.7 ± .4. In practical terms, this confidence interval means that if we were to replicate this survey using the same size sample, we would expect that the resulting percentage would fall between 15.3 percent and 16.1 percent 95 times out of 100.

Table E1. Estimated Standard Errors of Percentages for Norms Groups of Various Sizes

Unweighted size of norms groups	Percentage										
	1%	5%	10%	15%	20%	25%	30%	35%	40%	45%	50%
500	.445	.975	1.342	1.597	1.789	1.936	2.049	2.133	2.191	2.225	2.236
1,000	.315	.689	.949	1.129	1.265	1.369	1.449	1.508	1.549	1.573	1.581
2,500	.199	.436	.600	.714	.800	.866	.917	.954	.980	.995	1.000
5,000	.141	.308	.424	.505	.566	.612	.648	.675	.693	.704	.707
7,500	.115	.252	.346	.412	.462	.500	.529	.551	.566	.574	.577
10,000	.099	.218	.300	.357	.400	.433	.458	.477	.490	.497	.500
12,500	.089	.195	.268	.319	.358	.387	.410	.427	.438	.445	.447
15,000	.081	.178	.245	.292	.327	.354	.374	.389	.400	.406	.408
20,000	.070	.154	.212	.252	.283	.306	.324	.337	.346	.352	.354
25,000	.063	.138	.190	.226	.253	.274	.290	.302	.310	.315	.316
35,000	.053	.116	.160	.191	.214	.231	.245	.255	.262	.266	.267
40,000	.050	.109	.150	.179	.200	.217	.229	.238	.245	.249	.250
45,000	.047	.103	.141	.168	.189	.204	.216	.225	.231	.235	.236
55,000	.042	.093	.128	.152	.171	.185	.195	.203	.209	.212	.213
65,000	.039	.085	.118	.140	.157	.170	.180	.187	.192	.195	.196
70,000	.038	.082	.113	.135	.151	.164	.173	.180	.185	.188	.189
90,000	.033	.073	.100	.119	.133	.144	.153	.159	.163	.166	.167
110,000	.030	.066	.090	.108	.121	.131	.138	.144	.148	.150	.151
130,000	.028	.060	.083	.099	.111	.120	.127	.132	.136	.138	.139
240,000	.020	.044	.061	.073	.082	.088	.094	.097	.100	.102	.102

Note: Assumes simple random sampling.

---

[1] Calculated by $\sqrt{\dfrac{x\%(100-x\%)}{N}}$, where x is the percentage of interest and N is the population count from Table A3, column 2.

[2] Since the distribution of the standard errors is symmetrical around the 50 percent mid-point, for percentages over 50 simply subtract the percentage from 100 and use the result to select the appropriate column. For example, if the percentage we were interested in was 59, 100 − 59 percent yields 41, so we would use the column labeled '40%.'

[3] To calculate the confidence interval at the 99% probability level the critical *t* value is 2.56.

Appendix F

Sample Report Furnished to

Campuses Participating in the

2008 CIRP Freshman Survey

NOTES ON THE SAMPLE REPORT

The Standard Institutional Profile Report divides students into three basic groups, depending on how they answer question numbers 4, 5, 10, and 11 on the survey (see Appendix B). These groups are:

FIRST-TIME FULL-TIME. Students enrolled full-time who either graduated from high school in the same year as entering college *or* who have had no previous college experience.

FIRST-TIME PART-TIME. Students enrolled part-time who either graduated from high school in the same year as entering college *or* who have had no previous college experience.

NOT FIRST-TIME. Full- or part-time students who have had some college experience since graduating from high school.

The first section of a standard Institutional Profile Report (entitled "Total First-Time Full-Time) includes FIRST-TIME FULL-TIME students *only*. The first three columns summarize the results by gender for students attending the institution. The remaining six columns summarize results by gender for students in two comparison groups of increasing breadth (in the case of the sample, these are "nonsectarian four-year colleges of high selectivity" and "all nonsectarian four-year colleges").

The second section of the Report (entitled "Standard Breakouts," not included in this Appendix) includes results by gender for the FIRST-TIME PART-TIME and NOT FIRST-TIME (labelled "Transfer" on the report) groups, as well as results for all three groups combined. There are no comparative results displayed on this report, as the Higher Education Research Institute does not compute National Normative figures for FIRST-TIME PART-TIME or NOT-FIRST TIME students.

Whatsamatta University First-time Full-time Freshmen	# Resp- ondents	Your Institution			Private Univ-med			All Private Univs		
		Men	Women	Total	Men	Women	Total	Men	Women	Total
Number of Respondents		681	870	1,551	5,411	6,566	11,977	20,252	23,070	43,322
How old will you be on December 31 of this year?	1,547									
16 or younger		0.1	0.2	0.2	0.0	0.0	0.0	0.1	0.1	0.1
17		0.6	1.2	0.9	1.8	2.4	2.1	1.7	2.2	2.0
18		56.3	66.5	62.1	70.8	76.5	74.0	67.2	74.9	71.3
19		39.8	30.6	34.6	26.5	20.4	23.1	29.9	22.3	25.8
20		2.5	1.2	1.7	0.7	0.4	0.5	0.9	0.5	0.7
21 to 24		0.6	0.3	0.5	0.2	0.2	0.2	0.3	0.1	0.2
25 to 29		0.0	0.0	0.0	0.0	0.0	0.0	0.0	0.0	0.0
30 to 39		0.0	0.0	0.0	0.0	0.0	0.0	0.0	0.0	0.0
40 to 54		0.0	0.0	0.0	0.0	0.0	0.0	0.0	0.0	0.0
55 or older		0.0	0.0	0.0	0.0	0.0	0.0	0.0	0.0	0.0
Is English your native language?	1,546									
Yes		94.0	93.3	93.6	90.4	88.1	89.1	88.8	87.8	88.3
No		6.0	6.7	6.4	9.6	11.9	10.9	11.2	12.2	11.7
In what year did you graduate from high school?	1,547									
2008		95.9	97.6	96.8	98.9	99.2	99.1	98.6	98.9	98.7
2007		3.5	2.1	2.7	0.8	0.6	0.7	1.1	0.9	1.0
2006		0.3	0.2	0.3	0.1	0.1	0.1	0.1	0.1	0.1
2005 or earlier		0.3	0.1	0.2	0.1	0.1	0.1	0.2	0.0	0.1
Did not graduate but passed G.E.D. test		0.0	0.0	0.0	0.0	0.1	0.1	0.0	0.0	0.0
Never completed high school		0.0	0.0	0.0	0.1	0.0	0.0	0.1	0.0	0.0
How many miles is this college from your permanent home?	1,534									
5 or less		3.5	3.6	3.6	6.9	7.2	7.1	3.3	3.5	3.4
6 to 10		3.8	6.4	5.3	9.3	9.1	9.2	4.1	4.5	4.3
11 to 50		23.0	23.2	23.1	32.1	30.6	31.3	17.3	16.7	17.0
51 to 100		10.9	13.0	12.1	13.7	14.1	13.9	8.7	9.5	9.2
101 to 500		37.7	32.7	34.9	28.0	25.6	26.7	34.3	32.1	33.1
Over 500		21.0	21.1	21.1	9.9	13.3	11.8	32.4	33.6	33.0
What was your average grade in high school?	1,540									
A or A+		27.3	36.8	32.7	20.7	29.0	25.4	38.0	43.1	40.7
A-		29.2	29.2	29.2	25.9	29.6	28.0	31.5	33.7	32.6
B+		18.0	17.2	17.5	23.1	21.9	22.4	17.3	14.7	15.9
B		15.9	12.1	13.8	20.9	15.1	17.6	9.9	6.9	8.3
B-		5.9	3.3	4.5	6.1	3.3	4.5	2.3	1.2	1.8
C+		2.4	1.0	1.6	2.3	0.8	1.5	0.7	0.3	0.4
C		1.3	0.2	0.7	0.9	0.4	0.6	0.3	0.1	0.2
D		0.0	0.0	0.0	0.1	0.0	0.0	0.0	0.0	0.0
From what kind of high school did you graduate?	1,546									
Public school (<u>not</u> charter or magnet)		66.5	73.0	70.2	65.9	68.3	67.2	61.1	64.2	62.8
Public charter school		0.7	1.3	1.0	1.1	1.3	1.2	1.0	1.2	1.1
Public magnet school		1.5	1.8	1.7	2.4	2.8	2.6	3.9	4.1	4.0
Private religious/parochial school		13.3	9.8	11.3	22.7	21.9	22.2	18.1	16.9	17.4
Private independent college-prep school		17.4	13.5	15.2	7.7	5.5	6.5	15.6	13.2	14.3
Home school		0.6	0.6	0.6	0.2	0.3	0.3	0.4	0.3	0.4
Prior to this term, have you ever taken courses for credit at <u>this</u> institution?	1,547									
No		96.6	95.0	95.7	95.7	95.9	95.8	95.7	96.4	96.1
Yes		3.4	5.0	4.3	4.3	4.1	4.2	4.3	3.6	3.9

Whatsamatta University First-time Full-time Freshmen	# Resp- ondents	Your Institution			Private Univ-med			All Private Univs		
		Men	Women	Total	Men	Women	Total	Men	Women	Total
Since leaving high school, have you ever taken courses, whether for credit or not for credit, at <u>any other</u> institution (university, 4- or 2-year college, technical, vocational, or business school)?	1,531									
No		92.1	89.3	90.5	90.3	88.0	89.0	89.1	88.1	88.6
Yes		7.9	10.7	9.5	9.7	12.0	11.0	10.9	11.9	11.4
Where do you plan to live during the fall term?	1,543									
With my family or other relatives		7.2	9.5	8.5	20.9	21.7	21.3	7.1	8.0	7.6
Other private home, apartment, or room		0.1	0.7	0.5	1.1	0.6	0.8	0.6	0.4	0.5
College residence hall		92.5	89.2	90.7	77.0	77.0	77.0	90.8	90.3	90.5
Fraternity or sorority house		0.0	0.0	0.0	0.1	0.1	0.1	0.1	0.0	0.1
Other campus student housing		0.1	0.3	0.3	0.7	0.7	0.7	1.3	1.3	1.3
Other		0.0	0.2	0.1	0.1	0.0	0.1	0.1	0.0	0.1
To how many colleges other than this one did you apply for admission this year?	1,548									
None		19.0	17.4	18.1	6.9	5.5	6.1	8.7	7.8	8.2
One		8.5	13.6	11.4	7.4	6.3	6.8	5.6	5.4	5.5
Two		11.6	14.8	13.4	11.9	10.5	11.1	7.5	7.0	7.2
Three		12.1	12.9	12.5	16.4	15.8	16.1	10.4	10.2	10.3
Four		11.2	9.2	10.1	17.1	14.9	15.9	11.6	10.7	11.1
Five		7.7	8.1	7.9	12.3	14.1	13.3	11.1	11.4	11.3
Six		7.4	4.3	5.6	9.7	11.2	10.5	10.9	11.1	11.0
Seven to ten		16.3	14.2	15.1	14.6	17.5	16.2	25.5	27.1	26.4
Eleven or more		6.2	5.6	5.9	3.6	4.2	3.9	8.6	9.4	9.0
Were you accepted by your first choice college?	1,543									
Yes		77.7	88.9	84.0	75.2	78.8	77.2	66.7	72.2	69.6
No		22.3	11.1	16.0	24.8	21.2	22.8	33.3	27.8	30.4
Is this college your:	1,544									
First choice?		68.3	76.8	73.1	58.1	56.9	57.4	58.4	59.6	59.0
Second choice?		22.3	17.7	19.7	29.1	29.3	29.2	25.2	25.2	25.2
Third choice?		6.9	3.6	5.1	8.5	9.2	8.9	10.1	9.8	9.9
Less than third choice?		2.5	2.0	2.2	4.2	4.6	4.4	6.3	5.4	5.8
Citizenship status	1,547									
U.S. citizen		94.6	94.7	94.6	96.0	95.9	95.9	92.8	93.4	93.1
Permanent resident (green card)		1.0	1.3	1.2	2.5	2.9	2.7	2.9	2.8	2.9
Neither		4.4	4.0	4.2	1.6	1.1	1.3	4.3	3.7	4.0
Are your parents:	1,543									
Both alive and living with each other?		76.0	73.8	74.7	75.5	71.4	73.2	81.5	77.5	79.3
Both alive, divorced or living apart?		19.5	23.6	21.8	21.1	24.7	23.1	15.8	19.6	17.8
One or both deceased?		4.6	2.7	3.5	3.4	3.9	3.7	2.7	3.0	2.9

2008 CIRP INSTITUTIONAL SUMMARY

Whatsamatta University First-time Full-time Freshmen	# Resp- ondents	Your Institution			Private Univ-med			All Private Univs		
		Men	Women	Total	Men	Women	Total	Men	Women	Total
During high school (grades 9-12) how many years did you study each of the following subjects? [1]										
English (4 years)	1,530	97.9	97.8	97.8	98.7	98.9	98.8	98.6	99.0	98.8
Mathematics (3 years)	1,529	99.3	98.6	98.9	99.3	99.4	99.3	99.4	99.6	99.5
Foreign Language (2 years)	1,524	94.0	96.1	95.2	96.0	97.5	96.8	97.3	97.9	97.6
Physical Science (2 years)	1,515	68.4	62.9	65.3	65.7	59.1	62.0	74.9	68.3	71.4
Biological Science (2 years)	1,511	55.1	57.5	56.5	44.7	51.7	48.6	50.1	56.6	53.6
History/Am. Govt. (1 year)	1,509	98.6	98.9	98.8	99.4	99.4	99.4	99.2	99.3	99.2
Computer Science (1/2 year)	1,482	54.9	54.7	54.8	65.2	53.6	58.7	58.2	48.6	53.1
Arts and/or Music (1 year)	1,516	82.4	86.6	84.8	77.3	85.6	82.0	82.0	88.7	85.6
WHAT IS THE HIGHEST ACADEMIC DEGREE THAT YOU INTEND TO OBTAIN?										
Highest planned	1,346									
None		0.5	0.1	0.3	0.9	0.6	0.7	0.5	0.4	0.5
Vocational certificate		0.0	0.0	0.0	0.1	0.1	0.1	0.0	0.0	0.0
Associate (A.A. or equivalent)		0.3	0.1	0.2	0.2	0.2	0.2	0.2	0.1	0.1
Bachelor's degree (B.A., B.S., etc.)		21.5	18.6	19.9	18.5	15.1	16.6	12.9	11.5	12.1
Master's degree (M.A., M.S., etc.)		39.4	44.0	42.0	43.2	41.5	42.2	40.1	39.3	39.7
Ph.D. or Ed.D.		18.7	19.5	19.2	18.4	20.3	19.5	22.5	21.0	21.7
M.D., D.O., D.D.S., D.V.M.		10.2	9.6	9.9	8.7	13.3	11.3	13.6	18.0	15.9
J.D. (Law)		6.3	4.8	5.5	7.1	6.2	6.6	8.2	7.8	8.0
B.D. or M.DIV. (Divinity)		0.5	0.4	0.4	0.3	0.2	0.2	0.4	0.2	0.3
Other		2.5	2.7	2.6	2.7	2.5	2.6	1.6	1.6	1.6
Highest planned at this college	1,137									
None		1.0	0.8	0.9	1.1	0.8	0.9	0.7	0.5	0.5
Vocational certificate		0.2	0.2	0.2	0.1	0.1	0.1	0.1	0.1	0.1
Associate (A.A. or equivalent)		0.6	0.3	0.4	0.6	0.9	0.8	0.6	0.7	0.7
Bachelor's degree (B.A., B.S., etc.)		76.8	73.5	74.9	58.0	58.5	58.2	64.8	69.2	67.2
Master's degree (M.A., M.S., etc.)		15.4	17.5	16.6	28.3	25.3	26.6	22.7	18.7	20.6
Ph.D. or Ed.D.		2.0	5.0	3.7	5.2	6.7	6.0	4.8	4.4	4.6
M.D., D.O., D.D.S., D.V.M.		0.8	0.6	0.7	2.2	3.3	2.8	3.3	3.7	3.5
J.D. (Law)		0.8	0.2	0.4	1.9	1.9	1.9	1.6	1.4	1.5
B.D. or M.DIV. (Divinity)		0.0	0.0	0.0	0.3	0.2	0.2	0.2	0.1	0.2
Other		2.2	2.0	2.1	2.4	2.5	2.5	1.2	1.3	1.2
HOW WOULD YOU DESCRIBE THE RACIAL COMPOSITION OF THE:										
High school I last attended	1,537									
Completely non-White		2.4	2.3	2.3	2.4	2.5	2.5	2.3	2.5	2.4
Mostly non-White		5.9	5.7	5.8	10.4	12.5	11.6	9.7	11.3	10.6
Roughly half non-White		17.1	17.1	17.1	23.0	26.3	24.9	21.1	23.6	22.4
Mostly White		62.2	61.4	61.7	55.8	50.8	53.0	58.9	54.8	56.7
Completely White		12.4	13.5	13.0	8.4	7.8	8.1	7.9	7.9	7.9
Neighborhood where I grew up	1,456									
Completely non-White		4.4	2.8	3.5	4.6	5.3	5.0	4.3	4.6	4.5
Mostly non-White		5.9	5.6	5.8	11.5	12.5	12.1	9.3	10.1	9.7
Roughly half non-White		6.3	8.1	7.3	15.6	16.9	16.3	13.2	14.0	13.6
Mostly White		54.9	54.7	54.8	49.6	47.7	48.5	54.2	53.2	53.6
Completely White		28.5	28.8	28.6	18.7	17.6	18.1	19.0	18.1	18.5

[1] Based on the recommendations of the National Commission on Excellence in Education.

Whatsamatta University First-time Full-time Freshmen	# Resp-ondents	Your Institution			Private Univ-med			All Private Univs		
		Men	Women	Total	Men	Women	Total	Men	Women	Total
Do you have a disability?										
Hearing	1,551	0.9	0.2	0.5	0.6	0.4	0.5	0.4	0.4	0.4
Speech	1,551	0.4	0.2	0.3	0.5	0.2	0.3	0.3	0.1	0.2
Orthopedic	1,551	0.7	0.9	0.8	0.6	0.5	0.5	0.4	0.4	0.4
Learning disability	1,551	2.3	3.0	2.7	3.2	2.4	2.8	3.1	2.4	2.7
Partially sighted or blind	1,551	0.9	0.9	0.9	1.7	1.3	1.5	1.5	1.2	1.3
Health-related	1,551	0.7	2.2	1.5	1.3	1.4	1.4	1.3	1.2	1.3
Other	1,551	1.3	0.8	1.0	1.6	0.9	1.2	1.3	0.8	1.0
HOW MUCH OF YOUR FIRST YEAR'S EDUCATIONAL EXPENSES (ROOM, BOARD TUITION, AND FEES) DO YOU EXPECT TO COVER FROM:										
Family resources (parents, relatives, spouse, etc.)	1,551									
None		14.2	15.7	15.1	16.6	15.8	16.1	11.5	11.3	11.4
Less than $1,000		8.8	7.4	8.0	7.0	8.1	7.6	4.6	5.7	5.2
$1,000 to 2,999		10.3	10.9	10.6	10.0	11.3	10.7	6.7	7.6	7.2
$3,000 to 5,999		10.9	12.5	11.8	10.9	11.5	11.2	7.5	8.3	7.9
$6,000 to 9,999		9.7	10.8	10.3	10.8	11.7	11.3	8.3	9.1	8.7
$10,000 +		46.1	42.6	44.2	44.8	41.6	43.0	61.4	57.9	59.5
My own resources (savings from work, work-study, other income)	1,551									
None		33.0	29.8	31.2	36.1	32.9	34.3	38.5	37.0	37.7
Less than $1,000		22.6	28.5	25.9	21.9	25.9	24.1	21.0	24.3	22.7
$1,000 to 2,999		29.2	25.9	27.3	23.4	24.6	24.1	23.7	24.3	24.0
$3,000 to 5,999		7.5	8.4	8.0	10.5	9.4	9.9	9.6	8.3	8.9
$6,000 to 9,999		4.0	4.3	4.1	4.1	3.4	3.7	3.4	2.8	3.1
$10,000 +		3.7	3.2	3.4	4.0	3.8	3.9	3.9	3.3	3.6
Aid which not be repaid (grants, scholarships, military funding, etc.)	1,551									
None		30.5	22.4	26.0	18.9	14.6	16.5	29.1	25.8	27.3
Less than $1,000		2.2	2.9	2.6	2.7	2.8	2.8	3.4	3.6	3.5
$1,000 to 2,999		6.2	8.0	7.2	5.3	6.5	6.0	6.5	7.7	7.2
$3,000 to 5,999		8.1	7.6	7.8	6.7	8.1	7.5	6.7	7.2	7.0
$6,000 to 9,999		10.9	11.5	11.2	11.5	13.8	12.8	7.8	9.2	8.6
$10,000 +		42.1	47.6	45.2	54.8	54.2	54.5	46.5	46.4	46.4
Aid which must be repaid (loans, etc.)	1,551									
None		42.9	40.3	41.5	41.3	37.0	38.9	53.2	50.7	51.8
Less than $1,000		4.4	3.4	3.9	2.4	2.6	2.5	2.1	2.2	2.1
$1,000 to 2,999		9.3	9.1	9.2	8.2	8.2	8.2	7.7	7.7	7.7
$3,000 to 5,999		18.8	17.9	18.3	14.6	17.7	16.3	13.0	14.9	14.0
$6,000 to 9,999		10.7	11.4	11.1	11.0	10.9	11.0	7.9	8.0	7.9
$10,000 +		14.0	17.8	16.1	22.5	23.7	23.2	16.2	16.6	16.4
Other than above	1,551									
None		91.8	94.4	93.2	92.3	93.9	93.2	93.2	94.1	93.7
Less than $1,000		2.6	1.0	1.7	2.6	1.5	2.0	2.2	1.7	1.9
$1,000 to 2,999		1.8	1.6	1.7	1.6	1.1	1.3	1.4	1.1	1.3
$3,000 to 5,999		1.2	1.4	1.3	1.1	0.9	1.0	0.9	0.8	0.8
$6,000 to 9,999		0.9	0.8	0.8	0.8	0.7	0.7	0.6	0.5	0.6
$10,000 +		1.8	0.8	1.2	1.6	1.9	1.8	1.7	1.8	1.8

Whatsamatta University First-time Full-time Freshmen	# Resp- ondents	Your Institution			Private Univ-med			All Private Univs		
		Men	Women	Total	Men	Women	Total	Men	Women	Total
What is your best estimate of your parents' total income last year? Consider income from all sources before taxes	1,454									
Less than $10,000		2.7	2.6	2.6	2.2	3.2	2.7	1.7	2.2	1.9
$10,000 to 14,999		1.4	2.5	2.0	1.9	2.5	2.2	1.2	1.6	1.4
$15,000 to 19,999		0.8	2.5	1.7	2.0	2.5	2.3	1.3	1.6	1.5
$20,000 to 24,999		2.5	2.7	2.6	2.5	3.2	2.9	1.6	2.0	1.8
$25,000 to 29,999		2.2	2.7	2.5	2.3	3.1	2.7	1.5	2.0	1.7
$30,000 to 39,999		5.8	6.8	6.3	5.1	7.0	6.2	3.4	4.6	4.0
$40,000 to 49,999		5.5	8.7	7.3	5.2	7.4	6.4	3.8	5.0	4.4
$50,000 to 59,999		8.3	7.7	8.0	6.9	7.9	7.4	5.2	5.7	5.4
$60,000 to 74,999		9.7	10.5	10.1	10.7	11.3	11.0	7.5	8.6	8.1
$75,000 to 99,999		15.1	15.0	15.1	15.9	14.8	15.3	13.5	12.5	13.0
$100,000 to 149,999		17.8	15.1	16.3	22.5	17.6	19.8	21.8	19.3	20.5
$150,000 to 199,999		9.0	7.5	8.2	9.4	8.1	8.7	11.3	10.8	11.0
$200,000 to 249,999		5.1	5.4	5.3	5.0	4.4	4.6	7.9	7.5	7.6
$250,000 or more		14.2	10.3	12.0	8.5	7.1	7.7	18.5	16.6	17.5
Do you have any concern about your ability to finance your college education?	1,537									
None (I am confident that I will have sufficient funds)		40.9	33.5	36.8	37.5	25.7	30.9	44.3	34.2	38.9
Some (but I probably will have enough funds)		51.3	57.0	54.5	52.8	60.0	56.8	47.8	54.7	51.5
Major (not sure I will have enough funds to complete college)		7.7	9.5	8.7	9.7	14.3	12.3	7.9	11.1	9.6
Your current religious preference	1,522									
Baptist		6.1	4.7	5.3	3.4	4.3	3.9	5.0	5.8	5.4
Buddhist		1.0	0.6	0.8	1.4	1.3	1.4	1.5	1.5	1.5
Church of Christ		4.6	3.4	3.9	3.0	2.3	2.6	2.1	1.7	1.9
Eastern Orthodox		0.4	0.4	0.4	1.4	1.7	1.5	1.2	1.2	1.2
Episcopalian		3.4	2.2	2.8	1.1	1.0	1.1	1.7	1.9	1.8
Hindu		0.1	0.4	0.3	1.5	2.3	1.9	2.0	1.8	1.9
Jewish		2.7	3.1	2.9	2.7	2.4	2.6	7.2	6.0	6.6
LDS (Mormon)		0.0	0.2	0.1	0.1	0.2	0.2	0.2	0.1	0.2
Lutheran		3.3	2.8	3.0	2.5	3.3	3.0	2.0	2.5	2.3
Methodist		7.2	9.5	8.5	2.8	2.8	2.8	2.7	3.4	3.1
Muslim		0.4	0.6	0.5	2.5	2.5	2.5	1.6	1.5	1.6
Presbyterian		4.0	3.9	3.9	2.7	2.1	2.4	3.2	3.4	3.3
Quaker		0.1	0.4	0.3	0.2	0.3	0.2	0.2	0.2	0.2
Roman Catholic		28.4	30.4	29.5	41.3	42.1	41.8	32.1	33.1	32.6
Seventh Day Adventist		0.1	0.2	0.2	0.4	0.3	0.4	0.3	0.2	0.2
United Church of Christ/Congregational		0.4	1.6	1.1	0.4	0.4	0.4	0.6	0.6	0.6
Other Christian		10.3	12.1	11.3	7.6	10.2	9.1	7.5	9.4	8.5
Other Religion		2.4	3.1	2.8	2.6	2.8	2.7	2.6	2.7	2.7
None		24.8	20.5	22.4	22.3	17.5	19.6	26.6	22.9	24.6

Whatsamatta University First-time Full-time Freshmen	# Resp- ondents	Your Institution			Private Univ-med			All Private Univs		
		Men	Women	Total	Men	Women	Total	Men	Women	Total
Father's current religious preference	1,444									
Baptist		6.9	2.5	4.4	3.8	4.6	4.2	5.4	5.8	5.6
Buddhist		0.9	1.0	1.0	2.4	2.3	2.3	2.2	2.3	2.2
Church of Christ		4.4	3.4	3.8	3.5	2.5	3.0	2.6	1.9	2.2
Eastern Orthodox		0.8	0.5	0.6	1.7	1.8	1.8	1.3	1.4	1.3
Episcopalian		3.9	1.7	2.7	1.7	1.3	1.5	2.5	2.5	2.5
Hindu		0.3	0.4	0.3	2.0	2.6	2.4	2.5	2.2	2.3
Jewish		3.9	3.1	3.5	3.9	3.3	3.6	8.8	6.9	7.8
LDS (Mormon)		0.0	0.2	0.1	0.1	0.2	0.1	0.2	0.1	0.2
Lutheran		4.1	4.4	4.2	3.8	3.9	3.9	2.9	3.1	3.0
Methodist		7.5	10.0	8.9	3.5	3.2	3.4	3.5	3.8	3.7
Muslim		0.8	1.0	0.9	2.8	3.0	2.9	2.0	2.0	2.0
Presbyterian		4.5	4.1	4.3	3.4	2.6	2.9	4.0	4.1	4.0
Quaker		0.5	0.4	0.4	0.2	0.3	0.2	0.2	0.2	0.2
Roman Catholic		30.2	31.1	30.7	44.8	44.3	44.5	35.1	35.8	35.5
Seventh Day Adventist		0.3	0.4	0.3	0.3	0.6	0.5	0.3	0.3	0.3
United Church of Christ/Congregational		0.6	1.2	1.0	0.3	0.5	0.4	0.7	0.6	0.7
Other Christian		10.9	11.7	11.4	7.8	8.7	8.3	7.6	8.3	8.0
Other Religion		1.7	2.2	2.0	2.0	2.1	2.1	1.8	1.8	1.8
None		17.8	20.8	19.5	12.0	12.3	12.2	16.4	16.8	16.6
Mother's current religious preference	1,480									
Baptist		6.6	4.7	5.5	4.4	5.0	4.8	5.7	6.2	6.0
Buddhist		0.9	1.2	1.1	2.5	2.6	2.5	2.3	2.6	2.5
Church of Christ		4.0	4.1	4.1	3.6	2.7	3.1	2.8	2.2	2.5
Eastern Orthodox		0.5	0.7	0.6	1.5	1.7	1.6	1.4	1.4	1.4
Episcopalian		4.6	2.9	3.6	2.0	1.4	1.6	2.7	2.6	2.6
Hindu		0.5	0.4	0.4	1.9	2.6	2.3	2.4	2.1	2.3
Jewish		3.4	3.2	3.3	3.4	2.9	3.1	8.3	6.6	7.4
LDS (Mormon)		0.2	0.5	0.3	0.2	0.2	0.2	0.3	0.2	0.2
Lutheran		3.4	4.1	3.8	3.6	4.2	3.9	2.8	3.3	3.1
Methodist		8.5	9.5	9.1	3.9	3.7	3.8	3.8	4.2	4.0
Muslim		0.6	0.8	0.7	2.5	2.7	2.6	1.7	1.7	1.7
Presbyterian		6.2	4.6	5.3	3.7	2.7	3.1	4.4	4.2	4.3
Quaker		0.5	0.4	0.4	0.2	0.2	0.2	0.2	0.2	0.2
Roman Catholic		34.8	33.9	34.3	48.2	47.4	47.7	37.9	38.4	38.1
Seventh Day Adventist		0.2	0.5	0.3	0.4	0.5	0.5	0.3	0.3	0.3
United Church of Christ/Congregational		0.9	2.0	1.6	0.4	0.6	0.5	0.8	0.8	0.8
Other Christian		10.3	10.6	10.5	8.0	9.9	9.1	8.4	9.3	8.9
Other Religion		1.5	2.6	2.2	1.7	2.0	1.8	1.7	2.0	1.9
None		12.5	13.2	12.9	7.9	7.2	7.5	12.1	11.6	11.8

Whatsamatta University First-time Full-time Freshmen	# Resp- ondents	Your Institution			Private Univ-med			All Private Univs		
		Men	Women	Total	Men	Women	Total	Men	Women	Total
During the past year, student **"frequently" or "occasionally":**										
Attended a religious service	1,544	75.6	80.0	78.1	75.2	80.1	78.0	72.7	76.7	74.9
Was bored in class [2]	1,542	37.6	31.1	34.0	42.2	40.3	41.1	39.4	36.9	38.1
Participated in political demonstrations	1,537	26.6	23.2	24.7	25.5	26.2	25.9	26.0	26.8	26.4
Tutored another student	1,543	51.7	58.7	55.6	57.5	65.0	61.8	67.9	71.5	69.8
Studied with other students	1,542	87.5	93.1	90.7	82.9	90.2	87.0	88.1	92.9	90.7
Was a guest in a teacher's home	1,543	30.4	27.5	28.8	19.3	17.1	18.1	23.7	23.2	23.4
Smoked cigarettes [2]	1,535	2.1	1.7	1.9	5.4	4.8	5.1	3.3	2.7	3.0
Drank beer	1,534	52.1	35.3	42.7	49.6	37.7	42.9	47.7	37.0	42.0
Drank wine or liquor	1,534	47.9	42.5	44.9	50.3	48.2	49.1	48.5	46.7	47.5
Felt overwhelmed by all I had to do [2]	1,542	16.0	35.3	26.8	18.3	38.0	29.4	16.9	37.6	28.0
Felt depressed [2]	1,535	4.0	5.4	4.8	5.7	7.7	6.9	4.9	6.7	5.9
Performed volunteer work	1,541	85.3	92.4	89.3	83.0	89.9	86.9	88.3	93.7	91.2
Played a musical instrument	1,537	45.9	44.9	45.3	48.2	42.3	44.9	54.6	47.8	50.9
Asked a teacher for advice after class [2]	1,539	31.0	33.4	32.4	25.5	30.1	28.1	27.8	33.5	30.9
Voted in a student election [2]	1,529	22.6	24.9	23.9	21.9	25.4	23.9	23.7	27.9	25.9
Socialized with someone of another racial/ethnic group [2]	1,541	63.8	60.6	62.0	71.4	74.6	73.2	72.9	74.8	73.9
Came late to class	1,535	62.6	51.2	56.2	62.1	57.1	59.3	61.3	57.8	59.4
Used the Internet: [2]										
For research or homework	1,543	73.9	83.4	79.3	72.4	84.3	79.1	80.3	88.2	84.5
To read news sites	1,541	48.4	44.2	46.0	50.9	46.3	48.3	58.1	50.7	54.1
To read blogs	1,541	24.1	27.3	25.9	26.0	30.3	28.4	26.5	28.4	27.5
To blog	1,532	11.2	16.6	14.2	13.5	18.0	16.1	11.6	15.0	13.4
Performed community service as part of a class	1,539	60.1	63.5	62.1	59.6	65.8	63.1	60.3	64.9	62.7
Discussed religion [2]	1,541	32.5	31.4	31.9	31.4	35.2	33.6	36.0	37.7	36.9
Discussed politics [2]	1,538	41.9	38.2	39.8	39.6	36.7	37.9	46.2	43.3	44.7
Worked on a local, state or national political campaign	1,540	13.5	12.6	13.0	11.9	12.0	11.9	14.7	14.4	14.5
Student rated self "above average" **or "highest 10%" as compared with** **the average person of his/her age in:**										
Academic ability	1,542	77.9	74.2	75.8	79.7	73.5	76.2	89.6	85.8	87.5
Artistic ability	1,541	30.5	28.8	29.5	29.5	32.9	31.4	32.8	37.2	35.1
Computer skills	1,540	41.0	23.4	31.1	52.4	31.6	40.6	54.7	30.5	41.8
Cooperativeness	1,541	75.7	75.9	75.8	73.6	76.4	75.2	75.7	77.5	76.7
Creativity	1,542	56.5	53.5	54.8	59.7	58.2	58.8	61.7	60.5	61.1
Drive to achieve	1,544	78.6	83.3	81.2	74.5	80.8	78.0	80.8	86.4	83.8
Emotional health	1,543	65.6	52.1	58.0	61.9	48.6	54.4	66.1	54.6	60.0
Leadership ability	1,539	69.3	63.6	66.1	64.9	60.3	62.3	70.7	65.9	68.2
Mathematical ability	1,542	52.4	39.8	45.3	60.0	40.4	48.9	71.7	53.2	61.8
Physical health	1,541	72.1	52.7	61.2	64.5	45.9	54.0	67.5	52.5	59.4
Popularity	1,539	52.2	32.8	41.3	47.4	33.8	39.8	50.3	37.2	43.3
Public speaking ability	1,542	43.3	37.9	40.3	41.3	36.9	38.8	50.5	43.8	46.9
Self-confidence (intellectual)	1,538	72.6	53.5	61.8	69.8	55.8	61.9	77.7	63.7	70.2
Self-confidence (social)	1,543	60.9	45.4	52.2	56.4	48.8	52.1	57.4	50.5	53.7
Self-understanding	1,541	69.6	52.4	60.0	63.0	56.0	59.1	67.9	60.7	64.0
Spirituality	1,538	38.9	36.1	37.3	36.7	37.8	37.3	39.4	39.8	39.6
Understanding of others	1,541	64.9	67.2	66.2	67.6	71.0	69.5	69.3	72.8	71.2
Writing ability	1,541	47.3	47.6	47.5	48.9	52.9	51.2	57.1	60.5	58.9

[2] Percentage responding "frequently" only.

Whatsamatta University First-time Full-time Freshmen	# Resp- ondents	Your Institution			Private Univ-med			All Private Univs		
		Men	Women	Total	Men	Women	Total	Men	Women	Total
Student rated self "above average" or "highest 10%" as compared with the average person of his/her age in:										
Ability to see the world from someone else's perspective	1,539	63.3	63.5	63.4	67.6	69.4	68.6	73.7	74.5	74.1
Tolerance of others with different beliefs	1,540	73.8	78.0	76.2	75.6	79.0	77.5	80.2	82.6	81.5
Openness to having my own views challenged	1,540	63.0	55.9	59.0	61.8	59.5	60.5	66.0	63.2	64.5
Ability to discuss and negotiate controversial issues	1,538	72.5	54.5	62.4	71.9	63.4	67.1	77.0	67.3	71.8
Ability to work cooperatively with diverse people	1,537	78.7	77.7	78.1	80.4	82.6	81.6	83.6	84.7	84.2
WHAT IS THE HIGHEST LEVEL OF FORMAL EDUCATION OBTAINED BY YOUR PARENTS?										
Father	1,516									
Grammar school or less		3.3	1.8	2.4	3.5	4.0	3.8	2.0	2.2	2.1
Some high school		2.7	2.6	2.6	4.0	5.7	5.0	2.3	3.0	2.7
High school graduate		21.8	20.5	21.1	18.0	18.8	18.4	9.7	10.5	10.1
Postsecondary school other than college		4.5	3.6	4.0	3.4	3.7	3.6	2.0	2.3	2.2
Some college		10.2	12.8	11.7	14.8	15.5	15.2	9.7	10.8	10.3
College degree		26.4	27.1	26.8	29.7	27.9	28.7	29.7	28.6	29.1
Some graduate school		1.4	2.7	2.1	2.5	2.3	2.4	3.1	3.3	3.2
Graduate degree		29.7	28.9	29.2	24.1	22.1	23.0	41.5	39.2	40.3
Mother	1,527									
Grammar school or less		3.0	2.1	2.5	3.5	3.6	3.5	1.8	2.0	1.9
Some high school		2.9	2.2	2.5	2.9	4.3	3.7	1.7	2.3	2.0
High school graduate		20.3	18.4	19.2	17.9	18.2	18.1	10.1	10.4	10.2
Postsecondary school other than college		4.4	4.2	4.3	3.7	3.5	3.5	2.4	2.8	2.6
Some college		9.5	11.3	10.5	15.5	17.1	16.4	11.2	12.5	11.9
College degree		32.0	33.1	32.6	34.0	32.1	32.9	38.0	36.7	37.3
Some graduate school		3.3	3.7	3.5	2.7	2.9	2.8	4.0	4.2	4.1
Graduate degree		24.8	25.1	25.0	19.9	18.4	19.1	30.9	29.2	29.9
During the past year, did you "frequently":										
Ask questions in class	1,540	59.3	65.2	62.7	50.6	58.9	55.3	58.4	64.1	61.5
Support your opinions with a logical argument	1,543	66.1	60.9	63.2	63.9	60.0	61.7	74.6	69.2	71.7
Seek solutions to problems and explain them to others	1,538	51.0	54.1	52.7	53.5	56.9	55.4	65.0	65.7	65.4
Revise your papers to improve your writing	1,539	38.8	61.8	51.8	35.4	55.4	46.7	45.1	62.3	54.3
Evaluate the quality or reliability of information you received	1,537	38.8	39.9	39.4	38.7	39.3	39.0	47.9	47.7	47.8
Take a risk because you feel you have more to gain	1,539	43.2	37.1	39.8	43.8	37.3	40.2	45.7	39.0	42.1
Seek alternative solutions to a problem	1,540	43.5	43.3	43.4	48.2	46.3	47.1	52.7	49.5	51.0
Look up scientific research articles and resources	1,541	22.1	21.2	21.6	25.0	22.8	23.7	31.6	27.7	29.5
Explore topics on your own, even though it was not required for a class	1,539	36.3	29.4	32.4	37.8	31.5	34.2	44.3	35.8	39.7
Accept mistakes as part of the learning process	1,535	48.6	52.4	50.7	50.1	52.9	51.7	53.7	54.1	53.9
Seek feedback on your academic work	1,539	46.9	58.9	53.7	40.3	54.2	48.1	47.8	59.6	54.1
Take notes during class	1,536	54.7	81.5	69.8	54.5	81.1	69.6	57.4	82.9	71.1

Whatsamatta University First-time Full-time Freshmen	# Respondents	Your Institution			Private Univ-med			All Private Univs		
		Men	Women	Total	Men	Women	Total	Men	Women	Total
Your probable career occupation	1,479									
Accountant or actuary		3.7	1.7	2.6	3.9	2.7	3.2	2.2	1.7	1.9
Actor or entertainer		1.5	1.4	1.5	0.9	1.5	1.3	1.2	1.6	1.4
Architect or urban planner		0.6	0.5	0.5	0.8	0.3	0.5	1.5	1.5	1.5
Artist		0.8	1.9	1.4	1.3	2.3	1.9	0.9	1.8	1.4
Business (clerical)		0.6	0.4	0.5	0.9	0.7	0.8	0.6	0.5	0.5
Business executive (management, administrator)		12.1	3.4	7.2	12.1	6.2	8.8	13.4	7.7	10.4
Business owner or proprietor		2.2	0.5	1.2	4.6	1.9	3.1	4.6	1.9	3.2
Business salesperson or buyer		1.2	0.5	0.8	0.9	0.9	0.9	0.7	0.6	0.7
Clergy (minister, priest)		0.0	0.1	0.1	0.2	0.0	0.1	0.3	0.0	0.1
Clergy (other religious)		0.2	0.0	0.1	0.0	0.0	0.0	0.0	0.1	0.1
Clinical psychologist		0.2	1.2	0.7	0.6	2.1	1.5	0.4	1.7	1.1
College administrator/staff		0.0	0.0	0.0	0.0	0.0	0.0	0.0	0.0	0.0
College teacher		0.8	0.7	0.7	0.3	0.4	0.4	0.9	0.7	0.8
Computer programmer or analyst		1.2	0.4	0.7	3.4	0.1	1.6	3.4	0.4	1.8
Conservationist or forester		0.6	0.4	0.5	0.1	0.1	0.1	0.1	0.2	0.2
Dentist (including orthodontist)		1.4	0.5	0.9	1.6	1.8	1.7	1.1	1.3	1.2
Dietitian or nutritionist		0.2	0.2	0.2	0.2	0.4	0.3	0.1	0.4	0.2
Engineer		2.3	0.8	1.5	18.4	3.3	9.9	16.7	5.5	10.7
Farmer or rancher		0.2	0.7	0.5	0.1	0.1	0.1	0.1	0.1	0.1
Foreign service worker (including diplomat)		2.8	2.4	2.6	0.7	1.7	1.3	1.2	2.6	2.0
Homemaker (full-time)		0.0	0.0	0.0	0.0	0.0	0.0	0.0	0.1	0.0
Interior decorator (including designer)		0.0	0.0	0.0	0.0	0.6	0.4	0.0	0.4	0.2
Lab technician or hygienist		0.3	0.5	0.4	0.2	0.2	0.2	0.1	0.1	0.1
Law enforcement officer		1.5	0.2	0.8	1.3	0.4	0.8	0.6	0.2	0.4
Lawyer (attorney) or judge		4.6	3.1	3.8	5.2	5.5	5.3	5.5	5.9	5.7
Military service (career)		0.3	0.0	0.1	0.8	0.2	0.4	0.6	0.2	0.4
Musician (performer, composer)		2.6	1.1	1.8	2.7	1.0	1.7	2.4	1.3	1.8
Nurse		1.4	11.7	7.2	0.7	6.0	3.7	0.3	3.0	1.7
Optometrist		0.2	0.4	0.3	0.1	0.6	0.4	0.1	0.4	0.3
Pharmacist		0.8	0.2	0.5	3.8	5.6	4.8	1.5	2.5	2.0
Physician		7.6	8.7	8.2	6.4	10.6	8.8	10.6	14.0	12.4
Policymaker/Government		2.8	1.0	1.8	1.1	0.7	0.9	1.9	1.6	1.8
School counselor		0.0	0.1	0.1	0.0	0.4	0.3	0.0	0.2	0.1
School principal or superintendent		0.0	0.0	0.0	0.1	0.1	0.1	0.0	0.1	0.0
Scientific researcher		3.2	2.5	2.8	1.9	1.4	1.6	3.5	3.1	3.3
Social, welfare, or recreation worker		0.8	1.1	0.9	0.2	1.2	0.8	0.2	0.9	0.5
Therapist (physical, occupational, speech)		4.8	8.4	6.8	1.4	4.0	2.9	0.7	2.4	1.7
Teacher or administrator (elementary)		1.7	4.2	3.1	0.5	3.7	2.3	0.2	1.9	1.1
Teacher or administrator (secondary)		4.8	5.2	5.0	2.3	3.6	3.0	1.1	1.8	1.5
Veterinarian		0.5	2.8	1.8	0.0	0.6	0.3	0.2	0.8	0.5
Writer or journalist		2.3	3.1	2.8	2.0	4.1	3.2	2.1	5.0	3.7
Skilled trades		0.3	0.0	0.1	0.3	0.1	0.2	0.2	0.1	0.1
Laborer (unskilled)		0.8	0.1	0.4	0.4	0.1	0.2	0.2	0.1	0.1
Semi-skilled worker		0.5	0.1	0.3	0.3	0.1	0.2	0.2	0.1	0.1
Unemployed		0.5	0.5	0.5	1.0	1.2	1.1	1.0	0.9	0.9
Other		8.7	9.3	9.0	6.6	10.1	8.6	4.5	7.2	5.9
Undecided		16.7	18.1	17.5	9.7	11.4	10.7	12.8	15.6	14.3

Whatsamatta University First-time Full-time Freshmen	# Resp- ondents	Your Institution			Private Univ-med			All Private Univs		
		Men	Women	Total	Men	Women	Total	Men	Women	Total
Your father's occupation [3]	1,481									
Artist		1.8	0.6	1.1	0.8	0.9	0.8	1.4	1.2	1.3
Business		24.7	28.1	26.6	30.8	28.2	29.3	35.0	32.7	33.8
Business (clerical)		0.9	1.2	1.1	2.0	1.3	1.6	1.4	1.1	1.3
Clergy		0.3	0.7	0.5	0.5	0.6	0.6	0.6	0.7	0.7
College teacher		0.8	1.2	1.0	0.7	0.6	0.6	1.5	1.4	1.5
Doctor (MD or DDS)		6.5	4.6	5.4	3.6	3.6	3.6	7.0	6.6	6.8
Education (secondary)		1.8	2.9	2.4	1.8	1.7	1.7	1.9	1.7	1.8
Education (elementary)		0.6	0.6	0.6	0.7	0.5	0.6	0.6	0.4	0.5
Engineer		6.6	7.2	7.0	9.0	7.8	8.4	9.4	9.6	9.5
Farmer or forester		1.1	1.6	1.4	0.6	0.8	0.7	0.6	0.7	0.7
Health professional		1.5	0.6	1.0	1.5	1.8	1.7	1.5	1.6	1.6
Homemaker (full-time)		0.6	0.1	0.3	0.3	0.2	0.3	0.3	0.2	0.2
Lawyer		4.3	3.4	3.8	2.3	2.2	2.2	5.4	5.2	5.3
Military (career)		1.2	0.7	0.9	0.7	0.7	0.7	0.8	0.8	0.8
Nurse		0.5	0.5	0.5	0.6	0.6	0.6	0.3	0.4	0.4
Research scientist		1.7	0.7	1.1	0.6	0.6	0.6	1.7	1.5	1.6
Social/welfare/rec worker		0.8	0.4	0.5	0.6	0.5	0.5	0.5	0.4	0.4
Skilled worker		8.0	6.6	7.2	8.0	7.0	7.4	4.5	4.5	4.5
Semi-skilled worker		2.8	2.5	2.6	2.5	2.3	2.4	1.7	1.6	1.6
Unskilled worker		3.9	3.0	3.4	2.1	2.6	2.4	1.3	1.5	1.4
Unemployed		1.8	3.2	2.6	2.6	3.3	3.0	1.8	2.5	2.2
Other		27.7	29.6	28.8	27.8	32.4	30.4	20.7	23.6	22.3
Your mother's occupation [3]	1,506									
Artist		2.7	2.0	2.3	1.7	1.8	1.7	2.9	2.5	2.7
Business		12.9	13.8	13.4	16.2	16.0	16.1	17.0	17.4	17.2
Business (clerical)		3.0	3.8	3.5	4.4	4.0	4.2	3.7	3.4	3.5
Clergy		0.2	0.1	0.1	0.2	0.1	0.1	0.3	0.3	0.3
College teacher		0.6	1.1	0.9	0.5	0.3	0.4	0.9	1.0	0.9
Doctor (MD or DDS)		3.3	2.6	2.9	1.6	1.1	1.3	3.0	2.9	3.0
Education (secondary)		5.7	4.5	5.0	3.9	3.5	3.7	4.7	4.3	4.5
Education (elementary)		5.9	8.3	7.2	8.2	7.4	7.7	7.1	6.9	7.0
Engineer		0.5	0.7	0.6	0.9	0.7	0.8	1.5	1.4	1.5
Farmer or forester		0.8	0.4	0.5	0.1	0.2	0.1	0.2	0.2	0.2
Health professional		3.8	3.6	3.7	4.3	3.8	4.0	4.1	3.6	3.8
Homemaker (full-time)		8.8	7.9	8.3	8.0	9.8	9.0	12.6	14.0	13.4
Lawyer		1.7	1.4	1.5	1.2	0.8	1.0	2.6	2.3	2.4
Military (career)		0.2	0.0	0.1	0.2	0.1	0.1	0.1	0.1	0.1
Nurse		8.2	10.2	9.3	9.6	9.5	9.6	6.9	7.0	7.0
Research scientist		0.6	0.8	0.7	0.5	0.3	0.4	1.1	0.8	0.9
Social/welfare/rec worker		2.1	2.1	2.1	2.0	1.4	1.7	1.6	1.5	1.6
Skilled worker		1.5	1.7	1.6	1.7	1.1	1.3	1.1	0.9	1.0
Semi-skilled worker		1.1	0.9	1.0	2.3	1.5	1.8	1.6	1.1	1.3
Unskilled worker		2.3	1.2	1.7	1.3	1.5	1.4	0.9	0.9	0.9
Unemployed		6.8	6.3	6.5	6.5	7.0	6.8	6.8	5.9	6.3
Other		27.5	26.6	27.0	24.8	28.2	26.7	19.2	21.6	20.5
How would you characterize your political views?	1,516									
Far left		4.2	2.6	3.3	3.9	3.2	3.5	4.3	3.9	4.1
Liberal		33.7	35.0	34.4	28.9	40.0	35.1	33.4	42.6	38.3
Middle-of-the-road		41.1	43.3	42.3	45.4	41.6	43.2	38.9	36.5	37.6
Conservative		20.4	18.0	19.1	19.4	14.6	16.7	21.3	16.3	18.6
Far right		0.6	1.1	0.9	2.5	0.6	1.5	2.1	0.7	1.4

[3] Recategorization of this item from a longer list is shown in Appendix C of "The American Freshman."

Whatsamatta University First-time Full-time Freshmen	# Resp- ondents	Your Institution			Private Univ-med			All Private Univs		
		Men	Women	Total	Men	Women	Total	Men	Women	Total
Student agrees "strongly" or "somewhat":										
There is too much concern in the courts for the rights of criminals	1,510	53.1	52.8	52.9	57.9	52.7	55.0	54.2	49.7	51.8
Abortion should be legal	1,529	58.0	56.2	57.0	60.6	59.4	59.9	66.7	66.4	66.6
The death penalty should be abolished	1,525	42.7	43.6	43.2	35.0	44.0	40.1	40.9	48.6	45.0
Marijuana should be legalized	1,522	47.0	31.9	38.5	46.7	36.4	40.9	48.6	39.7	43.9
It is important to have laws prohibiting homosexual relationships	1,528	27.6	15.0	20.5	24.5	13.0	18.0	21.5	13.5	17.2
Racial discrimination is no longer a major problem in America	1,523	22.6	17.8	19.9	22.6	14.2	17.8	23.0	14.7	18.5
Realistically, an individual can do little to bring about changes in our society	1,525	25.8	20.2	22.6	31.3	22.7	26.5	27.8	19.5	23.4
Wealthy people should pay a larger share of taxes than they do now	1,522	66.4	63.3	64.7	61.4	62.3	61.9	58.0	58.6	58.3
Same-sex couples should have the right to legal marital status	1,524	61.5	74.3	68.7	64.4	78.4	72.3	68.5	78.2	73.7
Affirmative action in college admissions should be abolished	1,484	49.5	39.4	43.9	55.1	46.0	50.0	60.5	52.4	56.2
Federal military spending should be increased	1,511	27.6	21.7	24.3	28.8	21.2	24.5	27.1	19.3	22.9
The federal government should do more to control the sale of handguns	1,513	65.4	77.0	71.9	69.9	83.6	77.6	70.6	83.1	77.3
Only volunteers should serve in the armed forces	1,518	67.0	68.5	67.9	67.2	68.7	68.0	71.7	72.4	72.1
The federal government is not doing enough to control environmental pollution	1,517	81.3	83.0	82.3	77.1	83.7	80.8	79.6	85.5	82.8
A national health care plan is needed to cover everybody's medical costs	1,521	70.1	76.0	73.4	67.2	76.2	72.3	63.3	72.7	68.3
Undocumented immigrants should be denied access to public education	1,519	45.9	41.8	43.6	50.1	38.9	43.8	46.2	36.8	41.2
Through hard work, everybody can succeed in American society	1,524	75.1	74.1	74.5	78.6	76.6	77.5	75.1	72.5	73.7
Dissent is a critical component of the political process	1,451	68.0	58.9	62.9	66.1	58.3	61.8	76.7	71.1	73.8
Colleges have the right to ban extreme speakers from campus	1,515	41.3	37.4	39.1	41.8	34.3	37.6	44.9	37.0	40.7
Students from disadvantaged social backgrounds should be given preferential treatment in college admissions	1,509	46.2	34.9	39.8	38.5	35.6	36.9	38.9	34.6	36.6
The federal government should raise taxes to reduce the deficit	1,505	35.4	26.2	30.3	31.5	22.4	26.4	39.3	30.2	34.4
Addressing global warming should be a federal priority	1,518	76.1	80.0	78.3	74.7	81.1	78.3	75.7	82.2	79.2

Whatsamatta University First-time Full-time Freshmen	# Resp- ondents	Your Institution			Private Univ-med			All Private Univs		
		Men	Women	Total	Men	Women	Total	Men	Women	Total
DURING YOUR LAST YEAR IN HIGH SCHOOL, HOW MUCH TIME DID YOU SPEND DURING A TYPICAL WEEK DOING THE FOLLOWING?										
Studying/homework	1,519									
None		2.9	0.7	1.6	3.3	0.8	1.9	2.1	0.5	1.3
Less than one hour		11.1	6.1	8.3	13.8	7.3	10.1	8.2	3.6	5.7
1 to 2 hours		18.5	14.0	16.0	23.3	18.3	20.4	15.9	11.0	13.3
3 to 5 hours		25.5	24.2	24.8	27.9	27.9	27.9	24.8	21.7	23.1
6 to 10 hours		19.9	24.0	22.2	18.7	23.0	21.1	22.7	24.7	23.8
11 to 15 hours		12.3	17.7	15.3	7.8	11.7	10.0	13.3	17.2	15.4
16 to 20 hours		6.8	8.7	7.8	2.9	6.8	5.1	6.9	11.7	9.5
Over 20 hours		3.0	4.7	3.9	2.3	4.3	3.4	6.0	9.7	8.0
Socializing with friends	1,518									
None		0.3	0.2	0.3	0.4	0.2	0.3	0.5	0.2	0.3
Less than one hour		0.3	1.3	0.9	1.4	1.2	1.2	1.2	0.9	1.0
1 to 2 hours		3.8	5.3	4.6	5.5	6.2	5.9	5.4	5.5	5.5
3 to 5 hours		18.3	17.5	17.9	17.3	18.7	18.1	17.7	19.9	18.9
6 to 10 hours		26.4	30.9	28.9	24.7	27.7	26.4	28.2	29.9	29.1
11 to 15 hours		20.5	19.9	20.2	19.7	19.9	19.8	20.1	20.1	20.1
16 to 20 hours		13.7	13.1	13.4	12.3	11.4	11.8	11.6	11.5	11.5
Over 20 hours		16.7	11.8	14.0	18.9	14.7	16.5	15.3	12.0	13.5
Talking with teachers outside of class	1,518									
None		8.8	5.5	6.9	10.6	7.2	8.6	8.3	5.2	6.6
Less than one hour		36.9	34.3	35.4	41.6	40.7	41.1	39.3	36.6	37.8
1 to 2 hours		34.4	36.2	35.4	32.3	33.2	32.8	35.0	37.2	36.2
3 to 5 hours		13.9	16.8	15.5	10.5	13.0	11.9	12.5	15.4	14.1
6 to 10 hours		4.4	4.6	4.5	3.0	3.7	3.4	3.3	3.7	3.5
11 to 15 hours		0.3	1.8	1.1	0.9	1.2	1.1	0.8	1.1	1.0
16 to 20 hours		0.6	0.4	0.5	0.4	0.5	0.5	0.3	0.4	0.4
Over 20 hours		0.8	0.5	0.6	0.6	0.5	0.6	0.5	0.3	0.4
Exercise or sports	1,519									
None		2.1	3.0	2.6	2.9	5.2	4.2	2.5	4.0	3.3
Less than one hour		3.3	7.6	5.7	6.1	10.9	8.8	5.8	9.3	7.7
1 to 2 hours		7.5	12.9	10.5	13.3	18.2	16.1	12.7	15.9	14.4
3 to 5 hours		15.5	18.5	17.2	20.7	22.0	21.4	20.6	22.3	21.5
6 to 10 hours		19.5	18.9	19.2	19.9	18.3	19.0	21.4	20.3	20.8
11 to 15 hours		19.1	17.9	18.4	14.3	11.7	12.9	16.0	13.8	14.8
16 to 20 hours		14.1	10.7	12.2	9.2	6.9	7.9	9.2	7.6	8.3
Over 20 hours		18.8	10.5	14.2	13.5	6.8	9.7	11.8	6.9	9.1
Partying	1,509									
None		20.3	31.8	26.8	20.3	25.7	23.4	23.8	29.8	27.0
Less than one hour		17.0	17.1	17.0	14.3	14.2	14.2	15.9	15.9	15.9
1 to 2 hours		19.4	22.4	21.1	18.6	19.6	19.1	19.0	18.7	18.8
3 to 5 hours		22.3	18.2	20.0	21.4	20.9	21.1	20.9	20.2	20.5
6 to 10 hours		13.7	7.3	10.1	13.4	11.4	12.3	12.0	10.2	11.1
11 to 15 hours		3.6	2.2	2.8	6.0	4.5	5.2	4.2	3.1	3.6
16 to 20 hours		1.1	0.7	0.9	2.4	1.9	2.1	1.8	1.3	1.5
Over 20 hours		2.6	0.4	1.3	3.7	1.8	2.6	2.3	0.9	1.5

Whatsamatta University First-time Full-time Freshmen	# Resp- ondents	Your Institution			Private Univ-med			All Private Univs		
		Men	Women	Total	Men	Women	Total	Men	Women	Total
DURING YOUR LAST YEAR IN HIGH SCHOOL, HOW MUCH TIME DID YOU SPEND DURING A TYPICAL WEEK DOING THE FOLLOWING?										
Working (for pay)	1,516									
None		42.0	39.1	40.4	35.3	31.8	33.3	47.0	41.2	43.9
Less than one hour		4.5	2.9	3.6	3.2	2.0	2.5	4.4	3.3	3.8
1 to 2 hours		5.0	5.3	5.1	4.3	3.4	3.8	5.8	5.6	5.7
3 to 5 hours		6.9	8.2	7.7	7.3	8.0	7.7	8.7	9.4	9.1
6 to 10 hours		12.1	12.1	12.1	11.5	13.7	12.8	9.8	12.9	11.4
11 to 15 hours		7.7	11.2	9.7	11.4	14.3	13.1	8.6	11.4	10.1
16 to 20 hours		7.9	11.1	9.7	12.2	14.2	13.3	7.6	9.1	8.4
Over 20 hours		13.9	10.1	11.7	14.8	12.6	13.6	8.1	7.1	7.6
Volunteer work	1,519									
None		25.4	17.0	20.7	32.5	20.1	25.5	24.4	15.1	19.4
Less than one hour		26.5	21.3	23.6	23.1	19.1	20.9	22.5	18.9	20.6
1 to 2 hours		23.6	29.3	26.8	22.6	27.8	25.5	27.6	30.9	29.4
3 to 5 hours		12.8	21.0	17.4	11.2	18.5	15.3	15.3	21.1	18.4
6 to 10 hours		5.7	5.5	5.6	5.6	7.3	6.6	5.9	8.2	7.1
11 to 15 hours		2.7	2.3	2.5	1.9	3.1	2.6	2.0	2.8	2.4
16 to 20 hours		0.9	1.9	1.4	0.8	1.5	1.2	0.7	1.3	1.0
Over 20 hours		2.4	1.8	2.0	2.3	2.5	2.4	1.7	1.7	1.7
Student clubs/groups	1,510									
None		25.6	13.9	19.0	28.8	16.8	22.0	18.8	10.7	14.4
Less than one hour		15.8	11.4	13.3	13.8	12.1	12.8	13.0	10.8	11.8
1 to 2 hours		25.8	30.0	28.1	25.8	29.6	27.9	28.3	29.2	28.7
3 to 5 hours		17.0	22.9	20.3	17.5	21.4	19.7	21.8	25.6	23.8
6 to 10 hours		8.0	12.5	10.5	7.0	10.5	9.0	9.5	13.1	11.4
11 to 15 hours		3.9	4.3	4.2	3.2	4.2	3.8	4.1	5.2	4.7
16 to 20 hours		1.2	2.4	1.9	1.4	2.5	2.0	1.9	2.6	2.3
Over 20 hours		2.6	2.7	2.6	2.6	2.9	2.8	2.7	2.8	2.8
Watching TV	1,516									
None		7.8	10.3	9.2	6.3	6.5	6.4	8.0	7.3	7.6
Less than one hour		14.2	16.6	15.6	12.0	15.6	14.0	12.5	14.7	13.7
1 to 2 hours		23.5	28.4	26.3	22.8	24.6	23.8	22.6	25.6	24.2
3 to 5 hours		24.9	26.6	25.9	26.3	29.2	28.0	27.3	29.8	28.6
6 to 10 hours		15.8	11.8	13.6	17.7	14.1	15.7	17.6	14.8	16.1
11 to 15 hours		7.1	4.1	5.4	7.3	5.1	6.1	6.6	4.4	5.4
16 to 20 hours		2.4	0.8	1.5	3.0	2.3	2.6	2.5	1.8	2.2
Over 20 hours		4.2	1.3	2.6	4.6	2.4	3.4	2.9	1.6	2.2
Household/childcare duties	1,513									
None		23.8	14.7	18.6	23.3	13.2	17.5	23.5	14.8	18.8
Less than one hour		21.0	21.1	21.1	19.8	18.6	19.1	20.9	21.4	21.2
1 to 2 hours		29.5	32.9	31.4	30.3	32.0	31.3	31.1	33.7	32.5
3 to 5 hours		15.9	21.8	19.2	17.3	22.0	20.0	16.9	20.0	18.6
6 to 10 hours		6.8	5.9	6.3	5.8	8.1	7.1	5.0	6.3	5.7
11 to 15 hours		1.5	2.1	1.9	1.8	2.9	2.4	1.4	2.0	1.7
16 to 20 hours		0.2	0.5	0.3	0.7	1.3	1.0	0.4	0.8	0.6
Over 20 hours		1.4	1.1	1.2	1.1	1.9	1.5	0.8	0.9	0.9

Whatsamatta University First-time Full-time Freshmen	# Respondents	Your Institution			Private Univ-med			All Private Univs		
		Men	Women	Total	Men	Women	Total	Men	Women	Total
DURING YOUR LAST YEAR IN HIGH SCHOOL, HOW MUCH TIME DID YOU SPEND DURING A TYPICAL WEEK DOING THE FOLLOWING?										
Reading for pleasure	1,509									
None		29.6	17.2	22.6	30.1	17.7	23.1	22.0	14.2	17.8
Less than one hour		24.5	24.4	24.5	25.2	23.3	24.1	25.4	22.8	24.0
1 to 2 hours		22.2	26.6	24.7	22.8	25.6	24.4	26.2	28.4	27.4
3 to 5 hours		14.0	18.6	16.6	12.5	18.2	15.7	15.9	20.3	18.3
6 to 10 hours		6.2	7.2	6.8	5.3	8.7	7.2	6.6	8.9	7.8
11 to 15 hours		1.2	4.1	2.8	2.2	3.3	2.8	2.2	3.1	2.7
16 to 20 hours		1.1	0.9	1.0	0.9	1.5	1.2	0.7	1.2	1.0
Over 20 hours		1.2	1.1	1.1	1.2	1.7	1.5	1.1	1.1	1.1
Playing video/computer games	1,516									
None		23.1	61.9	45.0	16.0	56.7	39.1	17.7	62.4	41.8
Less than one hour		19.9	21.3	20.7	16.8	21.1	19.3	17.8	19.5	18.8
1 to 2 hours		19.9	10.0	14.3	22.1	11.8	16.2	21.8	10.1	15.5
3 to 5 hours		16.2	4.8	9.8	20.0	6.1	12.1	20.6	4.9	12.2
6 to 10 hours		12.7	0.9	6.1	12.7	2.5	6.9	11.8	1.9	6.5
11 to 15 hours		3.8	0.7	2.0	5.7	1.1	3.1	5.0	0.7	2.7
16 to 20 hours		2.6	0.1	1.2	2.5	0.3	1.2	2.1	0.2	1.1
Over 20 hours		1.8	0.2	0.9	4.3	0.5	2.1	3.0	0.3	1.5
Online social networks (MySpace, Facebook, etc.)	1,515									
None		11.6	8.3	9.8	12.1	6.3	8.8	10.1	6.0	7.9
Less than one hour		17.8	15.6	16.6	19.4	15.7	17.3	18.7	13.9	16.1
1 to 2 hours		29.2	31.5	30.5	27.2	27.6	27.4	29.2	28.1	28.6
3 to 5 hours		22.7	25.1	24.0	21.4	27.2	24.7	23.7	30.1	27.1
6 to 10 hours		10.9	10.9	10.9	10.7	12.5	11.7	10.5	13.1	11.9
11 to 15 hours		2.9	4.5	3.8	4.2	4.8	4.6	3.8	4.5	4.2
16 to 20 hours		2.1	2.3	2.2	1.8	2.4	2.2	1.5	2.1	1.8
Over 20 hours		2.9	1.8	2.2	3.3	3.4	3.3	2.4	2.3	2.3
Are you: [4]	1,524									
White/Caucasian		84.6	85.8	85.2	72.2	66.1	68.7	72.1	69.3	70.6
African American/Black		8.4	6.0	7.0	8.1	11.2	9.8	5.2	7.8	6.6
American Indian/Alaska Native		1.3	1.6	1.5	1.7	2.1	1.9	1.5	1.8	1.7
Asian American/Asian		6.0	6.7	6.4	13.0	13.9	13.5	17.5	17.0	17.2
Native Hawaiian/Pacific Islander		0.4	0.2	0.3	1.2	1.4	1.3	0.9	1.0	1.0
Mexican American/Chicano		1.8	0.9	1.3	2.4	3.1	2.8	3.3	3.5	3.4
Puerto Rican		1.0	0.7	0.9	2.8	2.9	2.9	1.7	1.8	1.7
Other Latino		1.9	3.3	2.7	5.1	6.1	5.6	5.1	5.8	5.5
Other		3.3	2.5	2.8	4.3	5.6	5.0	4.0	4.6	4.3

[4] Percentages will add to more than 100.0 if any student marked more than one category.

Whatsamatta University First-time Full-time Freshmen	# Resp- ondents	Your Institution			Private Univ-med			All Private Univs		
		Men	Women	Total	Men	Women	Total	Men	Women	Total
Reasons noted as "very important" in influencing student's decision to attend this particular college										
My parents wanted me to come here	1,528	10.6	9.5	9.9	13.6	15.8	14.8	13.1	15.2	14.2
My relatives wanted me to come here	1,523	4.9	3.5	4.1	5.6	5.1	5.3	5.3	4.7	5.0
My teacher advised me	1,518	8.7	6.0	7.2	6.4	6.0	6.1	6.7	6.4	6.6
This college has a very good academic reputation	1,532	74.4	83.6	79.6	67.2	74.8	71.5	78.6	82.1	80.5
This college has a good reputation for its social activities	1,526	34.8	37.3	36.2	34.6	39.3	37.2	38.8	40.4	39.7
I was offered financial assistance	1,528	52.8	58.3	55.9	58.5	66.5	63.0	44.5	50.6	47.8
The cost of attending this college	1,521	26.2	29.9	28.3	30.8	39.9	35.9	23.7	30.0	27.1
High school counselor advised me	1,521	12.9	12.0	12.4	11.2	11.7	11.5	10.4	10.3	10.3
Private college counselor advised me	1,514	5.9	6.8	6.4	4.7	4.1	4.4	4.9	4.2	4.5
I wanted to live near home	1,523	11.8	20.9	16.9	18.5	25.5	22.5	10.2	13.8	12.1
Not offered aid by first choice	1,510	4.8	4.5	4.6	10.3	12.0	11.3	7.5	9.2	8.4
Could not afford first choice	1,511	5.7	5.5	5.6	10.1	13.2	11.9	6.7	9.0	7.9
This college's graduates gain admission to top graduate/professional schools	1,515	40.8	44.8	43.0	39.2	50.1	45.4	47.8	54.8	51.6
This college's graduates get good jobs	1,519	56.3	64.5	60.9	64.2	70.2	67.6	66.9	71.3	69.2
I was attracted by the religious affiliation/orientation of the college	1,521	6.0	8.4	7.4	7.1	10.7	9.2	8.6	11.8	10.3
I wanted to go to a school about the size of this college	1,528	50.4	69.3	61.0	35.4	47.9	42.5	35.4	47.1	41.7
Rankings in national magazines	1,515	22.7	22.4	22.5	18.9	22.0	20.7	30.9	32.8	31.9
Information from a website	1,507	18.2	24.1	21.5	16.5	24.4	21.0	20.5	27.4	24.2
I was admitted through an Early Action or Early Decision program	1,517	18.6	16.6	17.5	12.6	16.6	14.9	20.5	23.5	22.1
The athletic department recruited me	1,522	29.4	16.6	22.2	7.3	4.6	5.8	6.9	5.3	6.0
A visit to campus	1,524	53.4	62.9	58.7	36.7	46.7	42.4	43.1	53.3	48.6

Whatsamatta University First-time Full-time Freshmen	# Resp- ondents	Your Institution			Private Univ-med			All Private Univs		
		Men	Women	Total	Men	Women	Total	Men	Women	Total
YOUR PROBABLE MAJOR										
Arts and Humanities	1,503									
Art, fine and applied		1.5	2.0	1.8	1.2	3.0	2.2	0.8	2.2	1.6
English (language & literature)		2.0	4.5	3.4	1.2	2.2	1.8	1.4	2.9	2.2
History		3.0	2.0	2.5	1.5	1.0	1.2	1.5	1.4	1.5
Journalism		0.3	0.9	0.7	1.1	3.1	2.2	1.1	3.1	2.2
Language and Literature (except English)		1.1	2.4	1.8	0.4	0.8	0.6	0.5	1.1	0.8
Music		1.8	1.5	1.7	2.4	1.2	1.7	2.4	1.6	1.9
Philosophy		0.8	0.0	0.3	0.5	0.2	0.3	0.6	0.3	0.4
Speech		0.0	0.1	0.1	0.1	0.6	0.4	0.1	0.2	0.1
Theater or Drama		1.8	2.0	1.9	0.5	1.2	0.9	0.9	1.5	1.2
Theology or Religion		0.2	0.4	0.3	0.1	0.1	0.1	0.2	0.1	0.1
Other Arts and Humanities		0.6	0.8	0.7	1.2	2.0	1.7	1.2	1.6	1.4
Biological Science										
Biology (general)		4.0	2.2	3.0	5.7	8.0	7.0	5.7	8.2	7.1
Biochemistry or Biophysics		1.5	0.9	1.2	0.9	1.3	1.1	1.8	1.8	1.8
Botany		0.0	0.0	0.0	0.0	0.1	0.1	0.1	0.0	0.1
Environmental Science		2.3	2.0	2.1	0.3	0.4	0.4	0.4	0.8	0.6
Marine (Life) Science		0.3	0.4	0.3	0.1	0.1	0.1	0.2	0.3	0.2
Microbiology or Bacteriology		0.5	0.2	0.3	0.1	0.2	0.1	0.3	0.3	0.3
Zoology		0.6	0.5	0.5	0.1	0.1	0.1	0.1	0.2	0.1
Other Biological Science		0.5	0.8	0.7	0.3	0.3	0.3	0.8	1.2	1.0
Business										
Accounting		3.3	1.3	2.2	3.7	2.4	2.9	2.0	1.4	1.6
Business Admin. (general)		4.0	0.7	2.1	4.6	1.5	2.8	4.3	2.0	3.0
Finance		3.2	0.9	1.9	4.6	1.6	2.9	6.0	2.1	3.9
International Business		2.1	1.2	1.6	2.2	1.9	2.0	2.4	2.4	2.4
Marketing		1.7	0.8	1.2	3.0	3.3	3.2	1.9	2.8	2.4
Management		4.3	1.1	2.5	5.4	1.9	3.4	3.4	1.5	2.4
Secretarial Studies		0.0	0.0	0.0	0.0	0.0	0.0	0.0	0.0	0.0
Other Business		1.1	0.4	0.7	2.6	0.9	1.6	1.5	0.8	1.1
Education										
Business Education		0.0	0.0	0.0	0.1	0.0	0.1	0.1	0.1	0.1
Elementary Education		1.4	3.3	2.5	0.3	3.4	2.1	0.1	1.7	1.0
Music or Art Education		1.1	1.1	1.1	0.4	0.5	0.5	0.2	0.3	0.2
Physical Education or Recreation		1.2	0.0	0.5	0.4	0.2	0.3	0.1	0.1	0.1
Secondary Education		2.1	2.8	2.5	1.3	2.4	1.9	0.4	1.0	0.7
Special Education		0.3	0.5	0.4	0.1	0.5	0.3	0.0	0.2	0.1
Other Education		0.0	0.4	0.2	0.0	0.2	0.1	0.0	0.2	0.1
Engineering										
Aeronautical or Astronautical Engineering		0.0	0.1	0.1	1.0	0.1	0.5	1.4	0.3	0.8
Civil Engineering		0.3	0.0	0.1	3.5	0.8	1.9	2.3	1.0	1.6
Chemical Engineering		0.3	0.0	0.1	1.6	0.4	0.9	2.6	1.5	2.0
Computer Engineering		0.0	0.1	0.1	2.3	0.1	1.1	2.3	0.3	1.2
Electrical or Electronic Engineering		0.0	0.0	0.0	2.0	0.1	0.9	2.4	0.4	1.3
Industrial Engineering		0.0	0.0	0.0	0.3	0.1	0.2	0.4	0.2	0.3
Mechanical Engineering		0.5	0.0	0.2	7.0	0.6	3.4	5.8	0.8	3.1
Other Engineering		0.5	0.4	0.4	3.4	1.6	2.4	4.3	2.9	3.5

2008 CIRP INSTITUTIONAL SUMMARY

Whatsamatta University First-time Full-time Freshmen	# Resp- ondents	Your Institution			Private Univ-med			All Private Univs		
		Men	Women	Total	Men	Women	Total	Men	Women	Total
YOUR PROBABLE MAJOR										
Physical Science										
Astronomy		0.2	0.0	0.1	0.0	0.0	0.0	0.1	0.1	0.1
Atmospheric Science (incl. Meteorology)		0.2	0.0	0.1	0.0	0.0	0.0	0.1	0.1	0.1
Chemistry		2.0	1.7	1.8	1.3	1.4	1.3	1.7	1.6	1.6
Earth Science		0.0	0.2	0.1	0.0	0.1	0.1	0.1	0.1	0.1
Marine Science (incl. Oceanography)		0.5	0.2	0.3	0.0	0.0	0.0	0.1	0.1	0.1
Mathematics		1.5	0.6	1.0	0.8	0.6	0.7	1.4	1.0	1.2
Physics		2.0	0.5	1.1	1.2	0.3	0.7	1.9	0.5	1.2
Other Physical Science		0.3	0.2	0.3	0.1	0.2	0.2	0.2	0.2	0.2
Professional										
Architecture or Urban Planning		0.8	0.2	0.5	0.6	0.2	0.3	1.4	1.5	1.4
Family & Consumer Sciences		0.0	0.0	0.0	0.1	0.2	0.1	0.0	0.3	0.2
Health Technology (medical, dental, laboratory)		0.3	1.1	0.7	0.5	0.5	0.5	0.3	0.4	0.3
Library or Archival Science		0.2	0.0	0.1	0.0	0.1	0.1	0.0	0.1	0.0
Medicine, Dentistry, Veterinary Medicine		5.9	8.6	7.5	2.9	4.8	4.0	4.5	6.6	5.6
Nursing		1.7	11.6	7.3	0.8	6.2	3.9	0.3	3.0	1.8
Pharmacy		0.5	0.1	0.3	3.9	5.0	4.5	1.4	2.1	1.8
Therapy (occupational, physical, speech)		5.3	9.0	7.4	1.0	2.9	2.1	0.5	1.6	1.1
Other Professional		0.8	2.7	1.9	1.6	2.2	1.9	0.6	0.9	0.7
Social Science										
Anthropology		0.5	1.5	1.1	0.2	0.4	0.3	0.2	0.8	0.6
Economics		4.7	1.9	3.1	0.6	0.2	0.4	3.0	1.3	2.1
Ethnic Studies		0.2	0.1	0.1	0.0	0.1	0.1	0.0	0.1	0.1
Geography		0.3	0.2	0.3	0.0	0.0	0.0	0.0	0.1	0.0
Political Science (gov't., international relations)		8.1	4.7	6.2	3.1	4.0	3.6	5.1	6.1	5.6
Psychology		2.1	3.7	3.0	2.4	6.8	4.9	1.8	5.3	3.7
Public Policy		0.2	0.4	0.3	0.1	0.1	0.1	0.3	0.4	0.3
Social Work		0.0	0.2	0.1	0.1	0.7	0.4	0.1	0.4	0.2
Sociology		0.9	0.6	0.7	0.2	0.5	0.4	0.3	0.6	0.4
Women's Studies		0.0	0.0	0.0	0.0	0.0	0.0	0.0	0.0	0.0
Other Social Science		0.2	0.1	0.1	0.1	0.3	0.2	0.2	0.5	0.3
Technical										
Building Trades		0.0	0.0	0.0	0.0	0.0	0.0	0.0	0.0	0.0
Data Processing or Computer Programming		0.6	0.0	0.3	1.0	0.1	0.5	1.0	0.1	0.5
Drafting or Design		0.0	0.1	0.1	0.2	0.2	0.2	0.1	0.2	0.1
Electronics		0.0	0.0	0.0	0.1	0.0	0.1	0.0	0.0	0.0
Mechanics		0.0	0.0	0.0	0.0	0.0	0.0	0.0	0.0	0.0
Other Technical		0.0	0.0	0.0	0.1	0.0	0.1	0.1	0.0	0.0
Other Fields										
Agriculture		0.0	0.5	0.3	0.0	0.0	0.0	0.1	0.1	0.1
Communications		0.9	0.9	0.9	1.6	3.1	2.5	1.2	3.0	2.2
Computer Science		0.8	0.4	0.5	2.0	0.1	0.9	2.3	0.4	1.3
Forestry		0.0	0.0	0.0	0.0	0.0	0.0	0.0	0.0	0.0
Kinesiology		0.3	0.0	0.1	0.1	0.1	0.1	0.1	0.2	0.2
Law Enforcement		0.9	0.1	0.5	1.4	0.9	1.1	0.6	0.4	0.5
Military Science		0.2	0.0	0.1	0.1	0.0	0.1	0.1	0.0	0.0
Other Field		1.5	2.2	1.9	1.2	1.6	1.4	0.7	1.0	0.9
Undecided		6.1	6.6	6.4	3.6	5.4	4.6	4.3	6.2	5.3

Whatsamatta University First-time Full-time Freshmen	# Resp- ondents	Your Institution			Private Univ-med			All Private Univs		
		Men	Women	Total	Men	Women	Total	Men	Women	Total
Objectives considered to be "essential" or "very important":										
Becoming accomplished in one of the performing arts (acting, dancing, etc.)	1,522	16.1	17.8	17.1	16.3	17.0	16.7	16.8	18.5	17.7
Becoming an authority in my field	1,519	60.6	54.5	57.2	64.5	61.8	63.0	66.9	64.9	65.8
Obtaining recognition from my colleagues for contributions to my special field	1,520	55.0	53.1	53.9	63.9	62.4	63.0	62.4	61.6	62.0
Influencing the political structure	1,519	22.4	17.7	19.7	27.1	23.1	24.8	26.8	23.0	24.8
Influencing social values	1,521	38.0	43.5	41.1	43.0	50.1	47.0	41.6	48.8	45.5
Raising a family	1,522	77.3	75.7	76.4	75.1	75.4	75.3	75.4	73.5	74.4
Being very well off financially	1,524	73.4	69.3	71.1	81.1	79.4	80.2	76.4	72.1	74.1
Helping others who are in difficulty	1,522	65.5	77.6	72.3	61.5	77.8	70.8	65.0	77.9	72.0
Making a theoretical contribution to science	1,520	20.5	21.9	21.3	26.9	22.6	24.5	29.5	23.2	26.1
Writing original works (poems, novels, short stories, etc.)	1,526	17.0	15.2	16.0	17.8	17.2	17.4	17.9	18.1	18.0
Creating artistic works (painting, sculpture, decorating, etc.)	1,524	13.4	14.4	14.0	14.9	17.2	16.2	14.9	17.1	16.1
Becoming successful in a business of my own	1,520	39.7	27.5	32.9	50.9	41.5	45.6	47.4	38.3	42.5
Becoming involved in programs to clean up the environment	1,520	29.3	31.7	30.7	28.7	34.0	31.7	29.7	35.9	33.1
Developing a meaningful philosophy of life	1,520	54.5	52.3	53.3	53.5	53.5	53.5	59.1	57.7	58.3
Participating in a community action program	1,521	28.6	37.4	33.5	27.1	38.5	33.6	29.5	43.5	37.0
Helping to promote racial understanding	1,519	36.3	34.1	35.1	36.2	43.1	40.1	35.8	43.7	40.1
Keeping up to date with political affairs	1,519	48.8	39.7	43.7	43.2	39.3	41.0	50.5	49.0	49.7
Becoming a community leader	1,521	39.3	36.3	37.6	35.7	38.2	37.1	40.4	43.3	42.0
Improving my understanding of other countries and cultures	1,518	55.6	56.7	56.2	50.1	60.9	56.3	56.6	69.3	63.5
Adopting "green" practices to protect the environment	1,520	46.0	50.9	48.8	43.5	54.5	49.8	46.4	58.2	52.7

Whatsamatta University First-time Full-time Freshmen	# Resp- ondents	Your Institution			Private Univ-med			All Private Univs		
		Men	Women	Total	Men	Women	Total	Men	Women	Total
Student estimates chances are "very good" that he/she will:										
Change major field	1,529	12.8	14.6	13.8	9.5	12.1	11.0	12.4	15.7	14.2
Change career choice	1,530	15.9	17.2	16.6	8.5	11.4	10.2	13.2	17.3	15.4
Participate in student government	1,525	4.2	7.0	5.8	6.5	8.6	7.7	7.9	10.1	9.1
Get a job to help pay for college expenses	1,526	41.5	57.6	50.5	42.5	55.4	49.9	38.5	50.1	44.8
Work full-time while attending college	1,525	1.9	5.8	4.1	6.3	7.7	7.1	3.7	4.4	4.0
Join a social fraternity or sorority	1,523	3.3	9.1	6.6	7.6	13.3	10.9	8.5	14.0	11.5
Play varsity/intercollegiate athletics	1,524	40.6	25.9	32.3	15.6	10.0	12.4	16.4	11.5	13.7
Make at least a "B" average	1,526	64.5	67.9	66.4	68.2	68.1	68.2	72.9	71.7	72.3
Need extra time to complete your degree requirements	1,525	3.9	5.5	4.8	5.3	5.8	5.6	4.0	4.0	4.0
Participate in student protests or demonstrations	1,530	7.1	6.5	6.8	5.7	7.3	6.6	6.6	9.0	7.9
Transfer to another college before graduating	1,524	3.1	3.0	3.1	4.9	4.5	4.7	3.1	2.8	2.9
Be satisfied with your college	1,519	58.0	69.4	64.4	50.2	57.6	54.4	63.8	69.1	66.7
Participate in volunteer or community service work	1,523	23.0	47.3	36.6	20.6	42.7	33.2	30.0	53.7	42.8
Seek personal counseling	1,526	7.3	8.8	8.1	6.7	9.1	8.1	7.4	9.9	8.7
Communicate regularly with your professors	1,521	42.9	50.0	46.9	31.3	39.3	35.8	42.9	50.0	46.8
Socialize with someone of another racial/ethnic group	1,527	65.5	71.5	68.8	60.3	71.8	66.9	70.9	79.6	75.6
Participate in student clubs/groups	1,526	42.4	61.4	53.0	42.0	59.1	51.8	54.1	69.5	62.4
Participate in a study abroad program	1,524	29.7	42.2	36.7	22.3	44.1	34.7	31.6	54.7	44.1
Have a roommate of different race/ethnicity	1,523	25.1	28.5	27.0	26.8	35.8	31.9	36.0	44.1	40.4
Discuss course content with students outside of class	1,527	46.6	58.6	53.3	40.2	54.1	48.1	56.4	68.0	62.7
Work on a professor's research project	1,527	24.3	24.3	24.3	27.6	32.5	30.4	30.2	33.6	32.0
Get tutoring help in specific courses	1,526	25.0	31.7	28.7	22.9	34.0	29.2	21.5	33.2	27.8
Do you give the Higher Education Research Institute (HERI) permission to include your ID number should your college request the data for additional research analyses?	1,378									
Yes		62.0	69.9	66.5	56.4	59.0	57.9	59.6	58.9	59.2
No		38.0	30.1	33.5	43.6	41.0	42.1	40.4	41.1	40.8

Higher Education Research Institute
3005 Moore Hall • Box 951521 • Los Angeles, California 90095-1521

Publications List

The American Freshman:
National Norms for Fall 2008*
December, 2008/189 pages $25.00

Provides national normative data on the characteristics of students attending American colleges and universities as first-time, full-time freshmen. In 2008, data from approximately 240,580 freshmen students are statistically adjusted to reflect the responses of 1.4 million students entering college. The annual report covers: demographic characteristics; expectations of college; degree goals and career plans; college finances; attitudes, values and life goals.

*Note: Publications from earlier years are also available: each year dating back to 1999 for $25.00; earlier years dating back to 1966 for $5.00 each.

The American Freshman: Forty Year Trends
March, 2006/261 pages $30.00

Summarizes trends data in the Cooperative Institutional Research Program (CIRP) Freshman Survey between 1966 and 2006. The report examines changes in the diversity of students entering college; parental income and students' financial concerns, issues of access and affordability in college. Trends in students' political and social attitudes are also covered.

Degree Attainment Rates at
American Colleges and Universities
January, 2005/74 pages $15.00

Provides latest information on four- and six-year degree attainment rates collected longitudinally from 262 baccalaureate-granting institutions. Differences by race, gender, and institutional type are examined. The study highlights main predictors of degree completion and provides several formulas for calculating expected institutional completion rates.

The American College Teacher:
National Norms for the 2007–08
HERI Faculty Survey*
February, 2008/160 pages $25.00

Provides an informative profile of teaching faculty at American colleges and universities. Teaching, research activities and professional development issues are highlighted along with issues related to job satisfaction and stress.

*Note: Publications from earlier years are also available: 2004-05, 2001–02 for $25.00; 1998–99, 1995–96 for $22.00 each; 1992–93 for $20.00

Advancing in Higher Education:
A Portrait of Latina/o College Freshmen at
Four-Year Institutions, 1975–2006
October, 2008/90 pages $15.00

The purpose of this report is to provide a portrait of Latina/o students entering four-year colleges and universities from 1975–2006. It is intended as a data resource for higher education in understanding the unique characteristics of the increasing numbers of Latina/o first-time, full-time freshmen. The national data come from the Cooperative Institutional Research Program (CIRP) Freshman Survey. For the first time, CIRP trends are disaggregated by specific Latina/o ethnic origin group and by gender, to highlight the heterogeneity in the population unavailable in other national reports on Hispanic college students.

Beyond Myths: The Growth and Diversity of
Asian American College Freshmen: 1971–2005
September, 2007/63 pages $15.00

The first-year student trends examined in this report help to address some common characterizations of Asian American students, particularly with respect to their educational success, that are often overstated and taken out of context. The findings suggest that Asian Americans still have to overcome a number of obstacles, such as levels of family income and financial aid, to earn a coveted spot in higher education. This report features data collected from Cooperative Institutional Research Program (CIRP) Freshman Survey. It is based on the 361,271 Asian/Asian American first-time full-time college students from 1971–2005, representing the largest compilation and analysis of data on Asian American college students ever undertaken.

First in My Family:
A Profile of First-Generation College Students
at Four-Year Institutions Since 1971
February, 2007/62 pages $15.00

First-generation college students are receiving increasing attention from researchers, practitioners, and policymakers with the aim of better understanding their college decision-making process and supporting their progress in higher education. This report explores the changing dynamic between first-generation college students and their non first-generation peers by utilizing longitudinal trends data collected through the CIRP Freshman Survey (1971–2005).

Black Undergraduates From *Bakke* to *Grutter*
November, 2005/41 pages $15.00

Summarizes the status, trends and prospects of Black college freshmen using data collected from 1971 to 2004 through the Cooperative Institutional Research Program (CIRP). Based on more than half a million Black freshman students, the report examines gender differences; socioeconomic status; academic preparation and aspirations; and civic engagement.

HERI accepts Visa, MasterCard & Discover. To order call 310-825-1925 or visit the HERI publications webpage:
www.gseis.ucla.edu/heri/research-publications.php